GOLDEN

GOLDEN

HOW ROD BLAGOJEVICH TALKED HIMSELF OUT OF THE GOVERNOR'S OFFICE AND INTO PRISON

Jeff Coen and John Chase

CHICAGO REVIEW PRESS

© 2012 by Jeff Coen and John Chase
All rights reserved
Published by Chicago Review Press, Incorporated
814 North Franklin Street
Chicago, Illinois 60610
ISBN 978-1-56976-339-1

Library of Congress Cataloging-in-Publication Data

Coen, Jeff.
  Golden : how Rod Blagojevich talked himself out of the governor's office and into
prison / Jeff Coen and John Chase.
      p. cm.
  Includes index.
  ISBN 978-1-56976-339-1 (hardback)
  1. Blagojevich, Rod R., 1956– 2. Blagojevich, Rod R., 1956—Trials, litigation, etc.
3. Illinois—Politics and government—1951– 4. Political corruption—Illinois. 5.
Governors—Illinois—Biography. I. Chase, John. II. Title.

  F546.4.B55C64 2012
  977.3'044092—dc23
  [B]

                              2012017760

Interior design: Sarah Olson

Printed in the United States of America
5 4 3 2 1

For Meredith and Liam and for Josephine

"We the People of the United States, in order to form a more perfect union, establish justice, insure domestic tranquility, provide for the common defence, promote the general welfare, and secure the blessings of liberty to ourselves and our posterity, do ordain and establish this Constitution for the United States of America."
—*Preamble of the U.S. Constitution*

"Always remember the rule of law is sacrosanct, nay it is more—it is F'n golden."
—*Inscription Rod Blagojevich wrote on a copy of the document at a book signing*

Contents

Part I: The Young Rod Blagojevich

Part II: A Public Rise

Part III: The Governor

Part IV: A Federal Probe

Part V: The Trials

Authors' Note

Sourcing for this project starts with the authors' almost total immersion in the Blagojevich story for much of the decade after 2001.

John was part of the *Chicago Tribune*'s team that began covering Blagojevich the candidate and then governor early in the decade, while Jeff was working the halls of Chicago's criminal courthouse covering the aftermath of the city's street crime. Their careers merged as John began covering the ongoing shenanigans in the Blagojevich administration and Jeff was sent to the Dirksen US Courthouse to monitor the swirling federal investigation.

In the days after December 9, 2008, the eyes of the nation and the world turned to the arrested Illinois governor. But what followed nationally was a mostly oversimplified version of the bizarre, Shakespearean downfall of Rod Blagojevich. Frustratingly, much of the telling was being done by writers outside Chicago or by Blagojevich himself. This project is our attempt to preserve a piece of city history—told by two Chicago journalists who were well positioned to do so. It's a great American political story detailing the rapid rise and meteoric fall of a man who touched the lives of millions, and one that carried lessons for future generations to heed.

The material in these pages came from a variety of sources. Many scenes that are replayed here we personally witnessed. Those we didn't observe came from scouring thousands of pages of court documents or from interviews with the players themselves. Not including the hundreds of notebooks we filled between 2002 and 2008, we conducted more than one hundred interviews specifically for this project with those who were part of the Blagojevich story from the political and the investigative sides. The interviews often took hours and sometimes were done with the promise that what would appear in this book wouldn't be directly attributable to those we spoke to.

The goal was to talk to sources on the record. And in the instances where the parties we interviewed agreed to be quoted by name, it is noted in the pages that follow. But where a quote appears without direct attribution, there was an agreement not to name a source. There were times when agreeing not to name someone freed them to speak and allowed that person to be forthcoming and provide even greater context for the story we wanted to tell. To verify information we were told in such instances, we checked court documents from Blagojevich's criminal trials, public documents, e-mails, and other correspondence, or interviewed others who were involved in particular scenes or who might have had direct knowledge about what was being said. If there was a disagreement over a set of facts provided by a person who wished to remain anonymous, we either made that disagreement clear in the pages or left the scene out.

In instances where dialogue is quoted, we took extreme care to ensure its accuracy by confirming it with either the speakers themselves or others who personally witnessed what was said. If we paraphrased a remark, it was because we felt we could not know with absolute certainty what was uttered, even if several people we interviewed confirmed a general idea or concept.

We quote heavily from the recordings that federal agents made on phones used by the governor and others. All of those quotes come from transcripts of those phone conversations or the recordings themselves. We are grateful to those who provided case material that was outside of the public record.

The authors also used information gathered from numerous interviews with Blagojevich himself over the years, including one in his home in the days before the start of his second trial. We also had access to transcripts of two extensive interviews with reporters from the *Chicago Tribune* in 1996 when he was first running for Congress. Those interviews proved extremely valuable, and we are grateful to those reporters and the newspaper for allowing us to use them.

We reviewed hundreds of stories about Blagojevich over the years, in particular from the *Chicago Tribune*, the *Chicago Sun-Times*, the Associated Press, the *Daily Herald*, and *Chicago* magazine.

A Legacy of Corruption

Rod Blagojevich belongs to Chicago.

Journalists, analysts, pundits, and comedians made him a national character, mocking his cartoonish hair and laughing at his reality-TV misadventures. They found his obsession with historical icons from Theodore Roosevelt to Elvis Presley somewhat endearing. And some fancied him a political Lazarus, dead but seemingly destined to rise again and keep the fifty states amused along the way. Maybe the impeached fortieth governor of Illinois says something about modern America.

But he belongs to Chicago. A back-alley jokester, yes, but one whose over-the-top persona always hid the kind of insatiable ambition that has made men of stronger character into great leaders. Like his city, he was tenacious and bold. He was steadfast and of good humor in the face of long odds. And it can be argued that nothing motivated him more than having someone tell him he couldn't do something. He was the young boxer who thinks he's twice as tough as he really is but when knocked down rises from the mat convinced he'll hit his opponent doubly hard in return. He was the city kid cliché; the charming son of immigrants who fought his way from tough beginnings on the Northwest Side to success and fame. Some days he shuffled through the slush of winter like anyone else, dreaming of being someone.

But there were other qualities, too, the ones from the shadowy places in Chicago's history: avarice, jealousy, vengefulness, and skill at manipulation.

1

The proverbial stacking of the deck and a very easy slide into moral ambiguity when it means dollar bills flowing from you to me. Blagojevich, like many before him, flew after power and after money, even when all wisdom should have told him not to. As a chief executive, he allowed influence to outweigh merit. And as a politician, he reveled in a world where backroom dealing almost always took precedent over front-room negotiation. If you can wink it, don't say it, and if you can nod it, don't wink it.

He came from a town whose city fathers pushed the Potawatomi out of the way to take the prairie and whose business leaders put labor rebels to death. It's a town built and sustained by power and run by those who have it. Even the do-gooders—the "goo-goos"—needed power to make things happen. Blagojevich knew that history better than most, though with outsiders he would discuss Alexander Hamilton more than Big Bill Thompson.

"Yankee and *voyageur*, the Irish and the Dutch, Indian traders and Indian agents, halfbreed and quarterbreed and no breed at all, in the final counting they were all of a single breed. They all had hustler's blood," Nelson Algren wrote of Chicago's founders.

It was penned five years before Blagojevich was born, but he learned it. And his politics were entirely Chicago's. He was the young man who grew up in the shadow of his smarter, stronger, and more serious older brother. He struggled with how to make something of himself until finally finding a place under the wing of a powerful alderman whose daughter he married. He rode that good fortune as long as he could until he figured out the game for himself and acquired associates beholden to him—not his father-in-law.

Blagojevich got wise and succeeded in a city that too often shrugs and says corruption is a built-in if you want potholes filled and garbage picked up and someone to answer a phone in a ward office when you call.

The Chicago that Blagojevich grew up in was one fashioned by Mayor Daley—the original—Richard J. It was a city where, in theory, the people elected the judges, but in practice even black robes were passed out by the Democratic organization Daley controlled. Patronage thrived. It was the backbone of the machine. City workers often served as the precinct captains for the local Democratic Party. They lived a few doors down or a few blocks away and handled the neighborhoods' problems. Trouble with the sewers or litter on the streets or in the parks? Your kid crossways with the law? They could all be solved with a simple call to the precinct captain.

But when election time came around, so did that precinct captain. He would have a few questions and a few requests. Did you like having all those problems solved? Do you want to make sure they'd be solved again? Well, sign your name on this petition, hang this poster in your window, and take this list of the party's slated favorites with you to the voting booth. Pull the lever for these fine candidates and Chicago will continue to be the city that works. The precinct captains came to the two-flat where Rade and Millie Blagojevich raised their two sons, just as they had years earlier when other immigrants lived in the five-room apartment.

And while the system had always kept the order of things, corruption flowed through nearly every vein in the city, and Chicago's bane became the state's.

During the nineteenth century, governors Joseph Duncan and Joel Matteson faced lawsuits and accusations, with Matteson allegedly owing the state a quarter-million dollars when he left office. Lennington Small, Illinois's governor during the Roaring Twenties, was indicted on charges he ran a money-laundering scheme during his days as the state treasurer. He deposited state funds in an inactive bank, lent the money to Chicago meatpackers, collected 6 percent interest, and refilled state coffers at a rate of 3 percent. But Small beat the rap, and it was only later discovered that four of his jurors had gotten state jobs for their bother.

Illinois seemed to forget to come of age in the twentieth century. Republican William Stratton, Illinois's governor during the 1950s, was indicted after he left office on income tax evasion. He was accused of mishandling campaign cash, but he too was acquitted. Stratton's successor, Otto Kerner, was convicted of bribe-taking, and in 1987, Dan Walker, who had been governor for a term the prior decade, was convicted of fraud related to his banking business.

So when Rod Blagojevich rose from middling lawyer and low-level Cook County state's attorney to a seat in Springfield and then from the US Congress to the governor's office, he knew exactly what he was getting into. In all, four Illinois governors—Republicans and Democrats alike—had been accused of crimes by the time Blagojevich took office. And the man from whom Blagojevich inherited the governorship, George Ryan, was on his way to becoming the fifth. Ryan was just months away from being charged when Blagojevich was sworn in as governor in 2003.

Those crooked governors took their place among hundreds of politicians—statewide officials, congressmen, city council members, school board trustees—in the class picture of Illinois's convicted political caste. There was an attorney general convicted of income tax evasion and a former state treasurer who pleaded guilty to a check-kiting scheme. There were federal probes with catchy names—operations Phocus, Incubator, Greylord, Gambat, Haunted Hall, Silver Shovel—that nabbed mobsters, aldermen, and judges. And then there was Paul Powell, the secretary of state whose Springfield hotel room was found filled with shoeboxes jammed with hundreds of thousands of dollars after he died in 1970.

Blagojevich got to the governor's mansion using a mind less adept at budgets and problem-solving than dissecting nearly every conceivable angle of campaign fund-raising in a state with few laws governing any of it. Controversy swirled around him early in his first term, but it didn't matter. Chicago and his fund-raising machine flexed their muscles again, and Blagojevich was reelected four years later despite a federal investigation that signaled to those paying attention that he might join that shameful class picture.

In today's histrionic, polarizing world of politics, Rod Blagojevich's unique fall from grace is a morality tale for the nation. His story is an object lesson on what can go wrong when voters elect leaders—for governor, president, even school board—based on superficial things like commercial sound bites and image-making spin that seem to dominate the country's current poisonous political scene. There is no better proof of the political adage that the candidate with the most money wins than Rod Blagojevich. He was a great campaigner and an even better fund-raiser, and he never lost an election.

And when his day in court eventually came, Blagojevich was not going to go easily. He had one more campaign to win. Staring out from under his trademark shelf of dark hair at a federal jury, he finally found himself very much on the ropes and ready to talk paint off a fence. Impossible to pin down, ready to fight, willing to play dirty, and seemingly wearing his heart on his sleeve.

How Chicago.

"I'm Rod Blagojevich. I used to be your governor," he said, dropping his voice in a tone that sounded like he was trying to either tell the jury or convince himself that everything was going to be OK. "And I'm here to tell you the truth."

PART I

The Young Rod Blagojevich

1

Our Kind of Guy

Chicago's city hall hummed with activity. Aldermen and bureaucrats clip-clapped across the marble floors inside the city's hulking, eleven-floor, Classic Revival seat of power. Alone and unnoticed, a young man sat in a hallway. Rod Blagojevich was definitely a nobody.

Home on summer break between his second and third years of law school at Pepperdine University in the summer of 1982, Blagojevich had a meeting. His father, Rade, a Serbian who emigrated from Yugoslavia after World War II, knew a friend who knew an alderman named Edward Vrdolyak. A personal injury lawyer who had become one of Chicago's most powerful politicians while representing the Southeast Side, Vrdolyak was a very good man to get to know. The alderman had come from a gritty neighborhood that bumped up against Indiana and was once filled with steel mills populated by working-class families with Eastern European roots. They toiled during the day and occupied the stools at corner taverns at night. Vrdolyak's parents had owned one of those taverns.

Since entering politics, he had become "Fast Eddie," and it was a nickname he had more than earned as a master of the city's nasty and complex political scene and a brilliant purveyor of the deal. Chairman of the Cook County Democratic Party, Vrdolyak made lawyers he liked into judges and businesspeople he favored into state reps. Out-of-work ironworkers who came to him often got city jobs.

And that's why Rod Blagojevich was sitting outside his office. The appointment was for 9:00 AM, and while the perpetually late Blagojevich had surprisingly arrived on time, it would be hours before he was invited in.

When the moment came, Vrdolyak sat in his office chair; papers were piled high atop his desk. Glaring at the young man with a ten-thousand-pound stare, Vrdolyak asked how he could help. Blagojevich explained the connection to his father's friend and wanted to see if Vrdolyak could get him a job for the summer, preferably as a law clerk for the city. He needed legal experience.

"You have my resume," Blagojevich said.

Sure, sure, Vrdolyak answered. "What ward do you live in?"

Blagojevich didn't have a clue. He told Vrdolyak he lived in "Ted Lechow-icz's" ward, name-dropping the powerful Northwest Side Democratic committeeman, Cook County commissioner, and former Illinois state senator, adding he thought that was the Thirty-Sixth Ward.

Vrdolyak looked at him incredulously. You live in the Thirtieth Ward, he corrected him before picking up the phone and instructing someone on the other end to come to his office. Minutes later, in walked George Hagopian, alderman of the Thirtieth Ward.

"This kid lives in your ward," Vrdolyak told him. See what you can do for him.

A week later, Blagojevich's phone rang. There was a city job waiting for him—driving a bus at night. It paid a healthy $11.25 an hour, but Blagojevich said there must be some mistake. He wanted a law clerk's job. It paid less but would give him the experience he needed, not to mention a political foot in the door.

A few days later, the city called back with the better offer. He could clerk for the city's law department that summer. Ecstatic, Blagojevich went back to city hall to thank Vrdolyak in person. Again he waited, this time unable to get by henchmen standing in front of the alderman's office door. When Vrdolyak appeared, he looked at Blagojevich like a man wanting to know what else this kid wanted from him. Hadn't he just gotten him a job?

"I know who you are," Vrdolyak said, stopping Blagojevich's attempt at a reintroduction. But Blagojevich continued, saying he didn't want anything more except to say thank you. "Ludicrous as it sounds considering your position, if there's anything I can do to help you, please don't hesitate to call."

Blagojevich was a breathless greenhorn, but he had clearly made an impression. Vrdolyak grabbed him and took him for a walk down one of city hall's large stairwells. The alderman asked what Blagojevich's plans were after he graduated from law school. Would he be coming back to Chicago? If he did, there could be a job waiting for him at the powerful alderman's law firm.

"We'll make you part of the family," Vrdolyak said. "You look like our kind of guy."

———

"How are you doing right now, Rod?" said the criminal lawyer, as a jury, a full courtroom, the state of Illinois, and, in fact, the country awaited a response. It was almost thirty years and a universe away from Vrdolyak's job offer and Blagojevich's baptism into Chicago politics.

"I'd prefer to be somewhere else, but I'm happy to be here," Blagojevich answered.

He was finally getting a chance to talk about everything that had happened to him, but by any stretch, Blagojevich certainly wasn't happy to be sitting on the witness stand in federal court. He had suffered the greatest political tumble in the state's history, beginning with the indignity of a predawn arrest at his home on corruption charges. Even in Illinois, Blagojevich was the only governor summarily thrown out of office after being impeached. Most of his closest friends had turned on him, helped the government, and testified against him; one was behind bars, and others were heading there. Still another had committed suicide under the pressure. And even the elusive Vrdolyak had been sent to prison in a scheme tied to Blagojevich's criminal case.

Blagojevich's finances were in shambles, and he was sitting through his second grueling federal trial. His wife, Patti Blagojevich, daughter of Chicago alderman Richard Mell, sometimes wept as she sat in support of her husband. Blagojevich's young daughters faced the prospect of losing their father for a decade or more. The former congressman and governor who had dreamed of being president of the United States had seen everything he had worked for crushed and had been forced to support his family by doing things like selling pistachios in television commercials.

"I grew up on the near Northwest Side of Chicago in the neighborhood around Cicero and Armitage," said Blagojevich, who was fifty-four years old that summer of 2011. "It was a working-class neighborhood back in the 1960s, a lot of small manufacturing companies and ethnically a diverse neighborhood."

The city Blagojevich knew was one filled with such sections. The kind created by blue-collar families who weren't looking for much beyond a job they could count on to help raise a family in a tidy house on a street filled with people they knew. Blagojevich came from LaCrosse Avenue, just south of Armitage Avenue in a neighborhood called Cragin, named for the Cragin Brothers' tin plate and sheet iron company that moved into the area around the Civil War. The streets were lined with two-flats and modest bungalows, and for decades served as a crucial base for white ethnics who couldn't afford to live closer to downtown but sought a stable family life. In 1960, when Rod Blagojevich was four years old, 99 percent of the neighborhood was white and nearly 40 percent were first-generation Americans.

Seventeen percent were foreign-born, like Blagojevich's father, Rade. Born in 1911 in a small town outside Belgrade, Rade Blagojevich lost his father at a young age and was sent off to military school when he was twelve to join his brother Milorad (after whom Rade would later name his younger son). Nazis had captured Rade, an officer in the Yugoslavian Army, and confined him to a POW camp for four years. After the war, he spent another three years in a refugee camp in Austria before coming to the United States in 1948.

He first moved to Waukegan, a northern suburb of Chicago, where a woman had set up a home taking in new immigrants. She was Croatian and Rade was Serbian—two ethnicities that often clashed—but in the New World they both recognized their shared roots and got along all right. Rade Blagojevich had come from a rough background, but America inspired a new energy inside of him. He quickly joined a Serbian church, and at an event there about a year later, the thirty-eight-year-old met a warm, handsome woman eleven years his junior, who quickly caught his eye.

Millie Govedarica was a Chicago girl with Serbian roots. Her father, Ilija, was a tall and slender man born in Serbia. He arrived in the United States in 1905, eventually working in Chicago as a bartender at a saloon on Fullerton Avenue just west of Ashland Avenue, right down the block from where he lived with his wife, Clara, and later at a coffee shop. Millie was a younger daughter of the couple and one of more than a half-dozen children. Her parents died when she was young, and she moved in with an uncle, Obren, who ended up taking care of several of the Govedarica children. She attended Lake View High School for a few years but dropped out to make money for the family. She had been bouncing around from factory job to factory job during World War II when she met Rade in 1949.

The two quickly fell in love and a year later got married. Five years after that, their first son, Robert, was born, followed a little more than a year later—on December 10, 1956—by Rod.

Rade wanted to give Robert a traditional Serbian name, Božidar, after Rade's father. It means "God's Gift." And he wanted Rod's formal name to be Milorad, after his uncle. It means "Happy Worker." But Millie refused. She was born in America, and she knew American culture and wanted her children to think like and be treated as Americans, not as immigrant children. Her children would have American names.

In the early years, the Blagojeviches lived with Millie's family in an apartment building on that same stretch of Fullerton, just west of Ashland. On the street level, two of Millie's brothers ran a diner. But Millie eventually decided she wanted her family to strike out on their own. They moved several miles west to a five-room apartment on the top floor of a two-flat at 1925 North LaCrosse Avenue. It was next door to a small, white Pentecostal church built in the middle of the block. About a half-mile away was Blackhawk Park, where later in life Rod spent countless hours hanging out with friends and playing basketball.

Millie got a job doing clerical work across Cicero Avenue at the Ecko utensils factory and later took a job as a ticket taker for the Chicago Transit Authority, working mostly at one of the CTA's largest El stops at Jefferson Park on the Northwest Side. Rade also worked factory jobs, including at the A. Finkl steel factory on the North Side. But Rade dreamed of more. He decided to give his best shot at the American dream and try his hand at being an entrepreneur, owning hand-washing laundromats.

After working his day job at the factory, Rade would make his way to his laundromat. Almost right away, the business was successful. Rade didn't see his wife or children much, but he was making money. He quickly bought two more, including one at Ashland and Grace on the city's North Side.

Unfortunately, hand-washing laundromats were quickly going the way of the horse-and-buggy. By the late 1950s, coin-operated laundries were popping up all over the city. A friend and business associate pulled Rade aside one day and told him he needed to change with the times. But Rade was still doing well enough financially that he didn't heed his associate's advice, not believing people would want to do their own laundry.

Instead, he decided to buy yet another laundromat, pushing the family's finances past the tipping point and driving him into bankruptcy. It was a major turning point for Rade and Millie and their two sons and would be a touchy subject for years, as Rod's parents argued about it in front of their boys. Even years later, a very stubborn Rade would try to explain to Millie why he didn't think he had made a mistake.

"No dead capital," he uttered over and over again as his business philosophy.

=====

Rade was strict with his boys. Having survived the atrocities of World War II, he felt discipline was important and constantly forced his will and their Serbian roots on his sons. He spoke only Serbo-Croatian in the house, and both Robert and Rod learned the language at a young age. The family also regularly attended Old Holy Resurrection, a Serbian East Orthodox church on Palmer Square a few miles away. In Rod's preteen years, Rade made him become a member of a local Serbian singing group along with other younger boys whose parents were recent Eastern European immigrants. Rod learned the tamburitza, similar to a mandolin, and in the summertime, he was sent to a Serbian camp in the northern suburbs.

Although he quietly despised some of the activities his father made him join, young Rod was always happy-go-lucky with other kids in the neighborhood and quick to make friends. But he also yearned to be free from his father's control and tried to embrace all things American.

He found the embodiment of all of it one night watching television with his mother. On the screen was an Elvis movie. And just like that, Rod was in love.

For years, mother and youngest son bonded as the two sat in front of the television watching the King's films. Rod would memorize Elvis's songs and sing them around the house, sometimes to the disapproval of his father. Eventually it grew to an obsession. Rod loved Elvis because he was cool, had great hair, and always got the girls. But unlike so many Americans, Rod's fixation never diminished, and he never permitted himself to view Elvis as the bloated, pill-popping, over-the-hill washout in a white jumpsuit that so many saw after his death. To Rod, Elvis was still the soulful singer on stage making the girls swoon or the rebel in the movie who had come to the beach town to shake things up and have some fun. Elvis was the embodiment of the American story. The rags-to-riches tale wasn't a cliché to Blagojevich. And, in Blagojevich's view anyway, Elvis's life would be his life. The poor kid who loved his momma, grew up with little, but made something of himself.

As governor, Blagojevich dragged one of Elvis's closest friends to a press conference about, of all things, prescription drugs. He also constantly quoted Elvis as an adult, tossing in phrases like "hang loose" and "a little less conversation, a little more action." After being kicked out of office, he actually got paid to do an Elvis impression, singing "Treat Me Right" on a loading dock for an office party being held in the street behind the Tribune Tower.

The real Rod Blagojevich could hide just fine inside the King's outsized personality. He could be as over-the-top as he cared to be, though those closest to Blagojevich often saw his flaws through some of his outlandish acts. There was the constant need to be reassured, the private self-doubt, and the inability to steer himself from the abyss when others could see his life coming down around him.

———

Rod and his older brother were inseparable as young children, mostly because Rod looked up to Robert so much. By many accounts, Rod idolized his older brother and followed him around the neighborhood wherever he went. But the two boys were dissimilar in almost every way. Robert did better at school and was a superior athlete who carried himself with more confidence. Physically, he showed off a cut figure, from his defined jaw line to his thoughtful, sometimes piercing eyes. Rod's face was rounder, with chubby cheeks and inset eyes that looked just a little too close together.

To make up for these inequities, Rod summoned a gregariousness to get attention and be liked. He became the funny, personable Blagojevich brother. It worked. Once while performing a tamburitza routine at a show where his brother also had been on stage, Rod got applause not for his musical ability but for hamming it up for a laugh. But the feeling of being second best caused Rod to develop a chip on his shoulder that he would never lose. Even when he was governor of the fifth-largest state in the nation, Rod always acted inferior to Robert, deferring to him and calling him "my older, more successful brother."

By 1966, Rod followed his brother around the Cragin neighborhood shining shoes. After school at Henry D. Lloyd Elementary School, a few blocks from their home, the Blagojevich brothers made their way to their mom's factory job at Ecko. For two hours nearly every day, the boys charged twenty-five cents a shine, plus tips. Rod eventually raised the rate to thirty cents.

Even on the witness stand decades later, Blagojevich recalled how one of his customers didn't like how he would rush through jobs. Rod got sloppy once and splashed polish onto the man's white socks. So the next time the worker arrived with cardboard to protect them.

Like so many children in the neighborhood, Rod obsessed over sports. In the winters, he played basketball; in the summers, little league baseball. When he was twelve, Blagojevich wrote a report about what he wanted to be when he grew up, a report he kept in his private possessions while he was governor. "When I grow up, I would like to be a lawyer," he wrote. "But moreso a baseball player. What position. Well maybe an outfielder. What team. Any team that will accept me."

On the witness stand in federal court, it was clear how much those days had meant to Rod Blagojevich the Chicago boy.

"Generally, how did you do in little league?" Blagojevich's lawyer, Aaron Goldstein, asked him.

"I was not anywhere near where I wanted to be. I was actually—they [had] a rule in little league where every boy had to play [and] at least get one at bat every game and there were twenty games a year, and I kept the statistics. I was one for twelve that year, which meant I couldn't even play in eight games," Blagojevich answered. "And when we would be ahead, the coach would exile me to right field because that's where fewer balls were hit. And I would hustle out there to try to impress him, and I just kept thinking that maybe if I could change my batting style I might actually be able to hit the ball, and it never quite worked out."

His one hit had been a roller between shortstop and third, Blagojevich recalled.

Even though he wasn't headed for the major league diamond, Rod demonstrated other skills and an early inclination for politics. One year he didn't like the team he was placed on, so he requested a trade. It was against the park district rules, but it went through anyway. Everybody at the park knew Rod through his brother, who was of course a park superstar. And while Rod wasn't nearly as good, he got by with his friendliness, charm, and upbeat personality. A North Sider, Rod also obsessed over the Cubs. On some summer days, he and his friends would board the Fullerton bus headed east and wend their way to the El stop at Armitage and Sheffield before heading north to Wrigley Field.

Rod also developed a passion for basketball, hoping maybe that was the pathway to athletic success. He was drawn to the game and especially the

American Basketball Association, the young upstart league best known for its freewheeling style, flashy players, and red, white, and blue basketball. He practiced incessantly, shooting hoops outside in the summer and inside neighborhood gyms when winter arrived.

"I felt I got actually pretty good," Blagojevich said proudly from the witness stand. "And I can't say this for sure, but I think when I was governor, out of the fifty of us, I was the only governor in America who could spin a basketball on all five fingers of his right hand. At least I had that going for me."

Around Blackhawk Park and on the streets around their apartment, Rob and Rod were well known and well liked by the neighborhood kids, forming friendships that would last well into their adulthoods. A few blocks away lived Danny Stefanski, who was part Serbian, and Michael Ascaridis, a Greek kid who, because he was raised orthodox, had cultural and religious similarities. And there were the Wolfer brothers and Danny Colla, who years later would hang out with Rod and constantly be mistaken in public for the male model Fabio. There were the Angarola brothers, Danny and Michael, who would later help Rod get a job with the Cook County State's Attorney's office.

At Lloyd, Rod was an average student still very much living in the shadow of his brother. But he began developing an uncanny knack for memorization. Millie had purchased a set of World Book encyclopedias, and Rod would sit down in the front room and read sections over and over, especially history and the encyclopedia's mini-biographies of American presidents. Rod would soon turn around and recite nearly all the facts back to his parents.

It was almost as if Blagojevich had a photographic memory, but his skill was different. Rod had developed a memorization trick that allowed him to take a piece of information and associate it with an object he wouldn't forget, thereby allowing him to remember the facts. He would most often do it with the presidents, playing an association game in his mind that allowed him to recite long lists seemingly with little effort.

"Give me a list of forty-two common words that I could picture, a mug or a tape recorder, and give me ten seconds with each word, and I can associate them with each president and I can give them to you backwards, forwards, you know, number 16, number 12," he'd later tell reporters. "I'd win bets doing that. I developed that interest. . . . I was very interested in presidents and birds. My favorite president was Lincoln, and my favorite bird was the scarlet tanager."

It quickly became clear Rod was headed more for a life in politics than orni-thology. And the skills he was developing as a child would come in handy as a politician. He'd amaze average people he had met only once, mentioning details about when they had met and where and who else was with them. It was a skill Blagojevich would use to connect with people, allowing them to feel like he wasn't the typical arrogant elected official but instead the down-to-earth neighborhood guy who had just happened to have gotten lucky and grown up to become governor.

As a boy, he also memorized famous phrases, inspiring sayings, and poems. Among his favorite was the well-worn poem "If" by Rudyard Kipling, which is known for its famous line, "If you can keep your head when all about you/Are losing theirs and blaming it on you." Rod didn't learn of the poem while reading it at school or the library. No, he became intrigued with it while watching an NFL Films television episode about running backs, in which the narrator delivered the line as the screen showed slow-motion action shots of football stars dodging tacklers and bolting down the sidelines.

Still, he memorized it quickly and would again try to impress his class-mates with his keen skills of recollection. This ability also helped him a bit in school, compensating for his lack of book smarts and poor performance on standardized tests, especially compared with Robert, who after grade school went on to attend one of the better public high schools on the North Side, Lane Tech. Though it had started as a technical school, Lane Tech's focus had become a college prep curriculum, something Rob and Rod's par-ents appreciated as they regularly talked about how their goal was to send both boys to college. Rob was doing well at Lane and just as well in athletics. He played all manner of sports but was especially good in baseball. By his senior year, though, he tore a bicep that cost him later.

Rod soon followed his brother to Lane. Built on more than thirty acres on the city's crowded North Side, Lane is a landmark in Chicago. The mas-sive red-brick school at the corner of Addison Street and Western Avenue looks like a castle. A little more than two miles west of Wrigley Field, it stood five miles—and several neighborhoods—away from the Blagojevichs' apartment. More than five thousand students attended the school—fifteen hundred in Blagojevich's class alone.

Although the school had high standards, it still had some rough pockets, and some of the Blagojevich brothers' fellow students joined gangs. One of the larger gangs on the North Side at the time that had members at Lane was made up mostly of white, greaser-type teenage boys who called themselves the Gaylords. Also a student at Lane, Rod's friend Danny Stefanski joined up with the group. The members hung out on street corners drinking, picking up girls, and getting into fights. Stefanski inked a small tattoo of the gang's main symbol, a cross, on one of hands with India ink and a small needle.

Years later, the Gaylords became a modern-day street gang as members carried guns, dealt drugs, and committed crimes all over the North Side. Increasingly, the nearly all-white gang got into racial and ethnic battles with black and Latino gangs that moved into Cragin and other North Side neighborhoods European immigrants were abandoning. Rod continued to hang around with Stefanski and the neighborhood guys who joined the Gaylords, but Blagojevich stayed on the periphery. It was clear to most of them he was no fighter.

"He'd hang out on the perimeter with the guys but not get into trouble," said one neighborhood friend who was in the Gaylords. "Rod never got into that. We socialized, but he wasn't in on that end of it."

Blagojevich's focus was more on making Lane's sports teams. He tried out for the baseball team but got cut right away. So he tried out for basketball. Rod wasn't much for attacking the boards or taking the ball to the hole, choosing to rely on his jump shot. And still trying to live up to his brother's standards, Rod practiced constantly in the gravel lot around his home, in the school parking lot, even in his bedroom where he looked at himself in the mirror and examined how good he looked shooting.

On Friday nights, Blagojevich could be found in the gym at the neighborhood high school, Foreman, which hosted after-school "activity nights." Rod was frustrated because he was riding the bench at Lane. Foreman's basketball coach saw Rod practicing one night and told him that if he transferred he could play on Foreman's varsity team. By his sophomore year, Rod was ready to leave Lane. Not only was he failing at basketball, but he also failed his drafting class.

Unlike Lane Tech, which was set back from the streets and had almost a college campus atmosphere, Foreman stood right on the corner of Belmont and Leclaire and lacked any distinctive architectural flair beyond average neighborhood high schools. Fewer kids attended Foreman, which meant less competition for the basketball team. Rod heeded the coach's advice and transferred. But before enrolling for his junior year he spent the summer— occasionally donning red Converse All-Stars that drove his anti-communist father nuts—wearing ankle weights when he practiced to make him quicker and jump higher.

At Foreman, he was good enough to make the team. He was also good at adding tricks to his basketball repertoire. He was remembered less for his play and more for a move in which he drove down the court, dribbled twice behind his back and once under his knee, and then swished the ball through the hoop. But Blagojevich's high school basketball career was brief. Early in the season he broke his wrist, officially ending his basketball dreams.

Rade was also struggling, but on much more serious matters. Rade's work brought in a steady income but not enough, especially with Robert already in college and Rod about to go. It was around this time in 1974 that Rade learned about lucrative jobs on the Alaskan pipeline. Rade and Millie talked it over, and Rade decided to go.

Rod was sad to see his father leave, but he was also caught up in his high school life. He took a summer job for $3.25 an hour at Stewart Warner, which manufactured vehicle instruments such as speedometers, working in the packaging department. Nights were still spent at Blackhawk Park, hanging out with friends from the neighborhood.

But with his basketball dreams dashed, Rod was looking for something else to pique his interest. Never finding his stride as a student, he enjoyed reading, especially history books about politicians. Rather than do his chemistry or math homework, Rod routinely whiled away hours in libraries reading about Winston Churchill and Abraham Lincoln. Entering his senior year in high school, he picked up a biography about Teddy Roosevelt and learned that as a young man Roosevelt was sickly, with terrible asthma and worse eyesight, and was bullied by other kids. Roosevelt took up boxing and vowed never to be weak again.

Blagojevich had no such inspiring story. But when he read about Roosevelt, he thought it would be cool to try the sport. His friend Mike Ascaridis was a good boxer and helped Blagojevich along. Ascaridis was so good, he'd fight regularly throughout the Chicago area and later be nicknamed Lou Nova after the amateur boxing champ from the 1930s.

With Ascaridis's assistance, Blagojevich hooked up with the Chicago Park District boxing program and the Golden Gloves tournament, the local amateur boxing competition. Worried his mother wouldn't allow him to fight, Rod got a girlfriend to forge his mother's signature on the application.

His first fight was at Clarendon Park, where Blagojevich lost in a decision. Afterward, Rod had to pick up his mother from her CTA ticket-taking job. When Millie got into the car, she looked at Rod's face and body. He had bruises and rope burns all over.

"What have you done?"

Rod explained his newfound boxing career. Millie was not amused.

"No more," she insisted.

But Rod persisted a little while longer.

Before a Golden Gloves match in March 1975—held in church gym near Wrigley Field—Blagojevich was sitting in the ring when he saw photographer Richard Younker hanging around the perimeter. With Blagojevich's coach, Jerry Marzullo, standing nearby, Rod made the unusual request of asking Younker to take his picture. The photographer wouldn't have taken Blagojevich's picture otherwise, having found Rod to be a particularly uninteresting subject. But Younker went ahead and took three photos of Blagojevich, including one in which Rod winks his right eye as Marzullo gives him some final instructions before a bout Blagojevich quickly lost.

In total, he had six fights in a decidedly unremarkable career, splitting two bouts in the Golden Gloves and two more in the Chicago Park District tournament. He won just two exhibition matches, and another coach, Pat LaCassa, explained why. During Blagojevich's final fight, he said, Rod lost because he spent far too much time with his gloves up, trying to protect his face.

―――――

High school graduation was just around the corner, and Rod Blagojevich was trying to figure out what to do with his life.

He wanted to aim high for college and go to Northwestern or the University of Chicago, but he had scored just an 18 on the college entrance ACT exam (out of a possible 36) and received a D in an algebra class—"a classic case of grade inflation," he would joke years later as governor. So he followed his brother to the University of Tampa, where Rob had tried to walk onto the school's baseball team but didn't make it due to his injured bicep.

By this time, Rade Blagojevich was working nearly year-round in Alaska on the pipeline, bringing in enough money for Rod to be able to go to college. On the witness stand decades later—a place where he never would have wanted his father to see him—Blagojevich still glowed as he talked about his dad. Blagojevich was strategically spinning the tale of his life story for the jury, but he was genuinely proud of his upbringing. He believed his parents had propelled him to high office through their actions while he was growing up and even from heaven after their deaths.

"I mean, your parents will, you know, they'll do anything for you," he testified. "So my dad—you know, it was hard for my dad to have to leave us. And he was the janitor up there. There was nothing fancy about the job that he had. He made beds and swept floors, ten hours a day, seven days a week for the next three years from the ages of sixty-three to sixty-six or sixty-seven, and he came home once a year, and we'd see him on what they call R & R for maybe a week during the Christmas holidays, and then he'd go back. It was what parents do. It's what we do. We love our kids; we sacrifice for our kids."

As Rod's graduation from Foreman approached, Rade told his youngest son there were jobs for him in Alaska, too. The money was good, more than ten dollars per hour. And he could work there all summer.

Rod had to move quickly to get the highest spot on the union list. So after the last day of school but before graduation, Rod traveled to Fairbanks. But he never got a job on the pipeline that summer because he wasn't high enough on the list. It would be the following year when he got a job but learned he wouldn't be working on the pipeline itself. Instead, he had to clean the pots and pans used to make food for the pipeline workers. He'd be stationed at Pump Station Six, about two hours north of Fairbanks, right by the Yukon River.

It was the middle of nowhere, Rod would say, a gorgeous landscape with nothing around him but mountains, trees, and water. It was nothing like Chicago, and Blagojevich was one of the youngest men in camp. He would later describe it like "a minimum security prison . . . because you're in the middle of nowhere and you can't go anywhere."

Blagojevich worked seven days a week that summer. When he wasn't cleaning pots and pans, he would clean up some of the portable offices set up around the pump station. He worked the night shift, starting at ten o'clock at night until eight in the morning. Rod was struck by the sunlight that still streamed across the landscape even late into the evening, with nighttime lasting from only two to four in the morning. One night, while cleaning the offices, he opened up the doors to air them out from all the dust that had gathered. Leaving the doors open, he walked over to the kitchen to complete his other tasks before heading back around four in the morning to close up the offices after their airing. As Rod walked back, he ran into another employee who asked Rod if he had seen the boss around. Rod hadn't.

"Why?" Rod asked.

"Because some fucking asshole left the doors open to the offices and there are two bears in there," the coworker said.

Rod walked over and saw the bears tearing apart the offices scrounging for food and making a complete mess. Security guards stood outside throwing rocks at the bears, trying to scare them off. But it was mostly useless. By the time the bears were done, they had demolished everything.

It was Rod who had to clean up, but he didn't answer the question about which idiot left the office doors open.

2

Leaving Cragin

As a politician, Rod Blagojevich spoke with pride about the hardscrabble neighborhood where he grew up, his immigrant father, his working mother, and the five-room apartment where he was raised. But as a youngster, Blagojevich was looking for a way out of Cragin. Test scores shut him out of a high-end university, and he wasn't going to be playing point guard for the Bulls or center field for the Cubs. Blagojevich feared getting sucked into the neighborhood's lifestyle and locked into a working-class job and common life.

At the University of Tampa, though, he began to gain some traction. He got good grades and dreamed of coming back to Chicago to make a life for himself—possibly in politics. Back home for winter break in 1976, Rod Blagojevich got absorbed along with the rest of the city with the news that Mayor Richard J. Daley had died. Daley had been mayor for twenty-one years, and his death caused a vacuum of power. One of the city's black aldermen, Wilson Frost, declared he would be the city's acting mayor, based on his reading of the city charter and the fact that he was president pro tempore of the city council. But Chicago wasn't ready for a black mayor—at least the white-majority city council wasn't—and they refused to allow Frost into the mayor's office. They said the keys to the office couldn't be found.

For several days, Frost's supporters and white aldermen debated and argued about whether Frost had the right to become acting mayor. It was a fascinating spectacle befitting the city. Already developing a negative attitude toward those in power, Blagojevich sided with Frost. So he and Ascaridis fashioned some makeshift stickers reading RETAIN WILSON FROST for mayor, passing the stickers around Cragin in a small sign of protest. A few days later, the city council made a decision. Michael Bilandic, the white alderman from Daley's home ward, the Eleventh, would be mayor.

———

While the excitement of the city was drawing Rod Blagojevich back home, Robert Blagojevich felt no such pull.

In his freshman year, Robert met a young coed from the South in his Western Civilization class. Her name was Julie Thrailkill. She was beautiful and charming and came from an upper-middle-class family. Her father, Walter, owned restaurants around Nashville, Tennessee, most notably a popular establishment called Arthur's.

Robert was beginning a new life without Rod. He had won a competitive military scholarship that paid for three years of tuition, launching an army career that lasted well into adulthood. He'd retire years later as a lieutenant colonel with the army reserves.

Soon after graduating, Robert and Julie married in August 1977 in Florida. Although the military scholarship and ROTC program required Robert to finish four years of active reserve, the newlyweds planned to move to Tallahassee where Robert would be attending graduate school in Eastern European studies at Florida State University. Robert and Rod were going their separate ways in life. Rod had just finished his sophomore year at Tampa, and with his big brother leaving and Chicago calling him home, he decided to transfer. He applied to both Northwestern University and the University of Chicago. Because he had a respectable grade point average at Tampa and didn't have to take the standardized tests at which he was clearly dreadful, Northwestern accepted him. Finally cutting away from his older brother, Rod was going to move back to Chicago and enter Northwestern as a junior majoring in history.

Blagojevich moved back home with $3,500 in his pocket, hooking back up with friends Mike Ascaridis and Dan Stefanski. He also met new friends at Northwestern, guys from other parts of the country and wealthier families. Tuition at Northwestern was high, so Rod lived at home with his parents and Millie's oldest sister, Helen. He delivered pizzas in his 1971 Dodge Dart for a neighborhood joint named Abondanza Restaurant and Pizzeria, where Stefanski also worked.

Though back in Chicago, Blagojevich felt out of place at Northwestern. A city kid, Blagojevich took public transportation or drove through much of the city to the stately Evanston campus, appearing in class wearing a black leather jacket and white T-shirts he bought at stores near Milwaukee Avenue and Division Street on the near Northwest Side. His Izod shirt–wearing classmates looked every bit the part of the preppies populating campuses all around the nation. While Rod listened to the King, they listened to Bruce Springsteen.

"I always felt that these kids at Northwestern, you know, they came from wealthier families, they came from better schools. I always felt a little bit intimidated that they were a lot smarter than me," is how Blagojevich put it on the witness stand in 2011. "And I hadn't been able to get in the first time, and so when I got there, I was afraid that, you know, maybe I wouldn't measure up to the other kids."

Still, Blagojevich's amiable personality enabled him to make friends and traverse the two distinct worlds. Among the friends he made at Northwestern was Bill Powell, who soon joined Blagojevich and Ascaridis carousing around Chicago, picking up girls and "being assholes," as Powell recalled. After some late nights, Blagojevich, Powell, and a few other friends wound up at a twenty-four-hour diner on the border between Chicago and Evanston called the Gold Coin. They called it the Cold Groin. Once or twice, Powell recalled, the young men would run out of the diner without paying the bill just for laughs. They called it "yo-ho"ing in an apparent pirate reference.

Blagojevich constantly talked sports, history, and politics. He played the field with girls but didn't have anyone steady. And he talked about his brother constantly. "He idolized Rob. That was key to Rod," Powell said.

Powell sometimes spent weekends in Cragin with Rod, sleeping over at the Blagojevich family apartment. Powell quickly realized the same thing Rod knew—he really didn't fit in at Northwestern.

"I think in some ways he reveled in sticking out on campus," Powell said. "He had such a chip on his shoulder, and he knew he had to do the work to be a success."

In addition to the obvious differences like taste in clothes and music, Blagojevich had adopted many of the conservative philosophies his father had embraced after coming to America. Because of what he saw the Soviet Union do to Yugoslavia, Rade Blagojevich deeply hated communism and embraced the Republican Party in America for their hard-line stance against reds. His conservative beliefs usually upset Millie, a New Deal Democrat who witnessed America's progress under FDR, and didn't match up well with the relatively liberal kids at Northwestern.

But Rade's influence and passion rubbed off on both Blagojevich boys, especially as they attended college during the tumultuous Jimmy Carter years. Studying politics and history, Rod gravitated toward men who made something of themselves from humble beginnings. He admired Alexander Hamilton, born poor in the West Indies, so much that he would later describe having a "man crush" on him and claim he memorized several of the Federalist Papers. Rod also identified greatly with Richard Nixon, confiding to friends a certain kinship with the shamed ex-president who had to work harder than everybody else to succeed.

In the post-Watergate era, it was more popular than ever on college campuses to be a Democrat. But Blagojevich went out of his way to debate his classmates and always took the conservative side. What the Kennedys did was just as bad as Nixon, he said dismissively. Nixon was a true American success story. His background and persona resonated with Blagojevich, who embraced the same chip-on-your-shoulder, up-from-nowhere attitude Nixon carried with him throughout much of his life. Blagojevich was embracing his role as outsider.

His uncanny ability to memorize always helped in his campus debates. Trying to sound smart, he'd recite another famous speech from Republican Teddy Roosevelt, declaiming verbatim Roosevelt's famous "Man in the Arena" speech.

"It is not the critic who counts; not the man who points out how the strong man stumbles, or where the doer of deeds could have done them better. The credit belongs to the man who is actually in the arena, whose face is marred by dust and sweat and blood."

To Powell and the rest of Blagojevich's buddies, Rod wasn't just trying to show off. He believed the words he was reciting. What's more, Blagojevich was collecting his odd stable of political heroes: Lincoln, Teddy Roosevelt, Nixon. He'd soon add a fourth: Ronald Reagan, for whom he'd vote for president in 1980.

═══

But as much as Rod was maturing in his political beliefs, he was still immature in many other ways. Blagojevich, Ascaridis, and other friends crank-called Chicago radio talk shows on WIND with Ascaridis trying to sound Latino and identifying himself as Rico La Verga.

"We would all dissolve in laughter. Mike had just gotten on the air calling himself Rico the Dick," wrote Powell, who became a foreign correspondent for *Newsweek* and *Time* and wrote an article about his times with Blagojevich in *Men's Journal*. Rod called another time, on St. Patrick's Day, when listeners were invited to talk about what they loved about the Irish.

"I think they're a bunch of sloths," Blagojevich said before hanging up.

The friends recorded the pranks and put them on a tape they called the Classics. Blagojevich also just liked screwing with people for sport, a character trait that continued well into his adulthood and political career.

At a Chicago Bulls game one night, Blagojevich and Powell brought along a nerdy friend named Rob, whom Blagojevich spent the entire first half trying to convince that a player had a fake nose because he was wearing a protective facemask.

"Seriously, Rob, this guy has no nose," Rod deadpanned. "Can you believe that? That's an artificial nose the guy's playing with."

———

By the time he received his degree from Northwestern, Blagojevich had decided politics was in his future and his best bet was to detach himself from the neighborhood. He would first have to go to law school, but he knew eventually he was going to run for public office. "I can't stand the sight of blood," he once said. "So I couldn't be a doctor."

Before his legal studies began, though, he wanted to make money to help pay the tuition. He continued to deliver pizzas for Abondanza on Wednesdays through Sundays and worked with Ascaridis doing construction work at Helene Curtis on the West Side. Among the perks there: an unlimited supply of free, fruity Suave shampoo.

"The stuff that smells like strawberries," Blagojevich wistfully told the jury in federal court. "You can have strawberry and watermelon. Remember that in the '70s? Maybe you don't."

Blagojevich loved his hair and enjoyed the perk, but he thought making connections in government probably helped his future plans more. He first got a job in the county recorder's office through a high school friend. Later, Blagojevich worked for the county's court interpreters program after his father found out about the job through a Serbian social organization he was active in. The county was looking for a Serbo-Croatian interpreter, and Rade thought his bilingual son was perfect for it.

One of his first cases, though, wasn't interpreting a fellow Serb or even a Croat. Instead, he was translating for a Bulgarian defendant at a courthouse in the South Loop at Thirteenth and Michigan. Blagojevich liked to say that his language skills were the next best thing to Bulgarian. Well, not quite.

During the testimony, two senior citizens said they were held up by a guy with a gun. But Blagojevich kept translating "gun" as "cannon."

=====

Between all the jobs and getting ready for law school, Blagojevich took acting classes at the Goodman School, lessons he would use years later, as Reagan used his acting skills, at press conferences and on television commercials. Unfortunately, those classes wouldn't help him on his law school entrance exam, the LSAT. As he had with nearly every standardized test he'd taken in his life, he did terribly, scoring in the lower half. He took it again and didn't do much better. It didn't matter. He still applied to several top-notch law schools, including Harvard. He thought it would be inspiring to learn law in Boston, a city so vital to the nation's founding. It was clearly a long shot, Blagojevich would remember later in court. But he relied on his essay.

"I tried to emphasize my background and diversity. . . . You can't have a lot of people with a name like mine in Harvard," Blagojevich testified. "It didn't work. And I like to say I applied on a Monday and I got my letter of rejection back on a Tuesday. I'm not literally saying that, I'm under oath, but it came back pretty quick."

He also was denied by the University of Chicago and even Northwestern, a snub he took personally because it dredged up his feelings of inadequacy and lacking the proper pedigree.

Blagojevich eventually got accepted to John Marshall Law School, a commuter law school in Chicago, and Pepperdine University in Malibu, California. Having spent the last three years living at home, he liked the idea of going west, even if it meant leaving his parents, who were going to be footing most of the law school tuition bills. As a kid growing up, he had always envisioned that one sign of making it in life was getting to California.

But before heading out, Blagojevich and Ascaridis took a trip to New York City. Beyond the expected tourist spots, Rod had one place he definitely wanted to go—Nixon's townhouse on the Upper East Side.

Blagojevich had read a magazine article that detailed Nixon's daily routine, including when he took his walks around the neighborhood. Rod insisted they show up and try to catch Nixon outside. Although they showed up plenty early, they both were still amazed to see him on the sidewalk. Wearing a wide grin and a white soccer-like shirt fashionable at the time with thick, dark stripes down the sleeves, Blagojevich cautiously approached Nixon and introduced himself and asked Nixon if he could take a picture with him. The thirty-seventh president had his hands filled with papers and a black binder, but he didn't mind at all. As the camera clicked, Blagojevich smiled while Nixon looked down, signing an autograph for the young men, his papers jammed between his chest and left arm.

It was nothing more than a brief interruption in an otherwise average day for Nixon. But for Blagojevich it was a highlight of a lifetime. Years later he would tell the story, acting out the parts of all three characters: himself, Ascaridis, and Nixon.

————

In the fall of 1980, with Ronald Reagan months from being elected president, Rod Blagojevich packed up his bags and moved west. He found himself blown away by the beauty of Pepperdine's campus overlooking the Pacific Ocean, and he was just as stunned by the women.

Blagojevich was once again easily distracted from his studies, choosing to read Charles Dickens novels and hang out on the beach over going to the law library. Later, he even got paid eighty dollars to be an extra in a TV movie, *Malibu*, in which he sat and watched a Chad Everett tennis match. It was a bit of a brain shift for Blagojevich.

"I had a job at a place called Malibu Nautilus," Blagojevich told the jury in 2011 before launching into one of his trademark rambles. "That was interesting because I'd clean up there and I'd help out, and, you know, they're working out there—I remember someone making a lot of noise, he was bench pressing, it was the late Michael Landon who played [on] *Little House on the Prairie*, and he was there. And Dyan Cannon, who was Cary Grant's fifth wife, she worked out once there. Olivia Newton-John, she would work out there. You'd see these movie stars. Farah Fawcett-Majors, you know, you'd see her. You know, it was completely different from Cicero and Armitage."

The first year of law school, which is traditionally the most difficult, ended up nearly catastrophic. Blagojevich found almost any excuse not to study. He got lost when professors tested students' logic and fashioned a legal debate in class, which was different from his undergrad lectures, where he had taken copious notes and memorized them for tests. By the end of his first year, he was on academic probation.

Blagojevich spent the summer painting porches back home but headed to England in August. Pepperdine offered law students the chance of spending a semester in London, and Rod seized on the opportunity. He later remembered thinking the "ambience of London" might make it easier for him to get in a legal mindset and concentrate on his studies.

Blagojevich was touring the city on a double-decker bus headed toward the Tower of London when he met Alonzo Monk.

Blagojevich recognized Monk as another student at Pepperdine, and the two started talking. Lon, as everyone called him, grew up in California. Monk's father was a rich, well-respected gynecologist who in 1962 delivered future tennis phenom Tracy Austin, an odd piece of trivia that somehow impressed Blagojevich. Later, the first time Rod visited the Monk family home, he was amazed to see peacocks patrolling the front lawn.

Despite their disparate backgrounds, Rod and Lon loved sports. Monk had played tennis in college while Rod talked about his mediocre boxing career. The following month, they watched the biggest match of the year—the "Showdown" welterweight championship fight between Sugar Ray Leonard and Tommy "Hit Man" Hearns—on a large screen in a movie theater at Piccadilly Circus. After being down at the start, Sugar Ray won a thrilling victory.

The two men bonded over the experience and forged a strong friendship throughout the semester. Despite being a year younger, Lon became a big-brother figure to Rod, who thought his friend was more mature and worth emulating.

After returning to Pepperdine, Monk and Blagojevich stayed close. But as they considered rooming together for their third year, an embarrassed Rod confided in Lon that he was close to flunking out. While Rod was back in Chicago between his second and third years, and Vrdolyak was arranging his clerk job with the city, Lon drove from his parents' home to Malibu to check Rod's final scores and see whether he had made it to his third year.

"I was on the phone and he was getting the grades, and I had tremendous relief when he told me that I survived. And I remember how he kinda yelled a little bit out of—you know, let out a yelp, you know, of cheerfulness for me," Blagojevich recalled for the jury.

"Those are little things that bond you with somebody. And that just—that and the previous experience with him began what I felt was a very close relationship. There are friends that you love in a real friend way, not—you know what I'm talkin' about. I loved Lon that way."

Rod and Lon lived together for their final year of law school. They lifted weights and ran together. Rod visited Lon's family in Palos Verdes and jogged with Lon's father, who still ran marathons despite being in his sixties. After graduation, Lon headed to Washington, DC, while Rod packed up his bags and headed back home to Chicago. But the two promised to stay in touch.

=====

Back in Chicago, one of Blagojevich's first stops was to see Vrdolyak. He wanted to know if that promise to make him "part of the family" still held.

By May 1983 the city's political landscape had changed dramatically. Just weeks earlier, Harold Washington had been sworn in as Chicago's mayor, the first African American to hold office in the city's history. And Vrdolyak was leading his contingent of white aldermen in a power struggle with Washington. In the fifty-member Chicago City Council, the "Vrdolyak 29," which included a brazen Northwest Side alderman named Richard Mell, was routinely defeating the "Washington 21" and stalling the mayor's initiatives. When Washington wanted to pass a piece of legislation to reform the city's infamously corrupt government, the Vrdolyak 29 blocked it. When Washington wanted an appointee to his cabinet approved, the twenty-nine aldermen wouldn't do it. City government was quickly coming to a standstill, and Washington couldn't do anything about it. Chicago was soon dubbed Beirut on the Lake.

Although Rod liked to think of himself as an anti-machine contrarian (and a Republican no less), he was quickly realizing political philosophy mattered little in Chicago. Connections, relationships, and getting ahead were all that really counted. Rod's only in was Vrdolyak, who did in fact bring Blagojevich out of law school to clerk on personal injury and workers' compensation cases. Lawyers in the alderman's office soon realized just how little Rod knew about the law.

"I gave one of the lawyers a case that was dated 1876, I thought it had a historic context," Blagojevich remembered on the witness stand. "It was ridiculous because it's no longer law, it hadn't been law for over a hundred years, and it was so not appreciated by the lawyers that they had me do other things like drop campaign literature in Hegewisch."

Vrdolyak soon made Blagojevich little more than an errand boy. He dropped off envelopes to Vrdolyak associates and picked up desserts for Vrdolyak's driver. It seemed unlikely Vrdolyak was going to hire him as an attorney for the firm. But the alderman still liked Blagojevich and promised to see if he could get him something with the Cook County State's Attorney's Office, where many young lawyers got their starts. By then, though, the office was being run by Richard M. Daley, son of the late Mayor Richard J. Daley, and Vrdolyak and the Daleys didn't get along.

"You've got to understand something about the Irish, the Daley Irish," Vrdolyak once remarked. "It's the Irish first, and everybody else is a Polack."

As Blagojevich killed time with Vrdolyak, he lived at home and studied for the bar exam. The first time he took it, he flunked. He studied more the second time, ensconcing himself at the august Harper Library at the University of Chicago even though it was miles away from his home. To him, the library, with its wood-paneled walls, *felt* like a law library and motivated him. Blagojevich passed the second time.

Done waiting for Vrdolyak, Blagojevich took a job with a firm in suburban Elk Grove Village in the shadows of O'Hare Airport, where he did mostly real estate work. Rod was quietly bitter about Vrdolyak not following through on his promise but also knew burning bridges with the alderman wasn't necessarily the smartest move for an upstart politician.

"He had promised the job in his firm, but apparently it never came through," Rod later said in an interview. "I sort of felt I was exiled in Elk Grove. . . . I just felt like I was Napoleon at Elba."

Blagojevich joined social groups and clubs in Elk Grove and discovered he was good at selling himself to clients. But he quickly tired of the suburbs and found a general practice to join run by well-respected Chicago attorney Marshall Moltz. Moltz's office was at Ashland and Addison, less than a mile west of Wrigley Field and just blocks from the gym where Rod had been pummeled as a senior in high school in the Golden Gloves.

While working for Moltz, Blagojevich's charming personality and ability to spin yarns were good for more than making friends or picking up girls. One of Blagojevich's first clients was a "little old lady" fighting her adopted daughter and son-in-law who were seeking conservatorship of the woman's estate because they felt she was squandering it.

In court, Blagojevich soon found himself in the middle of a jury trial. Blagojevich hadn't even participated in a moot court at law school and didn't know the rules of evidence or how to properly make an opening statement. But that didn't stop him. He decided to wing it.

While the daughter's attorneys introduced two dozen pieces of evidence and got doctors to testify against his client, Blagojevich had trouble introducing any evidence in court and had no witnesses. All he could do was establish that the daughter and son-in-law hadn't seen his client in over a year. But he made up for his poor performance with an hour-long closing argument where he paced the courtroom floor and yelled about evidence being kept from the jury due to "technicalities."

"Please don't hold her accountable for the rookie mistakes of her lawyer," Blagojevich recalled telling the jury. A little more than hour later, the jury came back in favor of Blagojevich's client.

Excited, Blagojevich ran back to Moltz's office and told his boss the story. Moltz smiled but weeks later fired Blagojevich, saying he was good at getting clients and he should go out on his own. Moltz didn't think Rod was focused enough on his work.

———

Dismissed but undaunted, Blagojevich began his own private practice. He did a little bit of everything—real estate closings, traffic cases, and criminal misdemeanor work. When neighborhood guys got into trouble, they hired Blagojevich.

He also got more involved in running, which he still talked to Monk about. On the witness stand years later, Blagojevich would say he ran the 1984 Chicago Marathon in a blistering time of two hours, fifty minutes, and thirty seconds. He said he did it wearing a T-shirt with the image of boxer Roberto Duran on the front, inspired not to repeat Duran's famous *"No más"* line when he lost to Sugar Ray Leonard. Unfortunately, he could never prove his time. He said he didn't know the rules of marathons and tore his number off his shirt, so judges never registered his finish.

While he enjoyed private practice, Blagojevich decided it was time to get a job with the Cook County State's Attorney's Office. He desperately needed the legal experience, and being an assistant prosecutor would give him the background he needed, not to mention possible political contacts in the office. Rather than go back to Vrdolyak, Blagojevich asked a favor from another neighborhood friend, Danny Angarola. His older brother, Michael, was first assistant in the office, Daley's right-hand man. Rod asked Danny if Mike could get him a job, providing another early lesson of the rewards of Chicago politics and the world of government favors.

In March 1986, Blagojevich got the job. His first assignment was anything but glamorous. He worked traffic court, often considered the lowest rung on the office ladder. Blagojevich prosecuted drunken drivers and suspended licenses—petty cases that didn't stir his soul. But Blagojevich struck his coworkers as ambitious, even overly so. Always energetic, he was a buzz of activity inside traffic court, running from case to case and always glad-handing with those around him—from public defenders and defendants to victims and even judges.

He was making connections, and that was important because politics were still at the forefront of his mind. On one Friday night after work, Blagojevich told his supervisor, John Budin, he wanted to be president of the United States one day.

═══

As Blagojevich built his resume, Chicago's political scene remained in turmoil. The Vrodolyak-Washington battle was still raging, and Blagojevich was being asked to take a side. Rade Blagojevich had done campaign work for Vrdolyak, and even though he didn't hire Rod as an attorney for his firm, the alderman asked Rod if he could help in the Twenty-Sixth Ward, a heavily Latino area on the city's near Northwest Side.

The Vrdolyak-Washington clashes had found their way to federal court, where a remap of the city's wards was debated. In May 1986, the courts ordered that special elections be held in seven wards that had been reconfigured to better enable blacks and Latinos to be voted onto the city council to reflect the increased population of both. One of those wards was the Latino-leaning Twenty-Sixth, where Washington had a candidate—Luis Gutierrez. Vrdolyak had one too—Manuel "Manny" Torres.

While the Twenty-Sixth Ward was geographically nowhere near Vrdolyak's Tenth Ward, the balance of power on the council was at stake, and each of the seven races mattered. "Do you have any friends who can help us in the Twenty-Sixth Ward?" he asked Rod. Blagojevich said he did. Vrdolyak told him to go visit another alderman on the Northwest Side to get his orders.

Rod called up thirteen friends—including Ascaridis and Stefanski—and they drove up to 2810 W. Fullerton Avenue. Inside was a rush of activity. Telephones rang. Dozens of men walked in and out the front door carrying piles of pro-Torres/anti-Gutierrez leaflets and signs.

A few feet away stood the man running the operation. Average-sized and in his late forties, he had a round face topped with a pile of white hair parted on the left. He had black eyebrows and piercing blue eyes. As he talked, his head bobbed up and down and his double chin wobbled. Not only was he talking a million miles a minute, he was talking about a thousand different topics. He needed no introduction to Blagojevich.

"Alderman Mell," he said. "I'm here to help."

Mell was a bundle of nerves and energy. It was his usual disposition.

A native of Muskegon, Michigan, Mell had moved to Chicago after graduating college. He landed in Chicago's Logan Square neighborhood after meeting a woman, Marge, who soon became his wife. In the 1960s, Mell was in Chicago when strife ruled the streets. But he was not a protester. He chose a path to power, joining a group called the Young Democrats of Cook County, which served as a sort of farm team for the city's politicians even though many of the Young Democrats viewed themselves as more independent-minded than those with the city's machine.

During the historic Democratic National Convention in 1968 in Chicago, Mell—then thirty years old—got a job through his post with the Young Democrats as a driver for US Senator Edmund Muskie of Maine. He drove Muskie around town in a Cadillac, wheeling over curbs as he steered through the crowds to deliver the senator for his speeches. When Democratic presidential nominee Hubert H. Humphrey picked Muskie to be his vice presidential candidate, Mell celebrated with Muskie, his wife, and his staff at the Conrad Hilton, dining on lobster brought in from Maine. Seven floors below, protesters battled with police in televised clashes that would stun the country, but Muskie, Mell, and the others didn't notice until several people at the table started crying. Teargas from police had begun wafting through the hotel's open windows.

Mell started a spring manufacturing company near Logan Square that quickly became successful. After a while, the business was running so smoothly Mell realized he didn't have to dedicate as much time there, so he decided to more fully engage in his love of politics.

He began where everyone in Chicago starts—he became a precinct captain in his neighborhood. The time-honored practice in Mayor Richard J.

Daley's Democratic organization called for spending years slowly rising through the ranks before making a jump for elected office. But Dick Mell was never a patient man. By 1972, he ran to be the Thirty-Third Ward's Democratic committeeman, a politically powerful post that controlled patronage and held the fate of ward candidates. Mell challenged the incumbent committeeman, John Brandt, who had previously been the area's alderman for two decades. Mell's bid was an affront to the organization, and he promptly lost. But he made a name for himself and three years later ran for alderman against the guy Brandt put up.

Alfred Ronan was a young assistant secretary for Illinois Democratic Governor Dan Walker's transportation department at the time. A mutual friend and Democratic political operative called Ronan to see if he would be interested in helping Mell run for alderman. The friend, Pat Quinn, said Mell was a hard worker and deserved a shot.

Mell had a half-dozen precinct captains and Ronan added another eighty men of his own to beef up the field operations. He was soon running Mell's campaign, and they eked out a victory. A year later, Mell became Democratic committeeman of the Thirty-Third Ward, and while Ronan lost for state representative that year, he won the seat in 1978, cementing a relationship between the two men.

When Blagojevich arrived at the ward headquarters to help him, Mell had grown to become one of the city's most powerful—and notorious—politicians. While known for being erratic and a nonstop chatterbox, he also had formed one of the strongest ward organizations on the Northwest Side, with scores of political soldiers (many who had government jobs thanks to Mell) who swore allegiance to him and would walk the streets and get his candidates elected.

He was also rich.

As Rod and his friends walked in to Mell's office, the alderman quickly gave them their orders. He pulled out a map of the Twenty-Sixth Ward and pointed out precincts in the Humboldt Park neighborhood where he wanted them to hand out materials promoting Torres's candidacy. In stark contrast to those Wilson Frost sticker days, the men spent the day jamming fliers inside the doors of homes, two-flats, and apartment buildings for the pro-machine candidate.

On the day of the special election, Blagojevich watched the results come in. It wasn't good for Vrdolyak. Gutierrez won. Not only that, but other races went in Washington's favor. By the time election night ended, the balance of power on the council had swung enough in Washington's direction that it was a 25-25 tie, giving the mayor the tie-breaking vote.

A year into his job at the state's attorney's office, Blagojevich had received a small promotion. He was now prosecuting minor cases—gun offenses, domestic violence, and prostitution—at branch courts in police stations like Fifty-First and Wentworth on the South Side and Grand and Central on the Northwest Side. They were still petty, but at least it wasn't traffic anymore.

He was beginning to realize he didn't want to be spending most of his early thirties as a prosecutor. It took hundreds of hours of court time and years of work to get ahead—five years alone just to get to felony court. Blagojevich wasn't that patient or, some felt, that hard a worker. He soon began cutting out early to do real estate closings on the side, which, while technically allowed, sometimes left his partners with the extra workload. Some of his fellow prosecutors nicknamed him the Shadow for his frequent absences. But Blagojevich's goal remained becoming a politician, not a prosecutor.

He was beginning to think about switching jobs yet again when he was stunned to learn his only clout in the office, Michael Angarola, had died. Angarola had been heading home to suburban Lincolnwood when he was involved in a car crash on the Kennedy Expressway. A twenty-year-old woman had lost control of her Datsun 280Z sports car, which jumped over a massive curb that split the expressway at Van Buren Street and smashed head-on with Mike Angarola's car. An hour later, both drivers were dead.

A few months after that, in February 1988, tragedy struck someone even closer to Blagojevich.

Rade Blagojevich, now seventy-seven years old, was out of town visiting Robert when he was cut down by a massive stroke. Robert rushed him to a hospital, but by the time doctors got to him, significant damage to his brain and motor functions rendered him unable to speak. They were able to stabilize him enough to transfer him back home to Chicago, to a nursing home where Millie and Rod would visit him on a regular basis. Then sixty-six, Millie retired from the CTA ticket-taker job she had held for twenty years to spend as much time with Rade as possible, though Rade still couldn't speak or eat.

After Blagojevich got back to work, he ran into Judge Saul Perdomo. While working at Fifty-First and Wentworth, the two loved to talk politics and lunched in Chinatown or Hyde Park. Perdomo was an associate judge at the time, a lesser judicial position than a full circuit judge. Perdomo wanted to run for a full-circuit post himself and asked Rod for help. In some parts of the country, asking a prosecutor who tries cases before you for political help might seem to carry inherent conflicts of interest. But not in Chicago. Blagojevich gladly agreed and picked up the phone to talk to a friend of his, Paris Thompson.

Blagojevich had met Thompson while working at Fifty-First and Wentworth. A young man who grew up in the Robert Taylor public housing homes near the police station, Thompson had been shining shoes there when he got kicked out over a misunderstanding with the police. Blagojevich's history as a shoe-shine boy instantly drew him to Thompson, and he had persuaded Perdomo to talk to the cops to let Thompson back in.

Now Blagojevich was wondering if Thompson had any ideas for where Perdomo could go on the South Side to get votes in the black community. Thompson suggested a church in Englewood, at Seventy-First and Halsted, the True Temple of Solomon. The temple's leader enjoyed allowing candidates to campaign from the pulpit. Perdomo loved the idea and wanted Blagojevich to join him. In fact, he wanted to see if Blagojevich would campaign with him all day on Sunday, March 6.

"Why don't you come with?" Perdomo asked.

Blagojevich had little going on that day, so he agreed.

Two more things, Perdomo added. He was going to a fund-raiser for a Northwest Side alderman, Dick Mell. Perdomo explained he had known Mell for years. They were members of the Young Democrats together. Rod said he knew Mell a little. Not only had he met him a few years ago during the Torres race, but he also met him in court when Mell showed up with residents upset about graffiti proliferation in their neighborhood.

The other thing, Perdomo said, was about Mell's daughter, Patti. She was engaged to a guy in Italy, where she had studied for a time, but they broke up and now she was moping around the house, brokenhearted. Mell wanted to see his daughter happy again and was bringing her to the event.

I told Mell about you, Perdomo said. "I said, 'I got this young assistant state's attorney.'"

Then thirty-one years old, Blagojevich had been dating around for years, meeting women around town or through work circles. A few relationships had been serious, with some women even meeting his parents. But Blago-jevich never thought of himself as the marrying type. All the same, he didn't mind being set up, especially with the daughter of a powerful alderman.

=====

After visiting the True Temple of Solomon, the two men steered north toward Mell's fund-raiser. It was being held at a famous Chicago German restaurant on Southport called Zum Deutschen Eck. It sat in the shadow of the historic, Gothic-style St. Alphonsus Catholic Church, its gray steeple hovering overhead.

Inside, the men passed under the wood-carved doorways that matched the solid oak, handmade bar and were instantly in the middle of the hundreds of people there for Mell's event. Perdomo scanned the crowd and spotted a brunette standing off in the distance, away from the throng. She was attractive and skinny and wore a red dress. She seemed disengaged with the festivities around her.

"That's Patti," Perdomo said, grabbing Rod's hand and pulling him toward her. Before either of them knew it, they were face to face.

About to turn twenty-three years old, Patricia Mell was the eldest daughter of Dick and Marge Mell. Patti had grown up in a household where her father was always a powerful alderman and kingmaker, and she was the princess. She was popular in school, attending St. Scholastica, an all-girls Catholic high school in Rogers Park run by the Benedictine Sisters. Chicago's first female mayor, Jane Byrne, graduated from St. Scholastica and even spoke to the students in 1982 while she was mayor and Patti was a junior.

Intelligent, Patti had shown some interest in French and the theater, especially Shakespeare. In her senior yearbook, she even quoted Hamlet's soliloquy contemplating suicide, "That this too too solid flesh would melt, thaw and resolve itself into a dew!" She went to the University of Illinois and studied economics before coming back to Chicago, where she found herself looking at her future husband.

"Patti, this is Rod," the judge said. "Rod, Patti."

Mell watched from a slight distance before saying hello to the young assistant state's attorney and then leaving the two to talk. Rod was quickly attracted to Patti. She was eight years younger but seemed smart and mature for her age. Rod did most of the talking, yammering on about work and politics and books. Patti listened intently. He was engaging and charming. The same way he was good at making friends and winning over judges, he was good at attracting women.

"If you go out with me, I'm going to show you the time of your life," Blagojevich said, smiling. After accepting the offer, Patti later parroted the line to her father, recognizing it as much for its braggadocio as for its cheesiness.

Two weeks later, Rod picked up the phone and called her, and they made plans to meet the following Sunday—three weeks after they had first met. Rod continued to bungle things and showed up thirty minutes late.

But despite the false start, Rod and Patti quickly grew close. Throughout that spring and summer, Rod broke it off with the few other women he had been seeing and began an exclusive relationship with Patti. Rod was constantly struck by how smart and well read Patti was. Maybe she couldn't memorize lines from poems or books like he could, but she knew what she was talking about. In Italy, she had spent a great deal of time at the library, she told him. After that, she and Rod would head over to a local library from time to time for dates. Rod was so excited, he'd call up Lon Monk to tell him about their outings together.

Just as he met Patti, Blagojevich decided to leave the state's attorney's office, feeling he could no longer get much out of the job. He joined a law firm run by attorneys James Kaplan and Sheldon Sorosky that focused on worker's compensation cases. Sorosky, himself a former assistant state's attorney, had met Blagojevich in his clerking days and knew him as an intelligent and capable young man who seemed to be very well read, especially when it came to history.

While Rod's life changed around him, his father lay in a nursing home, still unable to communicate or walk. Rod would see his father several times a week, almost always running into his mother there. And Rade's condition wasn't improving. One night as Rod sat at his father's bedside, he realized it was time to grow up. He had fallen in love with Patti, and he thought he wanted to one day marry her. And as he was losing his father, he was gaining a father figure in Mell, who was overjoyed his daughter had found a new man.

By that summer, Mell approached Rod with a job offer. Mell knew Rod was interested in politics and government, so why not join his team as a staff member? It was a part-time job, but it was a good opportunity, and he could open a private practice to make ends meet.

Rod didn't think twice. Workers' comp cases were boring him, and while he liked the firm, he told them he was going to leave just five months in. He hoped Kaplan and Sorosky understood.

As 1988 drew to a close, Rade grew frailer. Doctors at his nursing home couldn't do much more for him. On a cold Thursday night, December 29, Rod got news his father was having trouble breathing. He and Patti and Millie rushed to Columbus Hospital on the North Side. All three stayed there for hours, into the following morning. Doctors urged Rod and Patti to take Millie home. There was nothing they could do. At 7:30 in the morning, the doctors at Columbus called with the news that Rade had died.

In early 1989, Rod Blagojevich walked down Fullerton Avenue on the city's Northwest Side. Trucks, cars, and buses rumbled down the busy street just west of California Avenue in the city's Logan Square neighborhood as Blagojevich approached an unremarkable, single-story building with a wooden facade and glass front door.

"2810" read the address, and on the glass door were bold letters informing passers-by of the occupant:

33RD WARD
REGULAR
DEMOCRATIC ORGANIZATION
RICHARD F. MELL
ALDERMAN-COMMITTEEMAN

Three years earlier, Blagojevich had been here helping the white majority aldermen fight Harold Washington. That day, he was working as Mell's top staffer.

The office was typically a hive of activity. City workers hung out there for hours at a time. The phone was constantly ringing with politicians, neighborhood activists, and government bureaucrats all wanting something—or answering Mell's demands.

The office was nothing to look at. It was dusty, littered with paperwork and infested with mice. But to Blagojevich, it was exciting. He was finally really seeing Chicago politics from the inside, and he was part of it.

Beyond the front lobby area, Blagojevich looked down a long hallway dotted with doors on both sides. The first door on the right was the offices of a neighborhood newspaper, the *Chicago Post*, which Mell owned with James Boratyn, a precinct captain. The free, twice-a-month publication was a propaganda sheet filled with positive news about Mell's efforts to rid the neighborhood of crime, litter, and abandoned cars.

Across the hallway from the *Post*'s headquarters was Mell's wood-paneled personal office. His desk, also dark wood, was kept tidy. Slid under a glass topper sat a map of the city's Thirty-Third Ward, detailing every precinct, block, and alley. But there was no sign of what Mell was most famous for.

Mell's picture had been splashed around the country after the November 1987 death of Mayor Harold Washington. Chicago and the nation were stunned by the loss, and the days that followed shook the city to its core. With both allies and foes seeking to fill the resulting political vacuum, emergency meetings of the Chicago City Council suddenly became must-see local television as aldermen elbowed one another and lobbied behind closed doors to pick the next mayor.

As thousands jammed the streets outside city hall during the debate to pick Washington's successor, Mell stood up on his desk in the council chambers, waving several pieces of paper in an effort to be heard. Photographers captured the bizarre scene, which became symbolic of the city's wild and outrageous political landscape. Alderman Eugene Sawyer was eventually selected to replace Washington. He was an African American that white aldermen could agree on.

The next office down the hallway was Rod's.

As Mell's number one, Blagojevich's job was to show up at the ward office on Monday and Wednesday nights as well as Saturday mornings to deal with constituent complaints and services. On those weekdays, Blagojevich arrived around four in the afternoon and would stay until nine at night. On Saturdays, he would work from nine in the morning until two in the afternoon. Blagojevich loved the job and came off as earnest and interested. And his law degree didn't hurt either, helping him talk his way through the city's and county's bureaucracies. But at $13,000 in his first year, it wasn't a full-time career, and Rod was still trying to get his law practice off the ground. He opened storefront legal offices on the North Side, a little east of Mell's ward, at Montrose and Lincoln avenues, overlooking Welles Park, then at Lawrence and Ashland avenues. Millie answered telephone calls and helped organize things. He later rented space from his previous employers, Kaplan and Sorosky, downtown at 415 N. LaSalle.

Romantically, Rod and Patti were getting closer. The pair joined Perdomo to go skiing, their first time together, in Alpine Valley in Wisconsin. Mell was also getting closer to Rod. Mell was telling close friends and associates he was growing fond of the young man and felt like he was doing a good job at the ward offices.

"The kid has a knack for politics," he would say.

In Mell's family, Blagojevich at the time looked to be the closest thing there was to a successor to the alderman. Dick Mell's son, Richard, showed little interest for politics. Patti majored in economics at University of Illinois and was helping out the family's spring factory. She also was showing a little interest in real estate. Youngest daughter Deb was young and still trying to figure out what she wanted to be. Still, the Mell clan had several connections to government. Richard had a job with the city's aviation department. Patti had worked a summer at city hall, and even Mell's mother was on city payroll. Over the years she held numerous city jobs, despite questions about how often she showed up at work.

Blagojevich's job never entailed him going to city hall or working out of anywhere except Mell's ward office. But for a two-month period in 1989, his paychecks showed him being paid by four different City Council committees that did their work downtown, which indicated Blagojevich may have been paid for work he never did. Blagojevich later said that he never worked at city hall and never noticed he was being paid from the different City Council funds.

It was an oversight that wasn't going to be unnoticed forever.

———

At least one friend does remember Blagojevich being at the Hall in 1989. Judge Perdomo was at city hall with Blagojevich in July 1989 on the day when the thirty-two-year-old Blagojevich walked a few blocks east to Marshall Field's on State Street to buy an engagement ring for Patti. Blagojevich had already flown out to Washington, DC, to ask Monk about the idea, and Rod moved ahead with his plan.

Blagojevich scoured the jewelry case for the perfect ring. Scanning the shelves he finally found it. It cost about $5,000. The next day, Blagojevich was back at city hall, this time visiting Mell and telling him—not asking for permission—he was going to ask Patti to marry him.

"He was ecstatic," Perdomo recalled of the alderman's reaction. "He truly liked Rod and thought he would be great for Patti."

Later that night, Rod asked and Patti said yes. They set a date for a year away—August 25, 1990.

They married inside the Alice S. Millar Chapel at Northwestern University in Evanston, at the bend of the road leading into the heart of the campus. It was not a particularly political affair, especially for the wedding of a powerful city alderman's daughter and the man who would twice be elected governor. Only a few of Cook County's political class were invited, and Blagojevich invited Sorosky.

About one hundred people gathered inside the large chapel. Robert Blagojevich, Mike Ascaridis, and Danny Angarola all stood up as groomsmen, and Lon Monk served as an usher.

When father and daughter reached the end of the aisle, Mell looked at a smiling Rod Blagojevich. Rod took Patti by the hand and Mell walked back to his seat, where he watched the Reverend Thomas Parker take over the ceremony and marry the happy couple. During the ceremony, Monk read the Twenty-third Psalm: "The Lord is my shepherd, I shall not want."

Like the ceremony, the reception was not grand, held in a side room next to the chapel. But Rod and Patti looked overjoyed. Always outgoing, Mell stepped back for a few moments to take in the scene. His daughter was married, launching a new stage of her life with a man who seemed to share the same passion for politics and government as he did.

"He's made me a happy man," Mell told one guest about Rod. "They're an amazing couple."

3

A Tap on the Shoulder

Rod and Patti walked through the front door of Mell's Northwest Side bungalow and found the powerful alderman in the living room on his hands and knees.

It was early January 1992, and Mell had scattered maps all over the floor. He was clearly in a quandary. "Ronan left me," he told the couple, and they knew exactly what that meant. Every decade, the state deals with the results of the national census by redrawing Illinois's political maps. The shapes of the state legislative and congressional districts change to reflect shifts in population, but they also have a major political element. The Republicans had redrawn the maps after the 1990 census, leaving Democrats to battle it out in several legislative districts in Chicago. The 1992 election would be the first under the new maps, and Mell and his longtime ally, Alfred Ronan, couldn't agree on who should run where. Ronan wanted to run in a neighboring district and let his friend, incumbent Myron Kulas, take the seat in Mell's neighborhood. But Mell didn't care about Kulas. He thought it was time for Rod Blagojevich's entrance into politics.

"The kid could run," he had told Ronan.

The two men had been arguing about it for weeks when Ronan finally decided he'd had enough. He was packing his stuff up from the offices he shared with Mell and moving. He would run in the lakefront district, and Kulas, a seven-term incumbent, would run in Mell's neighborhood. If Mell didn't like it, then his son-in-law would have to challenge Kulas—which is exactly why Mell had invited Rod and Patti over to his house.

"You interested in running?" Mell asked Rod as the alderman continued to pore over the political maps that detailed the new boundaries.

Without hesitating, Rod said yes. He only had one reservation. He wanted to take his own positions on the issues and didn't want Mell telling him how to vote.

"I don't give a fuck about that," Mell answered.

It was decided then. Rod Blagojevich would run for the seat of Illinois Representative from the Thirty-Third District. But there was one other problem. Blagojevich didn't live in the Thirty-Third District. Mell and Blagojevich called Michael Madigan, the Speaker of the House and one of Illinois's most powerful politicians. They asked Madigan about the residency issue, and he told them that because the political boundaries were newly drawn, Rod was indeed allowed to run.

While dramatic and life-changing for those involved, especially Blagojevich, the decision amounted to little more than another daily twist in the city's political soap opera. The *Chicago Tribune* covered the unveiling of Candidate Rod Blagojevich on January 14, 1992, with a story that appeared in the "Chicagoland" section. They spelled his last name Blagojewevick.

For Mell, the 1992 campaign was about more than getting Blagojevich elected. Due to his split with Ronan, he feared his political powerbase was threatened. While not front page news, when an alderman and ward committeeman like Mell has a falling-out with a high-profile state legislator like Ronan, the city's political types were left to wonder if Mell was losing his grip. Mell needed to answer that question immediately. Not only did Rod have to win his race, but Ronan had to lose his.

The next day, Mell went to work at city hall, and the gravity of what he was getting into hit him. Other aldermen, including Terry Gabinski, whose Thirty-Second Ward held most of the precincts in the legislative district, made it clear Mell was on his own. Others sent the same signal.

That evening, Mell called Blagojevich, who had spent the whole day calling friends and lining up their support. A few had even said they'd donate money. Mell told him he was having second thoughts. "Maybe I should talk to Ronan and see if I can get him back," he told Blagojevich. "They're all against us."

Blagojevich said he'd do whatever Mell decided but that he was up for the challenge.

"I'm a big boy," Blagojevich said. "If it's bad for you politically, I understand. I'll support whatever you do."

"That's all I wanted to hear," Mell said.

As always, Mell had a plan. He called Nancy Kaszak, a community activist along the lakefront on the North Side who had made a name for herself in the 1980s in an unsuccessful effort to fight the Chicago Cubs' plans to install lights atop Wrigley Field. Now a lawyer for the Chicago Park District, Kaszak would be great against Ronan, who had earned a reputation as a wheeler and dealer in Springfield, the state capital. The "reformer" versus the "insider." In the yuppie neighborhoods along the lakefront, where residents frowned on stereotypical machine politics, Mell felt she had a chance.

Mell knew Kaszak was already thinking of running anyhow. He invited her to come over to his house, and when she got there, Rod and Patti were sitting on a piano bench. The couple said almost nothing as Mell held court. Ronan, he explained, still had a strong political army and if he had to fight on two fronts—for both his seat and the seat between Kulas and Blagojevich—that would give both of them a better chance to win.

Mell also promised to stake $30,000 for Kaszak's campaign.

In Chicago, the Democratic primary—being held in March—was the only election that mattered. Working-class residents, many of whom got their city jobs from their alderman or ward committeeman like Mell, owed their livelihoods to those elected officials, all of whom were Democrats. The general election in November was little more than a formality.

US Representative Dan Rostenkowski, the city's biggest political heavyweight in Washington, DC, whose political patronage army in Chicago was formidable, backed Kulas, who also had the tacit endorsement of Mayor Richard M. Daley, who by then had been elected mayor thirteen years after his father's death.

Still, Blagojevich had two things working in his favor: Mell's political army of precinct captains and Blagojevich's own ability to sell himself to voters.

From the moment the campaign began, Blagojevich plunged headlong into retail politics. In the morning, he went to coffee shops and El train stops. At night, he went to bowling alleys and restaurants. Part of the district was inside Mell's Thirty-Third Ward, but most of it wasn't. Blagojevich called Paris Thompson and asked him to get a few friends together to knock on doors inside the one public housing project in the district. Patti walked the neighborhoods too, knocking on doors and selling her husband to skeptical voters.

The whole thing had the atmosphere of a family business. Years later, while campaigning for reelection as governor, Rod and Patti talked openly about this first campaign as one of the happiest periods of their lives, when times were simpler, everything was new, and the constant pressure to raise campaign cash was nonexistent.

It was also during this campaign that Blagojevich first utilized that keen memorization ability he had cultivated as a child for political ends. Before groups small and large on the stump, Blagojevich recited the famous orations verbatim (or close enough that few people noticed). Blagojevich knew that while he was politically savvy, he was rarely the smartest man in the room.

Before Election Day, Blagojevich stood before a crowded hall of Thirty-Third Ward precinct workers and supporters after being introduced by Mell. Many in the crowd, loyal soldiers to Mell over the years, wanted the state representative job for themselves. But Mell picked his son-in-law. Those were the breaks, especially in Chicago politics.

Blagojevich didn't have much original to say, but he knew he could quote someone else to sound more substantive. As he stood before dozens of mostly hard-bitten city workers, he recited from Shakespeare's *Henry V* in which King Henry tried to rally his underdog troops before they battled the French.

"We few, we happy few, we band of brothers. For he today who sheds his blood with me shall be my brother and gentlemen in England now abed shall think themselves accursed they were not here, and hold their manhood cheap while others speak that fought with us on St. Crispin's Day!"

The city workers stood silent, not sure if Blagojevich was even finished and undoubtedly wondering if Mell had lost his mind putting this goofy guy up for the state rep seat. Then Blagojevich added one original line of his own: "Al Ronan never did that for you!"

They all cheered.

Blagojevich, who had a great ability to win crowds over through self-deprecating humor and telling audiences what they wanted to hear, had won over his first one.

Over the next two months, Kulas never even met Blagojevich, who nonetheless ripped the incumbent for being inattentive to voters' needs and not fitting in with the residents of the newly drawn district. As Election Day approached, Blagojevich felt the momentum building. The *Tribune* editorial board endorsed him, describing him as "an impressive young attorney who knows the communities in the district better." Mell's army, meanwhile, knocked on doors, jammed signs in yards, and pushed palm cards at the polling places.

Election Day arrived on March 17, St. Patrick's Day, a day when voters in Illinois would make history by nominating Carol Moseley-Braun to be the Democratic challenger for US Senate, defeating incumbent Alan Dixon. In what would be termed the Year of the Woman, Moseley-Braun would go on to become the first female African American senator in US history.

It was also a historic win for Blagojevich. He defeated Kulas by more than 4,000 votes out of more than 17,000 cast. One vote that Blagojevich didn't get was his own. Because he lived outside the district, he voted for Kaszak. Still, that night he picked up the phone and called his mother, Millie, to inform her of the victory.

"I won, Mama," he told her. Millie told him she was proud of him and wished his father was still alive to see his youngest son's achievement. Then, in a story Blagojevich would tell numerous times over the years, she exacted two promises from him.

"Now son, promise me you'll always be honest," Millie said. "And promise me you'll never take bribes."

"Of course I'll never take bribes," Blagojevich said. "Not only would that be dishonest, it would be illegal, and I'd never do anything to dishonor the memory of my father."

Then she asked one more thing: "Do you think you can get Aunt Daisy's son-in-law a job?"

Blagojevich would later tell the story as a joke. It garnered cheers and laughs from crowds who appreciated a sense of humor from a politician who winked about even his own family's duplicity regarding Chicago-style politics and patronage. Publicly, everybody condemned typical Chicago politics, but privately, everybody knew how the game was played. The Aunt Daisy joke fit perfectly within the story Rod loved to tell in selling himself to voters. He was a Chicagoan just like them. But he wouldn't break the rules.

It was a story Blagojevich wasn't always consistent in reciting. Before becoming governor, Blagojevich often finished the story by saying while he tried to help Aunt Daisy's son-in-law, he never got him a job because the son-in-law found another job. When running for reelection as governor in

2006, Blagojevich finished the story this way: "Thirteen years later, I'm governor, and my aunt Daisy's son-in-law, he's still unemployed!"

That version always got more laughs.

But on St. Patrick's Day 1992, it was Rod and Mell who were the ones laughing as they basked in the glow of the victory. What's more, Ronan lost to Kaszak. It was a highlight of Mell's career as a kingmaker. And the ward boss did it by selling to the public two candidates portrayed as reformers. Later that week, a sign could be seen in Mell's ward office: AL RONAN REST IN PEACE.

On Tuesday, November 3, 1992, Rod Blagojevich easily defeated Republican Daniel Reber by a more than 3-to-1 margin. When he arrived in Springfield two months later, Blagojevich took along with him the chip on his shoulder he had begun fashioning as a youngster.

Looking around the House floor, Blagojevich saw some of the same types of people he had met at Northwestern: men and women—even fellow legislators elected on a "reform" platform like he was—who he felt were elitist and didn't have to scratch for success like he did. They had this job handed to them by moneyed or powered interests. Occasionally he would mention these feelings to fellow legislators, some of whom had to bite their tongues. This was coming from the guy who had a House seat given to him by Dick Mell?

But Blagojevich didn't view it that way. Of course, Blagojevich acknowledged, Mell helped him. But he also went out of his way to let people know he felt he had won the seat by campaigning hard and raising cash. These North Shore and lakefront do-gooders who came from wealthy families didn't appreciate the plight of Chicago's working men and women. And because they didn't, they were hypocrites who didn't deserve his respect. They talked about helping the working class and the downtrodden, but they didn't really know what it was like.

"I do. I'm one of them," he said.

Also on the House floor Blagojevich saw Speaker Michael Madigan. Short and skinny with cold blue eyes, Madigan had been speaker since 1983 and ran the chamber like a fiefdom. Democratic members of the House swore allegiance to him and followed his every direction. And if they didn't, they soon found themselves on the outs and facing a well-funded,

Madigan-backed challenger in the next Democratic primary. Despite both the governor's office and the Senate being in Republican hands, many considered Madigan to be the most powerful politician in the state. A master of the process of governing, he killed legislation he didn't like in the House while he often figured out ways, through compromise or coercion, to get bills he supported passed and signed into law. If he wasn't the most powerful man in Springfield, he certainly was the smartest. The tired but true expression among legislators was: "Madigan plays chess while we're playing checkers."

To Blagojevich, Madigan embodied the authority he often fought against. And while Blagojevich said he would vote with Madigan most of the time, he told colleagues if there were issues he felt he could champion to challenge the state's power structure, he'd cross the party line. If it upset the speaker, it was a risk worth taking. And if it got him a little publicity, that was just another benefit.

Blagojevich's attitude about taking on the elites and Springfield's entrenched politicians came not only from his personal attitude but also from the fact that, at thirty-seven years old, he was still struggling to figure out what he stood for and what his political beliefs were—a pursuit that never really ended. He was the college conservative with the Republican father who had to blend his beliefs into the reality of being a politician in Chicago where Democrats ruled. Other than "fighting for the working guy," Blagojevich didn't have much of a political philosophy.

"He lacked substance. He rarely cared about issues except how they would help him politically," one ex-staffer recalled. "And that success only reinforced his behavior."

It didn't hurt that his North and Northwest Side legislative district was filled with middle-class folks who fit the definition of "Reagan Democrats," residents of the city's Bungalow Belt who held traditional values and hated taxes. Years earlier, many of these same men and women sent Mayor Richard J. Daley notes of encouragement for how he and the Chicago police handled those hippies protesting the Democratic National Convention in 1968.

Early on, Blagojevich focused mostly on two issues average folks in his district cared about—guns and gangs. But he also took occasional shots at Madigan and others in power. Though he had little chance of getting anything passed, the bills burnished his image as a reformer and satisfied that itch to stick it to authority. One bill specifically aimed at Madigan called for lawmaker term limits. Another would have required the state to auction off 10,000 low-digit license plates—a well-known political perk in Illinois doled out to those with clout. Yet another would have required lobbyists to disclose how much in campaign contributions they made to members of legislative committees they testified in front of. That bill tweaked General Assembly leadership, who one night happily attended fund-raisers where lobbyists contributed to legislators' campaigns and the following morning appeared before those same lawmakers to press their cases.

If Blagojevich's cocksure attitude came off as naive or vain, or both, lawmakers still generally liked Blagojevich personally. He was always go-along, get-along, friendly, and charming. And, in the end, he often voted along party lines on major issues such as school funding, gay rights, and crime.

He befriended downstate legislator Jay Hoffman and lakefront liberal Carol Ronen, who was his seatmate on the House floor. Both would become among Blagojevich's closest political confidants. His personality was such he was even good friends with several Republican lawmakers.

But Blagojevich wasn't the most serious lawmaker in the House. During session as votes were being debated, he often played games, challenging fellow lawmakers to use certain words or phrases in their speeches. He was also constantly on the phone at his desk on the floor, chatting away and ignoring most of the action around him. On more than one occasion, as legislators stood at his desk waiting to get his attention, they overheard Rod make the sound of two quick kisses. "I love you," he said. "Good-bye."

"Who are you talking to?" one legislator recalled asking.

"Oh, that was my mother," Blagojevich said.

———

Before Blagojevich even arrived in Springfield both he and Mell were dreaming of bigger things. He hadn't even been sworn in as a state representative and Blagojevich's name was being floated in a gossip column as somebody to keep an eye on to replace US Representative Dan Rostenkowski. Not long before, the idea of replacing Rostenkowski would have been unthinkable. A congressman from Chicago's North Side since 1959, the burly, no-nonsense Rostenkowski had brought billions of federal dollars back to Chicago and become head of the powerful tax-writing House Ways and Means Committee. Everywhere he went, people called him Mr. Chairman.

But for nearly a year, Rostenkowski had been under a cloud as his name was being connected with the ongoing Congressional Post Office Scandal.

By July 1993, the US House postmaster had pleaded guilty to helping several congressmen embezzle money as part of a scheme where congressmen converted stamps they received as part of their public office to cash. Though not mentioned by name, federal court papers cited "Congressman A" in the scheme. It soon became clear that "Congressman A" was Rostenkowski.

The controversy made the state's most powerful congressman suddenly somewhat vulnerable. Mell began pushing hard for Blagojevich's name to be in the mix of those in line to replace him. The strategy was that, even though he hadn't accomplished much in Springfield, Blagojevich would appeal to lakefront liberals who he had come to work with in the Illinois legislature as well as the district's working class, who bonded with Blagojevich over his name and status as Mell's son-in-law.

In October, Blagojevich sent out an open letter to voters criticizing the man everyone knew as "Rosty." Chastising Rostenkowski's support for President Clinton's North American Free Trade Agreement, Blagojevich said it would steal jobs from the city. "I have lived on Chicago's North Side my entire life," he wrote. "It is my feeling that the concerns and problems facing our community are not being adequately represented in Washington."

Mell's precinct workers jammed Blagojevich's brochures on doorsteps across the Fifth congressional district, from Lincoln Park to suburban Melrose Park. The pamphlets spelled Rod's last name phonetically four times: BLA-GOYA-VICH. It even carried a campaign-like slogan: "Blagojevich: hard to pronounce, easy to remember."

Other politicians were also mulling a run. Blagojevich's pseudo-running mate in 1992, Nancy Kaszak, was considering it, as was State Senator John Cullerton.

Blagojevich soon ramped up his game in Springfield, proposing more legislation, backing an effort to ban casinos from making campaign contributions, and calling for a statewide referendum on whether assault weapons should be banned. And by early December 1993, Blagojevich made it official—sort of. He would run for Congress, but only if Rostenkowski didn't. Kaszak also filed. Both Blagojevich and Kaszak filed to run for two offices—for Congress and for reelection to their state House seats.

One published report stated that Mell reached a private agreement with Mayor Daley, who supported keeping Rostenkowski in Washington because of his massive pull there: Blagojevich would drop out, but only if the mayor agreed to back Blagojevich for the congressional seat two years later. When Rostenkowski filed for reelection, Blagojevich and Kaszak both dropped out. Cullerton stayed in the race, as did three others. When time came for Mell and Blagojevich to endorse, they backed Rosty. The political calculation wasn't complicated. If anybody else won, he or she would be the new face of the Fifth Congressional District and Blagojevich's window for the seat wouldn't be open in 1996. If Rostenkowski won, his fate would be determined soon enough by federal prosecutors or voters.

A few weeks later Mell hosted his annual fund-raiser, an event that was quintessential Chicago politics. The alderman invited senior citizens from the neighborhood to come in from the cold Chicago winter to play bingo. The price of admission was that they had to sit there and listen to a bunch of politicians hawk themselves. After the candidates spoke for a few minutes, Mell would proudly announce how much money the candidate was throwing into the pot for the next game. Every year, the event drew more than one thousand seniors, giving the candidates a captive audience of loyal voters. The politically charged bingo game was always held just before the March primary in a large hall at Gordon Tech, a local Catholic high school close to Mell's house.

That year, Mell invited Rostenkowski. "We want a great ovation for the guy who can bring home the bacon," Mell bellowed as Rostenkowski made his way through the crowd of standing and applauding seniors. Mell slowly instructed the seniors that Rostenkowski's number on the ballot was twenty-two. "It's a very easy number," he said.

Blagojevich soon took the microphone and explained that while he had thought about running against Rostenkowski, he decided not to for the good of the congressional district. "I have to think about you first," he told the crowd. For his part, Rostenkowski kept his speech short. "I'd like your support," he said gruffly. "I'm not going to make a speech—let's play bingo!"

A few weeks later, Rostenkowski won easily and appeared safe to get reelected yet again in the highly Democratic congressional district. In the general election, he'd be facing some no-name Republican attorney named Michael Flanagan.

―――――

Blagojevich even had time to campaign for Rostenkowski because he had no primary opponent. The same couldn't be said for Kaszak, who had two primary opponents and had to fight off a challenge of her petitions by operatives with Mell's organization.

Kaszak had apparently upset Mell enough by filing to run for Congress, and she sought the advice of Speaker Madigan, who told her to talk directly with Blagojevich about it. But when Kaszak did, all Blagojevich did was nervously smile and swear he had nothing to do with it. "It's a Mell thing," he insisted. "It's not me."

Just weeks after winning the primary, Rostenkowski was indicted. While the charges as part of the post office scandal were not totally surprising, the news reverberated from Chicago's Northwest Side to Washington and weakened Rostenkowski's standing. Still, many Democrats and pundits thought an indicted Dan Rostenkowski had a better shot of winning than Michael Flanagan.

But on November 8, 1994, the nation witnessed one of the most decisive political victories by a political party in history. Republicans took over both houses of Congress for the first time in forty years. One of those wins was Illinois's Fifth congressional seat. On that night, Flanagan held his victory party at the Bismarck Hotel—a historic hotel near Chicago's city hall that was long used by the Democratic power structure for meetings, events, and victory parties of their own.

Asked whether he was trying to stick it to the Democrats by hosting his party there, the thirty-two-year-old Flanagan said, "That was the idea."

While Republicans were basking in the shocking win by Flanagan, Mell suddenly saw all his calculations for Blagojevich's political future falling perfectly into place. There was just one setback. Along with the Republican sweep in Washington, Springfield also witnessed a historic change in power as the GOP took control of the Illinois House, kicking Madigan out as speaker and making Blagojevich a backbencher in the minority party. Blagojevich feared any efforts to increase his profile through his work as a state representative would be limited to introducing legislation that might sound good to voters but never go anywhere.

Still, he quickly went to work in 1995, joining forces with some Republicans by introducing tough-on-crime legislation to get something passed. He then joined a group of lakefront and suburban Democrats who tried to distinguish themselves from the old guard with a more reformist platform that included requiring competitive bidding for state office leases and a casino license, as well as reforming welfare rules. But, as feared, they saw little success as the GOP moved forward with its own agenda and saw no reason to help the son-in-law of a Democratic city ward boss who was clearly setting his sights on a congressional seat now in Republican hands.

No longer having to tiptoe around the leviathan Rostenkowski, Blagojevich and Kaszak both began positioning themselves for a congressional
run in 1996 when Mell asked Kaszak to meet. The two got together at
the Ann Sather restaurant on Belmont Avenue, a Swedish-themed café
owned by a politically active leader in the city's gay community. Mell
asked Kaszak if she'd consider holding off running for Congress against
Blagojevich.

"I've got another seat lined up for you," he assured her. But with Mell not
offering too many specifics and having been stabbed in the back with the
petition silliness, Kaszak said no. With her solid record in Springfield and
her last name in a heavily Polish congressional district, she felt she had a
good chance to win and owed nothing to Mell. She was going to run.

By June 1995, just seven months after Flanagan's win, both Kaszak and
Blagojevich said they were running to get the Fifth Congressional District
seat back in Democratic control. Blagojevich made his announcement at
Foreman High School, his alma mater. Trying to show a cross-section of his
support and what Blagojevich would later call his "great combination," he
was joined by liberal lawmakers Ronen and Judy Erwin as well as longtime
Democratic machine aldermen Bernie Hansen and Bill Banks.

With Banks's powerful Thirty-Sixth Ward and his own Thirty-Third,
Mell was lining up the right support. He even met with Mayor Daley, who
rarely endorsed candidates in Democratic primaries but in this case promised to back Blagojevich. Tim Degnan and Jeremiah Joyce, two former state
senators who had become top aides to Daley, joined Blagojevich's campaign committee. Before long, Blagojevich hired one of Daley's top strate-
gists. David Axelrod was a former *Chicago Tribune* political reporter who
had become a go-to campaign consultant in Illinois since managing Paul
Simon's upset win over Republican US senator Charles Percy. Now he was
working for Blagojevich.

━━━━

While Blagojevich won his state representative race almost entirely because
of Mell, Axelrod said the race for Congress had to be different. Blagojevich
needed to raise money for television commercials.

Kaszak had received the backing of Emily's List, a national organization
with lots of cash that sought to elect more Democratic women to Congress.
Word also began trickling back to the Blagojevich campaign that Kaszak

was raising more money on her own, holing herself up in a basement with little more than a phone to make fund-raising calls all day.

Blagojevich had hired one of Daley's top fund-raisers, Kathleen Murray, to organize his fund-raising. One of her top employees, Joe Cini, was the point person. Soon, Cini was providing lists of potential donors and Blagojevich was burning up the phone lines and the event circuit raising cash. All the talk of fund-raising struck Mell as odd. He didn't dispute the campaign had to be different this time around, but he felt spending hundreds of thousands of dollars on television commercials in a congressional race was a waste. Axelrod argued Kaszak wasn't to be taken lightly and the notion that field troops would take care of everything was highly unlikely.

"The higher you go up the ladder, the less that is true," Axelrod recalled in an interview.

Blagojevich was left in the middle between Mell and Axelrod. But as he improved at fund-raising, he began to side more with Axelrod.

Some politicians hate fund-raising, apologizing as they embarrassedly ask for money. But Blagojevich quickly realized he was good at selling himself, always giving an upbeat, folksy, and strong pitch about how a contributor could help a struggling cause. And while Blagojevich might not have focused much on the details of his politics, he had a laser-like focus on his fund-raising.

As a major deadline approached for both campaigns to report how much money they had raised, Blagojevich was confident the hundreds of thousands he had raised would blow Kaszak away. But when she came in with her number, it wasn't far behind Blagojevich's.

"He was real freaked out," a campaign staffer recalled. "It was shocking how much she raised, and that pushed Rod to really ratchet it up."

Years later, numerous campaign aides and friends of Blagojevich pointed to this moment as a turning point in his career. Not only did Blagojevich realize he was good at fund-raising, but he also began to truly appreciate the power of the dollar in politics.

Perhaps it wasn't a coincidence that around this time, in the summer of 1995, Blagojevich first met Christopher G. Kelly.

It was a warm Wednesday evening, August 9, and Blagojevich was attending a fund-raiser for Chicago alderman Charles Bernardini. The alderman represented the affluent Lincoln Park neighborhood on the lakefront. Bernardini wore his Italian heritage as a badge of honor, and the fund-raiser was dubbed the Forty-Third Ward Polenta Dinner, featuring variations of the cornmeal dish from some of the city's best Italian kitchens.

As Blagojevich stepped out of the party at Moran's and into the cool air, he saw two men talking on the corner of Racine and Clybourn avenues. Blagojevich introduced himself. One man was smoking a cigar. He introduced himself as Ronald Rossi, a developer. The other was Kelly, who said he worked in the roofing industry.

Blagojevich explained who he was and that he was running for Congress next year. He'd love their support, he said. Kelly indicated he might be interested in helping out.

═══

As the race progressed, several colleagues noticed the dynamic between Mell and Blagojevich begin to change. The disagreement over television commercials and fund-raising was one thing. But Blagojevich also was starting to feel his oats as his own politician and to show some resentment toward Mell, who never let Blagojevich forget where he came from and who got him into the business in the first place.

"He almost resented the fact that he needed Mell," a campaign staffer said. "So he began to try to distance himself from him as much as he could."

The two men would fight and eventually smooth things over. "We both have thick skin," Blagojevich would confide. Blagojevich also knew he depended on Mell's help in the field. The lord of his ward, Mell's army of precinct workers continued to be impressive. They not only worked hard but they also were immensely loyal to Mell and, by default, Blagojevich. Among those who were helping Blagojevich's campaign was Dominic Longo, a longtime city worker who a decade earlier was convicted of federal vote fraud for stuffing ballot boxes in the Thirty-Third Ward.

Longo had bounced around city hall. He was a city truck driver and after the conviction helped oversee vehicle operations at O'Hare Airport. Throughout it all, he had stuck by Mell. When Ronan left Mell's organization, he took several precinct captains with him because he had the ability to get jobs. But Longo and others, including another top city precinct captain, Chuckie Lomanto, didn't bolt. While the men were Mell's friends, Blagojevich was now a member of the family, and they became his friend too. Longo and Lomanto and the others had been working city elections for years, and they were good at it. Blagojevich knew he needed their help to win.

"If Rod knew you could help him, he'd be nice to you," the campaign staffer said.

With the primary looming at Mell's annual bingo game and fund-raiser the following year, the mood was electric inside Gordon Tech as the seniors once again gathered inside the tile-walled room. Aldermen arrived. An old Mell friend, Aurelia Pucinski, was in attendance, as was Secretary of State Jesse White. Rod and Patti, who was four months pregnant at the time and just beginning to show, arrived and hugged Mell, who walked around wearing a fishing cap and loose-hanging jeans. After several speeches by other pols, Mell took the microphone.

"This is a great daughter and a great son-in-law," he started. "Five years ago, they fell in love, and because of that, my wife and I are going to become grandparents."

"He's done everything I've asked him in Springfield," Mell continued before handing the microphone to Rod, who instantly began blasting Flanagan and talking about Medicare payments before wrapping up his speech, "One last thing—" he began to say before Mell snatched the microphone from Rod's grip.

"Get to the punch line," Mell yelled to the crowd. "He's giving two hundred dollars to the next game!"

Snagging the microphone back, Rod yelled, "I'm not just a son-in-law. I'm giving three hundred dollars!"

PART II

A Public Rise

4

Congressman Blagojevich

March 19 was a nasty day in Chicago. Cold with a hard wind that was blowing trash through the streets, it was another typical early spring day in a city that rarely saw much of a transition between winter and summer. Voters hit the polls as soon as they opened, and so did Rod Blagojevich and Mell's crew of one thousand precinct captains and workers.

The closing weeks of the campaign had been a flurry between Blagojevich, Kaszak, and a third candidate, Ray Romero. Blagojevich embraced his underdog status, repeating, "It's us against the world" as he vowed to be a unifying force that would bring together the yuppies and working class of the Fifth District. Blagojevich undercut Kaszak's support among women by getting help from several female legislators, including Ronen and Erwin, who found Kaszak cold compared to Blagojevich's gregariousness.

By the time the polls closed, only a handful of people were inside the Thirty-Third Ward's new headquarters on Kedzie just north of Addison. While clusters of precinct workers were at a nearby tavern on the corner, Dick Mell, wearing reading glasses, wandered in and out of his back office area. The entire office was lit up, shining light onto the darkened street.

A few minutes after 7:00 PM, Blagojevich arrived, smiling. So was Mell. In Mell's office, Blagojevich took a moment to thank his father-in-law for all he had done.

"I don't know what else we could have done," Blagojevich told Mell. "If we lose you get to go fishing, and if we win we have to do this all over again in November."

Minutes later they both realized Mell wasn't going fishing anytime soon. Reports from his precinct workers were coming in from the liberal lakefront. Blagojevich, Mell, Axelrod, and his team had war-gamed that all Blagojevich had to do was win about 30 percent of the vote on the lakefront and he would win the whole race due to what they knew would be oversized support in the Bungalow Belt.

The first precinct came in from Lincoln Park. Blagojevich had lost by only three votes. He instantly felt vindicated. He'd done better with the yuppies and reformers than most in his campaign thought he'd do.

A jovial atmosphere quickly spread throughout the headquarters. Patti arrived, followed by Blagojevich's brother, Robert, and his family. Jammed inside the cramped ward headquarters with dozens of precinct workers, the Mells and Blagojevichs began to celebrate Rod's apparent victory. Cars were double-parked outside on the street, and the windows began to steam up. Vehicles driving by honked their horns. By nine o'clock, almost everybody headed over to Mell's house to watch the returns even though Mell stayed back, continuing to crunch numbers and take calls.

Though many finally began to feel confident about a Blagojevich victory, television reports still declared he was trailing. Those Bungalow Belt votes hadn't come in yet to turn the tide. At Mell's house, Blagojevich got on the phone with his mother, who was following the results on TV. She was in tears.

"TV has you losing," she told him.

"No, Mama, don't worry about it. We've got the numbers, we're going to win," Blagojevich said.

Incredulous, Mrs. Blagojevich asked her son, "Have you talked to Alderman Mell's precinct captains? Ask them, they'll tell you, you lost."

Blagojevich finally reassured his mother he had spoken to them and he was confident of his victory.

After Blagojevich took a shower, the remaining votes came in as expected. Calls were pouring in for him to make his way to the victory party, being held at an antique mall on Western Avenue. When Blagojevich arrived, Mell still wasn't there. Sitting in the car, Patti spoke to Axelrod, who told them to stay outside until Mell got there. Eventually, they called the campaign headquarters and discovered Mell was still there.

"You guys go without me," Mell told them. "I'll get there. Don't worry."

During his speech, Blagojevich used no script. He publicly thanked Longo, an acknowledgment that would come to follow him for years because of Longo's criminal and questionable past.

When Kaszak called to congratulate him on his win, Blagojevich began the conversation with, "Boy, you really know how to raise money."

The day after the win President Clinton called to congratulate Blagojevich. As he was talking to the president, Blagojevich watched while Mell took down campaign signs.

"You and I, Mr. President, share a common fondness for Elvis, and this is a district that Elvis would do very well in," Blagojevich told him, not mentioning that four years earlier he had voted for Clinton's Republican opponent, President George H. W. Bush. "Working-class, middle-income kind of district. We really want to help you."

"We're all trying to figure out how to say your last name out here," Clinton answered.

＝＝＝＝

With his primary victory in his rearview mirror, Blagojevich and his campaign staffers felt confident about their chances in the November general election.

Blagojevich pounded away at several themes: Flanagan's opposition to abortion rights and gun control and his signing of then–Speaker of the House Newt Gingrich's Contract with America, which upset unions. Axelrod also brought on Pete Giangreco, another well-known media consultant who specialized in direct-mail pieces.

"You need to go see Mell," Axelrod told him.

Inside Mell's ward office on the Northwest Side, Giangreco met Blagojevich for the first time and was taken by his drive for success. After joining the campaign, Giangreco discovered Blagojevich's immense talent for retail campaigning. He'd have boundless energy visiting El stops for hours at a time or Polish delis on Milwaukee Avenue. At parades, Blagojevich's skills as a runner paid off as he sprinted to both sides of the street, shaking nearly every hand. He fed off the crowd's energy with his affable personality and vigor. "It was unbelievable," Giangreco recalled later. "Some people just have this talent and some people have *it*. In front of crowds, when he turned it on, he had *it*."

Privately, though, Blagojevich would reveal the toll *it* took on him. He would become shy and reserved. Amid a flurry of campaign events one day, Blagojevich paused and looked at those assembled around him. "I'm the guy who has to go out there and perform," he said.

Axelrod was also concerned about something other than Blagojevich's opponent or his peculiarities. His old employer, the *Chicago Tribune*, was doing an exhaustive investigation into Mell and Blagojevich.

Several of the newspaper's best investigative reporters were pulling almost every piece of paperwork at city hall imaginable related to Mell, including timesheets and checks that Blagojevich received from the city while working for Mell's ward organization between 1989 and 1993 when he left to become a legislator. One of the motivations for the increased scrutiny was the fact that in a few months Chicago was hosting the Democratic National Convention for the first time since 1968. All the eyes of the world would be on the city and its politics, and the newspaper's highest editors wanted to give the city's visitors in August a taste of the city's sometimes infamous political scene.

Blagojevich saw it as little more than a vendetta being waged by a newspaper that years earlier had become identified with the Republican Party through its editorial page. Still, he felt the pressure as reports got back to him about all the calls and inquiries the reporters were making about him and his father-in-law.

"They're conducting a goddamned proctology exam on me," Blagojevich ranted to one associate. "I know they aren't looking this hard at Flanagan."

When he finally sat down for an interview with *Tribune* reporters Laurie Cohen and Robert Becker, Blagojevich was his sociable self. Meeting at Mell's ward offices at 3649 N. Kedzie Avenue, Blagojevich didn't come alone. Alongside him was John Kupper, an Axelrod associate, who wanted to know what the paper was *really* working on.

"Let's not conduct this under some facade of standard political reporting. Let's be straight about this," Kupper told the pair. "Our feeling was this was a request to follow a campaign to write a political story. There obviously was something else going on here that we weren't fully informed of."

Axelrod was particularly intense about advocating for Blagojevich. He closely followed the *Tribune* reporters' work and even conducted a shadow investigation of his own, interviewing Blagojevich and others who were also talking to the reporters. He questioned the entire premise of the effort, arguing the assignment itself placed big pressure on them to come back with a story, whether one was really deserved or not. He even wrote up a multipage memo that he sent to high-up editors arguing his case, which created some ill will among those reporters working on the story.

"I did it with reluctance because I was a reporter and I know it would piss me off," Axelrod recalled. "But I had a responsibility as well, so I sent it."

In the meantime, Blagojevich sat down twice with the newspaper's reporters. A focus of their questions was those payments he received from city hall while working as Mell's staffer. The records weren't clear about what exactly he did to earn that money. They showed Blagojevich getting paid by several city hall committees run by other aldermen even though Blagojevich insisted he never worked at city hall.

Blagojevich himself also fired off a memo, an eleven-page letter in which he answered a few lingering questions but also spouted off that he felt he was being treated unfairly. "The *Tribune* has devoted hundreds, if not thousands of hours, apparently pursuing every possible disparaging bit of information about me in almost an unprecedented game of 'Gotcha.'"

In August, the *Tribune* wrote a massive profile of Mell, declaring him the "Lord of His Ward," and in October, just weeks before the election against Flanagan, the newspaper carried an in-depth report laying out some of the questions surrounding Blagojevich, especially that questionable work at city hall.

———

Blagojevich, meanwhile, kept up the torrent of fund-raising. Even Joe Cini, still working as Blagojevich's fund-raiser, suggested putting the brakes on a little. But Blagojevich wouldn't relent.

"If a fund-raiser would give him $100, he'd want $150. If it was $150, he'd want $200. If it was fifty people at an event, he'd want a hundred," recalled a campaign staffer. "He was never satisfied. It was always more, more, more. He never let up."

Blagojevich raised $1.5 million—two times more than Flanagan. The money helped pay for commercials, including a controversial radio ad about Flanagan's vote to repeal an assault weapons ban. The commercial featured a Chicago police officer talking about how a semiautomatic pistol was used to injure him and kill another officer and implied that Flanagan was anti-cop.

Of all the winning challengers in the nation, Blagojevich was one of the biggest spenders. The $1.5 million he raised was third, behind only

California Democrat Ellen Tauscher ($2.5 million) and Utah Republican Christopher Cannon ($1.7 million).

As plans were made for the victory celebration, Blagojevich's campaign settled on the site of the party: A. Finkl & Sons Co., the same steel mill where Blagojevich's father had worked as a machinist. Everyone agreed it set the right tone for a campaign that was on the side of the working class that had been forgotten by a Congress led by Newt Gingrich, while portraying Blagojevich as a Jimmy Stewart–like everyman.

By Election Night's end, the Fifth District had a new congressman. Blagojevich won easily, garnering 64 percent of the vote. "This vote sends a clear message to Newt Gingrich and the radical right: Your revolution is over. Common sense has prevailed," Blagojevich told the hundreds at Finkl. After the celebration at his father's place of business, Blagojevich took time the following morning to honor his mother, thanking voters at the Jefferson Park train stop where she once took tickets. "Our next campaign begins as soon as we're done with this El stop," he said.

———

On the floor of the House of Representatives in early January 1997, the Democratic congressmen from Chicago huddled together and welcomed two new members to the delegation: Danny Davis, a former Chicago alderman from the West Side, and Rod Blagojevich.

Despite being the third-largest city in the United States, Chicago could sometimes be surprisingly parochial, especially when it came to its politics. It looked like Council Wars Redux as Davis and Blagojevich joined Luis Gutierrez and Bobby Rush in Congress, two former Chicago aldermen who made names for themselves fifteen years earlier during the original Council Wars. With his ties to Mell and Vrdolyak, Blagojevich was the clear outsider in the group. Davis, Rush, and Gutierrez had been staunch allies of Mayor Washington, as had been the father of another recent addition, US Representative Jesse Jackson Jr.

But on this chilly morning, there was no continuation of the bad blood from the previous decade, despite the odd scene of Mell sitting in the gallery excitedly waving his arms and hands like a schoolboy at his first baseball game.

The excitement had been almost too much for Blagojevich earlier in the day. He had jumped out of bed at 5:00 AM, before the sun rose, to take a long run around Washington, jogging around the Lincoln Memorial and allowing the moment to settle over him like a warm blanket. He was about to become a United States congressman. My dad would have been so proud to have seen this day, Blagojevich thought to himself.

Hours later, Rod thanked his childhood friend, Mike "Lou Nova" Ascaridis for coming and then on the House floor stood alongside Patti and five-month-old Amy, dressed in a cute little red suit, who had traveled from Chicago for the swearing-in ceremony. This would be his first act as a congressman and Rod was already breaking the rules: The House does not allow congressmen to bring spouses on the floor. They can only bring staffers and children under twelve years of age. So while Amy qualified, Patti did not. But a minute later, after he took the oath, Rod was officially a congressman.

———

One way Blagojevich tried to make his mark was by continuing to distance himself from his father-in-law. Around Christmastime, Mell had irked Blagojevich once again when the alderman joked to *Crain's* political reporter Greg Hinz that he wasn't sure he needed to buy Blagojevich a gift this year because "Don't you think I've bought him enough this year?"

It was another example of the types of comments that fed the up-and-down relationship between the two. And no matter how true the quip might have been, it only fueled Blagojevich's desire to do whatever he could to be his own man.

While Blagojevich compromised by hiring some Mell-connected people—like Chuckie Lomanto's wife Kitty—to run his offices in Chicago, he hired a group of young men and women for his staff in DC with no connections to Mell. As his chief of staff, he hired John Wyma. For nearly a decade, the mild-mannered and sharp Wyma had worked in DC in a variety of spots for congressmen from Wyma's home state of Michigan. Blagojevich's legislative director, Chris Davis, had worked in the office of House Democratic Whip David Bonior, also of Michigan. As his press secretary, he hired Matt Devine, a former political reporter who was the son of Cook County State's Attorney Dick Devine. Back in Chicago, he hired as his assistant Mary Stewart, who had worked for Blagojevich in Springfield.

Blagojevich asked Cini to join him, but Cini declined, not wanting to deal with Blagojevich's pressure tactics. Instead, Cini took a job with Mell doing constituent services, a move that upset Blagojevich so much the two wouldn't talk for years.

As a freshman congressman of the minority party, Blagojevich received a poor office assignment: fifth floor of the Cannon House Office Building. One of his first assignments for his staff was to find out if it had been occupied by John F. Kennedy when he was in Congress, but they never got a definite answer. Staffers soon discovered the same Rod Blagojevich that those in Springfield saw: a somewhat flaky person who was surprisingly conservative.

He stuck with hot topics in his district. He proposed pilot programs to fund "community prosecutors" to fight graffiti, pitched plans to curtail gun-running from the south, and introduced legislation to ban anyone younger than twenty-one from possessing a handgun. He also voted with Republicans on a failed effort to install term limits in Congress, on rewriting public housing laws that some said were anti-poor, and on renaming Washington National Airport in honor of former president Ronald Reagan, a move that stuck a finger in the eye of the air traffic controllers' union.

When staffers presented briefing papers on issues for upcoming votes, Blagojevich skimmed them, tossed them on his desk, and decided his time was better spent quizzing them about the topics at hand.

"I'm not a detail guy," he'd continually explain.

During staff meetings, Wyma, Devine, and Chris Davis explained all the pros and cons, almost all of which were already in the briefing papers. He'd also call up his old friend from law school, Lon Monk, and Ascaridis, as well as Axelrod and Kupper. And he would dial home to seek Patti's input.

In Blagojevich's mind, each of them fit into a specific political category or voting bloc. Wyma and Davis were DC people examining the issues; Devine was a Chicago suburbanite (even though he actually grew up in the city); Axelrod and Kupper were purely political; Ascaridis was a blue-collar guy from the neighborhood; Monk was a smart guy who wasn't political; Patti was a woman and mother. If Patti liked an idea but Ascaridis didn't, their opinions weighed on him as he decided how to vote. It'll piss off the neighborhood guy, but women support it.

Blagojevich often had these bull sessions on his speakerphone while he examined suit swatches fanned out carefully across his desk. Since leaving Springfield, Blagojevich had graduated from Armani to Oxxford.

The new congressman was quickly becoming a clotheshorse. He felt the Armani suits he wore in Springfield were a little too flashy and slick. Oxxford was more conservative and classic. A Chicago company headquartered in a nondescript factory in the West Loop, Oxxford Clothes was the preeminent clothier in the nation. Over the years, Clark Gable, Humphrey Bogart, and Joe DiMaggio bought suits from Oxxford. Individual suits, always tailored perfectly by hand, cost Blagojevich $3,000 to $5,000 each. And Blagojevich began purchasing a half-dozen or more per year. It wasn't something he advertised much to the outside world. It went completely against his "I'm a man of the people" routine. But when back in Chicago, he visited the head-quarters on Van Buren, just west of Racine, religiously, always showing up for a fitting with expert tailor Rocco Giovannangelo or asking him for more swatches.

Before Blagojevich's DC meetings began, male and female staffers sitting in front of him would have Blagojevich toss a suit swatch in their laps to see how it looked. "What do you think of that? Looks nice or not so much?"

It wasn't just suits that distracted Blagojevich in DC. Between meetings, he constantly complained about wanting to "get a run in." He was training for the Chicago Marathon that October. But more importantly, running kept him in shape and looking fit. "Vanity of vanities, all is vanity," he would say aloud, quoting Ecclesiastes and recognizing he too was victim.

Blagojevich was clearly becoming obsessed about his appearance. After media press events, he consistently asked staffers how he looked. He recorded any television coverage of his press conferences, watching the videotapes over and over, studying them to perfect his mannerisms and speech-making. He played the one-minute speeches he gave on the House floor, rewound them, and played them again. Inevitably, while watching the tapes with others, he'd ask, "Do I look fat?"

Before speaking to crowds, Blagojevich had to psych himself up. Even though he ended up being good at it, aides noticed it took a lot to get him out there. Before events, he described himself as "fundamentally shy, not very smart." He would say it almost as a mantra. Once he got out there, he was great. He could be almost transparently manipulative. But in a political setting, people found it charming.

One time, speaking before a group of mostly Italian voters in Melrose Park, Blagojevich stuck out like a sore thumb, looking like a yuppie amid a sea of men in Sansabelt pants. Still, he won them over. "My wife is one-tenth Italian, and today that's the part I love about her most!" It was clear pandering but the crowd laughed and went wild, finding him funny and charismatic as Blagojevich laughed along with them.

Blagojevich spent as little time in DC as possible. When Congress was in session, he flew in to Washington on Tuesday mornings and got on the first plane out on Thursday night. While in Washington, his days were filled with constant activity, though it was always disorganized and random. He was a whirling dervish in the halls of Congress, bringing up one issue with a staffer standing next to him and then calling another staffer five minutes later about doing something else. All the while he needed constant attention. He couldn't go to his meetings or votes by himself, demanding a companion, usually Wyma or Devine.

The only consistency to any of his thoughts was finding something to distinguish himself to move up the next step on the political ladder. When someone suggested he could be congressman for decades like Rostenkowski, Blagojevich bristled. "Are you kidding me?" he said. "I hate DC."

===

His frustrations stemmed mostly from his inability to get anything done, though that didn't stop him from voting himself a raise. He backed a bill to increase legislators' $133,600 annual salaries. But when Basil Talbot of the *Chicago Sun-Times* asked Blagojevich about it, he argued the 2.3 percent increase wasn't what it looked like. "It isn't a pay raise," he insisted. "It's a cost-of-living increase for federal employees."

His staffers, including Devine, Wyma, Axelrod, and Kupper, were mortified about the comments but Blagojevich was just happy to see his name in the paper. "We're in the mix!" he insisted. "It's fine. We're out there. People are talking about us."

In December 1997, Blagojevich found another way to get into the headlines.

The US Navy had to dispose of twenty-three million pounds of Vietnam-era napalm. It was in California, and they wanted to get rid of it at a facility in East Chicago, Indiana. To get it there, they planned to ship it on a train that would travel through parts of Illinois, including the Fifth District.

Blagojevich immediately sensed an opportunity. This was a safety concern. He fired off a letter to Defense Secretary William Cohen and held a press conference in a rail yard at Canal Street and Roosevelt Road. The navy insisted the jellylike mixture of gasoline and chemicals was not the "napalm bomb" Blagojevich described it as being. Not only would it be shipped safely, they asserted, but it was far less explosive than other chemicals being transported through Chicago every day. It was probably safer than most gasoline shipments.

But Blagojevich didn't let it go. The following day, he said the amount of napalm being shipped was enough to cause "an eleven kiloton explosion," sparking visions of Hiroshima. Some in Congress and even environmental officials shook their heads at the stunt they felt Blagojevich was obviously trying to pull, scaring people for no reason other than to make a name for himself. Still, he got Illinois's two senators, Carol Moseley-Braun and Dick Durbin, to write letters to Cohen seeking a meeting.

For weeks, the story stayed alive as the navy contemplated what to do. Naval officials held public hearings to calm fears after national television stations picked up the story, portraying Blagojevich as an environmental hero.

Amid the political pressure, the East Chicago waste-recycling company, tired of the bad publicity, decided to give up. It wouldn't accept the napalm and agreed to forgo $2.5 million.

Blagojevich had his trophy—and in less than a year in office. He also got his first—and what would become his only—piece of legislation passed by the House and Senate. It renamed a post office on Kedzie Avenue north of Addison in honor of slain Chicago police officer Daniel Doffyn. Although Doffyn was killed in the line of duty answering a burglary call on the West Side, outside the Fifth Congressional District, Blagojevich selected a post office in his district, just down the block from Mell's district offices.

Despite the modest successes, Blagojevich remained bored in Congress. He wiled away the hours running and cracking jokes and occasionally even pulling pranks on his fellow congressmen. In the early mornings he ran as much as five or six miles regularly with Jim Littig, a retired army colonel who served two tours in Vietnam. Littig had become a Washington, DC, lobbyist focused on military funding, so when Blagojevich was placed on the House's National Security Committee, Littig invited Blagojevich along to join him and his four or five running buddies. Littig and Blagojevich became fast friends, discussing national and international issues while on their runs around the Army Navy Country Club in Virginia, where President Eisenhower and later President Clinton often retreated to play eighteen holes. Sometimes, Blagojevich ran the full route around the golf course and then, when the others stopped, turned around and ran the course the other way.

Littig was impressed by Blagojevich's ability to recall certain facts and details about various issues, including later the war in Kosovo. Blagojevich always seemed starstruck, saying he was impressed that Littig had "five hand-to-hand combat kills in Vietnam!"

"That guy's a badass," Blagojevich would say, often repeating himself to aides who had heard the tales numerous times before. Years later, Littig demurred when asked about his service record. "I'd prefer not to talk about it. My basic rule was to kill [the enemy] from as far away as possible."

——————

The one thing Blagojevich did expend energy and time on was fund-raising. For him, it was like exercise: do a little every day. Blagojevich carried around a yellow legal pad with names of donors and others he thought should be donating. He wasn't afraid to cold call businesspeople and see if they wanted to meet or have lunch. He found it was always difficult even for successful men and women to turn down an offer from a sitting congressman—even a backbencher like Blagojevich. When they finally did meet, Blagojevich's disarming charm always did wonders. Inevitably strangers soon became donors.

National Democrats saw Blagojevich's skills and asked him to help the Democratic Congressional Campaign Committee, seeing if he could raise some money for the organization, which would then be divvied among the Democratic candidates around the nation in an effort to win back the House. Blagojevich bristled at the request. The DCCC hadn't helped him much during his campaign, so why should he help them?

He was at war with the world. He disliked his fellow Democrats and wouldn't help others in the Illinois caucus either. Yet at the same time, his fellow congressmen liked him personally. Face-to-face, he was funny and friendly, and his charisma and personality allowed him to avoid burning bridges.

Still, he sometimes took votes on bills simply to make a point that he wasn't owned by anybody and to show his independence.

"Rod never was very good with authority," Axelrod recalled. "He didn't get along with Madigan in the legislature and he didn't particularly get along with the leadership in the [US] House. He's not the kind of guy that likes to be told what to do. And so every once in a while he'd want to cast votes just to make a point, and sometimes they didn't make sense. He would do it just to say 'fuck you' to the leaders."

——————

As Election Day 1998 approached, Blagojevich had little to worry about. He was facing little-known attorney Alan Spitz, a Republican who worked on Flanagan's campaign two years earlier. Both major Chicago newspaper editorial boards endorsed Blagojevich for a second term, and in the heavily Democratic district, Blagojevich's campaigning was perfunctory.

Blagojevich's base was expanding. He had begun to solidify his relationship with Chris Kelly, the roofer he met outside Moran's a few years earlier. Kelly donated $1,500 to Blagojevich's congressional reelection campaign that year. So too had another Chicago developer he met, Antoin Rezko, who donated $1,000.

But the race in Illinois wasn't focused on Blagojevich. The state was in the midst of a campaign to elect a new governor, and the North Shore was electing a new representative in Congress to replace Sid Yates, who had served for forty-eight years. Jan Schakowsky, a state representative, was on her way to winning the congressional seat, but the race for governor was a tight-fought one between Republican George Ryan and Democrat Glenn Poshard.

A congressman from the downstate town of Marion, Poshard was struggling to get support in Chicago, where some traditional Democrats were leaning toward voting for Ryan because he was more liberal on social issues, including gun control, abortion, and gay rights. With just weeks to go before Election Day, Blagojevich offered to broker a meeting between Poshard and leaders of Chicago's gay, lesbian, bisexual, and transgender communities, a key constituency in Blagojevich's congressional district. But minutes after the meeting started, it blew up in Poshard's face as the activists hammered him on his opposition to legislation banning discrimination in housing and employment based on sexual orientation. Poshard left the meeting red-faced as the activists proclaimed their support for Ryan. Blagojevich came out a winner just for setting up the meeting, but Poshard, who later lost to Ryan, felt double-crossed. It wouldn't be a betrayal he'd forget.

Just days after the election, Blagojevich had other quandaries with which to cope. The impeachment of President Clinton was ongoing in Washington. Blagojevich initially made noise about voting with Republicans in favor of launching the impeachment inquiry. He argued that Clinton's actions with Monica Lewinsky led to an erosion of his moral authority. Eventually, though, he sided with the losing Democrats who opposed the effort. Days after that, in early January 1999, his mother died at Rush-Presbyterian-St. Luke's Medical Center on Chicago's near West Side. She had heart problems and recently had developed cancer.

Millie's death hit Blagojevich hard. Services were held at Old Holy Resurrection Church of Palmer Square, where Rob and Rod had long ago attended services with their parents, both of whom were now gone. After her death, Blagojevich found a box of his childhood belongings at Millie's place, including his baby shoes with his name on them. He was in tears while talking with staffers. "Nobody loves you like your mother," he repeated.

Though she was the more American of his two parents, Millie's service at Old Holy Resurrection was still filled with many traditional Serbian elements that made Blagojevich think more about his heritage and family, so a few months later when NATO forces engaged in heavy bombing in Serbia to stop Yugoslav President Slobodan Milosevic's efforts to ethnically cleanse Kosovo, Blagojevich felt a need to somehow get involved.

A few months after beginning his second term, that opportunity arrived, and so too a chance for Blagojevich to make a name for himself on a national and even an international level.

On March 31, 1999, three US soldiers patrolling the Yugoslavian border with Macedonia were captured and being held as prisoners of war by President Milosevic's forces. As a Serbian American member of the House, Blagojevich wanted to lead a mission to Belgrade to have the men released. Blagojevich still knew the Serbian language and had made contacts in his father's homeland through Chicago's Serbian community. But he recognized he couldn't spearhead the mission by himself. One man from Chicago, though, could.

The Reverend Jesse Jackson, the headline-seeking South Side civil rights icon, had found success in years past with similar mediation efforts. In 1990, he brought back about fifty Americans who had been stranded after Iraq left Kuwait. Six years earlier, he convinced Syrian leaders to release navy pilot Robert Goodman Jr., after he had been shot down over Lebanon. He also helped dozens of Americans and Cubans escape Fidel Castro's jails in Cuba.

Like most involved in Chicago politics, Blagojevich knew Reverend Jackson's reputation for having a taxing ego and taking credit for the work of others. But Blagojevich also heard Jackson had been unsuccessfully trying to meet with Milosevic. He decided Jackson's ability to command attention superseded his reputation for stealing all the glory.

On the floor on the House of Representatives, Blagojevich approached US Representative Jesse Jackson Jr. The two congressmen had become friendly since Blagojevich's election. Up-and-comer Illinois Democrats, Blagojevich and Jackson Jr. often sat next to each other and chatted on airplanes shut-tling them to and from Washington, DC. He asked "JJJ" if his father would be interested. "Absolutely," the younger Jackson replied. "Call the Reverend." As Blagojevich liked to tell the story years later, he paused dramatically for a moment with a quizzical look on his face. "You call your dad 'Reverend?'"

During their phone conversation, the elder Jackson indeed showed inter-est and in a matter of minutes turned the whole scenario back on Blagojev-ich and portrayed it almost like it was the Reverend's idea. "I want to take you with me," Jackson told Blagojevich.

Officials with President Clinton's administration publicly opposed the Idea. NATO had been bombing the nation, and the administration couldn't guarantee their safety. Blagojevich, Jackson, and a delegation of religious leaders pushed forward anyhow. Before the delegation's airplane landed, Blagojevich thought a great deal about how he had never been to his father's native country before and how he'd soon be walking the streets of Belgrade, much as his father did before being captured by the Nazis.

"This will be my first trip to the place my father came from. The last time my dad was there was in 1941, when Nazi bombs were falling on Belgrade," he told the *Chicago Tribune*'s Flynn McRoberts, who accompanied the group. "Now, decades later, I'm going there for the first time while Ameri-can bombs are falling on a government that, in many cases, is resurrecting some of the Nazi tactics."

Minutes after the delegation arrived, NATO warplanes knocked state television off the air. The group headquartered themselves at the Belgrade Hyatt on a Thursday and prepared for a meeting the following day with the soldiers and then, hopefully, Milosevic on Saturday.

When the meeting with Staff Sergeants Andrew Ramirez and Christo-pher Stone and Specialist Steven M. Gonzales occurred, it was punctuated by air raid sirens signaling the start of another NATO attack. The three soldiers told Jackson and Blagojevich this was only the second time they had seen one another since being captured four weeks earlier. They were being kept isolated at the Military Court of Belgrade.

Only Blagojevich and Jackson were allowed to meet the men, upsetting some of the religious leaders who had come along. But they delivered Bibles, some Chuckles candies, and three separate tape-recorded messages from their families. Blagojevich couldn't help cracking a joke, saying his posi-tion on military House committees authorized him to give them major pay raises.

The following day they met face-to-face with Milosevic. Sitting down in a formal room inside a palace in Belgrade, Jackson, Blagojevich, and others in the delegation listened as Milosevic complained about the media's portrayal of him and how nobody outside Serbia understood the national and cultural history. The delegation listened but tried to keep the powerful leader focused on the reason they had come so far: to bring back the three US soldiers.

Though Blagojevich's fluency in Serbian was invaluable, Jackson took a lead role in talking to Milosevic over three hours, trying to convince him to release the men as a sign of good faith. Jackson and Milosevic strolled through a garden, held hands, and prayed. Milosevic wanted guarantees from the delegation that if he released the soldiers the NATO bombing would stop. Jackson explained the delegation had no such authority. But Jackson said he would call US National Security Adviser Sandy Berger and Secretary of State Madeleine Albright to let them know what was happening. When he did, Berger and Albright said NATO's military campaign remained unchanged. Still, there was a sliver of hope. Milosevic never outright said "no" to their request the soldiers be released.

The delegation headed back to the Hyatt. About an hour later, the Yugoslav Foreign Ministry called members of the delegation to ask them to head back to the minister's residence immediately. Jackson, Blagojevich, and three of the religious leaders raced in cars through the streets of Belgrade. They were greeted at the residence by Foreign Minister Zivadin Jovanovic. "The government of Yugoslavia and President Milosevic have agreed," he told them. "It's my pleasure to inform you that you can take your soldiers home with you."

It was a stunning development. The mood in the room among the Americans was ebullient. Jackson soon greeted the three soldiers, who seemed amazed by the quick developments. The men stood with their arms behind their backs, and Jackson, in dramatic fashion, told them they were now free—and free to embrace one another. Jackson leaned against a lobby railing and wept openly, tears running down his face. Blagojevich saw the tears and the TV cameras rolling, catching the moment, and thought how good an actor Jackson was. "Total bullshit," he said years later. "He just turns on the tears and turns them off."

———

Days after Blagojevich got home from Kosovo, he and Patti finally found a home to buy in the congressional district he'd been representing for more than two years. Even though Blagojevich was elected to serve the Fifth Congressional District in 1996, he'd been living in the turn-of-the-century home he bought in 1994 on Logan Boulevard in the Logan Square neighborhood that was located in Fourth Congressional District. Though members of Congress are not required to live in the districts they represent, it was a political optics issue. During his primary run in 1996 versus Kaszak, Blagojevich was so worried that not living in the district would become a campaign issue that he and Patti temporarily moved into his mother Millie's apartment in the Fifth District and Millie moved into the Logan Boulevard home. To make sure she was safe there, Blagojevich had Cini live in the home with her.

Finally—on the corner of Richmond Street and Sunnyside Avenue—he and Patti found a house to call home in the Fifth. The Mediterranean-style, red brick bungalow was built in 1929 in the upper-middle-class Ravenswood Manor neighborhood. They paid $505,000 but took out a mortgage for $610,000 because Rod and Patti thought the eleven-room, three-bedroom home needed work. They wanted to move the bedrooms upstairs, and Blagojevich wanted to install a library that he was going to redesign specifically to his tastes.

It wasn't until October that Rod, Patti, and Amy moved in, but all the while Rod obsessed about the library. He asked staffers, friends, and even vague acquaintances their opinions about what he should do to decorate the room right off the foyer. He wanted bookshelves. Should they go all the way to the ceiling or only three-quarters high? What color should the walls be? What about decorations for the walls? Blagojevich became almost fanatical about the details, much more than he did about any legislation he was voting on in Washington. Blagojevich eventually decided: the bookshelves would go to the ceiling, the walls would be a dark red, and he would decorate his desk with a bust of Napoleon and his walls with pictures of Alexander Hamilton and Aaron Burr. He also bought scores of impressive-looking books to fill his new shelves.

"Now I guess I gotta read all these books, eh?" he joked as he flipped through book catalogues, picking out historical biographies.

As the century turned and the nation focused on electing a new president, Blagojevich focused on his next move. Just a little more than a year in office and the incumbent governor, Republican George Ryan, was becoming increasingly unpopular amid a growing scandal that focused mostly on his previous elected office, secretary of state.

Rod had disliked and shown such a disinterest in Congress, the only move that made sense to him was running for governor. The Senate was out of the question and staying in the House, even though he once again was going to face nominal competition in the fall, was not an option. He would still likely be a member of the minority party, and his patience, what little he had of it, was running ever thinner. Now was the time to move. But first he wanted to feel out some of his fellow Democrats and let them spread the word that if he did throw in, he wouldn't back down.

Blagojevich called up US Rep. Jan Schakowsky. The two met at her offices on Broadway in Chicago. Although she was new to the office, Blagojevich wanted Schakowsky's support. She also wasn't a threat. Of all the Democrats who might run, Schakowsky wasn't one of them. She was still too new.

Soon after the two sat down, Blagojevich sprung the news on her. With a fierce, almost crazed, look in his eye and a tenor to his voice that insisted he was serious, Blagojevich told her he was planning on running for governor. He wanted to do things, make a change in people's lives. This business of just voting on things and being a backbencher wasn't for him. Not anymore. And he didn't care what other Democrats ran against him in the primary. He was a good fund-raiser and he'd only get better.

"I'm going to roll the dice and do this. I'm not staying in DC, I can't," he told her. "I've got a death wish," is how he phrased it. Blagojevich didn't even care if he lost.

"A death wish?" Schakowsky said. "You've got to have a better pitch than that."

5

A Run for Governor

Milan Petrovic flipped on the radio as he steered his SUV down a northwest Indiana highway. A report on a Chicago station crackled across the speakers about young Chicago congressman Rod Blagojevich. Barren trees on the chilly spring day became a blur in the side-view mirrors as Petrovic's mind wandered.

A former Northwestern University basketball player who had become a well-known fund-raiser for Indiana Democrats, Petrovic was thinking of expanding into Illinois. When he heard Blagojevich's name, he thought he might have found a good fit. Blagojevich had made a name for himself, even in Indiana, with his mission to Kosovo. Petrovic was also Serbian. This could be his *in* into the world of Illinois politics.

When he got to work, Petrovic called Blagojevich's congressional office and got patched through to his chief of staff, Dave Stricklin. Petrovic said he was looking for Blagojevich's political office because he wanted to host a fund-raiser for the congressman. Stricklin asked Petrovic how long he had known Blagojevich.

"I don't know him at all," Petrovic said coolly.

Do you live in his congressional district?

"I live in Indiana."

Stricklin thought the call might be a joke. Why do you want to throw a fund-raiser for a congressman you don't know and can't even vote for? Petrovic tried to explain that there was a large Serbian community in northwest

81

Indiana and he liked what he'd heard about Blagojevich. Serbs like to help their own. "Go ahead and check my reputation among Indiana's congressional delegation," he assured Stricklin, who got off the phone without making any promises.

A few weeks later, Petrovic's phone rang. Blagojevich himself was on the other end and quickly got to the point.

"How much money do you think you can raise?" he asked.

"Ten thousand dollars," Petrovic said.

Blagojevich sounded impressed. OK, set it up. I'll be there.

Petrovic hadn't really thought it through but felt $10,000 wouldn't be hard to come up with, given his contacts. His plan was to host the fund-raiser at his home in Munster, Indiana. He'd invite all the businesspeople and Serbs he knew. Over the next few months, he invited friends and associates and fine-tuned the details but never heard another word from Blagojevich or his staff.

The day before the fund-raiser, Blagojevich called. "We have a problem," he said. Congress was going to be in session the next two days. He wasn't sure he could make it. Petrovic stammered and explained all the work he put in and all the people he invited.

"Do you think you'll hit your number?" Blagojevich pressed. Petrovic assured him he would. Blagojevich paused and exhaled. "OK, I'll make it."

The next day, partiers funneled into Petrovic's home around six in the evening, mingling and asking where the man of the hour was. Petrovic assured them Blagojevich would be there any minute. By 7:15 PM—fifteen minutes before the party was supposed to end—a white Cadillac pulled up in front of the house. Blagojevich got out and walked briskly into Petrovic's home, directly past his host, whom he still hadn't even met, and his wife, Anne. Petrovic had to tap Blagojevich on the shoulder to introduce himself.

The spacious home was packed with Democratic players and Serbs from the region. Blagojevich worked them all for hours, telling jokes, riffing about life in DC, and discussing his vision for the nation. The guests, as they always seemed to be with Blagojevich, were charmed. Several handed Petrovic checks and thanked him for the invitation.

Before anyone realized, it was 10:30 PM. A Blagojevich aide told Petrovic the congressman had to go. But first, they needed those checks. Petrovic had them gathered in a sloppy pile. He didn't want to just hand them over and couldn't fit them all into an envelope. Scanning the room looking for something bigger to put them in, he spotted a purple sack that held a bottle of Crown Royal Whisky. Petrovic grabbed the bag off the bottle and began jamming the checks into the sack, several at a time. By the time he was done, checks were flowing out of the top.

As the Cadillac headed off and curved around the corner, Blagojevich immediately turned to his aide and asked, "How'd we do tonight?" The aide held up the purple sack, still overflowing with checks. Blagojevich smiled and asked the driver to pull over. There, on the side of the road, Blagojevich turned on the car's interior lights and started counting. When he was done, the number amazed him: almost $30,000.

The next day, Petrovic's phone rang. It was Blagojevich thanking him for the splendid event. A few days after that, Blagojevich sent flowers to Petrovic's wife. And a few weeks after that, Blagojevich came to town and took Petrovic out to lunch and then to dinner. Then he asked Petrovic a question.

"When do you think you can throw me another fund-raiser?"

———

The money Petrovic raised in 2000 went into Blagojevich's congressional campaign fund. But by then, Blagojevich was already well on his way to running for the state's highest office.

Money would be key to winning. And Blagojevich was forming a plan that would blow away the competition by placing control of fund-raising in the hands of men such as Petrovic who were beholden to him—and not to Mell.

Since that first meeting five years earlier outside the North Side restaurant, Chris Kelly had also grown increasingly close to Blagojevich. They would talk on the phone about politics, business, and sports—mostly baseball and especially the Cubs. Blagojevich told others he looked up to Kelly, even admired him, for having made something of himself in the roofing business.

He saw a little bit of himself in Kelly. Here was a guy who is a lot like me, Blagojevich would say. He didn't have much growing up, but he hustled and worked at it, and now look at him. He was a player. He wasn't somebody who was born rich and had things handed to him. "He's a true American superstar," is how Blagojevich once described him.

While not from wealth, Kelly didn't grow up in the midst of poverty either. He came from an upper-middle-class family in downstate Champaign, where the University of Illinois campus is located. He studied landscape architecture there but decided to get into the roofing business, having dabbled in it through his father, who was a contractor.

He learned the trade and made friends with contractors and government officials over a decade of work with a firm run by William Cleary on Chicago's South Side. But by the mid-1990s, Kelly split with Cleary and started his own roofing firm, BCI Roofing. He teamed up with Ronald Rossi, the developer he was with the first night he met Blagojevich, and another buddy, Robert Blum, who owned Castle Construction. Blum and Kelly shared office space in south suburban Markham, and by 1998, BCI won a $7 million roofing contract at O'Hare Airport. Rossi and Castle were well on their way to collectively winning tens of millions of dollars in city contracts, much of it at O'Hare.

But Kelly also had a dark side.

Rather than behaving like he was raised well-off in a university town, he often acted like he came from the mean streets of Chicago's South Side. Tall and beefy, with slicked back salt-and-pepper hair and a crushing handshake, Kelly became successful with raspy-voiced tough talk, nonstop bluster, and incessant schemes.

When he dressed up, he wore fitted suits and fancy ties, looking the part of a successful businessman. But he preferred casual attire, typically untucked dress shirts, slacks, and sunglasses, which he often wore inside when meeting new people to prevent them from seeing his eyes.

He had battled demons in his past with addiction. When he drank to excess, things often got ugly as Kelly became loud and boorish. His efforts to become a teetotaler never stuck.

As Kelly made more money, he enjoyed it—and flaunted it. He bought a large home and took nice vacations with his wife and three daughters. He also wagered with Chicago bookies and took trips nearly every weekend to Las Vegas, where he was known by casino operators as a high-roller.

"He was almost a caricature of himself. Everything about him was exaggerated," one close Blagojevich confidant later recalled. "His voice was overly hoarse, like he was doing a bad impression of Marlon Brando from *The Godfather*. It's like he had an image of what a 'player' was supposed to be and then he tried to emulate it."

When he got introduced into the world of politics and got closer to Blagojevich, Kelly became more interested—even infatuated—with the power of this new world. He invited Blagojevich to various fund-raisers, and their friendship deepened. When Blagojevich discussed running for governor and asked Kelly to help quarterback his fund-raising, Kelly relished the idea. It was a perfect fit for both men. Not only was it a chance for Kelly to get more involved in politics, but also Blagojevich thought Kelly had the talents he needed to be successful. Although he hadn't done it before, Blagojevich felt Kelly's business acumen allowed him to one day schmooze businessmen and union leaders to donate to the campaign and then the next day pick up the phone and aggressively ask them "where is the fucking money?"

———

As he had with Schakowsky, Blagojevich began telling his fellow members of Congress his plans to run for governor in hopes of lining up their support. In the summer of 2000, Blagojevich called US Representative Luis Gutierrez's congressional offices. Since Blagojevich worked the streets for Vrdolyak and Mell against him in 1986, the two had mended fences. They now got along well, though Gutierrez privately was not overly impressed with Blagojevich's thin record as a congressman.

After Blagojevich told Gutierrez his plans to run for governor, Gutierrez pulled aside his top aide, Doug Scofield. "I just had a very interesting conversation with Rod Blagojevich," Gutierrez said, seeming almost stunned. "He's going to run for governor."

"Who is he kidding?" Gutierrez continued. Personally, Gutierrez liked Blagojevich, finding him an amiable colleague who had shown little interest in government and would be getting in over his head running for governor, except for the fact that he had Mell on his side. But Scofield, who had earned a reputation as a thoughtful aide who wouldn't dismiss ideas out of hand, told Gutierrez not to be so hasty to dismiss Blagojevich.

"It's a wide-open race," Scofield said. "He'll get lots of money from Mell."

Before joining Gutierrez, Scofield worked at the Strategy Group with David Wilhelm, who had made a name for himself successfully heading Bill Clinton's 1992 presidential campaign. The only thing Scofield knew about Blagojevich was his reputation as a fierce campaigner.

Gutierrez remained skeptical. Although the race was still nearly eighteen months away, the names being bandied about in gossip columns and over drinks at Gene & Georgetti, a steakhouse frequented by pols, was far more impressive: William Daley, President Clinton's commerce secretary and Mayor Daley's brother; Illinois Comptroller Dan Hynes, the son of long-time Cook County powerbroker Tom Hynes; Cook County State's Attorney

Richard Devine, who also happened to be the father of Blagojevich's press secretary, Matt Devine; even US Senator Dick Durbin.

But in general Scofield was right. It was a wide-open race, and Illinois voters were looking for something different, something new. Maybe Blagojevich could fill that void, that yearning. What was certain is that Democrats thought they finally had a real shot at winning the governor's mansion for the first time since Daniel Walker in 1972. Not because they had such a plethora of solid contenders, but because the Republican incumbent was so abysmal.

═══

George Homer Ryan was, to many, the embodiment of what was wrong with Illinois politics. A beefy man with a round face, thick neck, and thin white hair, Ryan—now in his late sixties—came from an old-school era of politics. He hailed from Kankakee, a small working-class city south of Chicago dominated by the local Republican Party.

In the early 1960s, he joined his brother Tom in running the family business, a pharmacy. But both men were interested in politics and befriended the county's Republican powerbroker, State Senator Ed McBroom. George became McBroom's campaign manager, and Tom became Kankakee mayor. Eventually, George moved up to county board and a state legislator, earning a reputation as a man happy to help friends and then come looking for their help when the time called.

George steadily climbed the state's political ladder, becoming speaker of the Illinois House, lieutenant governor, and secretary of state for two terms before defeating former US representative Glenn Poshard in 1998 and becoming Illinois's thirty-ninth governor.

All the while, Ryan seemed to embrace the image he carved out for himself as the backroom-dealing, cigar-chomping old political horse unafraid to make a deal over a drink. It was the way things got done, the way politics was practiced for decades. Nobody was getting hurt. Roads were being built, bridges repaired, and the state was better for it.

But to reformers and some federal prosecutors, those were simplistic explanations to rationalize the patronage and corruption that followed Ryan throughout much of his political career. And by 2000, Ryan's image was battered by scandal.

Investigators had been probing Ryan's eight years as Illinois secretary of state, an office with a long history of corruption. The secretary of state's office kept track of state records and business filings, but its biggest responsibility was overseeing auto license plates and drivers' licenses. That meant the secretary held sway over thousands of jobs and tens of millions of dollars in contracts and leases for the office's branches located throughout every corner of the state.

Perhaps Illinois's most famous secretary of state was Paul Powell. A former state legislator who famously cackled, "I can smell the meat a'cookin'" whenever the subject of state jobs was raised, Powell became secretary at the end of his political career. When he died in 1970, officials found $800,000 in cash stuffed into shoeboxes, strongboxes, and briefcases in the Springfield hotel where he was staying. Officially, Powell never made more than $30,000 a year.

By August 2000, the FBI and US attorney's office had been digging deep into illegalities that occurred while Ryan was secretary of state. What they found were office employees taking bribes in exchange for giving unqualified truck drivers their drivers' licenses. Some of the money, they discovered, was being donated to Ryan's campaign fund.

The US attorney's office called the licenses-for-bribes investigation Operation Safe Road. That name stemmed in no small part to an incident that occurred on Election Day 1994.

On the same day voters reelected Ryan secretary of state, an Illinois reverend, Scott Willis, and his wife, Janet, were driving a minivan with their children on an interstate near Milwaukee. Both had voted for Ryan. Ricardo Guzman, a Chicago man who prosecutors later alleged had paid a bribe to receive his commercial driver's license, drove a truck in front of them.

As the two vehicles sped down the highway, a mud flap–taillight assembly hung off Guzman's truck. At least one other motorist screamed and honked to alert Guzman about it. But Guzman couldn't speak English, and he ignored the warnings. Minutes later, the metal chunk split off Guzman's truck, flittered along the highway, and pierced the underbelly of Willis's minivan, striking its gas tank. In seconds, the minivan burst into flames with the Willis family trapped inside.

Almost instantaneously the flames engulfed Scott and Janet Willis. The couple fought hard to open the minivan's side door to get their children out. It was a horrific scene. The couple's oldest son, thirteen-year-old Ben, ran from the burning minivan while still swallowed up in flames before collapsing on the road as motorists who had stopped tried to help.

"His hair and eyebrows were gone," Janet Willis recalled years later. "His burned lips made it hard for him to talk. I was suddenly aware of searing, blinding pain in my burned hands. I could not imagine what my son, who was burned over much of his body, was going through."

Ben died. So too did five other Willis children in the minivan. The accident became national news, and when stories broke that Guzman may have bribed a secretary of state employee to get his license, it quickly became a massive scandal. By February 2000, federal prosecutors indicted one of Ryan's dearest friends, Dean Bauer, the secretary of state's inspector general, on charges he buried the investigation into the Willis accident.

It was looking less likely voters would reelect Ryan, if he decided to run at all. His popularity numbers were in the tank, and the feds were continuing to be on his tail. Democrats were excited. But who could win?

———

In mid-August 2000, Democrats from around the nation gathered in Los Angeles for the national convention and to nominate Al Gore to run against George W. Bush for president. When Rod Blagojevich arrived, he strode through the hallways of the Staples Center with the wide smile of a confident man.

In a way, this was going to be his coming-out party too. Word had begun to leak out that he was considering a run for governor. Democrats had thought of Blagojevich (if they thought of him at all) as someone who could be a congressman for life. With almost no effort, he was on his way to winning a third term in office. But few thought he could be more than that.

Blagojevich had arrived in LA to demonstrate he had no intention of being a lifelong congressman. But to do so, he'd have to convince the powers that be that he was a candidate to be taken seriously.

Accompanied by Chris Kelly, Blagojevich arrived at the convention amid news that Durbin wasn't closing the door on a run for governor. It stole some of the thunder Blagojevich hoped to produce, but he tried to take it in stride. To supporters there, Blagojevich dismissed questions that he had accomplished almost nothing in Congress, telling them he soured on the "legislative branch," especially being a member of the minority party. But if he got a job in the executive branch, he could finally achieve something.

The next morning, as the Illinois delegation gathered for breakfast in an orchestrated scene that played out before the media, Blagojevich cheerfully shook hands with delegates, laughing as a few greeted him as "Mr. Governor." He told reporters he arrived in Los Angeles later in the week to avoid the hubbub about possibly running for governor.

"I did not feel it was appropriate for me to promote my aspirations I may have in an election that comes after this one" in 2000, he said, trying to draw a distinction between himself and Durbin. Few reporters bought the self-serving comment, but many picked up on what Blagojevich said were his criteria before deciding to run for office: "What can I do for the people as governor? Do I have the support of my family? Can I raise enough money to be competitive?"

"If those three all come up 'yes,' it won't matter who's in the race or what they say, because I'm going to do it," Blagojevich said.

Of course, the last rule was truly essential. And Blagojevich's plan to be taken seriously was bolstered when he revealed he'd already amassed more than $1 million in his campaign fund. Still, it wasn't enough.

"We need to keep going," Blagojevich said to Kelly and others who had begun helping him in his fund-raising effort. "Keep pushing."

———

Among those who had questions about Blagojevich's ability to be governor was his media consultant, David Axelrod. When Blagojevich first broached the idea, Axelrod immediately thought it was bad. Blagojevich hadn't distinguished himself in Congress, he wasn't detail oriented, and he seemed to want the job more to have it than to do anything with it.

The two men discussed it over a series of meetings, and each time Axelrod refused to commit.

"Axelrod needs to get into this. Is he in or out?" Blagojevich would rant to close aides. During one meeting, Axelrod attempted to divert Blagojevich by suggesting he run for a lesser office—like president of the Cook County Board. Blagojevich fumed afterward. "Axelrod doesn't think I have the gravitas to be governor," he complained. "Well, who the hell is he?"

One of those Blagojevich privately complained to was Carol Ronen, who quickly came up with an idea for a replacement. Ronen knew Blagojevich needed a full-time, high-powered strategist, someone who would make him real in the eyes of the Democratic political establishment and the media. She called up an old friend, David Wilhelm.

Wilhelm's pedigree was as accomplished—or more so at that point—as Axelrod's. After successfully managing Bill Clinton's presidential campaign in 1992, he had become the youngest chairman of the Democratic National Committee. Like Axelrod, Wilhelm worked for Paul Simon in Illinois and

Mayor Daley in Chicago. Ronen had been Daley's deputy campaign manager in 1991.

Ronen and Blagojevich made their way downtown to Wilhelm's offices
just off Michigan Avenue. The men talked for more than an hour, breaking
down strategies and ideas about what issues Blagojevich should focus on
for the campaign. One of the few issues Blagojevich was active on in Congress was gun control. But that wouldn't play well in a statewide run when
Blagojevich would have to sell himself to downstate voters who distrusted
Chicago politicians, liked to hunt, and didn't like liberals who wanted to
take away their guns.

Before Blagojevich made a final decision, though, he met with Wilhelm
and Axelrod to talk it over one more time. During that meeting, Axelrod
asked Blagojevich a simple question: "Why do you want to be governor?"

"You can help me figure that out," Blagojevich answered.

Axelrod told him that was not what he did. "If you can tell me, I can
help you explain it to others," Axelrod said. "If you can't, then you really
shouldn't run."

Still Blagojevich tried to convince Axelrod to join the campaign, insisting he was "going to raise a lot of money" and "it'll be great," but Axelrod
said he couldn't.

There was no Axelrod-like come-to-Jesus question from Wilhelm, who
focused more on setting an agenda and developing a strategy to elect Illinois's first Democratic governor in a quarter century. But when the time
came to formally hire Wilhelm as campaign chairman, Blagojevich didn't
do it. As he and Ronen sat in Wilhelm's office, that odd, shy part of Blagojevich's personality presented itself again, and he never worked up the gump-
tion to offer Wilhelm the job. Finally, Ronen stepped in and did it.

"Absolutely," Wilhelm responded.

———

In terms of strategy, Wilhelm and Blagojevich quickly decided on the theme
of the 2002 campaign: Rod the Populist. Blagojevich won his seat in Congress pitching himself as an amalgam of a city ward boss's son-in-law and a
progressive yuppie. While that was fine for the Fifth Congressional District,
he would need more to win statewide.

Rod the Populist would hit on multiple issues: promising change to the
culture of sleaze in Springfield for those sick of the corruption; guaranteeing

affordable prescription drugs for senior citizens; and promising jobs and raising the minimum wage for working-class families.

To replace Axelrod, Blagojevich hired two experts from DC—media strategist Bill Knapp and pollster Fred Yang. The campaign, though, still needed a campaign manager. At first, Wilhelm sought out his former employee at the Strategy Group, Doug Scofield with Gutierrez's office. But Scofield balked. He and his wife had a one-year-old and another one on the way. The strain and stress of running a statewide campaign wasn't going to work for him.

"Talk to Axe," Wilhelm said, referring to Axelrod. Wilhelm thought maybe Axelrod or his partner, John Kupper, could help shed some light on what it was like working for Blagojevich.

When Scofield and Kupper spoke, Kupper talked about what a great campaigner and how energetic Blagojevich was. But there was another side, he warned. Blagojevich was an unbelievable handful. He didn't listen to his consultants, was unmanageable and unpredictable, didn't know the material particularly well, and didn't seem to care much about policy. "Think hard about it," Kupper told him.

Scofield called Wilhelm back, saying he appreciated the offer but was going to have to pass. By then, though, Blagojevich had gotten other ideas about a campaign manager.

As 2000 turned to 2001, he took a skiing vacation to Copper Mountain, Colorado, with Patti, Lon Monk, and Monk's girlfriend. Blagojevich, who wasn't much of a skier anyway, seemed preoccupied. He eventually dropped the bomb on Monk he was going to run for governor and he wanted Monk's help. Monk was skeptical.

He was a sports agent and didn't know anything about politics. But Blagojevich said he could handle that part of things. He wanted somebody who was organized, who felt beholden to him, and whom he could trust. But first, Blagojevich planned to place Monk on his congressional staff to get his feet wet. Blagojevich would transition Monk onto the political staff when the campaign was fully underway. Monk agreed, and by that spring, he was serving as Blagojevich's congressional general counsel, on his way to earning nearly $84,000 in taxpayers' money between May and the end of 2001.

Around the same time, Blagojevich was in Washington, DC, when he got a visit from an old friend—Paris Thompson. The two men had gone separate ways since Blagojevich joined Congress. Thompson's love of baseball had taken him to Florida where he tried his hand at umpire school. When that didn't pan out, he came home to Chicago to do community work and preach as a minister.

He also had some other news. His name was no longer Paris Thompson. It was Bamani Obadele. He had changed it after a trip to Africa. Blagojevich had some news of his own. He was running for governor. "I'm going to need your help in the black community. I'm going to need you with me," he told Obadele.

"I'm with you Rod," Obadele said. "But a lot of people in the community feel it is Roland's time."

Blagojevich knew exactly who Bamani was talking about—Roland Burris. The first African American to be elected to a statewide office, in 1978, Burris for years had been trying—and mostly failing—to ascend to a higher office. In 1984, he lost to Paul Simon for US Senate and in 1995 got crushed by Mayor Daley for Chicago mayor. He'd run for governor in 1994 and 1998 and lost both times in the primary. The only time he was successful was in 1990 when voters elected him Illinois attorney general.

Burris's name had recently floated to the top of the list of potential candidates. Some new names joined him. Michael Bakalis said he was going to run. A sixty-something suburbanite and Illinois's last superintendent of schools, Bakalis had gotten killed running for governor in 1978 against Republican James R. Thompson, a former US attorney who ended up holding the office throughout the 1980s. Paul Vallas, who made national headlines reforming Chicago's public schools, was also talking about running, which was ironic because years earlier Vallas was told he should run for governor by Dick Mell.

Burris was a good politician and not to be underestimated since he'd draw a large number of black votes. But he'd been a steady loser and was sixty-three years old; Blagojevich knew he could outenergize and outcampaign him. He also knew he'd crush him in the most important category—money.

Still heeding the lesson he first learned in the Kaszak race, Blagojevich told Obadele he was ready to make a splash with his cash. "It's gonna blow people away," Blagojevich said.

———

By the summer of 2001, Monk moved to Chicago and for nearly two months lived at Blagojevich's home on Sunnyside before finally buying a place in

Wrigleyville. The two friends became even closer, staying up late talking about old times and future plans. Blagojevich was becoming manic about money. He constantly talked about it, from gathering as much as possible to spending as little as possible. It was all with an eye on reporting the largest war chest to intimidate competition when campaign finance reports were released at the end of July.

Around the same time, Blagojevich decided it was time two of his biggest fund-raisers finally met. He called up Petrovic and said he needed to meet Chris Kelly, who, he told Petrovic, was going to be overseeing the campaign's fund-raising operation. The three men met at the Rosewood Restaurant in Rosemont, a high-end steakhouse in the small northwest Chicago suburb that had become a popular destination for conventioneers.

When Petrovic and Blagojevich arrived, Kelly was already sitting in a booth. Dressed casually, his graying hair slicked back, Kelly wore sunglasses and barely moved as Blagojevich and Petrovic sat down. Kelly didn't say a word as Blagojevich made small talk, and when Rod quieted down, the three sat in silence. Petrovic wondered what was going on. Kelly still hadn't even taken off his sunglasses. Then he looked in Petrovic's direction. "You gotta get up and leave. I gotta talk to Rod."

Petrovic looked at Kelly. He wasn't kidding. Then he looked at Blagojevich, who nervously chuckled and indicated he also didn't think Kelly was kidding. So Petrovic got up out of the booth and headed to the bar, thinking Kelly needed a few minutes before the three had their meeting. Nearly an hour later, after Blagojevich and Kelly sat in the booth speaking in hushed tones, Kelly stood up and walked out of the restaurant, ignoring Petrovic as he left. Blagojevich rescued Petrovic, still at the bar, and the two headed back to Petrovic's car. Sitting in the passenger seat, Blagojevich giggled nervously.

"Did I say something wrong?" Petrovic asked.

"No," Blagojevich responded.

"Well, what was that about?"

"He didn't like you."

"What do you mean he doesn't like me? I met him for thirty seconds."

"He doesn't like you because he doesn't know you," Blagojevich explained. "And because of that, he doesn't trust you."

Kelly's reaction wasn't unique to Petrovic. Almost anybody who Kelly felt could get Blagojevich's ear without going through him first got the same treatment. And Blagojevich did little to stop it. In fact, Blagojevich—ever the radio show prankster—often stoked the fires, egging Kelly on and watching just to see how people reacted as they vied for Blagojevich's attention.

But the meeting with Kelly wasn't enough to scare Petrovic off. He knew the business of fund-raising, and business with Blagojevich was good. Even Blagojevich's self-centeredness didn't make Petrovic get up and quit, though one Friday he wanted to.

Petrovic had driven Blagojevich to north suburban Gurnee for a fund-raising meeting, and following the meeting, Petrovic fought terrible Friday traffic for ninety minutes to drop Blagojevich off at his home. Just minutes later, though, Mary Stewart called to tell Petrovic there was an emergency. Rod had left his hairbrush up in Gurnee and needed Petrovic to drive back and retrieve it.

"You have to deliver it back to him," she said.

Petrovic was stunned but followed though with his task grudgingly. Nearly four hours later, after missing a night out with his wife, Petrovic was back on Sunnyside, knocking on Blagojevich's door, hairbrush in hand. "Thanks, handsome," Blagojevich said, grabbing the brush and not apparently noticing Petrovic's irritation. "I'll talk to you later."

But Blagojevich's push for fund-raising was paying off. By the end of June 2001, just days before he announced his bid for governor, he had more than $2 million in the bank. Roland Burris, by comparison, had less than $40,000.

———

As Blagojevich racked up the cash, Dick Mell was appearing at a Springfield restaurant for a meeting of the Democratic County Chairmen's Association.

Blagojevich's campaign had made the tactical decision that the primary would be won or lost downstate. Blagojevich had gotten the backing of friends from his state representative days, most notably Representative Jay Hoffman, who had roomed with Blagojevich when the two were in the legislature together.

An endorsement from the county chairmen's group, though, would be a boon. But Blagojevich didn't attend, instead allowing Dick Mell to show up in all his ward-boss glory. On the surface, some may have thought Mell and downstate Democrats would be opposites—the slick, big-city politician versus the country boys—but Mell still spoke the universal language of Illinois politics: patronage and power. And during his speech he tempted them about what the future would look like for all Democrats under a Blagojevich administration.

"He's a Jacksonian Democrat," Mell told the crowd. "Not necessarily a *Jesse Jackson* Jacksonian, but an *Andrew Jackson* Jacksonian, who said, 'To the victor remains the spoils.'

"He's a firm believer that, if the opportunity is there for a Democrat to have an opportunity to serve in state government, and he can do the job, [and] he's equal to the Republican, why shouldn't it be the Democrat? I mean, Republicans have done that for, I don't know, twenty, twenty-six years."

This wasn't Chicago politics, he explained. This was winning politics. "This is what builds parties," he continued. "It'll help you with your fund-raising. It'll help you build an organization."

Mell also let slip that Blagojevich was doing so well fund-raising he was going to exceed the campaign's original plan to raise $6 million for the primary.

Blagojevich wasn't pleased when the "Jacksonian" comments hit the *Springfield State Journal-Register*, but it didn't seem to hurt. The group was led by John Gianulis, a grizzled political veteran from the Mississippi River town of Rock Island. Nearly a year earlier, Blagojevich's campaign gave $2,500 to the Rock Island Democratic Party, which Gianulis controlled. When the association took its vote, it backed Blagojevich.

———

The dynamic between Mell and Blagojevich continued to be one of the more complicated aspects of the campaign. One reason was Blagojevich's increasing reliance on Kelly, including putting him in charge of fund-raising. One day Blagojevich and Mell would act like best friends, and the next they'd be refusing to speak to each other. It had gotten worse since Blagojevich entered Congress; the two men fought about everything from staffers in the congressional office to what gifts Amy received for Christmas. Blagojevich complained Mell acted like he owned him, and Mell complained Rod was an ungrateful jerk.

"The kid can be such a pain in the ass sometimes," Mell groused, sometimes out in the relative open of the anteroom behind the chambers of Chicago's city hall where aldermen gathered during council meetings. He's got talent but thinks the world owes him everything, Mell said.

Some viewed Mell's venting as jealousy. But others knew Blagojevich was trying to distance himself from Mell. Once again, it was good politics to not look indebted to a ward boss. But personally, it was what Blagojevich wanted. He'd been "State Representative Son-in-Law" and "Congressman Son-in-Law." He would not be "Governor Son-in-Law."

———

On Sunday, August 12, 2001, thousands of men and women jammed inside one of the rusting, hulking structures of the Finkl steel plant.

It would become a familiar setting for Blagojevich's campaign events, underscoring his blue-collar roots and populist agenda. Axelrod had used it when Blagojevich won Congress. Now Wilhelm was using it as Blagojevich announced he was running for governor.

Mell had packed the house with city workers and precinct captains who made up the backbone of the city's political scene, generating an electric atmosphere and a show of force. Four days earlier, Governor Ryan had announced in a much different setting—the courthouse square in Kankakee—that he wouldn't be running for reelection.

But, in Ryan, Blagojevich still saw a fantastic political foil that he wasn't going to let go to waste just because he took himself out of the race.

"The Republicans are hiding," he hollered to the animated crowd. "In Springfield today, the Republicans are running from Governor Ryan's record, but they cannot run and they cannot hide from a twenty-four-year legacy of corruption, mismanagement, and lost opportunities."

Afterward, Blagojevich was more keyed up than usual, shaking hands and hugging almost everybody he came across.

"This is gonna be fun!" he kept saying, even to some bystanders he didn't know. "Hold on to your hat!"

———

The field for governor was beginning to set.

On the Republican side, the state's attorney general, Jim Ryan, announced he was running for governor the day after George Ryan announced he wasn't. He was facing a highly conservative state senator from the southwest suburbs, Patrick O'Malley, and George Ryan's lieutenant governor, Corinne Wood, who positioned herself as the female moderate.

Jim Ryan was the immediate frontrunner. He had twice won office state-wide and was a proven commodity in Illinois politics. But the situation was hardly perfect.

Archconservatives who controlled a small but loud contingent of party regulars considered Jim Ryan to be closer to the "RINO"—Republican in Name Only—category than theirs. They preferred O'Malley. There was also a spectacularly controversial court case that haunted Ryan's career. Before becoming attorney general, he headed the prosecutor's office in suburban DuPage County. While in that job, Ryan prosecuted a suspect, Rolando Cruz, despite questions about his guilt in the killing of ten year old Jeanine Nicarico. The case got so far that Cruz was twice sentenced to death despite trials that raised questions about police and prosecutors' handling of the case. Cruz was finally found not guilty at a third trial when evidence emerged that lent credence to Cruz's claims. Jim Ryan's biggest problem, though, might have been his simplest—his last name. Even though Jim Ryan and George Ryan weren't related and weren't politically close, they shared the same surname and were members of the same political party.

Working to his advantage, however, was Jim Ryan's history and story. The Cruz case aside, voters had generally found him to be an ethical and solid government official, if not exciting. Personally, he had overcome a series of well-publicized tragedies, including bouts of cancer, his wife's heart attack, and the death of his youngest daughter, Annie. Voters respected him and saw his courage during trying times.

On the Democratic side, Blagojevich's opponents would be Bakalis, who portrayed himself as a reformer focused on education, and Vallas, who on paper was basically a younger, better version of Bakalis. The two men were Greek, had education bona fides, and hadn't raised much money or assembled much in terms of organizations.

A former budget chief for Mayor Daley, Vallas was selected years earlier to head the mayor's high-profile effort to improve Chicago public schools. It worked for a while but Vallas's relationship with Daley soured. Some close to Daley claimed school improvements stalled. Others said Daley wasn't too keen on the forty-eight-year-old Vallas's popularity being the same as or greater than his.

Other candidates were falling by the wayside. Daley's brother, William, decided not to run, after toying with the idea and, in the process, freezing up some critical fund-raising for Vallas. Dan Hynes was going to run for comptroller again, Durbin was going to stay in the Senate, and Dick Devine was staying state's attorney. Privately, Blagojevich took a lot of the credit, touting his fund-raising for scaring potential opponents off. That left only one more.

A few weeks after the September 11 terrorist attacks, Burris formally announced his candidacy in Centralia, the downstate city where he was born. He repeated his performance later that day on the porch of his home on Chicago's South Side, where Obadele's warning about how Burris would get massive support among blacks was on full display. Flanking him were congressmen Danny Davis and Bobby Rush, along with several state law-makers, including a tall state senator with big ears who stood in the back-ground—Barack Obama.

Even though it was still months before candidates had to officially file, the Democratic field was set: Blagojevich, Bakalis, Burris, and Vallas. "Two Greeks, a black, and a Serb," one Blagojevich fund-raiser noted.

One African American politician not standing behind Burris was US Representative Jesse Jackson Jr. Some in the media speculated Jackson and his father might end up endorsing Blagojevich, especially considering their friendliness with each other in Congress and their mutual ties from the Yugoslavia trip.

Publicly, Blagojevich downplayed a Jackson endorsement. But privately he coveted it, even having Wilhelm and the younger Jackson meet privately to talk about an endorsement. If the Jacksons backed him, it would almost assure a victory in the primary, he figured. Not only would it undermine Burris, but also it would virtually guarantee the 5 to 7 percent of the black vote Blagojevich estimated he needed to win in March.

Blagojevich decided to sit down with the Jacksons and their close ally James Meeks, who had also been on the Yugoslavia trip and was running for state senate in 2002. The younger Jackson told Blagojevich what he had told Wilhelm: he would strongly consider endorsing him, but he wanted something too.

He asked Blagojevich to back his plan for a third airport in Jackson's congressional district if he won the governor's office. It was a project vitally important to Jackson that he said would bring thousands of jobs to his district. It was also in political purgatory because Mayor Daley wanted an expansion of O'Hare International Airport to be the area's priority. If Jackson had an ally in the governor's office, the airport might get built.

Blagojevich agreed, even at one point calling himself a Peotone Democrat after the village in which the proposed airport would be built.

Jackson suggested Blagojevich should show his support for the black community by setting up a campaign office on Chicago's South Side. Blagojevich aides said the governor was also asked to hire campaign workers loyal to the Jacksons and to put some campaign cash into Seaway National Bank, an institution whose leaders were longtime supporters of Reverend Jackson. The younger Jackson denied requesting Blagojevich make the deposit in exchange for his support.

Wilhelm had wanted an early endorsement, but Jackson held him off. He agreed to endorse Blagojevich but at a later date.

Blagojevich was excited and called Obadele to tell him about the meeting. "Rod, they are going to fuck you," Obadele told him plainly. "They're full of shit. They aren't going to back you."

=====

In Blagojevich's congressional district, meanwhile, he was watching with great interest the race to replace him.

His former foe Nancy Kaszak was running against Rahm Emanuel. Blagojevich knew Emanuel. He was raised on the well-off North Shore, something that would typically make Blagojevich dislike somebody unless they were giving him money. But Blagojevich liked Emanuel because he was forceful and good at what he did. He had gotten into politics in Chicago by fund-raising for Mayor Daley. He was also a friend of Wilhelm and got dragged down to Little Rock in 1992 to help Bill Clinton get elected president. Emanuel stayed on with Clinton and moved to Washington, where his assertive nature made him stand out as a top Clinton aide and where he and Blagojevich got to know each other a little better.

Emanuel moved back to Chicago and waited for the right opportunity to reenter politics. In the meantime, he made millions of dollars as an investment banker. Emanuel lived only a few miles away from Blagojevich, so when Blagojevich decided to run for governor, that "right opportunity" was obvious.

"Should be a good race," he told one political insider. "Rahm's an aggressive asshole, and so is Nancy."

As the calendar turned to 2002, David Wilhelm tried one more time to get Doug Scofield to work for Blagojevich's campaign. There were only two months before the primary, and Blagojevich was about to put his first television commercial on the air. It was a bio ad, introducing a smiling

Blagojevich with his hard-to-pronounce last name to Democratic voters across the state. He was the embodiment of the American dream.

"My name is Eastern European; my story is American."

It was the first ad of the season, beating both Vallas and Burris out of the box. In just ten days, the campaign's internal polling showed Blagojevich moved from relative obscurity at 12 percent to contender at 28 percent. He was also showing a huge upswing among those key downstate voters. "He's moving," Wilhelm told Scofield. "He has a chance to win this thing."

Still, things weren't perfect. The campaign was disjointed. Blagojevich's current spokeswoman couldn't get along with either the press or the candidate. And, Wilhelm conceded, the candidate himself was undisciplined, unfocused, and self-absorbed. But just the same, he was brilliant at retail politics, had boundless energy, and tons of cash.

Work just until the primary in March, Wilhelm said, and after that let's see what happens.

Scofield agreed. The commitment was only for a few months, and the idea of helping elect Illinois's first Democratic governor in a quarter century was too tempting. He took a leave of absence from Gutierrez—who endorsed Blagojevich despite his previous skepticism—and days later sat down with the candidate, who was aware of the campaign's shortcomings. Except those that dealt with himself.

"The research shop is totally fucked up and completely disorganized," Blagojevich griped.

Scofield soon realized why. Blagojevich spent no money on research, paying only one staffer and relying on free interns to study the pressing issues of the day and develop policy positions. He didn't want to spend money on anything but commercials. A few days later, Scofield arrived at Blagojevich's home to accompany him to a meeting with the editorial board of Chicago's most prominent business magazine, *Crain's*.

As the SUV idled outside the candidate's home on the cold January morning, Scofield sat in the backseat flipping through the campaign's briefing books, familiarizing himself with Blagojevich's positions. John Wyma, whom Blagojevich had persuaded to leave his job in DC to be an adviser on the campaign, was also there.

Scofield glanced at his watch as they continued to wait for Blagojevich and realized they were going to be late. "Get used to it," Wyma said. When Blagojevich finally bounded into the SUV, he looked to Scofield and asked, "What are we saying?"

"Is this some sort of test?" Scofield thought to himself. "I've been with the campaign for seventy-two hours and he's asking me what he should say at this editorial board?"

Scofield soon realized this was the job. He quickly spouted some talking points about economic development and job creation to Blagojevich, who took mental notes and dashed into the editorial board meeting, which he nailed.

It was the first of several lessons Scofield would receive that made him realize two things: the campaign apparatus and the candidate were totally disorganized, and Rod Blagojevich could still become Illinois's next governor.

Blagojevich continued to raise cash at a blistering rate. By the end of 2001, he had collected nearly $4.3 million. Vallas and Burris each had raised about $1.1 million. He was even beating Republican Jim Ryan, who had raised $3.8 million.

He also was the voracious campaigner everybody promised Scofield he'd be. Whether in Chicago or downstate, Blagojevich leaned into the growing crowds and fed off their energy like his life depended on it. He shook every hand, summoned his keen memory skills to remember names of early supporters, and played up his working man shtick. When he did work downstate, he told crowds in VFW halls and small-town parades that if his father had moved to Marion instead of Chicago he would have been a coal miner instead of a factory worker.

The daily schedules were endless. Blagojevich dashed from event to event, rarely pausing and refusing to eat all day, somehow keeping up a high energy level. Unlike Blagojevich, Scofield, Wyma, and other staffers were starving. At campaign stops, they scarfed down energy bars they brought with them or darted off for a few minutes to grab a quick bite while the candidate worked a room.

Vallas was smarter than Blagojevich but came off wonky to voters. And he couldn't cover nearly as much ground campaigning because he hated to fly, especially in small puddle jumpers. Blagojevich could hit several corners of the state in one day while Vallas was stuck in one or two.

Downstate, the best thing Vallas had going for him was getting the endorsement of Poshard. The popular downstate congressman liked Vallas and still despised Blagojevich for that disastrous meeting Blagojevich had set up between Poshard and gay activists in Chicago.

But Poshard's endorsement would only go so far. And while downstaters were still concerned about this ward boss's son-in-law with the ridiculously difficult last name, Blagojevich was confident that wasn't enough to count him out in Vandalia, Pickneyville, and Alton.

"I can play in Peoria," he repeatedly assured staffers. "I'm an Elvis guy. I'm a working-class guy. These are my people. You really think Paul Vallas is going to connect with people in Rock Island? I understand these people."

———

Blagojevich had been killing himself, crisscrossing Illinois selling his "opportunities for working people" theme. His vision for creating jobs and making prescription drugs affordable for seniors, he thought, was starting to gain traction.

But he was still waiting to see some of that success in the polls. Burris had the highest name recognition and was the only black candidate, so early on he had held modest leads in the polls. But Blagojevich figured Burris would fade at the end, as he had in several previous races. Blagojevich and Vallas also got small bumps when Bakalis—running last—dropped out.

In early February, Blagojevich was sitting in his Washington, DC, office with John Wyma hoping for some good news as they awaited word from his pollster about the latest numbers.

As he nervously bobbed his right leg up and down, Blagojevich's mind drifted to a conversation he had just had with fellow Illinois US Representative Bill Lipinski. A powerful dealmaker from the city's southwest side, Lipinski endorsed Blagojevich but told him he better show improvement in the polls fast or endorsements and money would dry up quickly.

When the phone rang, Wyma answered it and Blagojevich apprehensively listened in.

"Twenty-four, twenty-four, thirty," Wyma read aloud. Blagojevich was relieved. He was tied with Vallas at 24 percent with Burris holding onto his lead at 30 percent.

No, Wyma explained, you are at thirty.

This was it. A surge of both excitement and calm washed over Blagojevich. He realized he could actually win.

Wilhelm, Mell, Monk, Wyma, Kelly, Petrovic, Scofield, and the rest of the campaign shifted into high gear. Though he suffered a setback when the Reverend Jesse Jackson and his son endorsed Burris just before Valentine's

Day, Blagojevich pressed on. Jackson and his father decided it was best to back Burris and not upset their political base by not backing the only black candidate. Blagojevich promised never to be fooled by the Jacksons again. "Those duplicitous motherfuckers," he said to one aide.

Angered, Blagojevich could still taste blood. The succeeding weeks were a blur of rallies, fund-raisers, and commercials as Burris stumbled as expected while Vallas and Blagojevich ascended to the top of the polls and slugged it out.

Vallas questioned Blagojevich's integrity and ability to reform Springfield, pointing out how Blagojevich never discussed his congressional gun control votes while campaigning downstate.

Blagojevich blamed Vallas for pushing a *Chicago Tribune* story less than a week before the primary that showed he hadn't used union workers for roughly $200,000 in renovation work he did on his Ravenswood Manor home in 1999, including the library he expended so much time and energy on. Blagojevich had big backing from unions, including the Service Employees International Union that had just dumped $250,000 into Blagojevich's campaign. The revelation could undermine some of that support.

Blagojevich claimed ignorance about who worked on his house, saying the work was "politically correct" because it included minority- and women-owned firms. "And the landscaper was a lesbian," he said, referring to Christy Webber, a politically active landscaper public about her sexual orientation.

The animosity between Vallas and Blagojevich grew stronger. When Blagojevich and Burris crossed paths as the two flew around the state for last-minute media hits, Blagojevich reached through the window of Burris's campaign van to shake his hand. "If I have to lose to someone, I hope it's you," Blagojevich said.

The weekend before Election Day, John Daley, a Cook County commissioner and the mayor's brother, endorsed Blagojevich, signaling where the city's top political family's support was. Vallas, meanwhile, was being backed by the powerful Nineteenth Ward, where he lived.

Not far away, Vallas ran into Jim Ryan in the Beverly neighborhood on St. Patrick's Day at the South Side Irish Parade. The two men were personal friends and, following the parade, saw each other at a raucous party hosted by Skinny Sheahan, a member of one of the Nineteenth Ward's most powerful political families. The two men crossed the crowded room and embraced, Ryan planting a kiss on Vallas's cheek.

Ryan was on his way to a victory, but it had been a bruising campaign. Ryan was forced to defend his decision-making in the Rolando Cruz case and to push back on conservatives backing O'Malley who suggested Ryan favored gay marriage. They sent out mailers with an image of two male plastic wedding figurines atop a cake. Ryan had to spend hundreds of thousands of dollars, weakening him for the general election.

=====

Two days later, clouds hung heavily in the sky on the chilly morning of March 19, 2002—Election Day. Blagojevich was nervous but optimistic as morning turned to evening. Polls continued to show him in the lead, but he knew it would be tight with Vallas. He hammered Vallas with a string of negative television commercials but cleaned himself up in the final weekend with a string of positive ads much like those first bio-commercials he ran.

Crowds gathered once again at Finkl steel, cramped inside the hangar-like building where he had announced his candidacy nearly fifteen months earlier. His brother, Robert, flew up from Tennessee and watched the returns with him, Patti, and Amy.

Early results were iffy. With suburban votes being counted first, Vallas was in the lead. But Blagojevich knew he wouldn't even think he was losing until downstate votes were counted. He also kept an eye on the race to replace him as congressman of the Fifth Congressional District. Emanuel was on his way to defeating Kaszak.

Across town at the Holiday Inn in downtown Chicago near the Merchandise Mart, a few friends and supporters gathered in Vallas's room as he sat and watched the movie *Training Day*. Now a *Tribune* columnist, John Kass was there working on a piece for the newspaper. When Vallas awoke from a nap and asked how things looked, Kass told him he was in the lead. Downstate votes still had yet to come in, but things looked promising. "Be a good governor," Kass said.

But by the time Vallas jumped in his car and made his way north to his election night party, the downstate votes had poured in. As Tuesday slipped into early Wednesday morning, the results showed Burris winning Chicago, Vallas carrying the suburbs, but Blagojevich scoring more than 55 percent of the vote downstate. It was, indeed, the difference. Blagojevich was the nominee, winning 37 percent of the vote to Vallas's 34 percent and Burris's 29 percent. He defeated Vallas by less than 26,000 votes.

Before heading onstage, Wilhelm and other aides counseled Blagojevich about his speech. Go immediately on the attack against Ryan, who hours earlier had won. Now is the time to begin shaping the campaign. Seconds after Blagojevich walked out to cheers, he opened up.

"Jim Ryan's fellow Republicans have it right," Blagojevich said, taking a tack from O'Malley and Wood, who had criticized Ryan for not doing more as attorney general to crack down on the abuses of George Ryan. "At a moment when leadership was needed most to fight corruption, the attorney general cut and ran."

Ryan's campaign was stunned by the quick assault. The following day, as a sleep-deprived Ryan rode in a black van to a meeting, he got visibly annoyed when a reporter repeated what Blagojevich said the night before.

"He hasn't even thanked his supporters yet and he's already attacking me," Ryan said. "Do I have a powerful alderman as a member of my family to help raise all my money? He spent millions and millions of dollars. Where did that come from? Come on, let's get real."

Blagojevich paid little mind. He had defied the skeptics and won. Even more important, he won with money from *his* people, especially Kelly. Now everybody in the Democratic Party was kowtowing to Blagojevich. Even Vallas eventually endorsed him, inviting him to attend a fund-raiser at the same Holiday Inn to retire some of his campaign debt. Blagojevich brought along Kelly and Petrovic, and the Democratic nominee sashayed through the crowd like a conquering hero.

Inside an elevator on their way out, the trio found themselves with several strangers, one of whom asked Blagojevich, almost as a joke, if he could get him a state job if Blagojevich won in November.

Blagojevich looked seriously at the stranger and raised the specter of Tim Degnan. A little-known name outside of Chicago politics, Degnan was renowned inside the scene as one of the most powerful men behind Mayor Richard Daley. Pointing to Kelly, Blagojevich told the stranger, "This is going to be my Tim Degnan. You talk to him."

6

Victory

At one-thirty on the morning after he declared victory in the Republican primary, Jim Ryan sat in his suite at the Sheraton Chicago Hotel & Towers listening to his closest lieutenants talk about his next opponent, Rod Blagojevich. They didn't have much to tell him.

John Pearman and Dan Curry were longtime aides of Ryan in the attorney general's office. Ryan's campaign director and good friend Stephen Culliton was also there.

A skinny, disciplined, thirty-one-year-old marathon runner, Pearman addressed Ryan as "General" and started with the obvious: he's Dick Mell's son-in-law. A quick look at his record in Congress didn't show much. The only bill he's passed was renaming a post office. Once he started campaigning, he often missed votes in Washington. Pearman also pointed out an intriguing story the *Tribune* did in 1996 when Blagojevich was running for Congress in which, Pearman said, the report made it sound like he might have been a ghost payroller. So we'll have to look more into that, Pearman told Ryan.

Ryan nodded and didn't say much. He had little to add. This is what he paid people like Pearman and Curry to do. He was the opposite of Blagojevich. Ryan had an aversion to the retail politics of shaking hands, kissing babies, and walking parades. He was disinterested in opposition research. He got visibly uncomfortable asking people beyond his closest friends and supporters for money. He realized he had to do all of it to get to the end goal. But that didn't mean he had to like it.

Ryan preferred to view the world through the lens of the law. There were evidence, rules, and black-and-white conclusions. Politics was messy and often unfair. There was no judge to rule something out of bounds. It was little wonder the public offices Ryan held were all in law enforcement. Before serving two terms as attorney general, Ryan was the state's attorney of DuPage County, the wealthy suburbs just west of Cook County.

Ryan hadn't paid much attention to the Democratic primary, but one thing he noticed was that Blagojevich spun yarns and sold himself well but didn't have much beneath the surface. It especially irked Ryan that Blagojevich talked about his time as a Golden Gloves boxer. Ryan also was a Golden Glove boxer, but, unlike Blagojevich, he had actually been a two-time champion.

Boxing is a great storyline for politicians. It lends itself to dramatic portrayals of men alone in the ring and fighting for what they believe in. If any politician has one organized fight in his childhood, he is sure to talk about it on the campaign trail. At fifty-six, Ryan was older than forty-five-year-old Blagojevich, but he had heard about Blagojevich's lackluster fighting experience from others involved in Chicago's tight-knit boxing community. It was a purposeful resume inflation on Blagojevich's part. And even though any politician would do it, it peeved Ryan that Blagojevich tried to play himself off as some kind of boxing aficionado when all he did was enter a tournament, something any chump could do.

So, after receiving Pearman's lowdown on Blagojevich, Ryan felt optimistic as he settled into bed. Indeed, the whole campaign thought they had dodged a bullet by not having to face Vallas, who was smart, had a strong grasp of the issues facing Illinois—especially the budget and education—and exuded a good-government nerdiness that would have played well with independents and some Republicans wanting to clean themselves off following the scuzz-show the state had endured the last three-plus years under George Ryan.

But there was no escaping that being a member of the same political party and having the same last name as George Ryan wasn't going to help. And Blagojevich showed he wasn't going to hold back trying to link the two men. The race was just hours old, and Blagojevich had already all but called Jim Ryan a crook for not bringing charges against George Ryan.

And it was just that sort of thing that annoyed Jim Ryan so much about politics. The attorney general's office didn't conduct major corruption investigations of statewide officeholders. More importantly, the feds were already neck-deep into their probe of George Ryan when some of this licenses-for-bribes stuff came to the surface. What was he supposed to do, launch his own investigation and get in the feds' way?

"Get real," Jim Ryan said again and again when Blagojevich laid out the accusation.

Ryan hoped voters would see through such silliness. And if they didn't, he wouldn't let the accusations go unanswered. Unlike Vallas, Ryan and his campaign aides felt they could at least compete with Blagojevich's fundraising juggernaut. Vallas couldn't win because he got into the race too late and couldn't raise enough money. People knew Jim Ryan. They knew his story. They knew his family's stories and its tragedies. And they knew how he had persevered.

As for fund-raising, he was getting help from some of his closest acquaintances, including one of his best friends, a man he'd known since they studied together in law school and who had gone on to become independently wealthy and a powerful behind-the-scenes player in Illinois politics.

Stuart Levine would be there for him.

———

Stuart Levine met Jim Ryan at their first day of law school in 1968 at Chicago-Kent College of Law. The two quickly became inseparable. "We were a study group of two," Levine once recalled. "Jim Ryan got me through law school."

After graduating, Levine worked as a lawyer and then as an administrative assistant for his mother's cousin, Ted Tannenbaum, and made millions of dollars in the health and dental insurance businesses. He started as a special counsel to Tannenbaum's Chicago-based HMO America Inc., the largest health-maintenance firm in the state, and quickly turned thousands into millions by investing. Later in life, he became a very public local philanthropist, serving on boards for the blind, the Lincoln Park Zoo, and several Jewish causes, including the US Holocaust Museum, which was built in a suburb near his home. In 1994, King Gustav XVI of Sweden knighted Levine for nurturing cultural and economic ties between the United States and Sweden.

GOP governors had placed Levine, a noted Republican, on several state boards, including those that oversaw teacher pension investments and hospital expansions. The positions didn't pay much but that wasn't the point. The posts on the state boards gave Levine power and influence.

Levine drove Porsches, traveled in chartered jets, and kept a private office on the twenty-ninth floor of the John Hancock Center at the northern end of Michigan Avenue, Chicago's Magnificent Mile. He looked the part of a distinguished, established businessman who had a perfect family, a two-story mansion in wealthy Highland Park, friends in high places, and seats on influential boards. He wore glasses, dressed impeccably, and kept his short hair neatly parted, appearing for all the world like he had been born with a silver spoon in his mouth and things had only improved from there.

While Levine got rich, Ryan entered politics. During Ryan's previous runs for office, Levine loaned or donated nearly $250,000 to his various campaigns. When Ryan decided to run for governor, he asked Levine not only for more money but also to serve as finance chairman of his campaign. He was the man in charge of finding donors and getting them to fork over cash. Levine was essentially playing the Chris Kelly role for Jim Ryan. And before the election was over, Levine would personally donate more than $540,000 to Ryan's bid to beat Blagojevich.

Few working for Ryan liked Levine. He was arrogant, brash, and abrasive with everyone in the campaign except the even-keeled Ryan. The two men couldn't have been more different, and close Ryan staffers chalked it up to an old friendship that was difficult to explain. But they were counting on Levine's aggressiveness to make Ryan competitive with fund-raising.

———

Just hours after Pearman and Curry's meeting with Ryan, both Blagojevich and Ryan awoke to a fresh start and the beginning of a new campaign season. The next election was more than seven months away, but both men engaged in post-primary election win clichés. How they went about it told everything a voter needed to know about how different Rod Blagojevich and Jim Ryan were.

Blagojevich had slept only forty minutes but showed no signs of it. With an earnest look in his eye, dressed sharp and bursting with energy, Blagojevich bounded up the steps of Union Station in downtown Chicago and eagerly shook the hands of every commuter he could buttonhole. He thanked them for their vote, whether they cast one for him or not.

A few blocks away, Jim Ryan stood at Lou Mitchell's, a famous breakfast diner in the West Loop jammed with businesspeople and construction workers fueling up for the day on coffee and omelets. But instead of charging into the restaurant to meet the public and revel in his victory with an eye toward another one in November, Ryan stayed by the front door where the management handed out little cartons of Milk Duds and doughnut holes to those waiting in line. Almost embarrassed, Ryan acted like he didn't want to intrude on patrons enjoying their breakfast. He gave a few television interviews for the morning programs before cutting the visit short and jumping into his campaign van.

It was a telling difference between the two men and was a scene that would repeat itself over and over throughout every corner of the state. But on top of retail politicking, Blagojevich felt he had another advantage. He had learned to fund-raise with the best of them, and he wasn't going to slow down now.

Kelly, Petrovic, Wyma, and another fund-raiser emerging onto the scene—Antoin Rezko—were spearheading Blagojevich's general election push for cash.

A savvy businessman who dressed in tailored suits and sported a trimmed mustache and a calm demeanor, Rezko became wealthy with a pair of enterprises. He developed housing in low-income neighborhoods, and he owned dozens of Panda Express and Papa John's pizza franchises. Tony, as most people called him, wasn't a Republican or Democrat. Instead, he subscribed to an anti-political philosophy that infused the state's character: "What's in it for me?"

For those in power, especially those of Rezko's ilk who orbited in the close circles around elected leaders, government was rarely about ideology. Rather, politics was a marketplace operated in the gray areas of power where Democrats and Republicans made deals away from the limelight. Elected officials, of course, officially belonged to one party or the other, but many of those close to them, like Rezko, moved seamlessly between Republicans and Democrats. All that mattered was who was in power at the time and how to gain access to them. Of course, what men like Rezko could do in return for politicians like Blagojevich was raise money.

But Blagojevich also liked Rezko personally. In Blagojevich's eyes, Rezko's story was much like his own and that of his parents—another great American rags-to-riches tale of success. Rezko was born in Aleppo, Syria, a historic city north of Damascus with a sizable Christian community. It was one of the country's larger cities, but Rezko dreamed of more. As a student, he became interested in engineering, and a teacher suggested he leave his native land to attend a good engineering school in America—the Illinois Institute of Technology in Chicago.

When Rezko arrived in the city, he was amazed at its size and how modern it looked. A good soccer player in Syria, he played at IIT but focused mostly on his studies. He dreamed of staying in America and making a life and career amid all the opportunities he saw around him.

After graduating from IIT, Rezko met Jabir Herbert Muhammad, the son of the famed and recently deceased Nation of Islam leader Elijah Muhammad. Since 1966, Jabir Muhammad had been managing the boxing career of Muhammad Ali, who became a member of the NOI. Rezko soon joined Muhammad in business, became a member of Ali's entourage, and helped manage the champ's affairs, including endorsement deals.

In the boom decade of the 1990s, Rezko formed a development firm with Chicago businessman Daniel Mahru. They called the company Rezmar, using portions of each man's surname. They quickly made millions, sometimes working with a well-known developer, Allison Davis, building and selling properties in the Woodlawn neighborhood on the South Side. As the development business grew, Rezko got involved in politics, an occupational hazard in a town where developers constantly need government help on everything from zoning matters to tax breaks.

Rezko had already dabbled in the world of local politics. In 1983, as Harold Washington was on his way to becoming Chicago's first black mayor, Jabir Muhammad encouraged Rezko to help. Rezko was instantly drawn to politics and fund-raised for Washington. In 1994, he donated nearly $70,000 and loaned thousands more to the Cook County Board presidential campaign of John Stroger, a Democratic ally of Mayor Daley, and then turned around and raised money for Republican governors Jim Edgar and George Ryan and later President George W. Bush.

Rezko also saw talent in a young man running for Illinois Senate from one of the neighborhoods where Rezmar worked. So when Barack Obama decided to run for state office, his earliest donations—$2,000 total—came from two firms Rezko controlled.

Rezko viewed getting involved in politics as good for business. What's more, he liked the feeling he got when the most powerful men and women in the city and state came to him looking for assistance. To him, politics and business were two sides of the same coin. You do favors for friends, you get something in return.

As Rezko got rich, he got to know Blagojevich. Rezko and his wife, Rita, regularly joined Rod and Patti for dinner and social events. In the late 1990s, Rezko even started using Patti as an agent for real estate work. Amy Blagojevich got to know Rezko's children.

Rezko stood on stage alongside Blagojevich on the night he won the primary, but few in the campaign were keenly aware of him. To them, he was just one of the dozens of faceless fund-raisers involved in Blagojevich's campaign.

And that's exactly the way Rezko liked it. Unlike Kelly, who craved attention and wanted a high-profile post with the campaign, Rezko enjoyed working behind the scenes and being the man sitting in the corner of the room barely noticed by others but whispering in the ears of those in charge.

———

Kelly and Rezko were soon becoming known to Ryan's campaign as well.

Sitting inside Ryan's campaign headquarters on the twenty-second floor of an old Loop office building next to the Oriental Theater, John Pearman had been talking to sources and looking at numbers and determined that Blagojevich's fund-raising wasn't just through Dick Mell. Two other names kept popping up over and over: Kelly and Rezko. "Everything goes through these two guys," Pearman told them.

Nobody in the room knew Kelly, and a few knew Rezko. The Ryan campaign had so far focused much of its attention on Mell and his associates, including the now infamous Dominic Longo and his Coalition for Better Government. Run by operatives with shady pasts, the coalition raised money and supported select candidates. They had helped Blagojevich but nowhere near what Kelly and Rezko were doing.

So now not only does Blagojevich have Mell's people helping him, he's got these two guys? We need to learn more about both men, Curry said. And we need something more to attack Blagojevich with.

———

A few months later, Pearman and others in the campaign thought they might have an answer on what to attack Blagojevich with. While chasing down tips from the six-year-old *Tribune* story that raised questions about Blagojevich's work at city hall, they kept hearing whispers that Blagojevich collected gambling debts for people with ties to organized crime. Nobody had any hard evidence, but it was an intriguing tip.

The campaign contacted Quest Consultants International, a suburban firm founded by four ex-FBI special agents. One of them, Jack O'Rourke, had been one of the agency's top organized crime experts. The guy you need to talk to, he told Pearman, was Robert Cooley.

Cooley was well known in Chicago's legal and political circles. In the 1970s and early 1980s, he was an organized crime fixer, an attorney who represented his clients during the day, partied with them at night, and in between doled out bribes and intimidation. He even bought off judges to fix murder cases. A former Chicago cop, Cooley was introduced to the mob through his police partner, who was a cousin of Marco D'Amico, a mob street crew boss on the rise. D'Amico took Cooley under his wing and taught him about bookmaking. It was a decision that would ultimately cost D'Amico—and many others—his freedom. In 1986, the bald, eccentric attorney who was once described in the *Chicago Tribune* as having a "near-photographic memory" began wearing a wire. For three and a half years, Cooley recorded mob bosses, their underlings, and politicians committing an array of crimes.

When the Ryan campaign tracked Cooley down, he had a tale both titillating and frustrating.

Cooley told them that while he was working undercover for the FBI, he witnessed Blagojevich meet Bobby Abbinanti, a mob-associated bookmaker, in a Northwest Side restaurant during the 1980s. Blagojevich was there to straighten out his bookmaking accounts, Cooley alleged, adding Blagojevich was likely a bookmaker and meeting Abbinanti to pay street tax to the mob.

Cooley acknowledged that while Blagojevich and Abbinanti never said outright that they were engaged in illegal sports gambling, it was clear that's what was going on. What's more, Abbinanti had a relationship with Dan Stefanski, Blagojevich's boyhood friend. Abbinanti had worked for D'Amico but was also active in Teamsters Local 726, which represented hundreds of city truck drivers. Stefanski ran Local 726, which donated thousands of dollars to the Coalition for Better Government.

What Cooley was saying made sense to Pearman. He learned Blagojevich was a sports freak, and his tricky way of remembering facts and figures (including that odd ability to memorize things based on the presidents) would be a perfect skill for a bookie to have, remembering bets without writing anything down. On the campaign trail, Blagojevich often showed off his memorization skills publicly by reciting Cubs starting lineups and individuals' batting averages from a quarter century prior. And while campaigning on Sundays he still took time to keep track of professional football scores, especially for his favorite team, the Dallas Cowboys. Ryan's campaign quickly determined that if they could confirm it, this story could end Blagojevich.

———

Ryan clearly needed the help.

Not only was he struggling to keep up in fund-raising with the Kelly-Rezko sleek jet Blagojevich had created, members of his own party kept getting into hot water.

Just weeks after the primary, federal prosecutors laid bare a grand scheme Ryan's fellow Republicans hatched four years earlier to get George Ryan elected governor. The indictment alleged some of the governor's closest friends and advisers diverted state employees to work on campaigns on state time, shredded documents, and tried to undermine an internal investigation into the licenses-for-bribes scheme. The feds even made the historic step of indicting George Ryan's campaign fund, though not the governor himself.

One way Jim Ryan tried to counter the bad news was by pulling a play from Blagojevich's book: he launched an early TV commercial blitz downstate. The commercial hit Blagojevich on supporting gay marriage and abortion and favoring gun control laws. Ryan's ad hit the air in the first week of June, a record at the time for the earliest political commercial airing in a general election for governor in Illinois.

Inside Blagojevich's campaign headquarters on Lincoln Avenue, Wilhelm, Monk, Blagojevich, and others decided how to respond. "We're not going to let any negative go unanswered," Wilhelm declared. Two days later, Blagojevich hit the air with a commercial that showed a split-screen. One side had Jim Ryan, the other George Ryan. "Jim Ryan didn't lift a finger" to stop George Ryan's corruption gone amok, it said.

It was the start of the Blagojevich campaign's nonstop strategy to inexorably link Jim and George.

———

Blagojevich's ability to so quickly respond to Ryan's commercials only cemented his burning desire to destroy Ryan in the race for funds.

With the help of a plane being donated by Blair Hull, a wealthy former securities trader and ex–Las Vegas card counter, Blagojevich continued crisscrossing the state raising gobs of money to sell his message on television. Hull loaned the plane because he was eyeing the idea of running for US Senate in 2004 and wanted to see how politics worked from the inside.

Blagojevich was happy to use Hull and his plane as he, Kelly, and Rezko also worked the phones, coaxing, manipulating, and straight-up pressuring fund-raisers to come up with more and more cash. In Springfield, one lobbyist was set to raise $35,000 for Blagojevich—an amount he and the campaign had agreed to weeks earlier. But when the event got closer, Blagojevich got on the phone and pushed for more.

"We need $70,000 from you," he told him. The lobbyist, not wanting to upset Blagojevich, said he could do $40,000. "You don't understand. I want $70,000," Blagojevich responded before slamming the phone.

Stories like that filled the taverns where politicians and insiders gathered. Blagojevich was doing more than demolishing every fund-raising record in the state. He was changing the dynamic of how fund-raising was conducted in Illinois. Even other politicians picked up on it. Less than two years later, as Barack Obama was running for US Senate, an Obama aide who knew Blagojevich saw a little hint of the governor in his candidate when Obama was on the phone squeezing a fund-raiser for more cash when he said, "I want you to feel a little pain, brother."

Even Blagojevich's favorites like Milan Petrovic weren't immune from the demands.

When Petrovic came up $7,000 short for an event at Harry Caray's Steakhouse that was supposed to raise $300,000, both Blagojevich and Kelly exploded in anger.

"What is wrong with you? Why are you falling short?" Kelly asked, in what Petrovic viewed as yet another attempt to undercut him in front of Blagojevich.

Petrovic held his tongue, refusing to yell back at Blagojevich that he was ninety minutes late and $7,000 in checks probably walked out the door because of it.

But there was little arguing the results. In just six months Blagojevich raised more than $7.5 million to Ryan's $4.8 million. Even worse for Ryan,

Blagojevich still had $3.8 million in the bank; Ryan had just $689,000. Those early commercials had taken a toll on Ryan's bank account.

———

Bars covered the windows and a tall black security fence surrounded the single-story, red brick office building at 853 N. Elston Avenue. Tucked between two nondescript apartment buildings, few neighbors knew what was going on inside the building that housed Rezmar Development Group where business was still booming for Tony Rezko. But on August 30, Rezko had an appointment on his agenda for a meeting that didn't have to do with real estate or development. He had invited his longtime friend Ali Ata over to talk about the future of state government.

Ata and Rezko were cut from a similar cloth. While Rezko came to America from Syria as a young man, Ata arrived from Jordan. He too wanted to make a better life for himself and came to America in 1970 to study engineering. After graduating, he worked for a suburban water treatment company, Nalco Chemical in Naperville, a job where he earned five patents and ascended the corporate ladder for a quarter century. Then came the terrorist attacks of September 11, 2001. Days later, FBI agents visited Ata, who shared a similar name to one of the hijackers, Mohamed Atta. Ata had nothing to do with the attacks, but two weeks later, his employer offered him an early retirement package. Only in his late forties, Ata got the message and took the buyout. But he was embarrassed and angry.

Ata had been involved in Illinois politics for years. In the 1970s, he met Dick Mell and supported him for alderman. The two men became friendly, so much so that in the early 1980s Mell had introduced his eldest daughter, Patti, to him while she was still in high school. In the 1990s, Ata got to know Blagojevich and supported him, contributing to his campaign for Congress. When Blagojevich was looking for money to get his campaign for governor off the ground, he and Mell visited Ata and asked if he would be willing to help. Ata quickly said he would. His friend Rezko also would be involved in the campaign, he learned, and Ata hosted a pair of fund-raisers at Rezko's request, promising Rezko he'd raise $25,000. He even contributed $5,000 himself. As the election proceeded, Ata noticed Rezko had even more sway with Blagojevich than he first realized. The two men began talking about what would happen if Blagojevich won.

Rezko suggested Ata identify a few posts in state government he might want. Since leaving Nalco, Ata was trying his hand as a self-employed financier, but he desperately wanted a post high up in state government to prove himself legitimate after his post–September 11 humiliation. After surfing the Internet, Ata came up with three: the Capital Development Board, which is the construction management arm of state government, the Department of Transportation, and the Department of Human Services.

As Rezko encouraged Ata to look for jobs he might like in a Blagojevich administration, he also harped on him to donate more money to Blagojevich's campaign. So when Ata showed up for the meeting in late August, he brought with him an envelope containing a check for $25,000. It wasn't the first time he'd been to Rezko's offices on Elston, Ata recalled years later while testifying in federal court. The modern offices, with glass everywhere and exposed brick walls, had been a hotbed of political clout, with movers and shakers like Springfield insider William Cellini frequently walking the hallways. And after Rezko greeted him at the door and took him to a conference room, he saw the state's new power structure: Lon Monk, Chris Kelly, State Representative Jay Hoffman, and Blagojevich himself.

Rezko told Ata these men were Rod's "kitchen cabinet." If elected, Blagojevich would have an official cabinet, but these were his most-trusted advisers. Ata sat down with Rezko and Blagojevich, and Rezko soon slapped the envelope with the $25,000 check inside down on the table between himself and Blagojevich.

Rezko and Blagojevich then began talking about Ata as if he weren't in the room. Looking at Blagojevich, Rezko said Ata was a good supporter and team player and he wanted to work for the administration if Rod won in November. Blagojevich nodded and told Rezko that Ata had indeed been a supporter of his and a friend. He then asked Rezko if Ata had identified any job opportunities. He had, Rezko responded.

———

While Blagojevich bounded across the state raising money, he was also busy selling his message of jobs and opportunities for the working class. But mostly, he was declaring that he—not Jim Ryan—would be the agent of change to bring reform to state government.

In doing so, though, he sometimes got his wires crossed. He told teachers that education would be his top priority. Business leaders later heard the same line about business. Even later he made the same pledge to social service advocates. He promised more money for everybody, even though Illinois faced a historic deficit.

It became so much that even Blagojevich himself acknowledged it as a joke.

"I've made 122,478 campaign promises in this race, and I am going to keep every one of them," he laughed during a speech before a crowd of teachers at a union picnic in Glenview, a northern Chicago suburb. At a fund-raiser later in the campaign, the number soared to "227,478 promises."

Blagojevich also looked to continue sticking it in the eye of the powers that be, which he felt also helped sell him as a reformer. Seizing on a series of *Chicago Tribune* stories detailing questionable state spending projects, Blagojevich slammed one that went to a former University of Notre Dame classmate of Speaker Madigan's for a livestock show. Blagojevich said the grants showed "arrogance" on the speaker's part.

The comment only rekindled the two men's general dislike for each other. Madigan, focused on getting his daughter Lisa elected attorney general, hadn't been helping Blagojevich's campaign, and Blagojevich was sending him a message that he wasn't to be trifled with. Two days later Madigan sent his own message on Democrat Day at the Illinois State Fair.

Madigan wasn't usually much for talking to reporters, but he took time to defend himself against Blagojevich's accusations and add that he wouldn't be attacking Blagojevich because he was going to take the higher ground.

"I don't plan to be critical of other Democrats. I don't plan to be critical of Blagojevich," Madigan said in his nasal Southwest Side accent. "I could talk about some of his indiscretions, but I don't plan to do that because I plan to be a strong party chair and work to bring all the Democrats together."

And just in case any reporters missed it the first time, he repeated the word: "Indiscretions."

Reporters hadn't missed it. What did he mean? Indiscretions? Speaker, what are you talking about?

It was a brilliant word for Madigan to use. It meant nothing and everything at the same time. The minds of reporters raced. Was he talking about sex? Rod used to be a state legislator, after all, and Springfield during legislative sessions wasn't much different from a college frat party for many of them. Something else?

But Madigan was gone, refusing to elaborate and coolly walking off from the media scrum. He left the word *indiscretions* hanging in the air like a gigantic stink bomb ready to explode all over the Democratic nominee for governor.

Minutes later, Blagojevich said whatever he could to stop the bomb from bursting, saying he didn't know what Madigan was talking about. The public was left with lots of smoke, no fire, but plenty of evidence the Illinois Democratic Party was happy to gather in a circle and shoot.

=====

Blagojevich's answer to "indiscretions" was to hit the road, once again barnstorming across Illinois to campaign and raise more money. He also chose to worry about more important things, such as his hair. The candidate constantly brushed it and was always in need of his black, oval hairbrush. It became so ubiquitous that Wyma, Scofield, and others in the campaign had a nickname for it—"the football"—a play on the codename presidents used for the briefcase containing the US government's nuclear launch codes. It was *that* important. In Blagojevich's case, he needed a brush so often, his staff kept nearly a dozen "footballs" stashed in his SUV, in the campaign office, and around the state.

Left out of the boys club, though, was Mell, who continued to feel slighted about being replaced by Blagojevich's new team, especially the brash Kelly. Mell had grown to dislike Kelly, viewing him not only as a threat for Blagojevich's attentions but also as a bad influence.

Kelly fed Blagojevich's ego, and they had grown so close they were becoming nearly inseparable. Kelly even purchased expensive Montblanc pens as gifts, telling Blagojevich that once he was governor he could use them for bill signings. Blagojevich kept losing the pens, and Kelly just kept buying more. The Kelly and Blagojevich families would eventually vacation together, traveling to Bermuda and Mexico.

It all left Mell with a growing bitterness and anger. "Fuck him," Mell said more than once when people asked him about Kelly.

Petrovic sensed the factions and his feelings were confirmed when Mell's assistant, Mary Hahne, called him out of the blue and asked him to meet the alderman at his office.

"Sit down," Mell said firmly when Petrovic arrived. Mell and Petrovic weren't close but also had shared a mutual respect for each other. Mell didn't waste any time getting to the point.

"I'm going to tell you something that you should never forget," he told Petrovic. "My son-in-law will never do anything for anyone unless it's in his self-interest."

Petrovic looked confused. Mell asked, "Do you understand what I just said?" Petrovic said no, in fact, he didn't. Mell just repeated what he had said: "My son-in-law will never do anything for anyone unless it's in his self-interest." And that was it. End of meeting. Petrovic walked out of the offices on Kedzie and stepped into his car where he sat for twenty minutes.

"I decided then to always keep distance between myself and Rod," he recalled years later.

—

As Blagojevich had problems behind the scenes, Jim Ryan's difficulties were evident for the whole state to see.

A Labor Day poll conducted by the *Tribune* showed Ryan down by 17 points, though he did slightly better when it was made clear to respondents that he was not George Ryan. That factoid only spurred a tit-for-tat between the Ryans. Curry and Pearman liked to see the fire in their candidate, though they wished it was aimed more at Blagojevich.

During one press conference, Jim Ryan was set to reraise the questions laid out in the six-year-old *Tribune* story about Blagojevich representing legal clients suing the city while moonlighting on Mell's city payroll. As part of the event, staffers brought along an oversized version of the famous 1987 photo of Mell standing atop his desk during the debate to pick Mayor Harold Washington's successor.

Ryan said he wouldn't use it. It was sinking to Blagojevich's level and had nothing to do with the campaign. Pearman and Curry were flabbergasted. This is the campaign theme, they said. This is an election about reforming state government. We have to remind people about this every chance we get.

"I don't care what you guys say about this," Ryan said.

Curry placed the photo next to the podium anyhow without Ryan knowing. He told campaign staffers he'd take the heat later. When Ryan walked into the room, he looked over at the photo and grimaced. And then he proceeded to ignore it until a reporter pointed to it and asked him what he was trying to say by having it standing there next to him. Ryan stammered for a second.

"I have questions in my mind of whether he is going to be able to say no to the person to whom he owes his political career," he dryly explained. "I think [Mell] will have a lot of influence over my opponent."

———

The next day, Mell was wreaking his own havoc within the Blagojevich camp.

Following Madigan's "indiscretions" comments, Mell had been hearing whispers about Ryan's campaign spreading rumors and reporters chasing other tips that involved some deep, dark secrets in Blagojevich's past. Some dealt with possible extramarital affairs or dalliances in Springfield; others had to do with Blagojevich's alleged bookmaking with mob associates. Mell had had enough. While driving downtown to the posh East Bank Club, he called in to the popular "Don and Roma" program on WLS-AM radio station and let loose.

"One of the stories was that he visited a house of ill repute and that I went down and ripped up the papers," Mell said. "That is one of the whispering campaigns I heard. Can you imagine that happening in the city of Chicago? That is the kind of gutter stuff that is being put out there by the opposition!"

Mell rambled on about how disgraceful the whole thing was and how it was upsetting him and his daughter. "Knowing Rod Blagojevich and knowing what he thinks of my daughter, I guarantee there are no indiscretions," he said. "He'd have it from my daughter. Patti is a very strong-willed young lady."

Before Mell had hung up the phone, he realized the call was a mistake. A lot of the rumors had been out there, but none had been published because they had not been substantiated. Now that Mell had opened his mouth, the mysterious "indiscretions" would be impossible to ignore. Boarding a plane in Springfield, Blagojevich got a call from Mell at the same time Scofield was getting a call from *Sun-Times* political reporter Scott Fornek.

"You might want to know that I was on the radio today," Mell told Blagojevich. He explained he was trying to help, trying to show how dirty Ryan's people were being. "But I might have screwed up."

Blagojevich hung up the phone and exploded. "Fucking Mell! Fucking Mell! Are you kidding me? Fucking Mell!"

Scofield tried to talk Fornek and other reporters who had gotten wind of the story out of picking it up. But by the end of the day, the best he could do was portray Mell as a frustrated parent defending his family. Mell promised to keep his mouth shut until Election Day. But the next day Scofield sent a top aide in the campaign's press shop, Billy Weinberg, to shadow Mell at city hall to make sure he held his tongue.

=====

While Ryan's people were ecstatic about Mell's gaffe, they hadn't gotten far enough on the mob bookmaking story. John Pearman had been trying for months to find any solid connections on the rumors, even once approaching Abbinanti and spending four days going through archived court files in a remote warehouse. Even years later, Abbinanti maintained the rumor was not true.

O'Rourke, the former FBI agent turned private detective, found others who heard the Blagojevich-bookie rumors, but nobody had any paperwork proving what Cooley was saying. Everybody only had indirect knowledge of it.

The *Tribune* had heard the same rumors and was running into the same problems confirming the story. With the paper apparently not going to run a story, Curry and Pearman got desperate and shared what little they had with other reporters all over town. After meeting with a reporter at the *Sun-Times* for hours, Curry and Pearman left with completely opposite ideas of how things went. Pearman thought there was a chance the newspaper might publish something. Curry didn't.

"Well, this fucking campaign is over," an exhausted and aggravated Pearman responded.

Adding to Pearman's frustration was the fact that it was clear by now the state's insiders and moneyed interests—those who cared more about themselves than political philosophy—were falling in line behind Blagojevich. Among them was William Cellini, who on paper was a longtime Republican but was just as well-known as the state's ultimate insider.

And he and Ryan hadn't gotten along. As attorney general, Ryan had killed a proposed settlement of a deal that would have bailed out a Cellini hotel project in Springfield, and Cellini apparently had not forgotten. In the last month of the campaign, he quietly held a fund-raiser for Blagojevich in suburban DuPage County just miles from Ryan's house.

Most in attendance at Cellini's money event were members of the Illinois Road and Transportation Builders Association, whose members knew him because of his long association with the powerful Illinois Asphalt Pavement Association. It was smart politics. And playing footsie with the Democrats was not entirely new territory for Cellini. As a Cellini insider once said: "It assured stability, no matter who was in office."

Still, it looked bad. If it got out that a man like Cellini was hosting a fund-raiser for Blagojevich just weeks before Election Day, people would ask questions and think maybe all that talk of reform and renewal coming from Blagojevich's mouth was just campaign rhetoric. So after the event Chris Kelly approached Kelly Glynn, the finance director for Friends of Blagojevich. Through a computer database, Glynn kept tabs on the campaign's "bundlers," the top men and women who got all the individual donors together to donate to the campaign. Kelly directed Glynn to muddy up the record of the fund-raiser. Instead of calling it a Cellini event, it was listed as Rezko-DeLeo-Roadbuilders, referring to Rezko, the roadbuilder attendees, and State Senator James DeLeo, a Northwest Side Democratic powerbroker.

Meanwhile on Ryan's side, Stuart Levine was doing well but not well enough. One day, he gathered a small group of men and women inside a private room on the second floor of Harry Caray's restaurant to pressure them to give to Ryan. "We can't wait any more! We just can't," he implored. "The time is now."

═══

At the outset of the election season, Blagojevich and Ryan had agreed to four debates. The first two hadn't generated many sparks, and the third was headed in the same direction when Blagojevich leaned in from his seat at WTTW-TV's studios and decided to change the subject.

"Let me tell you a story," Blagojevich began, spinning a yarn about that infamous Election Day 1994 when George Ryan won his second term as secretary of state, Jim Ryan was first elected attorney general, and the Willis family minivan crashed in Wisconsin, killing the couple's six children.

Throughout the campaign, Blagojevich recited his refrain that Jim Ryan didn't "lift a finger" to investigate corruption in the secretary of state's office under George Ryan in which drivers' licenses were traded for bribes. This time he took it up a notch.

"Neither George Ryan nor Jim Ryan did anything to change that failed system. And, and as every day passed, the corruption continued."

Ryan quickly interrupted. He hadn't even been attorney general when the Willis tragedy occured. "Have you no shame, Rod? Have you no shame? Are you talking about those Willis children?"

"Is this public television or *The Jerry Springer Show*? Can I finish?" Blagojevich asked.

"No, no, you can't," Ryan answered, his eyes widening and anger bubbling. "No, no, you're not going to say that. I'm not going to let you get away with that. No, I'm not. Not with my family sitting there, because that is an absolute shameful thing to say!"

Ryan then jabbed his right index finger in Blagojevich's face. "I don't care what your media meisters tell you. I'm not going to let you get away with that, Rod!"

It was as close to a turning point in the campaign as either side had seen. Blagojevich realized he had overreached, and Ryan sensed an opening.

When the debate ended, Ryan, still fuming, stormed into a holding room behind the studio where television and print reporters had assembled. This was the "spin room" where candidates declare victory and reporters attempt to clear up points made during the debate. "The voters of Illinois should be very worried about a guy who will sink to these depths to win an election," he said. "If they want him, they can have him!"

═══

After the debate, Ryan continued to muster energy he hadn't displayed for most of the campaign. But the difference between him and Blagojevich couldn't have been clearer.

In the small northwestern Illinois town of Sycamore, both marched in the pumpkin festival parade. Organizers separated the two campaigns, giving Blagojevich a ten-minute head start.

Before beginning, Blagojevich tossed off his loafers and slipped on some high-end running shoes. He then engaged in "battle," as he called it, running obsessively to both sides of the parade route to shake every hand and kiss every baby. He sprinted into the crowds standing on the side of the road or on their lawns. He even found himself in a few people's backyards as they cooked burgers.

"This is how hard I'll work for you if you make me governor!" he said.

Ryan, meanwhile, steadily walked down the center of the street, waving but barely shaking anybody's hands. As Ryan proceeded, he found himself catching up to Blagojevich, the two campaigns uncomfortably bumping up on each other. Ryan stopped for a while as Blagojevich continued to campaign but eventually got sick of waiting, finishing the parade before Blagojevich did.

A few days later, Curry had to all but beg Ryan to get out of his campaign van to do some retail politicking—shaking voters' hands outside Water Tower Place on Michigan Avenue. The plan was to for him to do it for a half-hour. After five minutes in the cold, Ryan said he was done and walked back to the van.

"I got ten votes and double pneumonia," he said.

=====

It was clear even to Ryan's closest backers that Blagojevich was going to win. Stuart Levine had continued to work for Ryan's campaign but was coming up short, and Levine, who had made a career being an insider, saw the dim prospect of backing the loser and being left without any connections to state government. That meant he would likely lose his influential roles on the state boards overseeing investing billions of dollars for the teachers' pension fund and multimillion dollar hospital expansion plans.

Then a door opened.

On the Saturday before Election Day, Levine was invited to a dinner party in Winnetka, a wealthy North Shore suburb. A friend, Dr. Ruth Rothstein, the former head of the Cook County Bureau of Health Services, asked Levine to come over to the home of Dr. Fortunee Massuda and her husband, Charles Hannon. A podiatrist who owned a massive chain of foot and ankle clinics around the Chicago area, Massuda asked Rothstein to invite Levine because he had helped get a project of hers past the board he sat on overseeing hospital expansion, the Illinois Health Facilities Planning Board. She wanted to thank him properly.

Nestled against Lake Michigan, Massuda's home was filled with players from Chicago's political scene. In addition to Rothstein and Levine, Orlando Jones, an adviser and the godson of Cook County Board President John Stroger, was there, as was another close Massuda friend, Tony Rezko.

With the statewide elections just three days away, politics was a main topic of conversation, and Levine and Rezko politely acknowledged their opposing allegiances but soon realized they had some shared interests too. Rezko dropped hints they were both friends with Cellini and another man, Robert Kjellander, a powerful lobbyist who was Illinois's GOP national committeeman and a close pal of President Bush's senior adviser Karl Rove.

Then they discussed business. Massuda talked about how she was interested in buying a valuable Gold Coast building on Dearborn Street in Chicago that had once been home to the Scholl School of Podiatry. Rezko was on the Scholl board, which was in the process of selling the building to Rosalind Franklin University. As a Rosalind Franklin board member, Levine knew about the deal intimately. The closing of the sale had been held up for some mysterious reasons, and as they talked, Levine began to suspect Rezko and Massuda might have been responsible for it.

Levine asked Massuda whether she had something to do with holding up the arrangement, and simultaneously she said, "No," and Rezko said, "Yes." After Rezko and Levine spoke briefly about what was going on, Rezko told Levine that if the building had been promised to someone else, Rezko could make the snag go away. Rezko told him he controlled the Scholl board.

How quickly could he expect the problem to evaporate? Levine asked.

By Election Day, Rezko answered.

It was the start of a relationship that would have mammoth implications for each of the men involved, not to mention the state's political structure. But at the time, it was just two businessmen working out a deal.

Both were seeing opportunity. In Rezko, Levine saw a man who would soon be on the inside of the new Blagojevich administration, someone who could help him stay on the state boards and keep his power. In Levine, Rezko saw a savvy businessman who had been working the system for years under Republican rule and knew where the bones were buried.

Indeed, even Rezko couldn't imagine how many bones.

Privately, Levine had worked out a deal for the property with none other than Edward Vrdolyak. Levine and "Fast Eddie" had secretly known each other and worked on schemes together for years, even after Vrdolyak left the Chicago City Council. In the Scholl property deal, Vrdolyak had found a developer, Smithfield Properties, willing to buy the building for $15 million, and he and Levine had arranged for Vrdolyak to receive a 10 percent—$1.5 million—finder's fee that he would then kick back to Levine and another member of the Franklin board.

But it wasn't the only secret Stuart Levine was keeping.

=====

The following morning, Jim Ryan was in Springfield for a high-profile rally with President George W. Bush, who was making his way across the Midwest to help Republican candidates.

About five thousand Republicans showed up for a rally of a slate of GOP candidates, from Ryan to US Senate candidate Jim Durkin to Judy Baar Topinka, running for treasurer. Ryan's people were hoping for a little bump from Bush. But the rally had been organized by Kjellander, who the Ryan people felt was doing all he could to minimize Ryan's role at the event. Indeed, Bush stressed the need to keep US Representative John Shimkus in Congress more than getting the vote out for Ryan, offering only a quick aside.

"And while you're in that voting booth, support a good man for governor. His name is Jim Ryan," Bush said. "He's got a record you can be proud of. You've seen him in action; you know he can do the job. A lot of folks around this state have written him off. I think they spoke a little too soon, don't you?"

———

Blagojevich wasn't going to let the president slow him down. Three days later, on Tuesday, November 5, 2002, he still couldn't get enough of campaigning. Most of the morning, he made last-ditch pleas for votes from commuters at Union Station in downtown Chicago, shaking hands and promising a new day was coming for Illinois, one filled with reform and renewal, not corruption. "We're trying to ensure that the people of Illinois have a government that's as honest . . . as they are," he said.

In suburban Elmhurst, meanwhile, Jim Ryan awoke early and decided to go to Mass. After services, he visited the grave of his daughter, Annie, who had died five years earlier at the age of twelve of a brain tumor. Tired of campaigning, Ryan returned home to spend the rest of the morning and afternoon with his wife and children. He told staffers he'd meet up with the campaign later and then they'd all gather that night at the massive Chicago Hilton and Towers on South Michigan Avenue.

Before the polls closed at 7:00 PM, Ryan's campaign gathered at the Hilton. Deputy campaign manager Glenn Hodas had established a massive war room in the International Ballroom next to the hall where partygoers were gathering. A large screen displayed a readout of Illinois's 102 counties next to percentage breakdowns of vote totals.

Early results were looking good for Blagojevich while Ryan remained cloistered in a hotel suite, watching the returns with his wife and a few close friends, including Stuart Levine and his wife.

Several miles away, thousands gathered—once again—at Finkl steel. They cheered wildly as they read that with 37 percent of the precincts reporting, Blagojevich was up 63–36.

Behind the stage, Blagojevich began to celebrate with Kelly, Monk, Petrovic, Scofield, Wyma, and Wilhelm. He had raised nearly $23.5 million from July 1, 2001. Ryan raised a little more than $14 million.

Back at the Hilton, at nine o'clock, Ryan campaign manager Carter Hendren, Hodas, and Steve Culliton had seen enough from the war room. They marched upstairs to Ryan's suite with a printout of results. He was getting crushed by more than 20 points. The two areas where Ryan was doing best—the suburbs and downstate—had the fewest precincts reporting, so undoubtedly it would get closer before night's end. But not enough to close the gap, they told him.

"Well, that's it," Ryan said. By 9:19 pm, he was on the phone with Blagojevich, wishing him luck and congratulations. Minutes later, Levine introduced Ryan to the lackluster crowd, and Ryan conceded. More than 1.8 million Illinois residents voted for Blagojevich—252,000 more than for Ryan.

Over at Finkl steel, it was a far different scene.

"My heart is full tonight," Blagojevich yelled to the screaming spectators, adding in an Elvis impression that same heart was filled with "nothing but a whole bunch a hunka-hunka burnin' love for each one of you!"

The dozens on stage with him celebrated wildly, including the state's new lieutenant governor, Pat Quinn. Blagojevich disliked Quinn, but the two had becoming running mates in March when Quinn won the separate nomination in the lieutenant governor's race, an odd coincidence given his early role in helping launch Mell's career.

The next morning—after only an hour of sleep—Blagojevich was back at it, shaking hands, signing autographs, and hugging anybody who wanted a hug at the Jefferson Park El stop. As hundreds filed past on their way to work, Blagojevich said those were the people he would fight for as governor. He'd help them reach their piece of the American dream just like they had helped him reach his last night.

When one person stopped and called him "Governor," Blagojevich turned with a smile. "You can call me Rod. I'm here to stay!"

PART III

The Governor

7

Taking the Reins

Lights blazed, music blared, and dozens of staffers, supporters, and fund-raisers jammed inside the house on the corner of Richmond and Sunnyside. So many people arrived that night in 2002, the front door was in almost perpetual motion as politicians and lawyers, downtown businesspeople and suburban union leaders, eased past bystanders and partygoers taking a break outside as they walked up the home's concrete steps to pay their respects.

Inside, the hosts—Illinois's governor-elect and first lady—greeted their guests graciously. The couple was euphoric. Almost everyone who was a player in Illinois, it seemed, was there to honor the winning couple and celebrate the coming-of-age of Rod Blagojevich, Illinois's fortieth governor.

The always affable Blagojevich proudly put his home on display, show-ing off the piano in the front room, the kitchen in the back, and especially the library he had spent so much time and energy renovating. Two men who didn't need the tour stood close by. Blagojevich showed them off as well. Chris Kelly and Tony Rezko had handed Rod Blagojevich the keys to the governor's office through their fund-raising and loyalty, and Blagojevich was making sure those who didn't know it before knew it now.

The always hoarse-voiced and boisterous Kelly was even more gravelly as he spoke but was also cordial and kind. Rezko stayed to form. Quiet and flawlessly dressed and groomed as always, Rezko lingered around Blago-jevich's home and stayed away from chit-chat. When introduced to strangers, he acted awkwardly. He attempted at one point to apparently try to ingratiate himself with a Blagojevich donor he had never met by explaining that even though he was from the Middle East, he was a Christian.

———

Days later, as Blagojevich and his campaign began the work of forming a transition team before the January inauguration, Kelly and Rezko were at his side once again.

Blagojevich's team rented meeting and office space in a modern sky-scraper across the street from the Thompson Center in downtown Chicago. Airy and made extensively of glass, the Thompson Center houses state agencies and board offices—including the governor's on the sixteenth floor. It features a massive atrium that allows visitors to see a cross-section of every floor, designed by architect Helmut Jahn to symbolize how Illinois government is "open" and transparent, something longtime insiders love to joke about given the state's sordid reputation. State employees hate the building, complaining the atrium is a massive waste of square footage and that the windows leak. Some Democrats also complain the building was named after a Republican, the former governor who got it built in 1985.

But Blagojevich wasn't one of them. In fact, Blagojevich named Jim Thompson the cochairman of his transition team. On the surface, Thompson seemed an odd choice since Blagojevich had just spent eight months hammering the living hell out of every member of the GOP he could find, blaming the party for plaguing Illinois with corruption and insider deals. But Blagojevich, who teamed Thompson up with liberal labor leader Marga-ret Blackshere, said bringing Thompson in showed he was already reaching across the aisle. He also said he planned to tap the expertise of the onetime governor who spent fourteen years in office about how best to establish a "firewall" between his campaign fund-raising operation and his state gov-ernment administration. He wanted to ensure politics never interfered with governing.

Thompson, the former US attorney, won election in 1976 by using his reputation as a corruption-buster. But after taking office, he became well known for successfully raising funds from state contractors. He even devised a new type of patronage—dubbed "pinstripe patronage"—that awarded no-bid contracts to politically connected consultants, lawyers, and bond dealers who received large fees for their work and ended up being top GOP contributors. While the fees never involved a stated quid pro quo, since that would be illegal, the state's political establishment was in awe of Thompson's political acumen, nicknaming him Big Jim.

In no small part because of Thompson's shrewdness, the GOP had dominated the governor's suite ever since. As a result, state government jobs were almost exclusively filled with Republicans, from executive assistants in the Department of Employment Security to the head of every agency in the state. One large task for those on Blagojevich's transition team was to start finding people for all those state jobs to replace the Republicans Blagojevich was going to get rid of.

Blagojevich made a public display of naming people high-up on his transition team. Wilhelm, Ronen, Monk, and Scofield all had roles. He even named Roland Burris as a vice chairman of a board of advisers. Kelly and Rezko barely got a mention publicly, but their influence was vast. Internally, few were surprised to see Kelly still around. He had played a huge role fundraising and had bonded personally with Blagojevich, but many were caught off guard by Rezko's involvement since his role during the campaign was muted relative to Kelly's.

During an early transition team meeting in mid-November, more than a dozen staffers, aides, and advisers sat around a large conference room table discussing strategy and hiring when Rezko uncharacteristically took it over and ran it. Some in the room didn't even know who he was. Soon enough, it became clear that the wishes of Tony Rezko and Chris Kelly were being taken very seriously by Blagojevich.

Nowhere was their influence more evident than in stacking the state payroll. Everybody close to Blagojevich had a say—Wilhelm, DeLeo, Jay Hoffman. Blagojevich himself, who had promised state jobs to even strangers he met on the campaign trail, made sure childhood friend Dan Stefanski got a post with the Illinois Department of Transportation and Bamani Obadele a job with the Department of Children and Family Services. His babysitter, a Mell family friend named Betty Bukraba, would get appointed to a $21,000 a year post on the state Civil Service Commission. John Gianulis, who had helped secure the primary win downstate, got a plum post overseeing hiring. Even Blair Hull got his exwife a job heading up the state's film office.

But Rezko's and Kelly's people were clearly jumping to the top of all the lists. Jack Hartman, a city official who Kelly knew from his days doing roofing work, became head of the tollway. Jack Lavin, who was Rezko's chief financial officer, became head of the state agency that doles out hundreds of millions of dollars in state grants.

And even more than in the high-end jobs, both men were cramming associates into low-level posts all over state government. A few were even qualified. But they all answered to either Kelly or Rezko because they knew who got them their jobs in the first place. They were like sleeper cells, put in position to bide their time for whenever a favor needed to be called in.

At the time, though, few within the administration saw it that way. They were just grateful at least somebody in the room knew some Democrats who wanted to work in government.

Mell was also tossing out names, and many were getting hired, a signal that the icy relationship between him and Blagojevich was at least temporarily thawed.

Several people who eventually joined the administration volunteered early on to help with the transition. One man Wilhelm recommended— John Filan—was described as a fiscal guru. He was a managing partner of the consulting and accounting firm FPT&W, and Wilhelm promised he would help Blagojevich balance the budget.

Another member of the transition team, who also seemed to come from nowhere, was Rajinder Bedi. An aggressive up-and-comer who ran an Indian newspaper that served Chicago's close-knit Indian community on the North Side, Bedi received a post in a state trade office. But his real job was after his state duties were completed for the day when he was supposed to build up community support for Blagojevich and compel wealthy Indian doctors and businesspeople to give Blagojevich campaign donations.

It wasn't that difficult a task. Blagojevich viewed the Indian community as an untapped political resource, and the Indian men and women saw a newly powerful man they wanted access to. It was a mutually beneficial relationship. And Blagojevich's story of a city kid who fought his way to success played well with many of the first-generation Indians and Pakistanis who owned the shops crowded on Devon Avenue.

Bedi worked with Brian Daly, another Blagojevich ambassador who had gotten to know many of the richest Indian business leaders in Chicago. An ex-marine who used to be an aide to US Senator Edward Kennedy, Daly joined Blagojevich's congressional staff and came to Chicago when Blagojevich ran for governor. He organized fund-raisers and passed messages between leaders in the Indian community and Blagojevich.

As Democrats lined up at the trough of state government jobs, those closest to Blagojevich were deciding their future as well. At the outset of the campaign, Wyma made it clear he had no intention of joining the administration, and Blagojevich never really pressured him to take a post as a senior adviser. It seemed obvious that Wyma, with his clear connections to the governor, was going to make a good living as a lobbyist. So too was Petrovic, who knew he stood to make good money despite his reservations about Blagojevich, Kelly, and others in the inner circle.

Monk also wanted to be a lobbyist. His work as campaign manager and history with Blagojevich made him closer to the governor-elect than even Wyma or Petrovic. But Blagojevich wanted Monk as his chief of staff. Monk took the job grudgingly, knowing that while he would be making a nice salary it was nothing like the millions a lobbyist stood to earn.

"Lon made the sacrifice, and he watched as Wyma did what he wanted to do," said a former top staffer. "Lon viewed his job as managing Rod. Rod was so all over the place that he needed somebody to keep things organized, and Lon took that on. Lon recognized that Rod had problems, and few people other than Lon could help him govern because Rod wouldn't listen to many people. But he would listen to Lon."

Blagojevich also wanted Scofield to join the administration. Burned out from the campaign and Blagojevich's behavior, Scofield wasn't sure he wanted to. He had considered rejoining Gutierrez or maybe heading up Navy Pier, one of Chicago's biggest tourist attractions. But Rod nixed that plan. He created a job he called deputy governor. Scofield would be in charge of policy and messaging, Blagojevich told him. Along with Monk, who would be overseeing day-to-day operations and personnel, Scofield would be essentially running the state.

"You are in charge," Blagojevich said.

Scofield wanted the job and wanted to believe it would be better than the campaign. He told Blagojevich he wanted to make sure the administration would be different from the election trail. They needed to establish a plan, hold regular staff meetings, and not do everything by the seat of their pants, like so much of what happened during the campaign. The late-night, hour-long phone calls had to stop too, Scofield said. That's the only way he'd take the job.

Blagojevich agreed. Things wouldn't be the same, he promised.

======

Amid all the changes, Blagojevich made one thing crystal clear to those around him: he wasn't going to move his family to Springfield to live in the governor's mansion. His daughter Amy was still in elementary school, and Patti was now pregnant with the couple's second daughter. Neither Rod nor Patti really liked Springfield. They had both grown up in Chicago and wanted their two girls to grow up in the city as well. Patti also had her real estate business, River Realty, and didn't want to jeopardize it.

Blagojevich knew the decision would anger downstaters, who took pride in the fact that the capital wasn't in Chicago, which so often sucked all the oxygen in the state in terms of clout and attention. Every statewide official—even the sole Republican, Treasurer Judy Baar Topinka—hailed from Chicago or the suburbs. But Blagojevich decided the negative press and bad feelings were worth it.

To him, his decision also signaled to voters that he was going to do things differently. It underscored the slogan that was becoming a theme of his first term: "Reform and renewal." Staffers were already in the process of making blue and white banners emblazoned with the phrase to be hung behind Blagojevich during his press conferences. In a world becoming more familiar with branding, "Reform and renewal" would be Blagojevich's.

Despite not caring much for Springfield, Blagojevich wanted to arrive there for his inauguration in style. On the weekend before, he boarded a train in Chicago and embarked on a two-hundred-mile whistle-stop tour to the capital. Leading up to the trip, Kelly and Mell had several arguments about who would be allowed aboard the train and who would get access to Blagojevich. Kelly won most of the fights.

At the Prairie Capital Convention Center in downtown Springfield on Monday, January 13, 2003, Blagojevich was joined by thousands of ecstatic supporters. On stage, Blagojevich stood alongside Patti as he took the oath of office with Mell nearby. Blagojevich lambasted the Republicans and outgoing Governor George Ryan specifically, though not by name. Several in the crowd giggled as Ryan applauded along even while Blagojevich excoriated him.

"I did not run for governor to be a caretaker. I did not run to manage a state of decline. I did not run to maintain the status quo. I am not here to serve just the few. The mandate we claim today from the people of Illinois and for the people of Illinois is simple and clear—no more business as usual," Blagojevich said to a cheering crowd of mostly Democrats. "I will tell it to you straight. I will give you my all. I will reach across party lines. I will seek out the best ideas. I will govern as a reformer."

Later, at one of two inaugural balls at the Illinois State Fairgrounds, the new governor and first lady celebrated with a first dance to Eric Clapton's "Wonderful Tonight." In Springfield covering the event, *Tribune* reporter Ellen Warren noted Blagojevich's love of fine clothing despite his humble beginnings. Blagojevich was wearing a pearl-gray silver Charvet tie—"he now buys only Charvet"—that cost $135 at Saks Fifth Avenue.

That night—and well into Tuesday morning—Blagojevich and his wife stayed up late celebrating with a small group of their closest friends, including Kelly, Wyma, and Monk. Sitting around a dining table at the Executive Mansion trading stories and laughing, Blagojevich was on top of the world. He sat at the head of the table, a man in charge. Nobody in the group had ever seen him this happy, this in control, this much in his element. Wyma felt Blagojevich was truly savoring the moment. He had a real opportunity to get things done and not just be a no-name congressman in the minority party in Congress.

As the evening wrapped up, Blagojevich spotted a bowl of oranges, grabbed one of them, and declared that now that he was governor he was entrusted with new powers he planned to use.

"Have a taxpayer orange," he said. "It's on me."

———

I, Rod R. Blagojevich, Governor of Illinois, order that no agency, department, bureau, board or commission subject to the control or direction of the Governor shall hire any employee or officer, fill any vacancy, create any new position, promote any employee or officer to any position or take any other action which will result in the increase or the maintenance of present levels in State employment or compensation (including benefits) payable in connection with State employment, including personal service contracts. All hiring and promotion are frozen. There will be no exceptions to this Executive Order without the express written permission of my office after submission of appropriate requests to my office.

Blagojevich signed "Executive Order 1," mandating a hiring and pay freeze for Illinois employees who reported to the governor, on his first full day in office. He also fired dozens of Republicans, including several men and women George Ryan had slotted into state jobs in the waning days of his administration. Blagojevich characterized the one-two punch as a stunning way to show voters and the state's political class that a new sheriff was in town. Things in Springfield had gotten out of hand, and he was supposedly putting cronyism to an end, starting with bringing state hiring under his control.

But behind the dramatic imagery of Executive Order 1 was a shrewd political calculation. Blagojevich was placing all personnel decisions within the purview of his office. Blagojevich, Monk, and others working directly for the governor now had even greater discretion to control hiring, firing, and promotions throughout state government, opening the door for many of those hundreds of Democrats and supporters who wanted jobs to find their way onto the state payroll. Not to mention all those friends of Rezko's and Kelly's.

With a wide smile, perfectly combed hair, and sporting a high-priced Oxxford suit, Rod Blagojevich strode through the halls of the Thompson Center on his way into work. It was afternoon.

Just a few weeks since taking the oath of office, Blagojevich's work habits were quickly becoming known. He rarely worked eight-hour days at the office, coming in late after having gone for a long jog in the morning. Or he wouldn't come in at all, instead choosing to work the phones from home, ordering Mary Stewart to get this person or that ("Rod wants you to call him," she said). Even some of Blagojevich's closest advisers weren't afforded the courtesy of a direct call from the governor. Mary was always the intermediary. And the calls were constant, just like during the campaign. Blagojevich would talk to Monk a half-dozen times and then hang up and immediately have Stewart call Scofield to go over what he just spoke to Monk about. Then he would call Kelly or Wyma.

At home, Blagojevich conducted business on the speakerphone. All manner of noises rattled around in the background, from children's cartoons to the clanking of iron as he lifted weights while conducting the people's business. Scofield already recognized things hadn't really changed from the campaign. There were no regular staff meetings that included the governor. When Monk or Scofield would mention it, Blagojevich waved them off. "I don't need to do that," he said. "That's your job."

Never once during his first term did Blagojevich meet with his entire cabinet.

The kinds of conferences Blagojevich did hold were mostly big-picture bull sessions at one of several upscale clubs in downtown Chicago. Kelly and Rezko were invited to attend and often did, where they displayed their influence for all to see. In one meeting early on in his administration, Lieutenant Governor Pat Quinn suggested Blagojevich at least consider raising taxes or fees to cope with the state's disastrous finances. The governor, who made no secret of his dislike for Quinn, quickly cut him off. "Tony," he said, gesturing to Rezko, "what do you think of that idea?" Rezko said it was a terrible idea. "I agree," Blagojevich said.

Some were put off by the growing influence of Blagojevich's budding "kitchen cabinet," though nothing was done about it. Meanwhile, Blagojevich continued to act like a candidate running for governor rather than someone who had just gotten elected. "Rod saw his job as the guy running for office. Then it was the job of everyone else who he hired to do the job of governing," recalled a former top aide. "So after the election, he basically viewed his job as being done until 2006."

With his fears rapidly being realized, Scofield would moan when his cell phone rang at ten at night after the governor had caught some story on the television news. "Nothing changed from the campaign," he recalled in an interview. "It was all still ad hoc, everything on the fly. No planning."

After less than a month in office Scofield wanted to quit. Almost everybody in the administration's upper echelon noticed, so much so that Blagojevich was asking around about replacements. One day, Wyma said he knew somebody who could be perfect.

———

In New York City, Bradley Tusk's phone rang. The twenty-nine-year-old Tusk was friends with John Wyma from their time working together for US Senator Chuck Schumer of New York. Tusk had handled communications, while Wyma served as Schumer's chief of staff. The two had stayed in touch since parting ways, Wyma rejoining Blagojevich and Tusk becoming a special assistant to New York City's newest mayor, Michael Bloomberg. And

Wyma didn't beat around the bush in asking Tusk if he wanted to move to Chicago to become Blagojevich's deputy governor.

"What's a deputy governor, and why are you calling me?" Tusk asked.

They were legitimate questions. Tusk's ties to Chicago weren't strong: He graduated from University of Chicago Law School but grew up in New York and worked politics exclusively on the East Coast. He had also met Blagojevich only once before, two years earlier when Wyma invited him to dinner to join Blagojevich and Monk at Mr. K's, a Chinese restaurant in Washington.

But Wyma noticed Tusk and Blagojevich got along well that night. They also shared a similar upbringing. Tusk was born in Brooklyn, the son of Gabriel and Nadine Tusk. Gabriel had been born in Siberia where his father and mother met at a Russian prisoner of war camp before coming to New York after World War II. Gabriel Tusk attended Brooklyn College, fought in Vietnam, and then made a living in New York City's schmatta business selling garments.

Bradley went to the University of Pennsylvania and caught the political bug after his freshman year when the Democratic National Convention was being held in 1992 at Madison Square Garden, where he met Ed Rendell, Philadelphia's mayor at the time. That meeting got Tusk an internship in the mayor's office, which he parlayed after graduation into several government jobs, including the New York City Parks Department and Schumer's office, squeezing three years of law school in between.

Tusk was smart, a hard worker, and extremely motivated, three qualities Wyma felt were needed to work for Blagojevich. But since that dinner at Mr. K's, Tusk had begun working for Bloomberg. He was doing well there, enjoyed the work, and hadn't thought much about the former congressman and Illinois's new governor. But Wyma's pitch was too much for Tusk to simply toss away. When Tusk asked, "What's a deputy governor?" the answer was enticing: he's the guy who runs the state.

Tusk flew into Chicago on the weekend before Presidents' Day. The series of interviews would be a quiet affair. Scofield hadn't gone anywhere, and even he didn't know the governor was bringing in people to replace him.

Tall and thin with dark hair, Tusk had a subtle New York accent and spoke so quickly people often had to ask him to repeat himself. He dressed well but disliked wearing ties. His first meeting was at the East Bank Club with Wyma and Kelly before the three later joined Monk and Blagojevich. Tusk understood everyone's role except Kelly's. But he didn't give it much thought. "I assumed his opinion mattered to the people making the decision," he recalled years later testifying in federal court. Then again, he wasn't overly impressed with Kelly, who struck Tusk as a successful businessman but politically unsophisticated. One of Kelly's main questions was what Rudy Giuliani was really like. Tusk thought to himself, "Should I tell him I work for Bloomberg?" He didn't.

Tusk had prepared heavily for the interviews, researching Blagojevich's congressional career and the promises he made on the campaign trail. Tusk was impressive from the outset, telling Blagojevich that he shared his desire to push for big programs that would have a significant impact on the state, not just tinkering on the edges. He had breakfast the following day with Monk and dinner at Blagojevich's home with the governor and Patti.

It was clear to Tusk that Blagojevich wanted somebody who would do the tough work, poke that stick in the eyes of other politicians, without worrying about offending anyone's sensibilities. Too often in politics, people in high-level posts like Tusk's would soft-peddle their plans with other politicians, either because they were friends with them or because they feared that being too tough could hurt them down the road in their career as lobbyists. Tusk made it clear from the outset he had no plans to join Illinois's insider political culture after he was done with the job.

While Tusk made his position clear, so did Blagojevich. He wasn't a detail guy. He was a big-picture guy. The details of these big programs and making them become reality were going to fall to Tusk.

Personally, Tusk and Blagojevich hit it off well. Blagojevich loved Tusk's stories of his grandfather and father. The POW camp. The schmatta salesman. It all reminded Blagojevich of his family's stories and his upbringing. The only thing Blagojevich didn't like was that Tusk was a New York Mets fan. But he could live with that. And Tusk could live working for a Cubs fan. This was a job that could make his career. Do well here and he could do almost anything.

Internally, the decision to replace Scofield came with little fanfare. Scofield talked to so few people about it that even his friends in the administration were caught by surprise. Scofield didn't even talk to Blagojevich about it directly, instead discussing it with Monk. Blagojevich often turned his back on people who left him, like a spurned boyfriend who got dumped before prom. He took it personally. In the weeks before Scofield left, Blagojevich stopped calling as much and demanding so much time from his deputy governor. When Scofield's announcement went public, though, there was no talk about Blagojevich's broken promises or atrocious management style. Scofield said he wanted to spend more time with his family. He soon discovered how truly mutual the decision was when Tusk was quickly named his replacement.

———

At the intersection of Madison and Halsted in Chicago's Greektown neighborhood, the driver of a large black SUV idling behind a taxi in the left turn lane turned on the vehicle's police lights, bolted around the taxi, and pulled up alongside a bank at the corner. "Can you believe that?" the cab driver asked his passenger, incredulous. "He put on fake police lights!" Seconds later, the cab driver discovered the lights weren't fake as he saw Rod Blagojevich hop out of the SUV and dash into the bank's front door.

"Oh my gosh! That's the governor!"

As usual, he was late. But Rod Blagojevich had arrived. Having inherited a $5 billion budget deficit and the largest public pension debt—$35 billion—of any state in the nation at the time, Blagojevich was holding an announcement event at the bank to unveil one of his first major ideas as governor. It was a controversial plan that was the brainchild of his new budget director, John Filan, who had conceived of it while working for Blagojevich's transition team.

Massive in scope and immensely complicated to pull off, the plan was also astounding in its simplicity: Illinois would borrow up to $10 billion at current low interest rates and use that money to pay off debt that was being collected at higher interest rates. It was no different from refinancing a home mortgage, Blagojevich and Filan said. The idea to buy so much in bonds spurred national headlines in the financial news world and raised questions about Blagojevich's sanity. He was in office just a few months and already saddling the state with massive debt in exchange for upfront cash and a hope the stock market wouldn't crash.

Blagojevich promoted the idea as a way for Illinois to balance the budget without raising taxes. But it had a major ancillary benefit for the financial industry: whichever company or companies got the bond business would make millions of dollars in, perhaps, just a few days. It was the biggest deal in the history of the state. And bond houses knew how Illinois worked. To get the business, they reasoned, they needed to hire lobbyists, preferably ones with close contacts to the governor and his administration.

Lehman Brothers hired John Wyma. ABN AMRO hired Al Ronan, who was once again on good terms with Mell. UBS Financial Services, Inc. hired Ungaretti & Harris, which employed big-time national Democratic fundraiser Joe Cari. Bear Stearns & Co. hired Springfield Consulting Group, which was headed by Kjellander, who despite being the GOP's national committeeman for Illinois and a close pal of Karl Rove was also good friends with Rezko.

The bond sale was so large it had to be approved by the legislature during the 2003 spring session, and after it was, Filan and his team began the process of prequalifying companies to get the work. Nearly a half-dozen firms were selected as "senior managers" after pitching their proposals. But one firm that didn't make the final cut was Lehman Brothers.

Blagojevich made a bold gesture of not allowing Lehman Brothers to get a piece of the work because he thought it would look bad to hire Wyma's firm. He was reforming the state's culture of insider deals, he said publicly. Officials with Lehman Brothers complained to Filan they were being unfairly targeted, but the decision was final.

For weeks Filan and his new deputy, a financial whiz named David Abel, watched the markets closely to see when the state should sell the bonds. In early June, Filan asked the governor if he would be available the following day because they might be ready to pull the trigger. Initially the plan was to sell $6 billion of the $10 billion, but as Filan and Abel looked at the numbers and the interest rates continued to sink, they recommend moving on the entire $10 billion that day.

Filan arrived on the sixteenth floor of the Thompson Center and entered Blagojevich's office, where he saw the governor as well as Tusk, Monk, and Kelly. Abel soon joined them and confirmed the numbers were favorable enough right now it was wise to move. But they had to move fast.

Everyone turned to Blagojevich, looking—needing—his approval. Blagojevich turned to Kelly, who Monk recalled had been huddling earlier with Rezko in the back of Blagojevich's large office. As discussions continued, Kelly pulled the governor aside for a few minutes, and the two quietly chatted. After that talk broke up, Blagojevich gave his OK. Bear Stearns would get all $10 billion. That meant $8 million for the firm and more than $800,000 for Kjellander.

8

A Scattered Leader

Rod Blagojevich was sweating.

Underneath the stands at newly named US Cellular Field, home of the Chicago White Sox, Blagojevich took warm-ups in preparation for accomplishing a near-perfect childhood dream: he would be throwing out the first pitch for 2003 Opening Day. Granted it was for the Sox, not the governor's beloved Cubs, up against the Detroit Tigers. But Sox owner Jerry Reinsdorf was a campaign contributor, and this was good enough. Dressed in a gray sweater, dark slacks, and dress shoes, Blagojevich sported a black glove on his left hand and paced out sixty feet in an empty private concourse used by ballclub staffers to get from one part of the stadium to the other. Crouched down playing catcher was Chris Kelly.

"Even if it is for the Sox, it's a dream come true," the forty-six-year-old governor said as he tossed several practice pitches to Kelly, who pounded his mitt and jokingly encouraged Blagojevich to "toss one in here!"

"I don't want to screw this up," Blagojevich said. "I don't want to be one of those politicians who can't throw the ball far enough and then people think I'm not an athlete."

When the time came, two hours later due to a rain delay, Blagojevich jogged out to the mound sporting a black Sox jacket, collar turned up. He was greeted with a hail of boos. Not only was he a politician, but he was also an unabashed Cubs fan. Blagojevich laughed. He figured he'd get that reception. With a big exhale, Blagojevich positioned himself on the mound, stuck his left index finger outside his glove just like the pros do, and tossed the ball. He bounced it. Blagojevich laughed again—this time at himself.

Several hours later, Blagojevich was still at the Sox game when Patti called. Ten days past her due date for their second child, she told Rod tonight might be the night. He quickly headed home and took her out for dinner to a Mexican restaurant—the same thing they had done before Amy was born. Again, it worked. By 5:00 AM Saturday at Northwestern University's Prentice Women's Hospital, Patti gave birth to the Blagojevichs' second girl, Anne. They planned on calling her Annie.

While Blagojevich was ecstatic over the birth of his second daughter, even taking time to enjoy the family's newest blessing with his father-in-law, something was bothering him. Several times he pulled friends and aides aside and asked them what they thought he should wear for the pictures the press was going to take when they left the hospital. "Should I be in a suit or go more casual? Sport coat? Jeans? What do you think?" Most didn't have much of an opinion. Blagojevich thought a casual look was better. And when the pictures were snapped, the state's young governor was wearing a sport coat and jeans with a dark turtleneck under the jacket.

———

With a new deputy governor in the office filled with energy and ideas, Blagojevich became more involved in the governing process. Though his general attitude remained that it was his employees' jobs to run government and his to win elections, Blagojevich came in to work at the Thompson Center most days.

But his harmful personality traits were still on display. He rarely put in a full eight-hour day, choosing instead to burn up the phone lines, especially with Tusk and Monk, about everything from press conferences to baseball games. Many in the administration came to think Blagojevich had some sort of learning disability that made him incapable of focusing; he continued to act like a manic depressive, unable or unwilling to leave his home and putting off public events to the degree he had to be coaxed into doing them; he was even a bit of a hypochondriac, constantly complaining of having a low-grade fever.

Usually, Blagojevich could pull it together, drawing his charm seemingly out of his suit coat and winning over a crowd of supporters or fund-raisers. But it frustrated those around him.

Tusk at one point in 2003 became so annoyed by the governor's antics that he asked Monk, "Can he work harder?" referring to Blagojevich. Monk had no answers. This is who he is, he said.

The only things Blagojevich seemed to be disciplined about had nothing to do with being governor. He was still energetic and organized about fund-raising, and he kept a tight regimen exercising at home, which mostly involved lifting weights and running.

Illinois State Police troopers assigned to protect the governor catered extensively to Blagojevich's life. They established a protocol for his jogs: as Blagojevich ran the Chicago streets, his detail followed in a tail car while one trooper rode a bicycle.

And because Blagojevich spent so much time at home, the state police rented an apartment down the street. Members of the "executive protection unit" had been idling in their cars outside the house for hundreds of hours as Blagojevich chatted away inside. So in mid-February 2003 the police began renting an apartment at 3016 W. Sunnyside Ave., about a block west of the Blagojevich home. The state police found an apartment even closer, at 3000 W. Sunnyside, in Blagojevich's second term in office. In the nearly six years he was governor, taxpayers spent more than $115,000 on rent for the two apartments.

Troopers could kick up their heels, warm up during the winter months, and watch football games on a color television. Both apartments also were filled with plenty of office equipment, including paperwork the troopers filled out on a regular basis and computers. The apartments also were outfitted with several phones, including a special red phone tied directly to Blagojevich's home. When that rang, it meant the consistently tardy governor was finally ready to leave. The troopers would jump in their vehicles—a black Chevrolet Suburban SUV and a tail car—circle the block, and wait for him out front of the house. Inside the Suburban, Blagojevich found an extra hairbrush—still called "the football"—in the glove compartment and a mirror specially installed in the backseat.

While Blagojevich's management style was off-the-cuff and chaotic, his political style was slash and burn. That chip on Blagojevich's shoulder was bigger than ever.

Rather than reaching across the political aisle and using the charm and charisma he had utilized so well in the state House and Senate, Blagojevich ran the governor's office like he was still running for office, relying more on spin and media manipulation than smart compromise and leadership. He blamed Republicans and even some Democrats for all the state's ills and threatened those who weren't on his side with being branded as agents of the corrupt status quo. On his proposed budget cuts, he flew around the state peddling an internal poll he commissioned that he claimed showed voters supported his plan. Anybody who didn't fall in line—including Democrats—should fear for their future come election time in 2004, he said.

There were early signs of Blagojevich's problems with sincerity as well. In the final days of the spring legislative session, the General Assembly approved a bill that allowed clout-heavy phone company SBC Communications, whose president was William Daley, to dramatically boost its revenue. The day it was up for a vote in the state senate, Blagojevich said he didn't know where he stood on the bill. "I need to look at it some more," he said. Four hours after it passed, Blagojevich quietly signed the bill into law.

A bill aimed at toughening aspects of the state's ethics laws also passed the legislature, and while Blagojevich said he didn't think it went far enough, he remained coy about whether he would sign it. Speaker Madigan, who backed the legislation, pulled Blagojevich aside at an event and asked the governor to call him before making his decision public. When Blagojevich decided to veto the bill, though, he refused to call Madigan.

"He couldn't bring himself to do it," Tusk recalled. "Rod hated calling people unless he only had good news. He also was afraid that if he called, Madigan would talk him out of vetoing the bill, which is probably true. So he simply refused to call him."

Madigan fumed, calling the governor looking for an explanation. But Blagojevich refused to accept the calls, a move that Blagojevich administration insiders felt permanently put on ice the already chilly relationship between the two. "Madigan felt he could no longer trust Rod's word," Tusk said in an interview.

Blagojevich then picked a fight with the state's other statewide officeholders, including Madigan's daughter, newly elected Attorney General Lisa Madigan. All were Democrats except Treasurer Judy Baar Topinka, and

Blagojevich sat them down like they were subordinates and tried to force them to cut their budgets. The sides agreed to a certain percentage of cuts, but after their meetings Blagojevich went behind their backs and cut even more. All were outraged, but Secretary of State Jesse White was most public about it. He said Blagojevich wasn't bargaining in good faith. He was violating "all laws of human decency."

When lawmakers later moved to reinstate $130 million in cuts he made to the budget, Blagojevich declared he was ready to go to war. In Springfield, he rebuked the General Assembly for their "spending orgy" and declared he would stop them from spending taxpayer money "like a bunch of drunken sailors." He then flew back to Chicago, spending thousands of dollars on a taxpayer-funded state plane to go home and to a political fund-raiser rather than spend the night at the Executive Mansion.

Politicians weren't the only ones who were the recipients of Blagojevich's sharp tongue.

In 2003, the Cubs were five outs away from going to the World Series for the first time since World War II. Then the unthinkable happened. Fan Steve Bartman reached for an apparent foul ball and deflected it away from outfielder Moises Alou. It opened the door for the Florida Marlins to rally past the Cubs and eventually win the National League pennant. Blagojevich was at the Bartman game, and although bad pitching and poor fielding probably contributed to the loss more than the young man's natural reaction, fans across the nation quickly blamed him, sending him into hiding. After the game, the governor found television news crews outside the ballpark and happily piled on to ridicule the hapless Bartman.

"If someone ever convicts that guy of a crime, he'll never get a pardon out of this governor," he said.

Legislators were quickly becoming frustrated with the new governor's leadership, and he soon found himself with few friends in Springfield. While Blagojevich supported some gun-control measures, they never went anywhere, and many groused Blagojevich never emphasized the one issue that filled his thin resume in Congress. They also were frustrated with the games they saw him playing related to expanding gambling in the state. Blagojevich hinted to lawmakers he might be open to the idea, but when several lawmakers actually presented plans, Blagojevich heaped scorn on them for being irresponsible and trying to come up with cheap and fast ways of making money rather than trying to solve the state's core fiscal problems.

A general impression was solidifying among the state's politicians that Blagojevich was less interested in solving problems and more interested in polishing his image, especially at their expense.

At a portrait unveiling at the state capitol for former governor George Ryan, legislators praised Ryan despite the scandal that chased him from office. With Blagojevich sitting in the front row, Senate President Emil Jones and Madigan both pointed to Ryan's ability to compromise as a quality the new governor might want to embrace. "His word meant something. You always knew where he stood," Jones said.

Even Ryan got in a dig. "You heard a lot of things I think you needed to hear here today," Ryan told the new governor before adding he was "only kidding" and that Blagojevich could look forward to such fanfare when his portrait is unveiled.

"I hope somebody shows up," Blagojevich laughed.

=====

Despite all the problems and distrust, Blagojevich still had success pushing through an agenda in his first year. He raised the state's minimum wage, signed legislation sponsored by State Senator Barack Obama reforming the state's tainted capital-punishment system, and devised a plan he said would save residents, especially senior citizens, money on prescription drugs. And after vetoing the first one, he even forged a new ethics bill he declared would finally help Illinois escape its notorious reputation for corrupt politics. On December 9, 2003, Blagojevich signed the legislation in Chicago with great fanfare and with most of the state's top lawmakers in attendance, though not Speaker Madigan. "Today we are reestablishing the primacy of principle over politics, and in Illinois that constitutes real change," he said exactly five years to the day before he was arrested.

By the end of his first year in office, a *Tribune* poll showed Blagojevich with a 55 percent approval rating. His replacement in Congress, US Representative Rahm Emanuel, seized on the governor's success and attempted to expand on it. Trying to become a rising star on the national scene, the freshman congressman recruited Blagojevich to join him in using prescription drugs as an issue to drive a wedge between voters and President George W. Bush. Democrats portrayed Republicans and Bush's Food and Drug Administration as siding with Big Pharma over taxpayers who were forced to spend too much on medicine while pharmaceutical companies made massive profits. To illustrate the point, Democrats pointed north to Canada—where price controls kept prescriptions cheaper—to show that some of the same drugs were sold for a considerably cheaper price.

Emanuel worked closely with Blagojevich and Tusk to fashion a plan in which Blagojevich challenged the federal government to stop the state from importing prescription drugs from Canada or Europe. The plan made head-lines around the world and helped bolster Blagojevich's image as a populist trying to help working men and women and seniors afford their medicine. It also gave Blagojevich a national platform to be known as "the health care governor."

Blagojevich didn't discuss it much, but it was clear the governor wanted the national attention for whatever his next step would be in politics. He was a young Democratic governor with a great ethnic-boy-makes-good tale to tell. He was a former congressman and a great fund-raiser. He could be on a national ticket. A run for president in 2008 wasn't out of the question.

Meanwhile, the men Blagojevich was setting up as insiders were only grow-ing in influence. Blagojevich told Chris Kelly he wanted him to be the point person on a controversial plan to build a new casino in suburban Rosemont. The governor knew Kelly was a big gambler in Las Vegas and somehow felt his knowledge of the industry would help him understand the negotiations.

It was unclear if Blagojevich knew it at the time, but Kelly was doing more than just occasionally going to Vegas. He was flying out there nearly every weekend, gambling tens of thousands of dollars at a time. Between 2000 and 2005, federal authorities would later allege, he gambled away more than $1.3 million. To cover it up, he cheated on his taxes and paid off bookies with his businesses' checkbooks. What also was not known publicly was that in early 2003 Tony Rezko had an option to lease a site for a hotel next to the proposed casino land.

The casino, to be called the Emerald, had been held up for years by state regulators who were concerned about mob influence. That delay, along with infighting among investors, created a legal morass. Blagojevich saw the Emerald as a way to help the state's struggling finances, but the pushy Kelly's sudden involvement rubbed regulators the wrong way.

Unconcerned that a bankruptcy judge had jurisdiction over Emerald, the governor's general counsel, Susan Lichtenstein, orchestrated a conference call between Emerald's bankruptcy attorney and two attorneys from the Gaming Board, Mark Ostrowski and Michael Fries. Also on the call was Oscar David, an attorney with Winston & Strawn, the law firm run by former governor Thompson. David said he was acting as outside counsel to the governor. Lichtenstein got on the phone and berated both sides to strike a deal, saying the matter had been "negotiated to death" and that she wanted to give the governor some "good news." David reiterated the point.

Around the same time, another attorney working for the state on the Emerald case revealed that he was asked to meet somebody connected to the governor to talk about the case. That was Kelly. Nobody in the room knew who Kelly was except the chairman of the Gaming Board, politically connected developer Elzie Higginbottom. "He's a roofer," Higginbottom said before explaining Kelly's ties to Blagojevich and recommending the attorney not break the appointment.

Kelly soon began bullying his way through Gaming Board meetings. He demanded answers and cut people off as they spoke. When others tried to find out why he was there, Kelly answered that the governor wanted him there as his emissary to ensure a deal got done. At one meeting at the Gaming Board's offices across the street from the Thompson Center, Kelly went so far as to individually point at Ostrowski, Fries, and the acting board administrator at the time, Jeannette Tamayo, and say, "I don't care about you, you, or you. All I care about is him," and then swiveling his pointed finger across the street toward the governor's office.

The Gaming Board staffers didn't take kindly to Kelly's involvement, and his presence and antics at meetings were eventually revealed in a *Chicago Tribune* story. Kelly did not waste time complaining to Ostrowski, Fries, and Tamayo that his "credibility [was] on the line" and insisted Gaming Board officials stop being so difficult toward Emerald and reach a deal, which would result in people with possible mob ties getting money.

Following one meeting, Kelly, clearly angry, got nose to nose with Fries and placed his right hand on Fries's shoulder. "So who do you think dropped the dime on the governor, Mike?" Kelly asked, clearly implying that Fries had spoken to the *Tribune*.

"I don't know, Chris. It could have been anybody," Fries replied.

Kelly stared for a few moments considering the response. He finally smiled, said, "Good answer," and abruptly left without saying another word.

After Kelly's involvement was made public, pressure from the governor's office lessened. Eventually, Lisa Madigan killed a deal that would have allowed another company to open a casino in Rosemont, saying Rosemont Mayor Donald Stephens and the town as a whole were too closely linked to organized crime. Three years later, Stephens died, having never seen a casino built in his town. The state eventually stripped Emerald of the casino license and awarded it to a company that opened up a casino in nearby Des Plaines, where it could be seen from Rosemont's city hall.

======

Blagojevich's lack of hands-on leadership and extemporized decision making was most evident in the department responsible for hiring employees—the office of intergovernmental affairs.

Blagojevich had put Joe Cini, his former congressional campaign fundraiser, in charge of the office. Since working for Mell, Cini had moved on to work for the city, but when Illinois's new governor called, Cini was excited to join the state's first Democratic administration in a quarter century and saw an opportunity to boost his career. Those concerns he had back in 1996 about working for the overly demanding Blagojevich faded quickly.

Still, Cini initially didn't want the intergovernmental affairs job. He twice turned Blagojevich down because he didn't think it was the right fit. But Blagojevich insisted, picking up the phone while on vacation in Puerto Rico to ask Cini a third time. That had done the trick. Cini couldn't turn down a governor three times.

Whether Cini wanted it or not, heading up intergovernmental affairs was a highly valuable position. In any government, but especially Illinois, doling out jobs was a big part and a big perk of being governor. In a previous era, Cini's title wouldn't have been wrapped up in ambiguous jargon; he would have simply been called what he was: "the governor's patronage chief." And Cini was finding himself in a stronger position than some of his predecessors because of Executive Order 1.

Blagojevich liked Cini because he was loyal. He also had good relationships with politicians all over the state, especially the old timers Blagojevich knew would come calling, looking for jobs from him for their friends and associates.

As expected, before Cini even started, the resumes began pouring in from nearly every politician in the state. Most were from Democrats, but a few came from Republicans who thought they were on good paper with the new governor. Ward bosses, suburban elected officials, Chicago aldermen, state legislators. Staffers got so inundated they didn't know how to organize the nearly twenty thousand names. They first piled their resumes based on what sorts of positions the people wanted—accountants, human services, corrections. But many didn't have a preference. They just wanted a government job. And when the politicians began to call Cini's office to check on the progress of their candidates, staffers had to comb through piles of paperwork.

Cini called Lon Monk and told him he had two choices: either eliminate the office of intergovernmental affairs altogether or start tracking all the names on state computers. It would list the names of the candidates, the status of their search, and which politician or person referred them. Not only would it help them get answers for the politicians when they called, it could help the administration keep track of whose favors were being granted.

What made matters worse was Cini, who had no experience in government hiring, didn't know the intricate rules and laws governing how it was supposed to be legally conducted. Some jobs, the high-level ones, could legally be straight political patronage. But many had to abide by restrictions ensuring all citizens had a fair shot at getting a state job. To try to navigate the morass, Cini was in constant communication with the governor's general counsel's office and even outside attorneys from the Chicago law firm Jenner and Block. "We did not know how to run state government," said one former intergovernmental affairs official. "It was chaos."

In just the first few months, Rezko submitted about a hundred people's names. On the lists kept by Cini's office, staffers placed the initials "TR" next to those he recommended. Rezko then followed up with phone calls to Cini. Both men were extremely busy so it wasn't unusual for Cini to miss the call and then miss Rezko when he called back. Eventually, they both decided it was easier to meet once a week—on Monday mornings between eight and nine—at Rezmar's offices so Cini could update him on the status of his names. Cini brought along an assistant, Jennifer Thomas, who carefully took notes.

The office of intergovernmental affairs soon existed for almost no other reason than to receive names of candidates from politicians and insiders. In Springfield, officials even set up a special room to receive faxes of resumes from insiders so they could jump to the head of the hiring line. Some connected employees—ranging in age from thirty-five to sixty—got internships intended for college kids. Military veterans who were supposed to get first crack at state jobs were shunted to the side for connected people in Chicago, who got hired for jobs in rural counties a hundred miles away only to then be allowed to work closer to home.

Among those getting jobs under questionable circumstances was the wife of Blagojevich's longtime friend, Michael Ascaridis—"Lou Nova." In August 2003, Beverly Ascaridis got a $45,000-a-year job as a state parks administrator. Hers was one of the names funneled through the special office. On top of that, less than two weeks after she started the job, Michael Ascaridis wrote a $1,500 check out to Blagojevich's daughter Amy for her seventh birthday, which the Blagojeviches cashed. It was a massive sum for a girl's birthday gift, and Beverly Ascaridis would say later that even she didn't know at the time her husband had written it. But after discovering it, the situation began to gnaw on her. Something was weird about it.

While there was no evidence anybody inside the office of intergovernmental affairs knew about the check, several felt similarly weird about everything going on with hiring, though none thought what was happening was illegal. This was just how it was done in Illinois. The Republicans did it for a quarter century. Now it was the Democrats' turn.

———

While Blagojevich was helping some legislators get jobs for friends, campaign donors, and constituents, that wasn't enough for them to begin trusting him. And Madigan was already becoming the top opposition leader.

When Blagojevich in early 2004 pitched a plan to take over the state board of education, making his case in a speech before the legislature in which he demeaned and insulted the board and its unsuspecting director as he sat in the audience, Madigan forced Blagojevich to accept a different version of the plan. But Blagojevich wasn't going to back down as easily on the biggest issue—the state budget.

From the outset, Madigan and Blagojevich were far apart. Blagojevich was pushing for several large programs while Madigan wanted to hold the line on spending. As talks continued with no progress and a deadline approaching, Blagojevich made a strategic decision he hoped would finally force the speaker to recognize his power as governor. He would essentially play chicken with the speaker, daring Madigan to not pass the budget and shut down state government.

"He still thinks I'm a backbencher," Blagojevich complained to one longtime contributor. "Well I'm elected. I'm now governor of Illinois."

Publicly, Blagojevich played it off like he was working hard to get things done for the people while Madigan was protecting business interests. But it was as much about gamesmanship, with Blagojevich trying to show the speaker who was boss.

The two men's differences were never on better display. During private meetings of the "Four Tops" (the Democratic and GOP leaders of both the House and Senate) Madigan was infatuated with the process of putting the budget together, obsessing over details and ensuring that things were just as he wanted them and then rarely talking about any of it in public. Blagojevich, on the other hand, showed no interest in the process of budget-making. He showed up late to those same meetings and talked about the 1962 Cubs lineup before leaving to make some splash for the press.

Blagojevich wasn't actually disinterested. He became energized by the fight with Madigan and his lawmakers. Using his powers as governor, he called special sessions, demanding legislators leave their homes to come back to Springfield even though there was nothing for them to vote on. As pressure mounted and the prospect of shutting down state government became more real, Madigan at one point whispered to Monk, "We think he likes this." That, of course, was exactly the impression Blagojevich was trying to give.

Lisa Madigan also wasn't off limits. When the attorney general's office declared unconstitutional Blagojevich's idea to raise $200 million by mortgaging the Thompson Center, he upset feminists and female lawmakers when he said he viewed the legal opinion as nothing more than a maneuver in his ongoing spat with the speaker. "It's her father, you know, I can't fault her," he said. "I've got two daughters. I hope they back me on stuff that I do."

The fighting wasn't unanimously endorsed by everybody close to Blagojevich. Chris Kelly complained to Tusk that fighting with Madigan was a bad political move, a sentiment Tusk disagreed with. Later, Kelly and Tusk got into another heated exchange when Kelly ripped several ideas Tusk had been pushing, such as the board of education plan and various health-care initiatives. Kelly called them "all smoke and mirrors," which caused Tusk to fly into a quick rage and then decide he and Kelly didn't need to speak much ever again.

Blagojevich wasn't totally alone in his fight. He had enlisted the support of Senate President Emil Jones. Since making his snippy comments at the George Ryan portrait unveiling, Jones had become closer to Blagojevich, especially with the governor realizing he needed somebody to have his back in the legislature given his poor relationship with everybody else.

As budget talks continued, the two men traveled the state making their case, portraying Madigan as the enemy of Democratic ideals. Blagojevich was back in campaign mode, keyed up and in the middle of a fight. "He showed he was willing to shut down government and he wasn't worried about the public perception," Tusk recalled. "He felt he could win that fight. Eventually, Madigan just wanted it to end."

Nearly two months past the deadline, it finally did, with Blagojevich getting much of what he wanted. But one of the bigger points Madigan made went right to the issue of Blagojevich's untrustworthiness. In an unprecedented move, Madigan and lawmakers forced Blagojevich to sign "memorandums of understanding" that detailed his spending promises. That way they had a piece of paper with his signature on it if he tried to renege on a budget pledge he made.

═══

Just days after the budget deal was finalized, Blagojevich, Kelly, Monk, Tusk, and Wyma arrived in Boston for the Democratic National Convention. Obama, now a Democratic nominee for US Senate, was giving the keynote address.

By that point, Blagojevich and Obama had become not-so-friendly rivals, and Obama's growing ascendance only made Blagojevich angry and jealous. Still, Blagojevich needed to be there. He was a Democratic governor of a large state and was building a resume for a possible national run. It soon became clear that national run wasn't going to be anytime soon. As Obama's speech was tearing the roof off the FleetCenter, Blagojevich sat in the crowd becoming more envious and crestfallen as it became clear he was being eclipsed right then as Illinois's most beloved Democrat.

Perhaps it was a coincidence, but upon returning to Chicago, Blagojevich became less and less engaged in governing. He retreated back to working almost exclusively away from the office, ordering people around on his speakerphone at home or working out of his new campaign office on Ravenswood Avenue.

Less than two miles east of his house, Blagojevich had poured more than $200,000 into renovating and decorating the third floor offices in an old loft factory building. He made sure nearly everything was in the mission architectural style, French doors separating his personal office from the rest of the space that featured a kitchen area/conference room and two small offices with computers that held massive fund-raising databases. Blagojevich's personal office, which looked out onto Ravenswood, was similar to his study at home—a grand desk, comfortable chairs, and a leather couch. A few friends and supporters liked to call the headquarters the Clubhouse.

Blagojevich worked out of the campaign offices on most Mondays and Fridays, arriving in casual attire, making calls for a few hours, and then changing into running gear to go for a jog. Then he went shopping.

Sometimes several days a week, he bopped around downtown buying new ties with the help of a personal shopper at Saks Fifth Avenue or picking up suit swatches from Oxxford. Since becoming governor, his taste for fine clothes had amplified. He was dropping thousands of dollars on ties and at least $4,000 for a single custom-fitted suit, of which he bought more than a dozen a year. During his six years as governor, Blagojevich and his wife spent $400,000 on clothes—more than they spent on their nanny.

Making a little more than $150,000 a year as governor, the costly clothing was pushing the Blagojeviches' budget. Patti was holding things together by bringing in as much or more than Rod in real estate commissions, including from Rezko, who met with the first lady when she showed up at Rezmar's offices with newborn Annie in tow.

Across town, Blagojevich would meet with Kelly at the Palace Grill, a well-known diner across the street from the city's 911 center and just blocks from the United Center, home of the Chicago Bulls and Blackhawks. While Blagojevich's security cooled their heels at the front of the restaurant, the governor and Kelly grabbed a table in the back and spoke in hushed tones for hours.

Although Blagojevich wasn't showing up for work, he still called relentlessly. It became so bad he and Tusk quarreled about it more than once. "I have to run the government," Tusk would bark at the governor. "Stop calling me."

While Blagojevich loved working the phone on his schedule, he still hated when the phone calls were coming in the other way. US Senators, cabinet members, and governors were constantly trying to contact him about various issues, and Blagojevich was ignoring all of them. "He figured they were all calling with bad news or were going to ask him to do something he didn't want to do. So he'd simply refuse to call them back," a former top aide recalled.

During the Hurricane Katrina crisis, then-senator Obama called Blago-jevich to ask his advice about what sorts of services Illinois could provide for fleeing New Orleans residents. The city of Houston was being overloaded, and he wanted to offer Illinois's help. Tusk, who was at Blagojevich's house at the time, took the call. When Obama asked to talk to Blagojevich, the governor waved him off, telling Tusk to tell Obama he wasn't available.

Another reason Blagojevich wasn't coming into work was that contro-versies percolating at several state boards were becoming troublesome.

9

Pay to Play

On April 18, 2004, one of the three telephone lines into a large home in Chicago's tony North Shore suburbs received a call. It was almost noon.

"Hello," a man there answered in an expectant voice.

"Stuart," came the reply. And Stuart Levine knew immediately who it was. Jacob Kiferbaum, a friend going back years who had gotten rich as a corrupt contractor, was on the other end sounding almost giddy.

Kiferbaum built hospitals. And at the time of the call, his construction firm was going to build a controversial one that many thought was unnecessary in Crystal Lake, northwest of Chicago. As part of that project for Mercy Hospital, he had agreed to kick back $1 million to Levine and Rezko in large part because Levine knew Rezko was very close to Blagojevich.

Now Kiferbaum and Levine, a powerful member of the Illinois Health Facilities Planning Board, were trying to worm into yet another proposal, a plan for an arm of Naperville's Edward Hospital, to be built in nearby Plainfield. The contractor was calling to go over a bit of theater they had just performed.

To make the deal happen, Kiferbaum and Levine had agreed to a "chance meeting" between them and Edward's chief executive officer, Pam Davis, at a local restaurant. Kiferbaum scheduled the breakfast meeting at the Egg Shell Café in Deerfield, where he pleaded his case to Davis that Edward should hire his firm because the approval Edward needed from the state board that oversees hospital expansions probably hinged on whether his company got the job. Kiferbaum and Nicholas Hurtgen, a senior managing director at Bear Stearns & Co. in Chicago, had been working Davis since the prior December. Kiferbaum wanted to build the $90 million hospital and medical office building, and Hurtgen's firm was in line to receive financing work in the deal. They told Davis they had a powerful connection on the regulatory board, Levine, and that he had the ability to push her project through if Kiferbaum were hired. To demonstrate they were serious, they had set up the breakfast where Kiferbaum would arrive with Davis, and Levine would be there with Hurtgen.

After finishing his breakfast and heading for the door, Levine stopped by the other table to stress to Davis that Kiferbaum's word was good and that he could do the job. He had done it before during a pair of construction projects at Rosalind Franklin University, where Levine and Kiferbaum both were board members, Levine told her. Of course, Levine didn't mention Kiferbaum paid a $1.7 million kickback to make sure he got that work, too.

The message was delivered, but the three men weren't the only ones hiding secrets that morning over their toast and coffee. Davis had been cooperating with the FBI for weeks after reporting that she was being extorted over her hospital's plans, and she was wearing a recording device in her bra. At agents' direction, Davis had first suggested a meeting where the men showed her that they really were working with Levine. The three men thought they were gaming Davis, but really it was the other way around.

Davis's cooperation allowed the FBI to get a court's permission to tap into the phones at Levine's home and capture the conversations that followed. It was one of the earliest pieces of an investigation that would last years, searing the earth of Illinois's political culture and toppling some of the most untouchable insiders in the state's notorious history. But on that mid-April 2004 morning, that ultimate outcome couldn't have been in the minds of Jacob Kiferbaum and Stuart Levine. Instead, they just wanted to gloat on the phone about that morning's scheme.

"It went perfectly," Kiferbaum told Levine as the FBI listened in. "She understood, uh, she's supposed to call her attorneys tomorrow."

Maybe there would be a deal after all. Kiferbaum had told Davis that if they came to some kind of an understanding that his firm eventually would be hired, Kiferbaum would wield his influence with Levine and the planning board for her. Reject Kiferbaum and expect a rocky road and a dead end.

"We'll find out what she's made of," Levine said.

Despite the well-known philanthropy, the posts on state boards, and the knighthood by a Swedish king, this was the true Stuart Levine. The illustrious business and family man in control of the universe was a personality Levine wore like a cloak, presenting a facade that allowed him to seemingly manipulate and cheat anyone who crossed his path. The real Levine was a chameleon, a political fixer of the highest order, a con man, and a drug addict. He had bribed his way to success. When he controlled a charity linked to drug interventions, he cheated it by writing a $3 million check from its account for an investment deal that would benefit him—and then blamed his secretary for it.

Levine had also used his relationship with Vrdolyak as leverage. While acting as special counsel for HMO America Inc., Levine hired the alderman and lawyer and other insiders, including Republican powerbrokers Kjellander and Cellini, as lobbyists. Levine's relationship with Vrdolyak also had a seedier side that few knew about. Levine later claimed to have given Vrdolyak bribes to pass along to someone at a postal union to get the union to enroll in the HMO and again to someone at the Chicago Board of Education, where a dental insurance business Levine worked for had government business.

Much of the money he stole went to fund his extravagant living style and secret life. He had a ferocious drug habit and a desire to break away from his daily routine for all-night drug and sex binges at hotels with young men. He would party in Springfield under the guise of being there for work, and he had a Chicago-area getaway—the famed "Purple Hotel," a brightly colored but dumpy place on Touhy Avenue in Lincolnwood. He paid the men cash, and his appetite shifted from mixing cocaine and Ecstasy in the 1990s to using crystal methamphetamine and the club drug ketamine in later years.

Much like Rezko, Levine was part of the "What's in it for me?" tribe. Despite his Republican ties and relationship with Jim Ryan, Levine cared little about political ideals or positions and was only interested in power and how he could get close to it.

Since that dinner in the fall of 2002 when he first met Rezko, Levine had pledged his allegiance to the new organization Rezko was helping build inside the Blagojevich administration. He and Rezko had made preliminary agreements to work together.

Among the chief reasons why Levine made his deal with Rezko was so Rezko could convince Blagojevich to allow Levine to continue sitting on the two state boards he had been appointed to by Blagojevich's Republican predecessors—the Health Facilities Planning Board and the $30 billion Teachers' Retirement System. Levine had invested a lot of time and effort cultivating power there. If Rezko could make that happen, Levine would be willing to do whatever Rezko wanted at the boards.

That setup still looked promising in April 2004, when Levine and Kiferbaum spoke on the phone after their little performance for Pam Davis of Edward Hospital.

"I am telling you that uh, I have never been in a better position that I am right now," Levine bragged, his voice suddenly sounding more earnest. "Part of the reason is because there's never been such a tight control of the uh, central apparatus."

And that was due to Rezko, he said.

"I mean uh, this guy is making decisions and can get anything done that he wants done," Levine continued. "He wants us to take whatever we can."

═══

What Levine meant when he used the term *central apparatus* was the hidden machinery inside the governmental process that, when secretly corrupted, turned political power into cash that was available to steal.

To some extent, government in Illinois had always been this way. Some state boards, commissions, or agencies were always corruptible. It was just a matter of knowing the right person in the right position of power to make it happen. Levine had made a career of it. And since meeting Rezko at Massuda's party, he was quickly learning that all the right people to find were in Blagojevich's immediate circle of friends and fund-raisers. Publicly, Blagojevich referred to this group as his kitchen cabinet, distinguishing them from his actual cabinet of department heads. In the simplest terms, they were the ones Blagojevich trusted.

Rezko and Kelly had never been elected to a political office, but with the governor giving them the power to appoint loyal people to decision-making boards, those who were in on the action could create situations where they could enrich themselves while no one was the wiser. After Blagojevich was elected in 2002, he had to name people to the hundreds of boards, commissions, and councils across the state. He was the first Democratic governor in

Illinois in a quarter century, leaving lots of pent-up demand for those loyal to the party to get a chance at a position. Many sought to be named to key roles on high-profile boards, while other positions on less glamorous panels were sometimes a challenge to fill at all.

But when it came to some of the most pivotal commissions, it was often Rezko and Kelly who had much of the say over which loyalists were named. In many cases, those they picked were not the best people for the job but *were* the best at taking direction from Rezko and Kelly when the pair communicated the wishes of "the administration."

At the hospital board, these Levine and Rezko puppets allowed Levine to steer a project toward approval once a contractor like Kiferbaum was attached to it and willing to pay to play. Lucrative contracts always had room for many to siphon away extra money. In many instances, even the board members who were following directions from men like Rezko and Levine would be kept in the dark about who was taking in illegal payments for themselves from state business. Levine found a way to take bribes through the hospital panel, but even more money was to be had at the Teachers' Retirement System of Illinois (TRS), which manages the retirement funds of most of the state's public school teachers. TRS has some 325,000 members and annuitants and in 2004 held more than $31 billion in trust. Among the responsibilities of the TRS board is to review and consider bids by private investment management firms to invest TRS funds. Its votes mean tens of millions of dollars for investment firms.

By rigging the system and picking which firms were deemed eligible for such large allocations, Rezko, Kelly, Levine, and others also chose bogus consultants on the deals to collect "finder's fees" when allocations were made. The cover was the consultants linked the investment firm with TRS. In reality, the consultants had done little to no work since the deals were already preordained by the insiders. Many of the firms agreed to hire the fake consultants and pay the fees knowing they might very well have been paying off somebody in exchange for access to state funds. That was just the way it was done in Illinois, many knew.

Among those allegedly scheming to influence things at TRS was Cellini, who had an association with Commonwealth Realty Advisers. Commonwealth controlled pension fund investments on behalf of state retired employees and teachers.

Cellini later invested in one of the state's first-ever legalized riverboat casinos, an investment he would turn around and sell in 2004 for $63 million.

The fit and trim Springfieldian for more than forty years made friends and money in every corner of the state from both sides of the political aisle. If men like Rezko, Levine, and Kelly abided by the "What's in it for me?" credo, Cellini could have been considered its architect.

At age twenty-eight in the early 1960s, Cellini became the youngest-ever member of the Springfield City Council and before long became the state's first secretary of transportation. A Republican in name, Cellini left state government to become executive director of the Illinois Asphalt Pavement Association, a powerful road-building group that became highly active in politics and political contributions. As Cellini got rich, he expanded into development projects and oversaw a firm that received state government leases. By the late 1980s, he had cofounded Commonwealth.

As he mastered the game, Cellini got to know everyone who played it, including Levine. By 2001, the two men had engineered what amounted to a coup on the eleven-member TRS board.

The panel is designed to have four members who are appointed by the governor, five who are elected by the thousands of members of the teachers unions, one who is selected by the board itself, and one who is the superintendent of schools. The board often split its votes along the appointed-versus-elected line, but Levine saw a weak spot in the summer of 2001 when one of the elected members was hurt in a motorcycle accident. Without its majority, the elected members saw Levine, with secret direction from Cellini, use his leadership of the appointed members to choose the single member selected by the board, as well as replace TRS's in-house legal counsel and executive director. Cellini leaked information to Levine that, in a snafu, the current legal counsel wasn't licensed to practice law in Illinois, a tidbit that Levine used to force the lawyer's resignation and the resignation of the executive director who hired him.

Replacing the men were Steve Loren, a lawyer and good friend of Levine, and Jon Bauman, a Cellini loyalist who would do what the men wanted when it came to reviewing and vetting potential investment firms to get massive TRS allocations. In the case of Bauman, he was rushed to approval by the Levine voting bloc when a candidate who had been selected by a TRS search committee was actually standing in the hallway waiting to be voted in. With Bauman in place, Levine would have his puppet to make investment recommendations to the board. And in case Bauman's loyalty ever slipped, Levine had himself named chairman of the TRS board's Rules and Personnel Committee, a position that made him responsible for giving

Bauman performance reviews and suggesting a salary for him. When things were going well in Levine's mind, he told Bauman that he could just write his own review and Levine would sign it as his own.

With their minions in place, Levine and Cellini effectively directed TRS staff toward certain investment firms and controlled the staff review of proposals. And when allocations came to a board vote, they had enough members under their control to get them approved. Then all that was left was to attach insider consultants to the deals who would share their finder's fees with the men that made it happen. Those fees typically were about 1 percent of the amount TRS was handing over for investment, but that's a nice sum when the investment amounts could be $50 million or more.

Levine and Cellini hadn't had their setup running for long when, just after Blagojevich was elected, his budget director, John Filan, pushed a plan to consolidate a number of the state's investment funds. That was a move that would have seen TRS disbanded and left Levine and Cellini without their influence. They weren't about to sit by and lose their new golden goose. Cellini simply went to Rezko and Kelly and explained how it would be better for all of them to leave TRS alone. If they would go to the governor and derail the consolidation plan, Cellini promised to allow the pair to select investment firms that would get TRS money. Rezko and Kelly could use that power to reward investment houses that made campaign donations to Blagojevich. The governor's advisers agreed, and the consolidation plan was shelved. By mid- 2003, Kelly was offering the names of firms that should have business steered to them.

So, with TRS locked down, Rezko turned his attention to other key panels, including the Illinois Health Facilities Planning Board and the Illinois Finance Authority, where he installed Blagojevich campaign contributor Ali Ata as president.

On the hospital planning board, Rezko placed Massuda, Imad Almanaseer, a Park Ridge pathologist who was an investor in Rezko's fast-food businesses, and Michel Malek, a neurologist and Rezko friend. Also on the panel was Thomas Beck, a former Cook County comptroller who had been appointed to his post by Governor Edgar and remained in place under George Ryan. He wanted to keep it after Blagojevich was elected, so he brought a $1,000 campaign check to Rezko's office on Chicago's North Side to ask that he remain in place. Together the three Rezko doctors, Beck, and Levine made up a board majority so tightly controlled by Rezko that he instructed Beck to have the bloc split its votes every once in a while on non-important matters just to make things look good.

The FBI and US attorney's office started tapping Levine's phones on April 8, 2004, and agents weren't exactly sure what kinds of conversations they might capture.

Among the first was on April 12, when investment fund manager and adviser Sheldon Pekin called Levine at home. Pekin had approached Levine about getting TRS money for a firm and was willing to do what Levine said with a finder's fee if Levine could turn on the TRS cash faucet for him. From the call, it was clear to the agents that Pekin had a lot of irons in the fire, acting as a finder on a number of deals Levine was orchestrating, and that Robert Weinstein, a doctor and businessman whom Levine defrauded the charities with, was playing a role. Investigators later learned Levine and his partner Weinstein were plotting to set up their own company to act as finders on such deals, with Weinstein as its public face and Levine steering it business. That would cut out the middleman and bring money off corrupt TRS deals directly into their hands without them having to share it with anyone.

"Listen, Shelly, are you around tomorrow?" Levine asked.

"I will be around," Pekin answered.

"I'm gonna stop by because um, I wanna talk to you about—a couple of things—you know, the arrangement with Bob," Levine stammered.

"There is no reason that Bob cannot [share] your finder's fees for LLR. And for uh, Stockwell," Levine went on, mentioning two firms he hoped to push through the TRS board and collect on.

Levine and Weinstein were hoping to bring in investment business from New York for their new company to latch onto, but at that point it hadn't panned out. Sharing what they had on the table in Illinois so far was the way to go, Levine said.

"So Bob can, you know, can enjoy the benefit of the fees from Teachers' itself," he said of TRS. "New York, ah, things may come through, but in Illinois we know what we got."

By that point, Rezko was passing word to those in the know around Illinois that it would take a $50,000 Blagojevich campaign donation for firms to even make a list to be considered for TRS investment, and he and Levine already had steered a $50 million investment to Glencoe Capital, with Pekin acting as the finder and bringing in a 1 percent fee of $500,000.

Rezko, Kelly, Monk, and Blagojevich also already had the experience of directing a finder's fee to the investment firm Bear Stearns in 2003. When it came time for the state to refinance the $10 billion in pension obligation bonds, the group made sure Bear Stearns would handle the deal. Acting as a consultant to the firm was Kjellander, who after taking in his $809,000 fee allegedly kicked back $600,000. Those funds went to Joseph Aramanda, a man linked to Rezko businesses who passed on most of it to people and entities that Rezko named. Kjellander would long deny he had any role in the illegal passing of funds, calling his movement of money a loan.

Over the next several days that April, agents picked up chatter on Levine's telephones as his various corrupt deals came together. They caught snippets of one arrangement after another. Levine gave directions and made promises to associates, getting them to have their own conversations with the people necessary to make things shake out as Levine wanted. He was not unlike someone moving chess pieces around a board, manipulating everyone he spoke to.

On April 14, it was political fund-raiser Joe Cari on the line. Cari had been Al Gore's national finance chairman in 2000 and would later be pressured by Blagojevich to take the governor's fund-raising national in front of a possible presidential bid. Levine was using Cari as a go-between on a TRS contract for JER Partners of Virginia, a firm that was in line for a TRS investment. Levine learned of the firm at a New York fund raiser Cari held for Blagojevich in late 2003, when Cari's partner at Healthpoint Capital, Carl McCall, mentioned it. Healthpoint was a private equity firm both Cari and McCall hoped could get TRS business with Levine's help, so they were eager to please him.

Levine later had Cari tell JER's leaders that they needed to sign paperwork giving a $750,000 finder's fee to a mysterious "consultant" in the Turks and Caicos Islands.

"All right, that's all set up, but I need to give uh, uh, Carl [McCall] the name of the guy their marketing people should call," Levine said, asking Cari to pick up the ball and pass messages to McCall and to JER. Cari agreed and said he would get things moving.

On April 15, Levine was on the phone with Joseph Senese, a Chicago area union boss and the son of Dominic Senese, a Teamsters official with reputed ties to the Chicago Outfit and underworld figures. Dominic was probably best known for surviving an attempt on his life that involved a shotgun blast to the face outside his suburban house.

Senese heard from one of the principals in an arrangement he and Levine were working on that would steer $200 million in TRS money to Investors

Mortgage Holding, a company that would turn around and make loans to developers. Everything was going perfectly, Senese promised.

"Well, my meeting last night went absolutely perfect too," Levine answered. "Full steam ahead."

Everything sounded like it was on track, the men agreed, and they were optimistic that once they pushed the $200 million from TRS in the direction they pleased, there would be many more deals later. "Better than a poke in the eye," Levine said.

Investigators later came to learn the meeting Levine mentioned had allegedly been with Rezko himself. Levine had gotten a private room at the Standard Club in Chicago, a posh members-only club with dining and rich amenities. He and Rezko met there over New York strip steaks and cabernet, and Levine took time to explain how the rest of the TRS deals he had lined up could work. Rezko—who later disputed that the meeting had happened at all—allegedly agreed and gave Levine a green light to do as he pleased. Phone records later showed Rezko called Tom Beck, head of the health facilities board, during the sit-down. And the next day, investigators captured another call between Levine and Weinstein.

"Great meeting last night," Levine said of the Standard Club get-together. "And I got everything all, uh, laid out and um, full speed ahead, fair and equitable, where everybody participates," Levine went on. "Whatever I want."

Levine and Weinstein would chat throughout the time the FBI had Levine's phones tapped. Two days later, on April 17, Weinstein and Levine discussed, among other things, a $220 million TRS allocation Levine hoped to make money on. And by the way, Levine told his friend, Levine was hoping to be named to a post with the US Holocaust Museum soon.

"You are a holocaust," Weinstein joked. "Good-bye."

10

The Pope and the Rabbi

In just the first few weeks of taping Stuart Levine, investigators were amazed by the amount of information that poured forth. It seemed that in any twenty-minute phone call, Levine would plow through fourteen or fifteen frauds as he chatted with someone close to him.

Leading the effort in the US attorney's office was Christopher Niewoehner, a Minnesota native who was Harvard educated and eager to work on public corruption cases. Niewoehner was often soft-spoken in public, but his quietness cloaked the deep intelligence of a shrewd prosecutor who was more than up to the task. Niewoehner was brought onto the case out of the narcotics division in the US attorney's office in Chicago because that experience left him knowing how to manage a wiretap. Levine had been captured talking about Rezko offering the keys to the kingdom, as it were, and Niewoehner would be in for the long haul.

That same April, Levine had been named vice chairman of the Illinois Health Facilities Planning Board, which Rezko sanctioned because it was necessary to drive the board's agenda if Beck, the chairman, couldn't run a meeting for some reason.

The five-member bloc on the panel voted Rezko and Levine's way, regardless of the merits of a particular project. That constituted a majority that could impose the administration's will on any question before the panel. If a proposal came up that the administration wanted to steer through or stonewall, Rezko told Beck which way to have the bloc vote. Levine and

Beck spoke before each meeting, and if there was an item of particular concern to the administration, Beck pointed it out and indicated which way the outcome should go. Beck often pulled the Rezko board members aside one at a time to tell them what to do at the meeting and sometimes even passed out note cards before meetings instructing the bloc which way to vote on particular agenda items.

It was supposed to run smoothly, though it didn't always.

What was supposed to be a behind-the-scenes scheme was nearly outed that spring when the first hospital Kiferbaum was to pay a bribe on came to a vote before the panel. Kiferbaum and Levine had been working on their plan to get an approval for the facility, to be built by the Mercy hospital system, as far back as the fall of 2003.

Levine had gone that spring to Beck to see about getting Mercy what was known as a certificate of need, or a CON, to build the hospital, and had been told Rezko was against it. Mercy submitted a poor application and didn't have the right clout behind it. So Levine visited Rezko that fall to see what could be done.

Others had been promised the Mercy plan would not get a go-ahead, Levine was told, but that wasn't the end of it. Levine later remembered asking Rezko if it would make any difference if he and Rezko could make a lot of money if Mercy got the CON. The two already had pushed the allocation for Glencoe through TRS, and Rezko siphoned money off that deal. In the Mercy matter, Kiferbaum paid a heavy bribe to get the plan pushed through and promised to make significant campaign donations to Blagojevich. The information that he could make money under the table did change Rezko's mind on Mercy, but he decided to keep even Beck, the chairman, in the dark that Mercy's fortunes were about to change.

With that assurance in hand, Levine went back to Kiferbaum with some direction. Mercy should start by hiring Steve Loren as its attorney on the proposal. That would get Loren a client and give Levine a lawyer he could communicate with behind the scenes.

In December 2003, a vote for Mercy came up for the first time. Kiferbaum wanted it approved immediately, but Levine and Rezko agreed they shouldn't push it through on the first shot. It wouldn't be wise to do anything unusual and draw attention to the plan. Most proposals making their first appearance before the panel would get what was known as an Intent to Deny from the board, directing additional work on a proposal before it would get approval. So Levine and Rezko decided to do nothing to help

Mercy the December before the FBI began its taping, allowing it to come for a vote and receive its first denial. But thereafter, Levine helped steer the project toward a better-looking proposal by giving Kiferbaum inside information he could take back to hospital leaders to guide them. That would help Kiferbaum's standing because the hospital would know the builder was getting them information they could not have gotten elsewhere, and Levine went as far as to appear at Kiferbaum's offices on one occasion to meet a Mercy leader there and show off Kiferbaum's influence.

By the time of the alleged Standard Club meeting between Levine and Rezko on April 14, 2004, Mercy was set to come for a board vote just a week later, on April 21. Beck hadn't been given his directions yet, Levine told Rezko, but by the time their meeting was through, he knew Mercy would be getting its approval.

Beck and Levine were caught on a recording just two days before the meeting, and it became clear to investigators that the wheels were in motion to get Mercy approved. The conversation began with Beck giving Levine some news.

"Uh, well we've got two new board members," Beck said.

Levine perked up and quickly asked who they were. One was named Pamela Orr, an African American woman who worked for a nursing home.

"And uh, I don't know, she's not one of Tony's," Beck said, seemingly first sharing with Levine the only thing they really cared about. "Tony told me she was from Balanoff," meaning Tom Balanoff, the local head of the powerful Service Employees International Union and one of Blagojevich's largest campaign contributors.

Beck told Levine he had called Orr to welcome her and to tell her not to be concerned about anything.

"Just vote the way we tell you to," Beck said, probably only half-joking.

Beck said he had spoken to Rezko about the meeting coming up on the twenty-first, telling Levine he had Rezko's "marching orders." Mercy was on the agenda and had come up in their conversation. "Our boy wants to help them," Beck said.

Levine answered with a calm "uh huh," giving no hint that he and Rezko already had their secret arrangement working on Mercy and that he knew Rezko was giving it a thumbs up because of the kickback. Beck thought he would just be doing the wishes of Rezko and the Blagojevich administration, and he did not know Levine and Rezko were to split Kiferbaum's bribe on the project.

Mercy had been given its cursory denial in December, but under the rules, they had been granted another six months to resubmit their plans. By that spring they had done so but had offered no changes, leading to a negative staff review not long before the scheduled board meeting. Altering the plan so close to the meeting would effectively knock Mercy out of the box for April and would mean having to call a special meeting in May just for Mercy, possibly drawing attention to it. So Beck and Levine discussed how they could ram the hospital through at the upcoming meeting without making things seem too blatant.

After hanging up with Beck, Levine immediately called Loren, who explained the hospital already addressed questions about whether the population in the area was large enough to warrant a hospital. Mercy was using newer standards on how to calculate whether a facility was needed, as recommended by the American Hospitals Association, not the older standards that the planning board's staff was using. Levine saw his opening to push the Mercy plan through. And as the FBI continued to listen, he called Beck back to tell him Loren dropped off a copy of the statement Mercy would be submitting at the meeting. Loren had brought his only copy to Levine's house and asked Levine to fax a copy back to him. Fine, Levine said, but it would have to wait.

"Spartacus is getting ready to march on Rome," he said. "And this is a very serious situation."

It wasn't some code that he was taking over the planning board or that Rezko was laying siege to Springfield. The odd Levine was actually watching the famous 1960 movie starring Kirk Douglas. He didn't want to be interrupted during what he later would call "an exciting time of the movie."

On April 20, just one day before the hospital planning board meeting, Levine and Beck spoke again. Eight of the nine board members were expected to be in attendance. The two talked about how they would manage the argument of the plans before the panel, which included both the Mercy proposal and another for a hospital in southwest suburban Bolingbrook. Even after their previous discussions, Beck sounded like he was leaning toward approving the Bolingbrook plan, a Mercy rival, and with a good reason of his own. Bolingbrook's consultant was lawyer and lobbyist Jeff Ladd, a former chairman of the board of Metra, Chicago's commuter rail system. He had gone to Beck about protecting his clients' interests in the face of Rezko's political dominance. Beck had a recommendation he thought could provide that protection—his cousin Ed Kelly, the renowned Forty-Seventh

Ward Democratic committeeman who knew Rezko—and Ladd had taken the advice. Beck told Levine he was going along with the program as they spoke the night before the meeting, but on the twenty-first, with the panel convening at a downtown hotel for its vote, Beck changed his mind and told Levine he was getting off the train. He couldn't go along with the plan.

Not so fast, Levine countered, and confronted Beck with the marching orders from Rezko. Beck said he hadn't been able to reach Rezko to discuss the situation one last time, but Levine pulled out a cell phone and got him immediately.

Beck later recalled telling Rezko that he didn't know how they could go against Ladd and his cousin Kelly. The pair had been promised that Mercy wasn't going to go ahead. Rezko answered that he understood but the pair couldn't get what they wanted all the time. There would have to be an IOU of sorts.

Beck was still upset.

"You can take this job and shove it," he would later recall telling Rezko as Levine looked on, watching Beck's half of the phone call. Beck was throwing in the towel if he had to approve Mercy over Bolingbrook. That would be the last straw, he told Rezko; he would resign.

Rezko called the bluff.

"You do what you have to do," came the answer from Rezko. Just get Mercy through the board vote as you were told.

Beck relented and handed the phone back to Levine. A short time later, before the vote, he was talking to Anne Murphy, the planning board's lawyer, and told her Mercy was going to get its approval and the board was probably going to be publicly flogged for it in the press.

"We're going to get creamed," he said. Murphy pointed out that the Mercy vote could be delayed, but the beaten Beck never answered.

When Mercy's proposal was up for its vote, the meeting was well attended. News reporters and the board's staff were there, as well as lawyers and staff of the various hospital plans, who started to weigh in on the plan. Levine was up first, immediately voting yes.

Two of the board members, Massuda and Malek, followed suit, throwing their support behind the plan. They were Rezko backers, even though they had no hint of his secret stake in the outcome. Next, Orr, the newest member, voted no, as did two board members who were not in the Rezko bloc.

Then the vote hit a snag. Dr. Imad Almanaseer was somewhat confused. Mercy still had an overwhelmingly negative staff review, leaving Almanaseer thinking it was something he should vote down. He was concerned enough about the situation to try to call Rezko earlier in the day, but he had been unable to reach him. So when it came to be his turn to vote, Almanaseer passed.

That put the Mercy plan in front of Beck, who also seemed confused. The plan was stuck with just three yes votes—two shy of approval—and the three nos. "Where are we?" Beck said out loud, looking down at his tally sheet in front of him. He leaned over to ask Murphy whether Mercy could be deferred at the last moment if need be. Even if Beck voted yes, it wouldn't be enough, and Mercy would be locked in with a denial and defeated.

So with scores of onlookers scratching their heads, Beck got up from his seat and walked over to whisper to Levine, telling him what was going on, and Levine in turn got up from his chair and walked over to whisper to Almanaseer.

Beck had already told Almanaseer to follow Levine's lead on the Mercy plan because "Tony" wanted it that way, and Levine whispered to the doctor that Beck wanted him to vote now. An embarrassed Almanaseer answered, "Fine, I'll vote," and changed his abstention to a yes. A moment later, Beck gave the Mercy plan its fifth and decisive approving vote, sending up an audible gasp from those watching the meeting.

Afterward, a shocked Murphy went up to Levine to try to find out what in the world had just happened. Levine just shrugged.

"Sometimes you have to be a good soldier," he said.

———

With the meeting behind them, Levine and Beck drove to Rezko's office on the North Side to try to straighten out the issue that had nearly led to Beck scuttling the Mercy plan and ruining Levine and Rezko's secret payoff. He had been afraid his cousin's reputation of having political influence would be ruined because he had been hired to try to stop Mercy and promote the Bolingbrook plan. Both proposals had come before the board in a political shoving match.

Levine later remembered being ushered into a conference room, where Rezko soon joined them.

"We'll make it up to him," Rezko told Beck, a comment Levine took to mean that Ed Kelly could get taken care of the next time around. Ladd also would be taken care of, because he was an attorney for a hospital group wanting to build in Bolingbrook and that project was on Rezko's radar.

That night, a prideful Levine was still relishing his victory. Aside from the theatrics, things had gone well. Even inside observers might believe that Mercy had been pushed through by a consultant the hospital had hired for its plan, Victor Reyes, a former close adviser to Mayor Daley. They would assume his clout had led the governor to push buttons for Mercy. Levine called Mercy's lawyer, his friend Steve Loren, starting the call with "You have no idea" instead of saying hello.

"From the minute I walked in there, Beck—wanted to resign," Levine tried to explain, stuttering through the dramatic tale. "And of course nobody, nobody knows that it's me. And nobody really knows that it's Tony for the reason that it's Tony."

"I kept the whole thing together, boy," Levine said.

———

A few days later, on April 24, federal agents tapping Levine's home telephone captured one of the few calls where the careful Rezko could be heard speaking about any of the business involving Levine and the boards he controlled. There wasn't much to it, just Levine inviting Rezko out for coffee sometime that weekend. Levine had heard that Children's Memorial Hospital was looking to refurbish or even replace its facility—and the tab could be $500 million. It was a ripening fruit that had Levine salivating, and he was eager to tell Rezko about it.

"I wanted to uh, to talk a little bit about, about uh, some stuff that happened I think needs to be done and may be a giant opportunity also," Levine said.

"Very good," Rezko answered. And although a meeting on the topic never materialized, it wouldn't be the last time the children's hospital was targeted by members of Blagojevich's inner circle or even the governor himself.

Two days later, on April 26, Levine was back on the phone with Joe Cari, the former finance chair for Al Gore who Levine was trying to use to pressure JER Partners into paying a finder's fee to get TRS business. Levine didn't yet have a name of a consultant for him to pass to the firm, but maybe he would that afternoon. Levine's talent for keeping multiple plates spinning was apparent to anyone who listened to his calls, as three minutes later, he was talking to Sheldon Pekin, who had done the first crooked TRS deal with him. Pekin was a little late in getting a payment from the deal involving the investment firm Glencoe Capital to Joseph Aramanda, the Rezko associate who was getting cut in on Rezko's share. An agitated Levine heard Pekin was sarcastic with Aramanda, joking about getting him a check by asking whether Christmas was coming early. Word had gotten back to Rezko, who apparently wasn't amused.

"If we don't get it finished today, uh, Tony's gonna, not gonna do business anymore like that," Levine told Pekin, who promised to fix things quickly and make the payment.

On May 1, agents recorded Levine and Weinstein talking about what would be the largest TRS investment that Levine and Rezko would try to influence. Capri Capital was an investment firm with a history of doing business with TRS. But one of its principals, Thomas Rosenberg, a Chicago businessman and Hollywood film producer best known for bankrolling the movie *Million Dollar Baby*, had a very chilly relationship with Levine. Levine thought Rosenberg had previously stiffed him out of $500,000 in one of the firm's TRS deals. So in early 2004, when Capri had a $220 million investment from TRS lined up, Levine made sure it went nowhere. One of the ways he had derailed it was to tell Rezko and Chris Kelly about all the business Capri was getting from the state—all while contributing zero in campaign funds to Blagojevich. Levine was recorded telling Weinstein he had told Rezko that Capri had gotten nearly a billion dollars in TRS business and not done anything for the administration.

"He said, you know, fuck him!" Levine said.

Rosenberg later said he called Cellini to find out what was going on and that he was told Rezko and Kelly had found out that Capri wasn't doing anything under the table to support the level of business it was getting from Illinois. He would eventually be given a choice. Make a $1.5 million campaign donation or agree to pay a $2 million finder's fee to whomever was dictated to him.

Levine and Weinstein were still talking about getting their own investment management company put together, with their interest in it hidden, to take in TRS money. Levine told his friend he saw no obstacles to getting $500 million in TRS business. Rosenberg might have to scrap the business Capri was doing.

"Or do a deal," Levine said of the corrupt arrangement. "And I'm fine. I would prefer he would not, to tell you the truth, we can take, uh, this money and put it as part of the $500 million. I don't give a shit anymore."

Rezko was supportive of the plan to create a firm that could take in finder's fees itself, Levine said. That would cut out annoying middlemen like

Pekin and Rosenberg. Levine said he had explained to Rezko how it could work: they could direct TRS money to the investment firms they picked, with those firms being directed to pay a finder's fee to the shadow company that was only there to collect the fees.

"And he said to me, orchestrate the whole thing, Stuart," Levine told Weinstein on the call. "Just do it. Let me know what I gotta do."

Weinstein agreed it could potentially be perfect. Rezko and Kelly and those close to them would control both ends of any deal coming before TRS and its massive coffers, with the corrupt Levine as their point man. It would be a looting of state money on an unprecedented scale.

———

On May 6, Levine spoke to Cari again on the phone. There was trouble with JER and its $80 million allocation from TRS, which was to be voted on at the board's meeting later that month. The agreement for JER to pay a "consultant" chosen by Levine and Rezko had yet to be finalized, and Levine admitted to Cari that he was getting nervous. Somehow the leaders at JER— including principal Debbie Harmon—had gotten the idea that they were fine without paying a finder's fee.

"I hate to undo things," Levine threatened. "But I, I'll have to do it, uh, real fast, and . . . I'd hate to have to do that."

Levine was more than a little irritated that Harmon and others had been told all along that they would need to hire someone he called a "marketing person." Never mind that was really code for the bogus finder. Now JER magically thought they could get away with not making the payment they had been directed to make? Levine would pull the plug with extreme prejudice if that kept up. No need, Cari answered. They'd get the message. It was just a misunderstanding, and everything would be just fine. Cari could call his friend and Healthpoint partner, McCall, who was former New York state comptroller, who could tell JER and Harmon to communicate the urgent need to pay the finder's fee.

Good, Levine said. People he was dealing with were waiting to hear about results.

"I don't wanna be in the middle of something that doesn't happen after I tell people it's gonna happen," Levine warned.

"I understand," Cari answered.

A few minutes later, Cari called again. He had spoken to McCall, who had been exchanging voice mails with Harmon all day. They had been told they needed to work with the "marketing person" they would be given, and Cari told Levine the contract would be as he had laid out earlier, with half of the fee paid at closing and half six months later. Levine knew that Rezko had selected Charles Hannon—Dr. Fortunee Massuda's husband—to act as the collector of the kickback. All of JER's potential roadblocks had been removed, Levine said again. But that could change.

"You know how upset people can get—the political powers that be," Levine said.

Cari would get several messages to leaders at JER that this was simply how things were done in Illinois and "how the governor handles patronage." It made no one at JER comfortable to deal with that kind of pressure, and those handling the TRS business for the investment firm found it strange that they received a copy of the proposed contract from a company called Emerald Star International, whose representatives they had never met, and that the company's fax machine apparently was in the Turks and Caicos Islands.

———

The next day was May 7, and Levine was on the phone with Cellini, his long-time ally. The men were so close and controlled TRS so tightly that the head of the TRS staff referred to Cellini as "the Pope" and Levine as "the Rabbi." The men had been going back and forth a bit on one of Levine's projects, and Cellini told Levine he had just had an interesting conversation with someone.

As the FBI continued listening in, Cellini said he told the angry movie producer Rosenberg he had checked to find out what the problem was behind the TRS issue and learned people in high places were "flabbergasted" to learn how much state business Capri was bringing in while doing nothing in return. "Doing nothing" of course meant not making any kind of political donation to Rod Blagojevich. Cellini said he told Rosenberg he planned to reach out to Rezko to get a fuller explanation but that Rosenberg had cut him off.

"He said, 'And let me tell you, I don't want any interfacing with that guy,'" Cellini recalled. "He said, '[Rezko] would never be somebody that I would go to. There are two people in this administration that, in my opinion, if they're not under investigation already they're being monitored every step of the way, and that's Tony Rezko and Chris Kelly.'"

Cellini said he had led Rosenberg to believe that someone else could have reached out about the problem and alerted Rezko and the rest of the machinery under Blagojevich to the fact that Capri was all play and no pay. Rosenberg had said he would find out and get back to Cellini, who had told Rosenberg he had linked up to Rezko and Kelly and been asked to do fund-raising on behalf of the state road builders. Whatever, Rosenberg had answered. He had said in no uncertain terms that if he thought he had to go through Rezko or Kelly to pry the $200 million allocation out of TRS, he was willing to walk away without his money.

By late the next afternoon, Cellini called Levine at his home again, after just speaking to an irate Rosenberg, who said he had learned through an intermediary he did in fact have a problem with Rezko and Kelly. And the more Rosenberg talked about the situation, the angrier he became on the call. He let Cellini know he was going to fight. He was being shaken down, and it was outrageous.

Rosenberg insisted he wouldn't be blackmailed. And if they pressed the matter, he would stand at the corner of State and Madison in the heart of downtown Chicago and shout out what was happening. He had gone on so long, Cellini said, Rosenberg's cell phone had started to cut in and out.

Cellini told Levine he was nervous about the whole situation. Rezko and Kelly were "essentially hammerin' people for contracts." There was so much going on, eventually someone would probably take a look at it. And who knows where things could lead then?

The message from Rosenberg would be passed to Rezko and Kelly, and Levine even wondered out loud what kind of effect it would have.

"Maybe this conversation becomes, uh, a little bit sobering for them," Levine said. "Does it have that potential?"

"For twelve minutes," Cellini answered.

===

It was May 12 by the time the men had had separate conversations with Rezko and were again going over the scenario involving Rosenberg and how to handle him. Levine had been in a meeting with both Rezko and Kelly, and the personalities of the pair and how they handled this kind of fund-raising had clashed. Rezko was ever the careful, measured analyst.

"He just said uh, solve this with your head, not your heart," Levine told Cellini of his conversation. "The other guy [Kelly] says, 'Smack'em over the head.'"

Cellini said Rezko's position seemed to be that Capri would get its $220 million allocation in an attempt to placate the volatile Rosenberg, but there would be no more state business for the firm. With no promises from Capri's leaders that it would take care of the people pulling the strings in Illinois, they would quickly find themselves on the outside looking in.

And then Cellini made a comment that would perk the ears of investigators hoping to weave a case together and push it as high as it might go. Rezko had said something else in their conversation, Cellini told Levine.

"Did he tell you too that the big guy said Rosenberg means nothing to him?" Cellini asked, referring to Blagojevich himself. It told investigators that the governor had been briefed on the Rosenberg situation and apparently had blessed cutting Rosenberg off at the knees.

"Of course, it seems like nobody means anything," Cellini said with a laugh.

It was an important moment for many on the investigation. It wasn't completely confirmed that the "big guy" was Blagojevich, but it was certainly reasonable to suspect that Cellini meant the governor was aware of what was happening and had passed some kind of word down the food chain about it.

———

On May 19, just before the TRS board was supposed to meet next and vote on proposals Levine was running, Levine and Cari were on the phone. Levine still hadn't heard for sure whether Debbie Harmon of JER had signed the contract that would send money to Rezko associate Charles Hannon. McCall was getting off a flight just then, Cari explained, and even though it was after five o'clock in New York, the state's former comptroller was going to go to JER's offices in person to make sure it would be taken care of. Apparently that's what it was going to take.

"Well, I look forward to seeing you tomorrow," Levine said. The next day would be May 20, 2004, but Cari wasn't the only person Levine would be seeing. Answering a knock on his door at 7:00 PM, Levine was greeted by FBI agents. One of them was Daniel Cain, who had been with the bureau for nearly twenty years after leaving a job as an accountant at a small firm in central Illinois. The agents would play some of the recordings they had made so far, showing Levine a photo of himself with other targets in the investigation the month before and throwing some names at him. For Levine, they were all the wrong ones: Jacob Kiferbaum. Nicholas Hurtgen. Tony Rezko.

The wiretaps were discontinued the next day, but not before authorities captured a final call between Levine and Weinstein. The FBI had been by, a shellshocked Levine said, and they were looking for a "big fish." That was Rezko, Levine told Weinstein, the political patron who had opened up so many doors for him over the past months. Just a couple of weeks later, subpoenas landed at the offices of the Illinois Health Facilities Planning Board in Springfield, asking for documents related to the odd Mercy vote Levine had participated in. Levine would resign his post that June before the next hospital board meeting, even with four hospital plans up for a vote, and he would leave TRS, too, in July. He gave no official reason for stepping down.

News of Levine's woes and the subpoenas to the hospital board quickly reached Rezko's ears, those of Blagojevich's chief of staff, Lon Monk, and the governor himself. All the IHFPB members were considering hiring criminal lawyers, and everyone knew that bad publicity was coming. The members whose actions during the Mercy vote were most in question were Blagojevich appointees, so there was little doubt that he was going to catch some of the heat for the Levine debacle. Monk, Rezko, and Blagojevich were on a jet at O'Hare International Airport when Blagojevich asked Rezko to tell him what he knew about the situation. Rezko wasn't that concerned.

"Don't worry about it," he said.

And there was only slightly more anxiety not long after when news spread that Levine's phones had been tapped. Rezko thought about conversations he might have had with the targeted insider and could only think of one. It wasn't a conversation he thought he had to worry about, but he did toss out his cell phone and get a new one. He told close associates he thought he was being watched and sometimes showed them bug-detecting devices he had installed in his office.

On October 30 of that year, federal agents arrived at Cari's home to question him. They asked about Stuart Levine and what Cari's relationship was with him. Having no idea where the investigation was going or what the agents were getting at, Cari lied and said he had no relationship whatsoever with Levine. He said he had no idea whether Levine was behind the promotion of a mysterious consulting firm to get a fee in a TRS deal with JER, but wanting to be in a decent position if things got bad, Cari promised to help the agents and give them any documents he had collected in the arrangement.

But at that moment, Cari had decided to keep to himself what he knew about Rod Blagojevich and the fact the Illinois governor was dreaming up creative ways of making it to the White House.

PART IV

A Federal Probe

11

"Public Official A"

In the midst of Rod Blagojevich's budget battles with Michael Madigan, federal prosecutors had made their approach to Stuart Levine, compelling him to resign from the state boards Blagojevich had reappointed him to and forcing Blagojevich to explain his relationship with the longtime Republican. Blagojevich said he didn't know Levine well and was just trying to bridge the gap with Republicans by reappointing him. But that excuse didn't completely fly because since the election Levine had become a Blagojevich donor, including picking up the tab for a plane ride to and from New York City for a curious fall 2003 fund-raiser there.

A few weeks later, a whistleblower lawsuit filed by Edward Hospital detailed some of the accusations against Kiferbaum and Hurtgen and stated that a hospital official wore a wire. And the media began reporting on Rezko friends Massuda and Malek getting appointed to the Health Facilities Planning Board after each made $25,000 campaign donations to the governor—one of the first indications of what would be known as Blagojevich's $25,000 Club. In all, Blagojevich received more than two hundred individual donations of that amount, and a majority of the contributors got something from state government, from appointments to boards and commissions to state contracts.

Indeed, while Blagojevich was often an absentee governor he was still fully engaged in fund-raising, as he'd always been.

Rezko and especially Kelly continued to lead the push, assisted closely by Petrovic and Wyma, both of whom had picked up major clients with interests before the state. Blagojevich's main goal was to raise millions of dollars in one night each year by inviting hundreds of people to and hosting "the big event" during the early summer at major Chicago locales like Navy Pier or under the skeletal remains of the T. rex Sue at the Field Museum. Blagojevich was always successful, collecting $4 million or $5 million a pop, which even for Illinois was a colossal sum that was already scaring off potential competitors for the 2006 election.

But one man who wasn't overjoyed was Mell, who by now was being fully pushed to the side. With all the governor's men raising so much cash for Blagojevich, Mell's influence wasn't needed. And still portraying himself as a reformer, Blagojevich didn't want to even appear indebted to Mell. But perhaps mostly, Blagojevich *wanted* the separation, still resenting the feeling that others thought he was Mell's tool.

With Blagojevich's blessing, Kelly cut Mell out wherever he could. When the Thirty-Third Ward office staff, proud to have close ties to the sitting governor, placed Blagojevich's name on ward stationery, Blagojevich had legal counsel draft a letter to Mell's people declaring that was illegal. Then he had Kelly set up a meeting with Mell to explain the new order of things and stress the governor's independence from his original sponsor, which incensed Mell even more.

The old-timers and precinct captains loyal to Mell and who had helped Blagojevich win his state rep and congressional offices were livid. Some probably had been edged out of jobs or some other sort of benefit they felt they were owed, but many also felt Blagojevich was turning his back on those who had helped make him a success. Mell and Blagojevich were barely speaking, and the alderman wasn't talking with his daughter much either. He vented to friends that putting Blagojevich up for governor was the worst decision he'd ever made and that his son-in-law had turned into an "ungrateful son-of-a-bitch."

But the two men put their disagreements aside briefly for the holidays. It was a very temporary thaw. During dinner on Christmas Eve 2004, Blagojevich overheard Mell talking about how successful one of his wife Marge's cousins was running a landfill in Will County near Joliet. Blagojevich quickly became suspicious. After talking about it with several friends, including Kelly, Blagojevich came to believe the relative, Frank Schmidt, was telling construction waste haulers that they could dump whatever they wanted in the landfill because he was related to Mell and the governor.

Blagojevich said nothing about his suspicions that night. But two weeks later, he announced publicly he was closing the landfill. It was a highly unusual move for a governor to make even if there hadn't been any family ties. But Blagojevich said he was trying to send a message: nobody gets special treatment—not even his family.

The on-and-off hostility that had been brewing quietly for a decade between Mell and Blagojevich had finally reached its boiling point.

A seething Mell, vacationing in Florida, called reporters all over Chicago, blasting Blagojevich for being an ingrate and repeating to the press what he had previously said only privately: Blagojevich uses people and then throws them under the bus if he thinks it will help his career. He also took several swipes at Kelly, telling the *Sun-Times* he felt like one of those wives who for years supported a struggling husband only to be dumped for a trophy wife once the man became successful.

"I am the old wife," Mell said. "The new wife is Chris Kelly."

He then added even more fuel to the feud when he accused Kelly of trading appointments to state boards and commissions for "$50,000 campaign contributions" to Blagojevich's campaign fund.

Illinois's First Family was in full-on meltdown.

In the following days, Blagojevich demanded Mell retract the statement about the campaign contributions, which essentially accused Kelly of breaking the law. Kelly hired high-powered attorney Robert Clifford to threaten a defamation lawsuit. Clifford had known Mell for years. The two men had summer homes next to each other in Lake Geneva, Wisconsin, where Clifford had gotten to know both the alderman and Blagojevich. Clifford was one of Blagojevich's biggest campaign contributors and had met Kelly through the governor. When he arrived at Clifford's plush downtown offices, Kelly was righteously indignant. He said he was innocent, he told Clifford, and he wanted to sue to prove it.

Mell soon realized what he'd done. His pride prevented him from immediately taking back what he had said about Kelly, but he also realized he may have gone too far. When Clifford and Mell spoke, Mell said, "I get going sometimes, and maybe I took it out on the wrong guys." Less than two weeks later, Mell officially recanted, and Kelly didn't sue.

The Mell accusations had virtually no impact on the ongoing federal probe. With Levine, Cari, and others already in the fold, agents and

prosecutors were well on their way into looking into the Blagojevich administration.

But Mell's words did spur the Cook County State's Attorney and Attorney General's offices. They couldn't unhear what Mell had said, and both
offices launched their own probes.

Privately, Blagojevich became obsessed with the landfill spat, constantly
talking to Kelly and aides about it. If one of the city's new major newspapers
wrote a story on the issue, Blagojevich would churn it over and discuss every
detail. While other business in the government had to get done, Blagojevich
focused only on the landfill and the fallout.

"The whole situation was all driven by hatred of Mell," one former top
staffer recalled. "But that doesn't mean Mell wasn't up to no good. The two
things aren't mutually exclusive."

It was also a turning point for Blagojevich. Although the investigations by Lisa Madigan's office and county prosecutors never resulted in any
charges, Mell's accusations—combined with the brewing investigations at
the state boards—began to focus public attention away from the governor's
policies and toward his growing scandals.

A few weeks later, a *Tribune* poll showed more voters than not wanted
to see his administration end after one term. Blagojevich, who polled internally through Fred Yang's firm three to five times a year, seemed unfazed.
He didn't blame the bad poll numbers on the ongoing investigations. Rather,
he said, it was just the typical ups and downs of politics. What he did, taking on Mell, showed how different he was from other politicians who would
have looked the other way to help a relative. Of course, Blagojevich had his
own unique way of making his point.

"Do you have the testicular virility to make a decision like that, knowing
what's coming your way and then stick to it?" he asked. "I say I do."

———

At the end of the school year in 2005, a press conference was held on the steps
of the Chicago Academy High School in the city's Portage Park neighborhood. The experimental school at 3400 N. Austin Boulevard was run by the
Academy for Urban School Leadership and was a training ground for teachers. Incoming instructors would spend a year there under veteran teachers before going out and spending five years in underperforming schools
around the city. It had a big backer in the neighborhood's congressman.

"We're talking about a program that was on the cover of the US Department of Education's newsletter recently as one of the most innovative teacher training programs in the country," said Rahm Emanuel, who attended the press conference to announce a $2 million state grant that would turn a large parking lot at the school into athletic fields. "I'm a smitten convert."

Arne Duncan was there, too, the Chicago schools CEO who would go on to be US education secretary under President Obama. Emanuel had made getting the state grant into a pet project and had successfully gotten it from Blagojevich. Or at least it seemed like Emanuel had gotten the money.

Work on the athletic fields started just after school got out the following spring. An engineer was hired, plans were finalized, environmental work was done, and the concrete was broken up. In short, bills were coming in, but the promised grant funds weren't materializing.

Emanuel was livid and contacted Tusk, the deputy governor, to see what the holdup was. When Tusk spoke to Blagojevich about it, the governor said something so outrageous that even Tusk—who had been listening to Blagojevich's craziness for two years—was taken aback. Blagojevich said he was holding up the grant until Emanuel's brother, Hollywood movie agent Ari, held him a fund-raiser.

Tusk felt what Blagojevich was suggesting was illegal. He hung up the phone and made two calls—to Wyma and to Bill Quinlan, the state's general counsel. If Blagojevich persisted with his plan, Tusk thought the governor might turn to Wyma for his help. So Tusk called his friend to make sure Wyma knew what just happened and didn't do anything to help Blagojevich. As for the call to Quinlan, Tusk wanted to report what happened; he knew Quinlan was good at talking to Blagojevich. "You need to get your client under control," Tusk told him.

———

Tusk never told Emanuel about Blagojevich's scheme even as Emanuel was joining the legions of politicians beginning to distrust Blagojevich. The two were still working together to thumb their noses at President Bush over the issue of importing prescription drugs into the United States.

Blagojevich was happily using his bully pulpit to grab national headlines promoting health-care issues. One was a state-initiated website that allowed consumers to buy medicine from Canada and other foreign nations. The other was his decision to buy $2.6 million of flu vaccines from overseas in the middle of a national flu vaccine scare. Both had dubious success. Few people used the online service, and the Bush administration never allowed the flu vaccines to enter the country, forcing Blagojevich to donate the medicine to earthquake-ravaged Pakistan. But even there it didn't help anybody as Pakistani health officials burned the half-million doses because they had expired.

The governor then launched All Kids, a showpiece health-care program that made state-subsidized health insurance available to all Illinois children. Blagojevich promoted the program for months and felt that it alone could win him reelection. But he didn't stop with the attention-getters. He introduced legislation to ban the sale of violent video games to minors, even though both he and Tusk realized it was likely to get knocked down by the courts as being unconstitutional. Still, it pushed the conversation.

But soon enough the conversation was back to the tidal wave of scandal washing over the governor, with either him, Kelly, or Rezko always seemingly drowning in it.

News broke about a California firm, owned by Rezko friend Jay Wilton, delivering a $50,000 personal check to Blagojevich's campaign fund. The money had come in not long after the governor announced plans to allow Wilton's company to redevelop state tollway rest stops. The firm, Wilton Partners, then picked men with close ties to Rezko, including one named Al Chaib, to run two of the fast-food businesses that were planned for the redone "oases" on the tollway system.

Stuart Levine was also indicted on sweeping fraud charges, and federal subpoenas were issued to numerous people with ties to the administration, including Rezko. A few weeks later, Blagojevich was forced to acknowledge Rezko and Patti had been working together on real estate deals for eight years, a disclosure that began to increase scrutiny and ultimately hurt Patti's real estate business, River Realty.

———

A few months earlier, in the fall of 2004, federal investigators had not been actively and specifically targeting Rod Blagojevich himself, though their probe into Stuart Levine's various schemes was branching through the governor's administration and many agents had a sense of where things might lead.

The Levine investigation had started as a look at the possibility there was a rogue cell of corruption inside the administration. It was clear to investigators that Levine had help in high places from men like Rezko in the governor's inner ring of advisers, as well as from government insiders such as Cellini. But at first, they discovered precious little to implicate Blagojevich. The tape of Cellini mentioning "the big guy" was tantalizing but still provided no absolute evidence that the big guy was Blagojevich, or at least nothing that could be taken to a jury.

Investigators continued to work and follow what they had. They sifted through reports of fund-raising irregularities and hiring abuses. Word had circulated throughout the state's political channels about what kind of powerbrokers Rezko and Kelly were, and much of the talk had filtered to those trying to peel back the layers of Blagojevich's fund-raising organization.

Clues included Cellini also being taped talking to Levine about a roadbuilder he had vouched for to Kelly and who promised to do a fund-raiser for Blagojevich. The business got a state contract but later backed out because of all of the chatter in the industry about getting state work in exchange for making contributions. Things were getting too open. Cellini had told Levine that law enforcement was sure to start sniffing around, and he had gone as far as telling Kelly to think about a cover story. If Kelly were ever asked about Cellini, he couldn't say he didn't know him if the feds had hundreds of calls between them show up in phone records.

Cellini and Levine talked about how Rezko and Kelly were doing things much more blatantly than the two of them had under prior Republican administrations.

"We would not call somebody after they got something or before they were gonna get something," Cellini said. "As the general rule they do. That will set up a pattern that could be used and then all [the feds] gotta do is ask some of these people and these guys will cave in like a herd of turtles."

But for all the reliance on taping and technology during the Levine probe and in the final acts of the probe years later, the early stage was more like a standard criminal investigation relying on the compiling of information and turning suspects into cooperators and cooperators into good witnesses. Investigators searched for intelligence and information, going as far as looking into unsubstantiated rumors of Blagojevich mistresses.

One of those turned by Niewoehner and those working with him was Levine. He was flatly informed even by his own attorneys that there was virtually nothing to do to blunt the evidence against him, and he was easily facing spending the rest of his life in prison. He admitted what the government accused him of. The tapes compiled by investigators were nearly impossible to get around. He would tell them how he had the blessing of Blagojevich cronies to make illegal money at TRS and the health facilities board and that he believed Rezko and Kelly were doing things with the governor's knowledge and approval. After an early hiccup in his cooperation when he lied about schemes with Vrdolyak, Levine sat for more than three dozen sessions with investigators, spilling his secrets.

But just as pivotal was the cooperation of Joseph Cari.

In late 2004, Cari was only offering the feds documents showing his attempts to secure a consulting fee from JER. He was hopeful that he could ride out whatever storm was gathering around him. But he was wrong. The documents alone would not appease investigators.

During long criminal investigations, different people respond differently depending on who is doing the questioning, and so it was with the onetime national Democratic fund-raiser. Cari was much more willing to bend when faced with a delivery of the facts by the formidable Reid Schar. The Standford-educated Schar already had made a name for himself in the office of US Attorney Patrick Fitzgerald when he was brought in to be the "bad cop" of sorts to question Cari. He was the lead investigator in the case against Muhammad Salah, a Palestinian American accused of funding overseas terrorism.

Schar oozed the kind of harsh, no-nonsense intelligence and energy that put real fear into potential defendants. He was tall and had a shaved head and features that reminded some of a walking, talking federal eagle—and one that was more arrows than olive branch. To him, the US attorney's office was "the family," and a perceived crossing of it brought righteous anger. Some lawyers in the case would derisively refer to Schar as "Chicago's one-man morality police" behind his back, but he was highly focused and seemingly always on task. And the evidence was on Schar's side.

The people Cari had threatened at JER were real victims, and he was the one who had tried to extort them. Schar quickly communicated that Cari was not going to get a free pass. There was no yelling, but Cari was told in no uncertain terms that he was going to be charged. There would be a real prosecution and real prison time if he chose to try his luck. He could help the government and the government would help him, or he could spin the wheel and wind up at a defense table with Levine and Rezko. In other words, you can either be on the train or under it.

And in early 2005, Cari gladly took his ticket.

He flipped, and he was to be the one to provide prosecutors with the first real evidence that Blagojevich could be going above and beyond what was allowable in the fund-raising arena. Cari described being on a flight with the governor in 2003, on Levine's private plane, no less. Chris Kelly was there, too. Cari had gotten the message that he could have just about anything he wanted if he were to dive in and help Blagojevich set up a national fund-raising apparatus for a presidential run. The governor was interested in raising a lot of money and didn't seem to have many scruples about how that happened. Bill Clinton, who had been governor of Arkansas, was a model for Blagojevich, who noted it was much easier for a sitting governor to raise the giant piles of cash necessary to run for the White House because he could give out contracts and all kinds of state business to help bring it in.

It was a watershed moment for investigators, who now had a firsthand account of Blagojevich talking about using the powers of his office to bring in campaign dollars. Their suspicions about Blagojevich were confirmed, and prosecutors and the FBI dug in for a long probe of how it might be happening.

———

By fall 2005, Joseph Cari was dropping a bombshell in court that for the first time publicly brought the investigation of corruption right into the governor's office and campaign. Pleading guilty to the extortion scheme at TRS, Cari acknowledged that state pension business was steered by two associates to favored companies in exchange for campaign contributions to a high-ranking public official described in court documents only as "Public Official A."

Several news outlets quickly identified the two associates as Rezko and Kelly and "Public Official A" as Blagojevich. The following day, Blagojevich held a press conference at the Southeast Asian Center on North Broadway in Chicago to discuss state programs to help needy seniors heat their homes during the upcoming winter. But the heat was entirely on the governor, as dozens of reporters and television news crews jammed inside a small former restaurant to ask Blagojevich if he was "Public Official A."

"Thank you for caring about the poor who need help," Blagojevich deadpanned before reporters launched into thirty minutes of questions. "I don't know who A, B, C, or Z is," he continued. "I have on my side the most powerful ally that exists and that is the truth . . . and the truth is that we do things legally. We do things ethically. And we do things right."

At one point during the flurry of questions, an elderly immigrant woman attending the event scolded the media for not asking questions about senior heating. With a smile on his face, Blagojevich placed the woman between himself and the reporters. "That's right," he said.

Blagojevich may have thought he dodged a bullet. But a month later the *Tribune* disclosed that a federal grand jury had launched an investigation into Blagojevich's hiring practices, specifically Joe Cini's shop.

Even Blagojevich's friends were getting in trouble. The feds were subpoenaing records tied to David Wilhelm's venture capital firm, Hopewell Ventures, which had teacher fund business. Dan Stefanski earlier in the year was arrested for drunk driving, which looked bad since he had a six-figure salary working for the Department of Transportation. And Bamani Obadele was forced to resign from his job with the Department of Children and Family Services after an internal investigation discovered he had steered tens of thousands of dollars in state cash to companies he had a stake in.

———

Scandal was now coming from seemingly every direction, and some of Blagojevich's backers were worried it would hurt his ability to raise money.

Kelly was also acting paranoid, refusing to talk to fund-raisers on the phone and demanding they talk to him only in his car. Sometimes, while they talked, he even demanded they remove the batteries from their Blackberries so he was sure he wasn't being recorded.

During one fund-raising meeting in 2005 at the Friends of Blagojevich campaign headquarters, Blagojevich met with more than a half-dozen advisers, including Kelly. At one point during the meeting, Pete Giangreco suggested the governor stop accepting campaign contributions from state contractors. It would help Blagojevich stem the tide of negative stories about scandal and help retell the story that won him the first election—that he was a reformer.

But Kelly would hear none of it. He stood up, clearly angry, his face beet red.

"We've built a money-making machine in there!" he screamed at them, pointing to the pair of windowless rooms containing computers jammed with data of state contractors and contributors. He wasn't going to just give that up for one positive story in the press. Blagojevich sat silently, and the idea was dropped.

Federal authorities were still pushing hard as well.

In March 2005, agents finally got access to Blagojevich, whose lawyers allowed him to meet with investigators and answer some basic questions. Investigators, including Cain, met with the governor at the offices of his high-powered legal team from the Chicago firm Winston & Strawn, sitting across from him at a conference table. The agents were prepared to record the gathering, but the lawyers told them that wouldn't be happening. Not much was expected from the interview, but investigators hoped to lock in some statements the state's chief executive might make on how money was raised inside his administration.

It was the day before St. Patrick's Day, and supervisory agent Patrick Murphy was doing most of the questioning. Murphy, like Cain, worked out of the FBI's satellite office in west suburban Lisle, which had begun leading the probe because the first complaint had come from Edward Hospital CEO Pam Davis in nearby Naperville.

Blagojevich's chief lawyer, Brad Lerman, had prepped the governor, but Blagojevich also had occasionally sought the advice of Sheldon Sorosky, his old friend who had given him one of his first law jobs. Sorosky would hang around Winston meetings and basically help translate Blagojevich for the firm's attorneys, but he wasn't there when Blagojevich met with the FBI.

Murphy wanted to know whether it could be true that illegal pledges were being made by Blagojevich's office. Did it take a sizable campaign donation to do business with Illinois under him?

As he had done many times before when answering similar questions put to him by reporters, Blagojevich told the FBI that was simply not the case. He stayed a million miles away from the handing out of contracts. He didn't keep track of who was giving him money and didn't know how much he might be getting from each individual donor, Blagojevich told Murphy and Cain. The way he described it, there was a "firewall" between fund-raising and governing. And under him, Blagojevich said, the two did not mix.

There were times when information might splash up on him, Blagojevich said, such as when he went to a fund-raiser and noticed someone there who was more than likely going to be giving money to the campaign. Sometimes campaign staff would tell him how an event was going, he said, but wouldn't give him details. When he was running for office that kind of stuff was important to him, but not when he had the business of the state to attend to as its leader. Politics was politics, and when it came to campaign cash, Blagojevich told the agents he simply didn't want to know.

———

Word of the FBI interview wouldn't become public for some time, and, despite the swirling probe, Blagojevich's fund-raising momentum continued unbroken as he racked up millions of dollars for his 2006 reelection bid. By the time January 1, 2006 arrived, Blagojevich had $15.5 million in the bank.

It was enough to scare off the few Democrats who whispered about running against him. The only one who did was Edwin Eisendrath, a former Chicago alderman from Lincoln Park. In 1990, Eisendrath was an up-and-comer who had moved too fast when he took on US Representative Sidney Yates for Congress and got thumped. He eventually left city government to work for the Clinton administration's Department of Housing and Urban Affairs and hadn't really been heard from since. But Eisendrath was deciding to run because he was sick of the scandals. He was massively underfunded and being ignored by Blagojevich, who refused to debate him, but he didn't seem to care.

In March, just days before the primary, Dick Mell invited Eisendrath to attend his bingo fund-raiser at Gordon Tech. It was an obvious tweak to Blagojevich even though Mell wasn't endorsing Eisendrath over his son-in-law. It didn't matter, of course. Blagojevich won with 70 percent of vote.

With the primary in his rearview, Blagojevich was facing Judy Baar Topinka in the fall. The state treasurer and Illinois's only Republican statewide officeholder, Topinka had excelled in Illinois politics because voters thought of her as a solid financial steward of their dollars who talked straight just like Aunt Judy who lived across the alley. Unfortunately for her, as voters got to know her better many began to think of her more as Crazy Aunt Judy.

At sixty-two years old, she had flaming orange hair and wore dark makeup around her eyes and clothes from thrift stores. She tripped up several times on the campaign trail, giving flippant answers to serious questions and making fart jokes. Even when she tried to criticize Blagojevich she ended up insulting millions of voters by comparing him to the Chicago Cubs, saying, "They're a bunch of losers too."

That was really all Blagojevich and his millions of dollars needed. One of her quirky responses in a discussion about gun control found its way into a Blagojevich television commercial when she said "a rolling pin" could be considered an assault weapon. Another time she compared the state's minimum wage to a government "giveaway" program. Blagojevich's DC strategist Bill Knapp took the sound bites and placed them in short, light-hearted, but still negative fifteen-second television ads that repeated Topinka's words and asked a simple question: "What's she thinking?" Blagojevich ran the rolling pin commercial five hundred times in two months in the Chicago area.

At the same time, Topinka couldn't respond in kind because she couldn't raise the kind of money Blagojevich had.

Between January and July, Blagojevich raised $6.5 million and spent nearly $10 million, much of it on those commercials. It still left him with $12.2 million to spend between the summer and November. During the same time, Topinka raised $3.1 million but spent almost all of it, leaving her with only $1.5 million in the bank for the final months of the campaign.

Blagojevich had brought back much of his winning team from 2002. Monk left his post as the governor's chief of staff to be campaign manager again. He was replaced by John Harris, who was recommended by Kelly and came over from Mayor Daley's administration. Scofield, who since leaving had done public relations for nonprofits and the pro-Blagojevich labor group, Service Employees International Union, also returned. He helped train the campaign's new spokeswoman, Sheila Nix, who had worked for Hull's failed 2004 Senate bid. Wyma was always a phone call away. Tusk and Blagojevich's newest general counsel, William Quinlan, never officially joined the campaign but assisted whenever they could.

And Blagojevich still had his political charm, gracefully manipulating crowds wherever he went, even children. When speaking to parents and youngsters about his All Kids program, he tried to connect with white audiences by asking if the kids watched *Hannah Montana*. When it was a group of mostly African American children, he asked if they watched *That's So Raven*.

While keeping his offices on Ravenswood intact, Blagojevich opened up a campaign headquarters above a bank in an old building at Milwaukee and Division, just around the corner from where he bought that black leather jacket and white T-shirts he wore in college.

But the 2006 campaign lacked the energy of his first run. Blagojevich went through the motions but essentially counted on his massive campaign fund and sharp television commercials to carry him through. In the last six months of the year, Blagojevich spent $16.4 million; Topinka spent $6.2 million.

======

The one arrow Topinka had in her quiver, though, was what Blagojevich himself gave her: his scandals.

In May, the hiring investigation that had been highlighted the previous year made its way back to the front pages when a list of people recommended for state jobs—and their political sponsors—was leaked.

Both Chicago newspapers began digging into the quickly growing story. The *Tribune*'s Ray Long disclosed a 2004 report by Blagojevich's inspector general, Zaldwaynaka Scott, that stated Blagojevich's office tried to circumvent hiring laws in myriad ways. She said they falsified hiring records, found work-arounds to ensure veterans didn't get priority, hired unqualified employees, and faked some workers' experience. She said the administration's strategy "reflects not merely an ignorance of the law but complete and utter contempt for the law."

Curry and Pearman from Jim Ryan's campaign were working behind the scenes too, pushing tips to reporters and even feeding information they found hinky to the feds. Curry would end up speaking to FBI agents twice.

The next month Attorney General Lisa Madigan made public more details about the federal investigation into hiring. Madigan's office was stepping back on its own probe into the matter to allow federal prosecutors to take the lead. To prove her point, she released a letter from US Attorney Fitzgerald that said the feds were probing "allegations of endemic hiring fraud" and that they had "developed a number of credible witnesses."

Little of it, though, had much impact. Legally, Blagojevich didn't think anybody could make a connection to him, and politically, the stories were difficult for voters to get their heads around, which was reflected in Blagojevich's internal polling.

But just two months before the election, the questions about hiring came into quick focus when the *Tribune* wrote a story about the Beverly Ascaridis job and the $1,500 birthday check. Having been bothered by the check, Beverly Ascaridis told the FBI of her suspicions she received her job because of it. The story quickly gained traction because it was so easy to understand and highly questionable. Who gives a young girl a $1,500 check for her seventh birthday?

Privately, Blagojevich was stunned by the story and worried it could hurt him. He stopped talking to Lou Nova, especially after he read quotes from his wife in the *Tribune* in which she said she hated Blagojevich with every fiber of her being. After the story broke, Blagojevich attended an event at a downtown Chicago hotel and faced reporters, defending his decision to accept the check and then muddying up his original story that the money was for Amy. He said he also thought it could have been a christening gift for Annie.

Staffers for Topinka's campaign following the governor around with small video cameras caught the melee with the usually smooth-talking governor totally stymied and stammering. That was one little commercial Topinka could run against Blagojevich.

"It totally sent him over the edge. You couldn't even talk to him about it to try to get the story from him," one former campaign staffer recalled. "Lou was like a brother to him. He was actually closer to Lou than he was to his own brother, and this whole thing ruined that."

As Election Day neared, Patti's business continued to take heat amid revelations by the *Tribune*'s David Kidwell that she had made $113,000 in real-estate commissions from a woman whose company had no-bid state contracts and whose banker husband was a major Blagojevich contributor. The story of Amrish and Anita Mahajan was the second time Patti's business came under scrutiny, unfurling a portrait of the First Lady as being more than an innocent bystander in the growing scandals.

But the escalating background noise of possible corruption reached a crescendo in October, less than a month before Election Day, when Fitzgerald charged Rezko as part of the Levine case, laying out in the most detail to date Rezko's involvement with the Blagojevich administration and Levine. Fitzgerald said Rezko used his influence with the administration to seek millions in kickbacks for himself and business partners and campaign donations.

The ten-page announcement from the US attorney's office in Chicago highlighted the corruption at the Teachers' Retirement System. It described Rezko as a businessman who "was involved in political fund-raising in Illinois" and said he was added as a defendant in "a pending federal corruption case." But still nowhere in the document was the name Blagojevich.

The pending case was Operation Board Games, so named for the shenanigans at the state boards that Levine had spearheaded. The probe was orbiting the governor and was officially shifting to target what he knew about the corruption of some in his administration. Levine's cooperation was by then public, and federal investigators' efforts to use him to record politicians —including Vrdolyak—were at an end. Levine would admit guilt within weeks of the Rezko indictment. And in his plea agreement came a clear signal that investigators knew that both Rezko and Kelly were part of an effort to turn their influence in the administration into cash payouts. Rezko was listed in the document by name and Kelly as "Individual B." It was not welcome news for Blagojevich, who had to field and spin the developments while in the midst of a campaign for reelection.

But there would be other worries for the governor as well. Throughout the same period, federal investigators would come to learn, money seemed to be moving in arcs from people and businesses associated with Rezko toward the Blagojeviches. Rezko money started moving right around the time Kjellander got his cut from the giant Bear Stearns deal with the state.

Some in Rezmar—Rezko's development company—would tell the feds that they were asked to add dummy commissions to contracts in order for Patti Blagojevich to be paid for work she didn't do. In one deal in 2004, Rezmar took in a $40,000 commission, and that same amount was paid to Patti Blagojevich's company, River Realty, the very next day. The $40,000 was then paid to Patti herself from River Realty another day later. Federal prosecutors would allege that such Rezko arrangements were where the rubber met the road—clear examples of pay-to-play funds winding up in the pockets of the state's first couple.

Schar, Niewoehner, fellow Assistant US Attorney Carrie Hamilton, FBI case agents, and investigators from the IRS Criminal Investigations Division and US Postal Inspection Service worked for months to chase leads in the case and round up all the witnesses necessary to bring Rezko to trial. There was a long series of complicated financial schemes to unravel, and the team worked long hours to gather statements from those who could corroborate Levine's story. Insiders such as Beck and other members of the hospital board were turned into witnesses, and the investigators pooled accounts of hiring and fund-raising going through Rezko's office. The case against him would feature recordings corroborated by authoritative testimony by key players in the plans, a structure many prosecutors considered the bread and butter of the US attorney's office under Patrick Fitzgerald.

It was a stunning blow, but Blagojevich was relieved the indictment didn't mention him by name. Inside the campaign headquarters at Milwaukee and Division, it was all hands on deck—except for Blagojevich himself, who was still at home. Monk, Scofield, and others were even joined by former governor Thompson, who was still with Winston & Strawn and sat in well-worn campaign furniture reading the indictment, talking with advisers, and looking for spots of weakness in the prosecution case.

That evening, Blagojevich finally arrived at the campaign offices to publicly address the charges. While acknowledging Rezko was a supporter and a friend, Blagojevich attempted to minimize Rezko's vast influence with the governor personally and the administration as a whole.

"If, in fact, these allegations relating to Tony are true, he betrayed my trust," Blagojevich said. "He lied to me. He deceived me. But a lot more important than that, he violated the public trust."

Topinka tried to seize on the developments, but her accusations ended up flat. Following Rezko's indictment, she overplayed her hand when she built up expectations that Stuart Levine's guilty plea would likely carry even more bombshells. When the plea agreement was made public, it was filled with tons of juicy details about Levine's illegal schemes but nothing close to a stake through Blagojevich's political heart.

That night, Blagojevich attended the Thirty-Sixth Ward Regular Democratic Organization's annual fund raiser in Rosemont. John Wyma stood by his side most of the night. Packed inside a convention center ballroom, Blagojevich was as cocky as he had been all campaign. Glad-handing with some of the old-timers who originally backed Blagojevich because of his father-in-law, they were still there for him even though Mell was gone. And Illinois voters were going to reelect him without his father-in-law's help.

"They got nothing—nothing!" he howled.

———

Four years earlier, the Democrats with Rod Blagojevich as their ostensible leader arrived in Springfield acting as conquering heroes, controlling both the House and Senate and all but one of the statewide offices. In 2007, they controlled everything, with Topinka's treasurer's office now in the hands of a young Democrat named Alexi Giannoulias. Yet as the crowds gathered on a bright and chilly January morning, a pall hung over the Prairie Capital Convention Center in downtown Springfield. It was in no small part because of that ostensible leader and his baggage.

At Blagojevich's first inaugural the convention center was filled to the banisters. His second inauguration was nearly half-empty. Blagojevich had almost amassed 50 percent of the vote to Topinka's 39 percent, but it was no mandate. Perhaps the biggest sign of voters' discontent was that 10 percent voted for enigmatic Green Party candidate Rich Whitney.

Even Blagojevich seemed uninspired. By then, Monk had left to become a lobbyist. Tusk headed back to New York City for a job with Lehman Brothers. For deputy governor, Blagojevich got two people to take his place: Nix and Louanner Peters, a longtime aide who had come back to Chicago after running into problems in Washington, DC, using government credit cards on personal expenses while working for Mayor Marion Barry. With Rezko under indictment, Petrovic was keeping his distance. Even Kelly wasn't hanging around as much anymore.

The governor tried to build momentum and take attention away from his scandals by proposing a universal health-care bill. While Blagojevich hewed to his promise not to raise taxes on "the working class," he said he would pay for it with a $7 billion tax on "gross receipts." Blagojevich argued the tax would hit businesses, not consumers. But businesses and many Democrats recognized that the businesses would likely just pass the tax burden onto consumers.

None of it worked.

======

The feds stayed focused, and on a personal level, their work was starting to damage the Blagojevich family's finances. Publicly, River Realty came under greater scrutiny. It was discovered that Patti received at least $30,000 in commissions from John Wyma's purchase of a $650,000 Chicago condominium. The funny thing about the arrangement was that Patti Blagojevich didn't find the condo for Wyma. He had found it himself because he purchased it from one of his clients who owned an architectural, engineering, and construction firm that later won $10 million in state contracts.

A month later, it became clear that federal authorities were looking at River Realty as part of their investigation into Blagojevich and his personal finances. The feds had already subpoenaed Blagojevich's campaign records.

All the controversy over Patti Blagojevich's real-estate business was truly now taking its toll. Her business was drying up, and it was having an impact on the Blagojeviches' income. Blagojevich lashed out at those asking questions, calling their inquiries "Neanderthal" and sexist.

By the end of 2007, the noose closed even tighter.

Just as the Levine tapes and witnesses had made it clear who Rezko was in the Blagojevich administration and what he was doing, the same harsh spotlight was shining on Chris Kelly. Investigators had spent much of 2007 looking at questionable practices in Kelly's businesses and issues in his personal life. And there was plenty to find. Kelly was indicted in December 2007 on tax fraud charges, with federal prosecutors alleging he had understated his income by $1.3 million, sometimes using corporate funds to cover gambling debts. Kelly had wagered millions with a bookmaker and used funds from his roofing company to help pay losses, debts that Rezko also sometimes helped him with. It was just the first volley in what would become a series of federal shots against the intense and troubled Kelly, who had remained one of the governor's most trusted confidants.

In late 2007, just prior to being charged, Kelly spoke with federal prosecutors. They wanted to tell him he was in hot water and that he should assume that things were going to get worse for him and not better. He could still help himself, but it would mean cooperating. True to form, Kelly said very little, choosing to keep his tough exterior intact. Instead of telling the assistant US attorneys he would do what they wanted, he just stared them down.

On top of the breaking scandals involving those closest to him, Blagojevich's political agenda was going nowhere. With no friends other than Emil Jones in the legislature, Blagojevich's universal health-care plan flopped, with the House voting 107–0 against it. Blagojevich didn't know how to handle the massively embarrassing loss so he gave an answer that made sense to absolutely nobody. "Today, I think, was basically an up," he said. "I feel good about it."

Another series of budget battles broke out, but Blagojevich, acting more erratic by the day, wasn't going to defeat Madigan this time with his crazy games. Instead, Madigan outfoxed him, getting lawmakers to approve a budget over his opposition. They argued he hadn't negotiated in good faith— not a difficult argument to make. Blagojevich vetoed some of the spending, especially the money Madigan and House Democrats wanted. He also sued Madigan for convening a special session of the House a few hours earlier than Blagojevich wanted him to. Blagojevich then antagonized lawmakers again by calling his own special sessions. But this time they just ignored him and refused to show up. The only thing he got passed was a massively expensive plan that gave seniors free rides on public transportation regardless of their income level. It ended up costing the transit agencies tens of millions of dollars.

Springfield was burning. And instead of fiddling, Blagojevich was fundraising and hanging out at his house. He was showing up at work maybe two to eight hours a week. When he did show, he sometimes hid in the bathroom to avoid meetings or making tough decisions. With Obama running for president, living Blagojevich's own dream, he was depressed. One bright spot he had was the Cubs, who were on their way to the playoffs both in 2007 and 2008.

Since becoming governor, Blagojevich had indulged his boyhood fantasy of being a baseball player by doing the next-best thing: hanging out with the players, coaches, and manager of his favorite team. He befriended Dusty Baker, who was managing the team when Blagojevich was first elected, and attended players' charity events. One night, at such an event, Blagojevich introduced himself to Dave Kaplan, the host of a popular sports program on the Cubs radio station, WGN. Kaplan quickly realized Blagojevich knew something about baseball and invited the governor to cohost a radio show with him and his partner at the time, Tom Waddle, a former Chicago Bears wide receiver. "Absolutely! I'd love it," Blagojevich responded. Kaplan suggested he could sit in for thirty minutes of the two-hour show. "Oh no. I want to do the whole two hours!"

A Blagojevich scheduler soon settled on a date but on the afternoon of the show called Kaplan with disappointing news. The governor was going to have to cancel. Something important had come up. Kaplan said that was too bad because he had arranged for Dusty Baker to call in. Thirty seconds later, the scheduler called back: "He's in. The full two hours."

Baker was replaced by Lou Piniella, whom Blagojevich also got to know. Blagojevich and Baker kept in touch. The governor also became friendly with Cubs General Manager Jim Hendry, going so far as to dedicate a street in his hometown in his honor. As the state melted down but the Cubs won, Blagojevich watched dozens of games at Wrigley Field or at home. After tough losses, he would call Kaplan and others to talk Cubs baseball. "Why did Lou bring in Remlinger there?" he said once, complaining about a pitching change. During much of 2008, Blagojevich constantly harassed his communications director, Lucio Guerrero, to get him on ESPN's national radio morning show, *Mike & Mike*, to talk about the Cubs.

Even when games weren't being played, Blagojevich was hanging out at Wrigley. Having suffered a leg injury while running, he routinely showed up at the ballpark in the morning and asked Cubs trainers to work on him and help him heal. They obliged.

The players would joke to broadcasters who covered the games, "The governor was here again today."

12

Stuart the Bizarre

A long line of people ran down a hallway on the twelfth floor of the Dirksen US Courthouse on March 6, 2008, waiting to see if they could get a seat in the courtroom where Tony Rezko's trial would be held.

Many were surprised the trial was happening at all. Most thought Rezko was too smart to ever be caught in a federal net, and others had figured the last thing he would do was stick around for a trial. When prosecutors had been ready to have a grand jury indict him, Rezko was on a long trip to the Middle East, and his return date was uncertain. They finally unsealed the papers against him while he was still overseas, hoping it would coax him to return to face the charges. Fears that he had engineered an escape from his legal troubles by burying cash in the sand in Syria were soon proven to be unfounded, however, as Rezko returned to the United States and his plane was met by FBI agents at O'Hare International Airport.

Rezko posted bond, but investigators remained unsure of his true intentions. They watched his finances closely and eventually moved to have him taken into custody again just weeks before his trial was to begin. They found that he had brought into the country $3.5 million from Iraqi-born billionaire Nadhmi Auchi, who had business links to Rezko, and believed he had concealed it. That was enough for Schar, Niewoehner, and Hamilton, who would take the Rezko case into court. The last thing prosecutors wanted to do was prepare for a lengthy corruption trial striking at the heart of the Blagojevich administration, only to have Rezko skip out on them just as he was to sit in front of a jury. Rezko was held in solitary confinement at Chicago's Metropolitan Correctional Center downtown, a highrise federal jail in the Loop. Those who ran the facility said it was for Rezko's own security, while some around him wondered if it wasn't a final attempt to crack the stubborn Rezko and get him to tell authorities what he knew about Blagojevich.

Whether that was or wasn't the intent, it didn't work, and Chicago was soon braced for its biggest public corruption trial since George Ryan had been convicted two years earlier.

Right away, prosecutors sought to put an approachable face on their case and turn the head-spinning detail of investment contracts into something that made sense to normal people. They chose Hamilton, who had come up through the office handling child exploitation cases, to give the opening statement and remind the jury what part of the case was really all about. Every day, thousands of public school teachers go to work instructing the children of Illinois. And while they're concentrating on their jobs, other people were supposed to take care of their retirement money by trying to find safe places to invest it and help it grow. Likewise, there's a state panel that is supposed to make decisions about where health facilities should go in Illinois, looking at how to make sure patients get the best care. They are supposed to think about where it's appropriate to have a hospital or clinic and how big it should be. They, too, should not be basing decisions on whether they or someone allied with them should be able to make money off a project to build a health facility. Both systems are based on a foundation of public trust, Hamilton went on, her voice sharp with indignation. It wasn't supposed to be about whose pockets got lined.

Tony Rezko had worked with an insider to corrupt both of those organizations. So instead of decisions with the right aims, decisions at TRS and the Illinois Health Facilities Planning Board had been made with the best interests of Rezko and his insider in mind. Rezko was one of Blagojevich's top fund-raisers, she explained to the jury, dropping the name of the governor early and often, and after he was elected, Rezko was given access to the very highest levels of power in the administration. When it came time to fill hundreds of vacancies on boards and commissions after the election, Rezko was one of the trusted few who was in meetings putting forward names of those he believed should be appointed. Rezko would give a name, Hamilton said, and "more often than not" that person found themselves on a state board. Hamilton showed the jury a diagram of the hospital planning board, with the five members of Rezko's voting bloc able to carry any vote on any proposal that came before the panel. And she explained how the group was able to push the plan for Mercy through, even as stunned onlookers watched the insider, Stuart Levine, whispering into the ears of other members of the panel to swing the vote. That plan had been approved just because Levine and Rezko had agreed to split a bribe.

"Rezko was the man behind the curtain, pulling the strings," Hamilton said. "Stuart Levine was out in front."

Hearing the allegations spelled out in such clear detail for the first time did little to rattle Rezko. He sat at the defense table with his chin resting in his hand, looking as calm as someone waiting for the second act of a boring play.

Rezko's lawyer was one of Chicago's most affable, Joe Duffy, a gentlemanly attorney with friends all over the Dirksen US Courthouse. A former IRS agent and federal prosecutor, Duffy had broad experience and the kind of personality that would make anyone want to share a beer with him. His friendly and witty demeanor did much to hide his considerable legal skill. Juries loved him, and even prosecutors liked him—even while he was quietly figuring out ways to eat their lunch. At the IRS he had worked on the prosecutions of politicians for income tax fraud. And all the while he was attending nighttime law classes, emerging as a hungry young attorney. He landed at the US attorney's office, where he rose to its number-two spot. And in private practice he had done well, defending cases as varied as fraud in Chicago's yen trading pit and the prosecution of a man accused of diverting charity funds to Muslim extremists. In other words, if anyone could figure out a way to get Rezko out of trouble, it might be Duffy.

Right off the bat, he made the case all about Stuart Levine. It was Levine who was out to scam Edward Hospital and Levine who repeatedly sold his clout, both real and imagined. Duffy knew that very little was recorded linking Levine to Rezko, so he tried to interject doubt about just how much a man like Rezko would pay attention to Levine.

Levine was a Republican, and by 2003, when Edward was making its proposal, the Republicans were out of power in Illinois. That left him with only one choice, Duffy said; he had to lie about having a connection to a Blagojevich power broker to convince Edward to go along with him. The hospital's Pam Davis had gone to the FBI, and the shakedown attempt was recorded. Rezko had nothing to do with it.

"It was a lie by Stuart Levine that he had a corrupt relationship with Mr. Rezko," Duffy said. It was Levine who had asked his old friend Vrdolyak to set up a meeting with Rosenberg, even before Rosenberg had his problems getting investment funds from TRS. In fact, Levine had cheated his way through everything he had ever done. Levine had even made a bad buck while handling the estate of Ted Tannenbaum, the second cousin of his mother.

"You'll see Stuart Levine hasn't worked an honest day of labor in the last twenty-five years," Duffy said.

———

The government's first group of witnesses was meant to quickly demonstrate the kind of power Rezko had in the administration and how he got it. Kelly Glynn, a thirty-four-year-old former finance director for the Blagojevich campaign, was called first. She told the jury that Lon Monk was Blagojevich's campaign manager in 2002 and that Rezko was a top "bundler," meaning a fund-raiser who could find other donors and pool their contributions. Glynn had moved on to New York since the 2002 campaign, she said, working in finance for the committee overseeing Democratic senatorial campaigns. But she still recalled the events of that campaign and how money was raised. One event was hosted by Bill Cellini at a Wyndham Hotel in the suburbs, Glynn said, but it hadn't gone on the books as a fund-raiser for the Democrat Blagojevich hosted by the Republican Cellini. Instead, the event for state road builders was listed as being hosted by Rezko, Glynn said. Chris Kelly had told the staffers to list it that way.

She remembered a number of meetings at Rezko's office, where staffers talked about targeting top fund-raisers and meeting money goals. And after the election, Monk helped host a party at Rezko's Wilmette mansion for campaign leaders.

That was all well and good, but no one really doubted that Rezko was an important figure in the Blagojevich administration. What was important was what he had done with his influence. And to prove that Rezko had breached what was allowable, there was really only one witness.

———

Underrated on the long list of shady political characters in Chicago history, Stuart Levine was still largely an enigma when he took the stand at Rezko's trial. He stood stiffly to be sworn in at the front of the courtroom and sat down in the witness chair with a somewhat smug look on his face. Even with everything that was known about him, Levine still carried himself with a slight aloofness and not a hint of shame or introspection.

He told Assistant US Attorney Niewoehner that he was sixty-two, living in Highland Park to the north of Chicago, and that he graduated from the University of Illinois in 1968. After law school at IIT Chicago-Kent, he worked as a lawyer and then as an administrative assistant for Tannenbaum. He said he handled some of Tannenbaum's business interests and banking. And after that, Levine said, he was a consultant and an investor.

Between 2000 and 2004, Niewoehner asked, how much money was he making?

"I would estimate between $9 and $10 million," Levine answered, still without much emotion.

But since he had been charged in Operation Board Games and some of his schemes had been exposed, things hadn't been going as well. He had gotten a job, any job, to say he had one while he was on bond in the case. The former high roller was working for the Chicago Messenger Service, he said.

"I deliver packages," Levine said, telling Niewoehner he was now making only about $800 a week. "Minus expenses."

Levine told the jury he had first been indicted in May 2005 for the attempted extortion of Edward Hospital, the Rosalind Franklin University scams, and siphoning money away from a student charity. Then he was charged several months later and accused of scheming to defraud the Teachers' Retirement System. Levine was doing his best to maintain a dignified air, answering questions on the stand as one would expect a lawyer would, seemingly with a lot of respect for the process and what was unfolding in front of him. Every yes or no response he gave Niewoehner had a "sir" at the end of it, and Levine occasionally gave a slight head bob as he replied.

Niewoehner went over Levine's plea agreement with him, the one that would see him spared from a long prison term, and then immediately moved to get ahead of some of the damaging material that Rezko's defense had promised to attack him with and tell the jury about it first. Levine acknowledged he had committed crimes he had never been charged with and said he had used drugs from 1972 to 2004.

"I experimented with LSD, marijuana, cocaine, Quaaludes, Ecstasy, crystal methamphetamine, ketamine," Levine said flatly. It was definitely like it was no big deal—and to him it probably wasn't. He could have been a doctor or a treatment expert reading the names of the substances off a clipboard.

Between 2000 and 2004, Levine said his drugs of choice were crystal meth and ketamine, known on the street as the designer drug Special K and used commercially as a horse tranquilizer. He said he used them once or twice a month.

Levine had decided to cooperate in January 2006, he told the jury, and had been interviewed by the government "certainly more than one hundred times." He had tried to be truthful, except in one instance regarding Vrdolyak, Levine said, and he often had to go back and listen to recordings or review documents to get his memory straight. Niewoehner had Levine again track through the early stages of his legal career, stopping in 1976 when Levine began sharing office space with Tannenbaum, who had been a founding shareholder of McDonald's of Canada. It was while doing work for Tannenbaum and some of his businesses that Levine had begun bribing public officials.

One of the companies was the Consumer Tire Company, Levine remembered.

"It wanted contracts from the city of Chicago—certain departments, Streets and Sanitation—to supply tires," Levine testified. Another company, called Willett, wanted contracts with the Chicago Board of Education to supply school buses. And then there was Chicago HMO, an insurer that had Dr. Robert Weinstein as its president and COO. That company wanted members of the postal union to sign on as subscribers to its insurance plan, so Levine said he passed a bribe to Vrdolyak to make that happen.

"Was it your understanding Mr. Vrdolyak was going to give that bribe payment to someone else?" Niewoehner said.

"Yes, sir," Levine answered matter-of-factly. And Chicago HMO also paid three lobbyists to try to influence lawmakers on its behalf, he said—Cellini, Kjellander, and Vrdolyak.

Levine had also worked for a dental insurance company owned by Tannenbaum, Dental Care Plus, that Tannenbaum eventually sold. The company became known as CompDent in about 1996, and Levine said he stayed on to maintain its government accounts. The state of Illinois and the Chicago Board of Education both were clients, and Cellini and Kjellander were lobbyists. And on the city side, Levine said he again passed a bribe to Vrdolyak for him to take elsewhere and help secure the contract with the city schools.

The testimony was coming off fine, with a fairly polished and seemingly well-rehearsed Levine rattling off facts for Niewoehner without a problem. But then, just a few minutes into his questioning, came the first hiccup. In normal circumstances it would barely have been noticed. But in Levine's case, his drug-addled memory was going to be an issue. Levine said he stopped working for CompDent several months after he was first indicted—in 2004.

"I think you earlier said you were indicted in 2005. Is that right?" Niewoehner said, keeping Levine on track.

"I'm sorry. Yes, sir," Levine replied, the expression on his face not changing much.

Levine said there had been a number of times when he had violated laws on campaign financing, by contributing money through straw donors.

"It was simply easier for me to give the money myself, through others, than to go out and raise it," Levine said. Other times, Levine said, he would give money through others that would wind up in the coffers of Democrats. Levine, a Republican for the sake of appearances, didn't want his name attached to the funds.

"Did you expect to get anything when you made significant contributions to candidates?" Niewoehner asked in a tone that made it very clear that he and everyone else in the courtroom knew the answer already.

"Yes, sir," Levine said, stopping.

"What did you expect to get?" Niewoehner continued.

"Access," answered Levine, uttering the word that probably singularly embodied what he was really about when it came to the world of Chicago and Illinois government. He believed he was buying the opportunity to worm his way into the political world and get in a position to make even more money for himself.

He had been named to the Illinois Health Facilities Planning Board, the state Gaming Board, and the board of the Teachers' Retirement System. And yes, Levine said, he did know Tony Rezko. The men had met at a dinner party in November 2003, Levine said confidently. And here it went again, as Niewoehner stopped to ask the judge if he could show Levine his own office calendar to refresh his memory about the date.

"I'm very sorry, sir," Levine said. "That was 2002."

Levine told jurors how during the dinner conversation, Massuda had interjected that she had a clinic in the Scholl building and was interested in buying the property herself. Levine recalled that he asked whether she had something to do with holding up the arrangement he was behind.

"Simultaneously, Dr. Massuda said, 'No,' and Mr. Rezko said, 'Yes,'" Levine told the prosecutor. The two then had a short discussion, Levine said, and Rezko turned to tell Levine that if the building had been promised to someone else, Rezko could make the snag go away. Rezko controlled the Scholl board, Levine said he was told, so he asked his dinner companion when he could expect the problem to evaporate.

"Mr. Rezko told me by the following Tuesday morning," Levine recalled, and said that in fact the issue was solved the next week and the deal closed shortly thereafter.

The power play apparently impressed Levine, and he said he sought out Cellini to ask if he knew Rezko. Cellini said he did, "very well," and Levine went on to describe the meeting with Rezko and how Rezko had promised to take the brick off the property sale to the medical school. Levine said he had wanted to know whether Rezko was trustworthy and could be believed when he made a promise.

"Mr. Cellini's response was that he found—had always found—Mr. Rezko to be reliable, a man of his word," Levine said.

Levine had arranged to meet with Rezko again after the Massuda dinner. On his mind was an attempt to get another county contract for CompDent. Kjellander had told Levine again about Rezko's influence, he said, telling him to go to Rezko to get things done in Cook County. So Levine imagined a two-for-one, where he could go to Rezko for help either with county issues or to get a contract with the state under Blagojevich, who had won the election by the time Levine had Kjellander set up another meeting with Rezko for him. Levine said the next sitdown was in Rezko's conference room at Rezko's offices at Elston and Milwaukee on the North Side. Cook County was about to bid out for dental insurance, Levine testified.

"I indicated to Mr. Rezko that any fees that I would make in the event of a successful contract with the county of Cook, that I would share with Mr. Rezko," Levine said. Rezko said he was willing to go forward with the plan, according to Levine, and that he would put Orlando Jones in charge of it. Levine had met Jones at the same dinner party at Dr. Massuda's home, he told the jury, but it didn't matter anyway. CompDent withdrew its contract application after Levine was approached by the FBI.

But in the wake of their Cook County conversation, Levine said he began to try to bring more opportunities for inside dealing to Rezko's attention. One key meeting was the following summer, he said, when he was in Rezko's Chicago office explaining what they could do together at TRS, at least in theory. He said he brought lawyer Steve Loren with him, TRS's outside counsel, to detail how TRS went about choosing investment firms to give funding allocations to. Rezko had an associate named Mike Winter take in what Loren was explaining, Levine recalled, and then walked out of the meeting room they were using and into his own office. Levine said he followed and immediately began to tell Rezko that up until that point, he had not personally made any money off TRS dealings.

Rezko quickly gathered what he was getting at, Levine recalled.

"Mr. Rezko said to me, 'Stuart, anything that I decide to do at TRS, you will be a partner in,'" Levine said, adding that he saw it as a green light from Rezko that they could cooperate on schemes at TRS and elsewhere, such as the Illinois Health Facilities Planning Board, where Levine still was a member.

"I told Mr. Rezko that I was extraordinarily pleased to know him and to have gotten to know him better and that I thought we could do a lot of business together."

And with their relationship having progressed, Levine said he began spending much more time at Rezko's office, talking about ways to make money at TRS and about state politics. Rezko explained how he had been given the power to make key recommendations to have people appointed to state boards and to have others hired to jobs in state agencies. He went over his picks directly with Lon Monk. In fact, Levine said, Rezko told him that "all major decisions that were made in the governor's office" were cleared by him. There were more conversations than he could specifically remember about such things, Levine said, though he did recall Chris Kelly was there for some of them. Rezko told Levine not to worry about Kelly's presence, Levine remembered, saying he was told there were no secrets between Rezko and Kelly. Money that they made was shared, and Levine should know he could speak freely. Both men were a part of Blagojevich's "kitchen cabinet" of advisers and were obviously its most influential members.

Levine said he had been reappointed by Blagojevich to the health facilities planning board in August 2003, after a phone call he had with Cellini. He remembered telling Cellini he had decided he wanted to be reappointed and that he had gotten a response that Levine thought was unusual.

"He said that he would call Mr. Rezko and see if that were possible," Levine said, remembering telling Cellini to pass the message to Rezko that he would cooperate with anything the Blagojevich administration wanted to do on the planning board.

"That meant that if there was an application pending before the Illinois Health Facilities Planning Board that the governor's office wanted to either have approved or not approved, that regardless of the merits, I would do as the governor's office asked," Levine said, remembering that Cellini called him back within days and told him Rezko had said he would see to it that Levine stayed on the board.

The appointment came through as promised, and two months later, Levine said he chartered a flight for himself, Blagojevich, and others to take to New York to attend a fund-raiser there. This was the flight Cari had described for prosecutors, the one that helped send the Blagojevich probe into overdrive and that the media later dubbed the "shakedown shuttle."

The trip had been an in-and-out affair, Levine remembered, and on the flight back with him were just Blagojevich and Kelly. It was then, Levine said, that he took the chance to thank the governor for reappointing him to the hospital planning board.

"The governor said, in response, 'Never discuss any state board with me,'" Levine recalled. "'You discuss them with either Tony Rezko or Chris Kelly. But, you stick with us, and you'll do very well for yourself.'"

———

Levine spoke in detail about each fraudulent deal he helped steer through TRS, beginning with the Glencoe allocation with Sheldon Pekin. Levine had begun meeting with Pekin about the private equity firm in late 2002 and was interested to know that Pekin would be getting the finder's fee if Glencoe was able to get tapped into funds from TRS. Levine wasn't shy about asking to share the fee in exchange for helping Glencoe and arranged for his longtime associate Dr. Robert Weinstein to take in his fee and get some separation between himself and the illegal payment.

He talked to Cellini about it too, Levine said, and Cellini saw the potential deal as a way for him and Levine to ingratiate themselves with Rezko and Kelly, who clearly were the men to negotiate with in connection with the Blagojevich administration when the Glencoe deal was coming together in the spring of 2003. Cellini told Levine that Mell, Blagojevich's father-in-law, had been complaining about wanting to make money after Blagojevich's election, and this might be a way for cash to be directed to him. Rezko was feeling the pressure, Cellini had said, and this would mean good things if they were the ones to help him help Mell. Cellini had conversations with Rezko about it and learned that it was acceptable and that Rezko wanted an actual contract drawn up between Mell and the firm that would look real and specifically mention that Mell wouldn't bring in any money in connection with state business.

Mell—who has always denied being involved in the deal—eventually withdrew, Levine said he was told. He met Rezko at his office and learned Rezko would choose someone else to get the money. Glencoe did receive $50 million in August 2003, but when the amount was split into two allocations of $25 million, Pekin only got to collect $250,000 and not $500,000 as Levine and the others had expected. Levine didn't want to go back and tell Rezko to expect less. So Levine took a hard line.

"I told Mr. Pekin that he had promised to pay a $250,000 fee, and that's what I expected him to pay," Levine recalled, telling the jury that Pekin agreed. It meant Pekin would get nothing in that deal but still had the promise of getting future TRS business with Levine's assistance.

So at Rezko's direction, Levine had a consulting contract drafted between Pekin and Rezko associate Joseph Aramanda. A dummy version read that "X has agreed to retain the services of Y for the purposes of assisting X with identifying institutional investors who may have an interest in making investments in the private equity and other investment funds with whom X maintains a marketing relationship." And while all the language made it seem like someone must be getting paid for doing something official, the entire document was concocted solely to make it look like Aramanda was being paid for something legitimate.

Levine saw dollar signs when he thought about them repeating the TRS model at other boards controlling pension funds. Pekin and Weinstein could start a business with the goal of collecting finder's fees, and Pekin and his son would be responsible for finding the firms that could accept investments. Levine could use Rezko's access to power to help steer those firms toward sure approvals. At the Illinois State Board of Investment in particular, Levine said, Rezko knew he could be helpful, because its board already contained many of his "friends" and its chairman had been helpful to the administration.

Rezko and Levine had their eyes on the State Universities Retirement System (SURS) as well, which handles the retirement benefits of university and college employees. Levine said he spoke to Rezko, who told him of his plan.

"That—ultimately at SURS there would become vacancies, trustees, whose terms would expire, and, at such times, he would have the opportunity to suggest appointments for new trustees," Levine remembered. "And at such time that there was a controlling number of his friends, he might be able to do something at SURS."

It was the prior month when Levine had met Rezko at the Standard Club at an intimate dinner where he had allegedly laid out what kind of money the two could make together at TRS and the Illinois Health Facilities Planning Board. Niewoehner had Levine describe that meeting in detail, as Rezko's attorney, Joe Duffy, objected to no avail.

Levine said he brought notes on several investments he was trying to line up for the TRS board meeting on May 24, and he seemed to have a good recollection of what had happened when he sat down with his political patron. "It was in a private room on the fourth floor that had a table in it that could seat six," Levine testified. "It had a buffet with a telephone on it and the general things that a waiter would need to set up. And the table was set up for two people, with chairs one right next to the other."

Levine said he told the waiter that once dinner had been served, he didn't want to be interrupted. He told Rezko that they had already made a good bit of money on the Glencoe and Mercy Hospital deals and they stood to make a lot more if all of Levine's various plans for the boards came together.

One deal involved a company called Stockwell, and Levine said he told Rezko he would be "very pleased" to see a $1 million finder's fee split three ways, between Weinstein, Rezko, and Pekin. Another was an $80 million allocation for JER, the real estate group that Cari had been dealing with in Virginia. Yet another was for Investors Mortgage Holding, Levine said, a company that lent money to developers and could be in line for as much as $200 million from TRS. That finder's fee could be as high as 2 percent, or $4 million, Levine said he told Rezko.

Capri Capital was supposed to be getting $220 million, although Levine and company would run headlong into the angry Tom Rosenberg before that plan would get airborne.

Levine acknowledged he didn't really need Rezko to do anything to make the deals happen, he just wanted to further ingratiate himself with the fund-raiser and the Blagojevich administration. Rezko said nothing about being concerned about fees coming in the way things were laid out at the meeting, Levine said, and he certainly didn't raise a hand and ask whether it was legal. Levine said he simply finished explaining what he was planning, Rezko agreed, and Levine drove him home.

"And did you keep your notes from that session?" Niewoehner asked.

"No," Levine said. "I ultimately destroyed them."

Levine said he had met Rosenberg in the 1980s, and he, too, had done some lobbying on behalf of CompDent. Rosenberg had been a business partner of Tannenbaum, and Levine said that in exchange for supporting a $100 million TRS allocation for Capri in 2001, Levine had expected Rosenberg to pay him and Weinstein a fee. It was supposed to be $500,000, but instead Rosenberg just told Levine he no longer had to pay him anything to lobby for CompDent, and that was it. Levine took it as Roseberg backpedaling out of a deal, and he had never forgotten it.

So when Capri was lined up for the $220 million allocation in early 2004, Levine and his vendetta against Rosenberg decided to stall the TRS outlay. He told Niewoehner he had thought Vrdolyak, who spoke regularly to both Levine and Rosenberg, could be the conduit for Levine to finally get money out of his nemesis. Shortly before the Capri allocation was up for a vote, Levine said he told Bauman, TRS's executive director, that he knew Capri was actually on the block. Not disclosing a possible management change to TRS staff before getting an allocation was against the rules, so Rosenberg and Capri's investment money were shelved.

Within weeks of the meeting, a very unhappy Rosenberg reached out to Cellini to see if "Big Bill"could be of any help to him. Cellini then told Levine he thought messing with Rosenberg was probably a bad idea and reached out to Bauman to see if the situation could be fixed. But meanwhile, Levine said, he was already moving to tell Rezko and Kelly about Rosenberg and the $220 million, knowing that the pair would think it was a very interesting amount to be going to someone who had done nothing to help the Blagojevich administration, which could certainly think of more "loyal" people and firms to give it to. That spring, Levine told the fund-raisers in a meeting at Rezko's office that Rosenberg was managing $1 billion in real estate for TRS.

Niewoehner asked what Kelly's reaction had been.

"Mr. Kelly's reaction was that . . . this was a company that should be contributing a great deal of money—or an individual who should be contributing a great deal of money—to Governor Blagojevich," Levine answered. So the three decided that Rosenberg should be given a choice before the Capri deal could go ahead. Rosenberg could pay a $2 million finder's fee or raise $1.5 million in campaign funds. Levine was to tell Cellini that was the decision, Levine recalled, and Cellini would then inform Rosenberg about the behind-the-scenes machinations. Rezko believed that developer Allison Davis already had reached out to him on Rosenberg's behalf, though

Rosenberg would later dispute that idea. So Cellini could just tell Rosenberg that a Davis message that Rosenberg was willing to help the governor had been received and that he should call Levine, who would then put the fundraising choice to Rosenberg.

To show the jury what happened next, Niewoehner walked Levine through the series of calls Levine had with Cellini in May 2004, including the one where Cellini described how a furious Rosenberg had said Rezko and Kelly could or should be under investigation for their fund-raising. In a second call, after Cellini had again heard from Rosenberg, Cellini said Rosenberg had told him he had found out that Davis had mentioned his name to Rezko as someone who could be asked to contribute to the campaign. Rosenberg had again flown off the handle and said he would never, ever go to Rezko or Kelly and that he would take the extortion attempt public if pressed.

The plan had started to come apart after word spread among the men that Rosenberg probably meant business with his threat, and Kelly in particular had gotten involved, at one point calling Levine and Cellini simultaneously on separate cell phones to set up meetings and conversations to try to clear things up.

Levine met with Rezko and Kelly in person on May 11 in Rezko's office, he testified, and Cellini joined in by phone. Kelly wanted to try to get tough with Rosenberg, but Rezko had advised everyone to take a breath, Levine recalled.

"Mr. Rezko felt that the situation should be dealt with dispassionately and that the situation should be disarmed, that Mr. Rosenberg was a dangerous individual and nobody wanted to be put in a dangerous situation," Levine said. "And that nobody should talk with Mr. Rosenberg about a campaign contribution and that Mr. Rosenberg should get his allocation from TRS, but in fact, that should be the last business that Mr. Rosenberg does with the state of Illinois."

Niewoehner also wanted to know about Cellini's mention on the call that "the big guy" was aware of that plan. What was Cellini saying?

"That the governor was aware of this, and he had indicated that Rosenberg means nothing to the governor," Levine answered.

Levine had later spoken to Rezko about it at his office, too, he said.

"Mr. Rezko indicated to me that he had made the governor aware of the situation and the things that Mr. Rosenberg had said and that the governor agreed with the way Mr. Rezko wanted to handle it but that he felt that this was the last thing that Mr. Rosenberg should get from the state," Levine remembered.

===

By the time Joe Duffy got a crack at Levine, the calendar had turned from March to April, and he was more than ready. After Niewoehner finished up his last few questions, Duffy refused the offer of a break from the judge and instead launched right into his attack, giving Levine no chance to catch his breath.

"Mr. Levine, you have been involved in criminal activity your entire adult life, is that right?" Duffy asked.

"No, sir," Levine answered.

OK then. In what part of Levine's adult life had he not been a criminal?

"In no part of my adult life was I not involved in criminal activity," a suddenly puzzled Levine said.

If this was how it was going to go, there was a chance Duffy was going to be questioning Levine until Christmas, but the lawyer didn't let up. He had just asked the same question and gotten a different answer. So was Levine changing his answer for the jury?

"No, sir," Levine said flatly, finally offering that he was confused by what Duffy had meant by "adult life."

Duffy pressed by asking about Levine's first crimes, and Levine said he thought he was in his early thirties when he had started. But that seemed to be a reference to the activity in the case. What about drugs? Duffy asked whether Levine thought using illegal drugs was a crime, and after Levine agreed, he agreed with the lawyer that he had, in fact, been a criminal his entire adult life. It had seemed like a labored point, but Duffy wanted the jury to have an absolutely clear view of the kind of person who was accusing his client. It wasn't going to take much to make Levine look like a scattered man with a sometimes limited grasp of what was going on around him.

Levine had spent months preparing to testify, meeting with prosecutors dozens of times, and he was having trouble telling Duffy which years the tapes even covered. After first answering that the tapes were from early 2004, Levine agreed they actually started in late 2002. And he agreed there had been some that the jury didn't hear, including one when Levine had been caught on the phone asking a man Levine did drugs with whether the man had bought some.

"And he was one of the drug buddies that would go to these hotel rooms, where you'd have these drug binges, is that right?" Duffy asked.

"Yes, sir," Levine answered. The narcotics had come up again, but Levine disagreed that his years of using could have had any kind of adverse impact on his ability to remember things. The two men continued their back and forth discussion for the jury, with each speaking with the kind of forced cordiality that made it clear they didn't much care for each other. Almost every answer about Levine's past was answered by Levine with a passive-aggressive bent. Even seemingly straightforward questions from Duffy were met with veiled and less-veiled sarcasm from the witness stand. Duffy asked, for example, what Levine thought a bagman was, using the Chicago term for someone who carries cash bribes between two parties or otherwise acts as a go-between passing money from an illegal deal.

"My definition of a bagman is a homeless person," Levine said. "But that is not what you are referring to, and therefore, sir, I'm perfectly willing to use your definition."

Levine finally relented that a total of three people had acted as bagmen for him, including his partner Dr. Weinstein. But Duffy quickly pointed out that Levine had forgotten to list a fourth: Vrdolyak, who was the one who collected money on a fixed deal for the sale of the Scholl building.

"You forgot, is that right?" Duffy asked.

"Yes, sir," Levine said again.

"Even though you don't have a memory problem?"

Duffy then listed all of the people he knew Levine had been involved in crimes with, much of it public corruption. Tannenbaum and Loren were among them. They had been a part of crimes that had been committed years earlier, with Duffy's point being that Levine hadn't needed Rezko's help to pull them off. Levine hadn't needed Rezko to learn how to take a bribe, pay one, get a kickback, extort someone, or lie, he agreed. Rezko hadn't been needed to teach Levine how to be a corrupt board member or to be a con-man. The capable Levine had done all of that on his own. And through much of it, Levine had been a serious substance abuser. Cocaine. Crystal meth. LSD. Special K. Quaaludes. Had Duffy forgotten any?

"I believe you missed ketamine," Levine said. And just like that, Duffy had him again. Special K is ketamine, right? Levine reluctantly agreed, realizing his mistake. Duffy asked whether Levine had just forgotten the drug's street name, and Levine said he apparently had.

"Does Special K affect your memory?" Duffy asked.

"It's possible," Levine answered, as spectators in the courtroom tried to suppress a few chuckles. The odd Levine was proving to be a fairly easy witness for the smart Duffy to chop away at. Many lawyer-witness exchanges—even in heated criminal trials—can be fairly predictable. Most of the time, both the lawyer and the witness have a pretty good idea of what's going to be covered. The witness has been prepared by whichever side calls them, and both the defense and the prosecution know all of the essential facts. Rarely does the questioning look like what happens on your average TV courtroom drama, where every witness gets crossed up in some unscripted moment that scores significant points for one side or the other. But that's what was happening to Levine, over and over again. Every few minutes he would stumble over something basic. It was Duffy's goal to make him seem incredibly conniving with a healthy dose of space cadet, and the message was getting across. Even after being tagged with the Special K flub, Levine continued to dig in his heels and open himself up. He disagreed that there would be a "smorgasbord" of drugs at his hotel parties, leaving Duffy to rattle off the long list of substances that would be on the table in his rented rooms.

Levine also testified that he did not recall ever having one of his drug binges on a Saturday. That's because he wanted to be home on the weekends to deceive his family into thinking everything was OK with him. Once again, Levine was playing into Duffy's hands. The lawyer had a copy of a credit card receipt of Levine's showing a charge at the Purple Hotel on Saturday, November 2, 2002. That was the very day Levine had told the jury he first met Rezko at the dinner party at Massuda's home. Duffy was insinuating that not only was Levine again either lying to the jury or forgetting something, it was possible he was drug addled that evening after spending the day using and didn't have clear recall of the events at the dinner. Levine said he had no memory of a drug binge earlier that day.

"Well, you would agree with me, Mr. Levine, just based upon the first fifteen minutes of my cross-examination, that your memory fails you at times, doesn't it?" Duffy said.

Duffy then turned to 2004 and specifically to the supposed meeting Rezko and Levine had in Chicago on April 14 at the Standard Club. Levine had talked about explaining a number of insider deals to his new political patron, including taking money in the form of bogus finder's fees from firms that got TRS investment capital. Levine agreed with Duffy that he had been the one to set those up, not Rezko, and that none of those ideas had been consummated with anyone getting any illicit funds. That was because the FBI had come to his home a little more than a month later, Levine agreed. If not for the agents, Levine could have pulled the deals off with or without Rezko. In fact, Duffy said, the only thing Levine needed Rezko for was to try to dodge a long prison term. Levine was getting a sentence of five and a half years and agreed that probably wouldn't be happening without Levine bringing forward information that would put someone like Rezko on the hook. The government was building a case that led to Rezko and beyond, to the man who was really responsible for his power. That was Rod Blago-jevich, and everyone knew it. Duffy wanted to plant the thought in jurors' minds that Levine, the druggie weasel, would do anything to try to help himself. That included constructing a case against Rezko, the government target. It was Levine who sat before the jury as a convicted felon.

Levine said he was confident the jury knew he was a felon, whether someone had told them or he had read them information from his plea agreement. Again, Duffy saw an opening. He asked whether Levine remembered looking at his plea agreement while he was on the stand, and Levine said he was sure he had. Well, that would mean the plea agreement was in a large cart of government exhibits in the courtroom. Levine agreed that it should be there, so Duffy told the judge he wanted to ask Niewoehner to retrieve it for him.

"Your honor, we'll stipulate that there is no such exhibit," answered Niewoehner, who knew the agreement was not a trial exhibit and that Levine hadn't looked at it during his testimony. The prosecutor had a look on his face that suggested he might want to jump off a tall building—or, preferably, to shove Levine off one.

———

Levine hadn't agreed at first to cooperate with the government after the FBI dropped in on him just as some of his corrupt schemes were about to bloom. Like any true cunning conman, he had tried to keep his cool at first. He had taken a step back and tried to get a handle on what his position was and what his possible options could be. He was quickly recorded by agents calling Weinstein after the visit and telling him that the government was interested in a "big fish"—and that was Rezko. Duffy tried to point out that it was only after prosecutors found and interviewed one of his "drug bud-dies" that Levine finally decided to be a flipper. In addition to that, he had the realization that if he were charged with everything the government had on him, he would most likely spend the rest of his days in prison and then die there by himself. Levine must have been imagining a world that would start with the embarrassing exposure of his secret life and end with solitary death behind bars.

What would most people say to avoid such a fate? Maybe the answer was just about anything, or at least exactly what the prosecutors wanted him to say. That was Duffy's aim anyway, to embed that idea in the minds of the jury. At best, Levine was a drug-influenced serial liar and crook who spent most of his time deciding how to fleece people. At worst, he was all of those things while now being cornered and desperate. You couldn't trust him before, and you definitely couldn't trust him now.

And even in the face of that kind of pressure, Levine still hadn't been completely honest with prosecutors. At first he had failed to disclose his dealings with Vrdolyak. He hadn't reported the kickback he was due from the Smithfield Properties sale, maybe because he was holding out hope that he could somehow still receive it. Levine still had half of a $1.5 million bribe out there uncollected, and true to his nature, he thought he could outsmart the US attorney's office even that late in the game. It was a foolish last ditch effort to keep Vrdolyak out of trouble, a friend who was holding $750,000 for him. The government was aware of it anyway, and Levine's first substantial interview with prosecutors had stopped after it became clear Levine was holding back.

But under lengthy cross-examination by Duffy, Levine tried to be steadfast about what he thought was happening to him, repeatedly resisting the idea that he was just a tool for prosecutors.

"I don't know if I'm hurting them or helping them," he testified. "What I do know is that what I'm saying, in the confines of this courtroom, is the truth. And if the truth helps the government, then it aids them. And if the truth does not help the government, then it does not aid them. That is why I'm here, sir."

Levine said he knew his plea agreement was a benefit to him, but he denied being obsessed with his ultimate penalty or even that he had been part of the actual negotiations between his lawyer and prosecutors about what his final time in prison was going to be. He remembered being interviewed for the first time in early 2006, in an out-of-the-way secret location. It was a nearly empty government building in the West Loop. He had agreed to wear a wire for the government, attempting to catch both Vrdolyak and former Chicago alderman William Singer—who was lobbying for Smithfield—in discussions of their schemes. He went to meetings with a battery pack strapped to the small of his back and a recording device sewn into the tailoring of his clothes. He had gotten little of much use and once told investigators that his device had failed as he talked to Singer.

Meanwhile he continued to give prosecutors as much information as he could, eventually being interviewed forty-one times. Sometimes he told agents and prosecutors that he wanted to go home and think about the details of what they were asking him, returning at their next session with notes about the things he could recall. In ten of those interviews, Levine had been asked for details of his meeting with Rezko at the Standard Club. All of it had led to Levine pleading guilty in his own criminal case and then testifying against Rezko, a man who at one point had been about as close an insider to Blagojevich as a person could be. Kelly, one of the governor's best friends, may have shared a deeper connection. But for a time, almost nothing of importance had happened inside the administration without Rezko knowing about it. Levine had laid bare some of the inner workings of corruption in Illinois, even if he did have those pesky memory problems.

As he testified, he revealed to Duffy that he couldn't even recall for the jury the day he had pleaded guilty in federal court.

"Can you tell them the month you pled guilty?" Duffy asked.

"No, sir," Levine said, with the same glassy, lizard-like calm he kept throughout his days on the stand.

Duffy paused for second and decided to go ahead and swing for the fences. "Can you tell them the year you pled guilty?"

"No, sir," came the answer again.

"Have you pled guilty?" Duffy said, teasingly.

"Yes, sir."

———

The Rezko trial, which would predictably end in a conviction, remained a drag on Blagojevich, but fund-raising was another outlet for him to get his mind off things. He may have hated governing, but he didn't lose the drive to raise cash, still feeding off—almost needing—the adoration he got from events where people still lauded his leadership and handed over a check.

While some supporters were staying away due to the scandals, he was hitting up a group of wealthy Indian businessmen more and more. The men, some doctors, pharmacists, or bankers like Mahajan, felt aligned with Blagojevich because of his family's ethnic background and his support for their causes. Many were first-generation Americans and simply liked to be near the power of a sitting governor, giving them bragging rights over their friends.

Brian Daly had always been the contact between the campaign and the Indians, who sometimes acted like a cohesive group but often carried baggage and jealousies that divided them. But Blagojevich had also been dealing with Rajinder Bedi, who was still with the administration and successful at trying to bring the community's divergent elements together.

Blagojevich called Bedi "my Sikh warrior" in helping round up the donors, which included businessmen such as Mahajan, Babu Patel, and Raghu Nayak, who owned a group of surgery centers in and around Chicago.

But as Blagojevich continued to raise money, the scrutiny from prosecutors and the press also continued. At one fund-raiser in the summer of 2008 hosted by Wyma at the upscale restaurant Naha, Blagojevich spotted a photographer and reporters from the *Tribune* out front. Trying to avoid having his picture taken, Blagojevich had his security detail drive around the block and drop him off. From there he briskly walked down the block around the corner from the restaurant, blending with a group a people walking by before dashing into Naha.

The fund-raising was at full tilt even while Rezko's trial was ongoing just a few blocks from Naha, with witnesses detailing Rezko's activities and Blagojevich's shady campaign operation. The pressure was becoming so much that legislators fashioned a bill aimed directly at the governor and his fund-raising activities. It prohibited anybody with state contracts worth $50,000 or more from contributing to the politicians who oversee those contracts.

But Blagojevich wasn't worried about it passing because he still had Senate President Jones in his corner. Then Jones got a call from Barack Obama.

It was just a few months from Election Day, and the Democratic nominee for president urged his onetime mentor, Jones, to call the bill despite Blagojevich's efforts to have the Senate block it. Trying to get rid of the stink of Illinois's corruption that had often dogged him, the vote would help Obama show his home state was doing something proactive to stop it. The bill passed the Senate 55–0 and would take effect January 1, 2009.

Blagojevich was livid. His last remaining ally in state government had abandoned him for Obama. His jealousy raged. He decided he now had to raise as much money as possible before January 1 from all the sources of income he had tapped for six years. State contractors, hospitals, anybody. He also had almost nobody he could trust to do the work of raising money. So he turned to the only member of his family left, his big brother, Robert.

"I need your help."

13

Endgame

They arrived for the meeting early. Dew still rested on the windshields of the cars parked along quiet Ravenswood Avenue in front of the old brick industrial building that housed the Friends of Blagojevich headquarters.

Dressed in jeans, a white T-shirt, and a baggy black golf pullover, John Wyma parked his car down the street and hustled toward the front door of 4147 North. Lon Monk, also in jeans, pulled his Volkswagen SUV into a spot directly across the street from the four-story building with the red-brick facade. Both men climbed three flights of stairs for their meeting with Rod Blagojevich.

October 22, 2008, was a crisp autumn day in Chicago. Trucks dropped off piles of dirty clothes for cleaning next door at a uniform-rental business. Commuters made their way to the nearby CTA train station.

Ninety minutes after he arrived, Wyma emerged by himself. Grasping a piece of paper and a Blackberry in his left hand, he headed toward his car. The last thing he was expecting was a pair of newspaper reporters and a photographer. He looked stunned. His eyes widened and he stopped cold, glancing to his left and right as if looking for an escape. But he was trapped.

The *Tribune* reporters were there seeking his reaction to being named in a new subpoena issued by a federal grand jury, one that was interested in his work for Provena Health some years before. Still standing in the middle of Ravenswood Avenue, Wyma turned and took a few steps toward the political offices. Perhaps worried how bad it would look for him to run back into the headquarters, Wyma turned around again and walked quickly toward his car.

"I have no comment," he mumbled, before he disappeared.

Wyma had done his best to keep a swirl of emotions suppressed. Just days earlier, he had become what amounted to the last domino falling in Blagojevich's line of defense against the federal government.

In September, he had immediately suspected Rezko when he got the subpoena. A grand jury wanted to know about his dealings as a lobbyist with Provena Health, a hospital and medical center group he had worked with in 2004, when the company was trying to get approval for a heart surgery facility in Elgin. Back then, two years into the first Blagojevich administration, dealing with that board meant Rezko, and it meant Stuart Levine. Often it meant money moving to Blagojevich's campaign fund before things loosened up and proposals could get by the board. Provena had gotten its approval, and its political arm had made a $25,000 donation to the governor weeks later.

Wyma couldn't have known all that Rezko had told authorities by the time October had rolled around, but his suspicions were right.

After weeks of testimony from Levine and others, Rezko had been convicted of money laundering, fraud, and aiding bribery in his own case that summer, and the trial had lasted long enough for prosecutors to flip men like Ali Ata, who testified about giving the governor the $25,000 check and getting a big state job.

And facing mounting pressure and a long prison term, Rezko could no longer afford not to cooperate, despite such resistance being ingrained in his very nature. Perhaps no one in Blagojevich's inner circle had been as mentally tough as Rezko, but even he had his limits. Pressure from prosecutors and his family had begun to mount. He had been loyal to the end, even through a criminal trial that had ended badly for him, and where had it gotten him? His family thought enough was enough. No one had helped him when he needed it most. Rezko began talking with his lawyer, Joe Duffy, about what cooperating with the feds would mean. He had gotten a further wakeup call from prosecutors in his early meetings with them. If he ever wanted to see his family again outside a prison visiting room, he needed to tell them the truth about his past, holding nothing back.

Before Rezko's decision, the investigation officially known as Operation Board Games was running out of string. Decisions had been made inside the FBI to run things out as best they could, but there wasn't much traction.

Supervisors thought there were plenty of arrows pointing to Blagojevich, and cases had been made all around him, but there wasn't enough evidence on him specifically. Some thought a possible route was investigating money that had been given to Patti Blagojevich by Rezko's company, a strategy some called "balls to the wall on Patti," but that wasn't a sure thing.

Enter Rezko. By July, he was in full discussions with prosecutors, and a new avenue was opening. Rezko was talking about his history with Blagojevich and his role in the machinations inside the governor's administration. In the beginning, Blagojevich had come to him three times seeking his help. Rezko had said no each time, he explained, before he had eventually decided he could help Blagojevich navigate the political waters of Illinois. If Rod wouldn't pull out of the race, Rezko told his new friend, he wouldn't pull out either.

Rezko, who had dealt with Republicans in the Edgar, Thompson, and Ryan administrations, knew that meant going to Bill Cellini, who had been entrenched with some of the same players for decades. Cellini was going to have a new political boss, Rezko told him. His name was Rod Blagojevich. He was going to win the election, and Cellini was going to be able to work with him.

Meanwhile, Rezko had become deeply involved in Blagojevich's campaign. He was responsible for bringing in millions, and after Blagojevich was elected, Rezko acknowledged he was among those trusted to name people to boards and commissions in the state. He had turned his actual power into even more power, knowing that appearances often were as good as reality. Blagojevich had known of many of his ideas in general and endorsed them, Rezko told prosecutors, but wasn't always up on the details. It was widely believed that Rezko had the governor's ear. And while he did, Rezko used his position as well. There had been times when he would tell people to do things, he said, knowing they wouldn't check with the governor.

Rezko's version of events was that he had outlined broad strategies for making money through Blagojevich's official actions and that he had shared these with Monk, Chris Kelly, and the governor. Any money that was brought in was to be paid to all of them in the future. Rezko told prosecutors he kept a kind of marker in his head of what everyone might be owed. But by and large, there was no real method to the madness and no money to divide. Dollars that Rezko brought in he often used himself. When he pulled corrupt money out of state deals, he had used it in a shell game to move cash around and cover his own business losses.

Rezko discussed a lot of politicians, including dealings with former governors and Obama. He had been a fund-raiser for many, a fixer for others, and a trusted ear. But prosecutors and the FBI were not completely impressed with what he delivered. Rezko did say he knew that Chris Kelly had told Blagojevich about the effort to get campaign money from film producer Tom Rosenberg and said he then checked with Blagojevich himself about holding up the TRS investment with Rosenberg's firm. But at times there were frustratingly few details, as if Rezko were holding back. Chiefly, Rezko withheld that he actually had paid cash to one member of Blagojevich's inner circle, Lon Monk.

Other times Rezko absolutely refused to agree with some of what Levine had said against him at his trial. Rezko would serve the rest of his life in prison, it seemed, before lining up behind everything that Levine had said. That didn't make Rezko a promising witness, and neither did a letter he had written to the judge in his case, Amy St. Eve, complaining months earlier that the government was pressuring him to lie about Blagojevich and Obama. Some investigators thought Rezko might have had the ability to deliver the dagger they needed on Blagojevich, and his sentencing was delayed again and again as he worked with them, but he just wasn't providing a finishing blow.

Still, there were some interesting things Rezko had said that moved the investigation forward. Among them was that he'd had conversations with Wyma about what it would take to move a plan through the Illinois Health Facilities Planning Board years before. Rezko said Wyma had gone to Monk first asking what to do and had been pointed in Rezko's direction. Rezko said he had communicated the going rate—meaning how much it would cost—and told Wyma there was a dispute between one member of the IHFPB and Provena. The government eventually would contend they could not substantiate Rezko's claim that he had communicated a dollar amount to Wyma, but they had never approached Wyma about his Blagojevich connections, despite his history as a Blagojevich staffer in Washington and as a lobbyist.

Because of Rezko, Wyma wound up as a subpoenaed subject of the government's investigation, and through his lawyer, Zachary Fardon, set up a date to have a preliminary talk with prosecutors about his past and what they were looking for.

In the meantime, Wyma had a pair of fund-raising meetings set up with Blagojevich, including on October 6, at the Friends of Blagojevich offices. The governor told Wyma about a plan to expand the Illinois Tollway. He was going to roll out his proposal slowly, teasing the road builders with a $1.8 billion program, with the promise of another much larger plan. He wanted to see what the group might give to his campaign fund by the end of the year, Blagojevich said. "And if they don't perform, fuck 'em."

Meeting later with Wyma and the governor that day was one of Wyma's clients, Michael Vondra, a construction executive in the asphalt business. Vondra was looking at a deal for one of his companies with British Petroleum for a distribution center in Chicago's south suburbs and wanted Blagojevich to get behind the idea and smooth things out with state regulators. Blagojevich thought it was a great idea but had more to say after Vondra left the meeting. Wyma should ask his client for $100,000 in campaign money for the governor by the end of 2008.

On October 8, Wyma was back at Friends of Blagojevich with the governor, Lon Monk, and Robert Blagojevich. Another Wyma client, Children's Memorial Hospital, was on the agenda. Blagojevich had been called on behalf of the hospital by former Cubs manager Dusty Baker, who had connections to the hospital. Baker asked the governor to back a pediatric rate increase that would mean more money for the facility to care for sick children.

Blagojevich's decision was that he was going to approve an increase that would mean another $8 million a year for the facility. But again, there was a catch. "I want to get the CEO for fifty," Blagojevich had said, meaning the governor wanted $50,000 in campaign cash from CMH executive Patrick Magoon in exchange for the rate increase. It might be better to wait a year after the hospital got its boost for Blagojevich to get that kind of thank you, so Wyma told Blagojevich to maybe give the request some time.

"How much time do you mean, ten days?" Blagojevich answered.

It was at the same meeting that talk had turned to whether Rezko had actually begun helping the government, as Chicago's newspapers were starting to report. There was nervousness but not too much worry. Blagojevich thought he had kept his nose clean enough, he told the three. "Unless, prospectively, somebody gets you on a wire," Robert replied.

The meetings were a graduation for Wyma, who had a just received the subpoena and was scheduled to meet with federal prosecutors. He knew it was time for him to get out of the way. The Blagojevich express was headed for a cliff, as it were, and the last place he wanted to be was on the train. Within days, he told prosecutors all he knew about Blagojevich's aggressive moves to make money that was attached to his duties as governor and that Blagojevich wanted some $2.5 million by the end of the year when new ethics legislation was going into effect. Prosecutors were impressed and wanted more of Wyma's help. The October 22 fund-raising meeting at the Friends of Blagojevich was coming up, and prosecutors wanted Robert's premonition about a wire to come true. If Wyma would agree to wear one, they might capture some of what Blagojevich said on tape and launch their case into overdrive.

Wyma was trying to protect himself, but he decided that wasn't going to include wearing a wire against a longtime friend. Instead he let prosecutors record his voicemails. One became especially important in the early stages of the government's final efforts against the governor.

"I know that you're gonna be following up with Children's Memorial and just wanted to know what the next steps are and what it is kind of we're looking to accomplish there," Robert Blagojevich said in the message. "So when you get a chance, give me a call so that I can at least kind of document it and you know make sure I'm following up on you so you get it done. Hey man, you know I'm jerking your chain, but I think they have potential to do well by us. Give me a call."

To investigators it was a link between the fund-raising request and the state action Rod Blagojevich was promising. Wyma was supposed to hint to the hospital that if a donation were made, they had the chance to get what they wanted from the administration. That message, along with what Wyma had told them about Blagojevich's fund-raising tactics, gave pros-ecutors enough ammunition to get approvals from the Justice Department in Washington to approach a judge and receive approval to plant hidden microphones at the Friends of Blagojevich offices. In some ways, Wyma's refusal to wear a wire wound up forcing the feds to write up an extensive affidavit on why Blagojevich should be recorded with no willing party help-ing them.

Their plan was successful, but there was one problem. Chicago's chief federal court judge approved the bugging request just a day before the Octo-ber 22 meeting. An FBI team was quickly assembled from Quantico, Vir-ginia, to get bugs in place. They would be able to record conversations for thirty days in two rooms at the Friends of Blagojevich headquarters—Blago-jevich's personal office and a conference room.

In Chicago, coordinating the planting was left up to longtime supervisor Pete Cullen, who quickly got the bureau's assistant special agents in charge in Chicago into a meeting. On the phone were technical advisers, as Cullen sought to get as much expertise into one room as he could. Some knew locks and security cameras. Others had experience defeating alarms, and still others were acquainted with where to plant hidden microphones. The FBI had to establish a contact on the Illinois State Police to give Blagojevich a bogus all clear when he asked for a sweep for bugs, which he had done that very week. Late at night on October 21, the team made what the FBI calls an "orchestrated entry" into the building, surreptitiously planting small microphones inside the offices, including in the phone right on Blagojevich's desk. It wouldn't record calls but sounds in the room and at least Blagojevich's half of anything said into the phone.

———

At 10:17 AM, October 22, the government bugs had been in place for hours before Wyma arrived. FBI agents were monitoring their equipment from a car outside and could hear as the Blagojevich brothers and Monk were making fund-raising calls. On their list was Gerald Krozel, a roadbuilding executive who often represented the state's road companies collectively when it came to politics and Blagojevich. The governor told Krozel he was excited about the plan to expand the state's tollway system, and there were pauses as Krozel answered. Blagojevich said things were going ahead and then asked for money. The new ethics law was coming online at the end of the year and would make it illegal for the governor to raise money from companies and organizations that were doing business with the state.

"The good news is, we're off and running, we've got something going, and there's gonna be more," Blagojevich said into the phone. "And the good news for you guys is—which is the bad news for us—is after the first of the year, this level of it will, you know, pretty much be over, we won't be able to bully you guys."

Blagojevich hung up, immediately telling Monk to be the one to follow up. He hadn't given Krozel a number, he told them.

On October 28, investigators scored another hit. This time, Robert was taped in the conference room on the phone with his brother. The 2008 presidential campaign was drawing to a close, and signs were pointing to Obama emerging as the winner. To say the least, this was expected to have an enormous effect on Illinois and Chicago, and Blagojevich would be expected to appoint someone to replace Obama when he gave up his seat in the US Senate and headed for the White House to become the country's forty-fourth commander in chief. Investigators weren't even exactly sure what they were hearing when they captured the half of the conversation they could hear from Robert.

"Now here's the big issue he came up with, and I don't know if you want to listen to this or not," Robert was heard to say.

"But it has do to with a particular person who is lobbying to be the senator, um, and wants to talk to you about his resume, Jackson," Robert said, talking about Jesse Jackson Jr. "And Raghu Nayak evidently supported it, and he had communicated through Rajinder that if in fact, um, that would be the case, ah, there would be some accelerated fund-raising on your behalf between now and the end of the year, through his network. And I said look, and, uh, they haven't even, and I, I completely told him, you know, we don't even know who the president is gonna be yet."

The men Robert was talking about were Raghu Nayak and Rajinder Bedi, two players in Chicago's Indian community who had become major Blagojevich supporters.

Nayak was a businessman from west suburban Oak Brook who owned surgery centers all over Chicagoland. He had been friends with Blagojevich and Jackson for years, donating more than $200,000 to the governor and $22,000 for Jackson. Bedi was a Blagojevich fund-raiser and had received a state job after Blagojevich became governor.

Prosecutors were constantly adding new information to their requests to expand the recording operation. And the day after Robert's call, October 29, the judge approved the broadening of the taping to permit the interception of telephone calls to Robert's cell phone, to the governor's Chicago home where he was conducting most of the state's business, and to the campaign offices. He would occasionally conduct meetings at the James R. Thompson Center, the state's main government building in Chicago, but liked to avoid it if he could. An appearance in Springfield was an even rarer occurrence, as Blagojevich stayed away from the capital as much as possible.

The wiretaps were activated that same day by 6:00 PM, with calls to both numbers being routed into the FBI's satellite office in Lisle, a suburb west of Chicago. It was from there that Supervisory Agent Pat Murphy and Agent Daniel Cain and others had been running Operation Board Games. All of the files were there, so it made sense to have Lisle be the center of the listening effort. The FBI suddenly found itself monitoring a total of nine phone lines, needing two agents available for each from early in the morning until around eleven o'clock at night. It didn't take long to run through one hundred agents a week, and Cullen found himself shifting agents from squads handling health-care fraud and bank fraud to cover listening shifts. Agents from all over the bureau in Chicago were volunteering because of the high-profile nature of what was happening and because of how profitable to the investigation the calls quickly became.

The idea that Blagojevich could be illegally attempting to get something for himself for the Senate seat was still a new concept. Some agents on the case were listening only for calls about fund-raising irregularities. The rules on wiretapping require agents monitoring phone lines to stop recording, or "minimize" the calls, when something personal or unrelated to the investigation comes up. So as the taping began, prosecutors who were getting discs of the calls were finding that the new agents to the case were minimizing when Senate discussions began. The assistant US attorneys quickly rectified the situation. They told the agents to let the recordings continue when a replacement for Obama came up.

=====

The Rod Blagojevich who would be captured on hundreds of federal recordings was becoming a desperate man, a politician at a crossroads who was seeing the best years of his career ending and only questions ahead. His original presidential aspirations had never developed, and worse yet, another dynamic politician from Illinois was riding the wave to the office that Blagojevich himself had hoped to catch. And Obama was taking some of the state's best and brightest with him for his cabinet, adding to Blagojevich's sense that he was being left behind. Obama was headed for Washington and the history books Blagojevich loved so much, while he seemed destined to be a historical footnote.

Blagojevich was also simply tired of being governor. He felt underappreciated, as polls showed just a fraction of the state's voting public liked what he was doing. He had taken to political gimmicks, like giving seniors free passes to public transportation, to try to recover his image. Meanwhile, he was feeling the pressure of the federal investigation, reading regularly about Rezko's possible cooperation. His own legal bills were mounting, as he was paying some of the city's top lawyers to handle federal requests for documents. It was a tab he could pay from his campaign fund, but he was facing problems there, too. His coffers were dwindling, and his ability to refill them was about to be seriously curtailed. With the new ethics bill going into effect at the end of the 2008, firms doing business with the state would no longer be allowed to make large campaign donations.

By the fall of 2008, Blagojevich was separated from his lawyers at Winston & Strawn, as he had become embroiled in a dispute over their pay. Also factoring in the split from Winston's perspective were complaints from federal prosecutors that the same law firm should not be representing Blagojevich and Cellini, who remained under investigation and was represented by one of its top lawyers, Dan Webb. Blagojevich was left with Sorosky, who had previously remained on the sidelines for the governor and now found himself front and center. "I may just be a finger in the dike, but I'm his lawyer," he told federal prosecutors.

Blagojevich had appeared at a second meeting with the FBI while being represented by Winston & Strawn, not long before his reelection in 2006. But when investigators asked to see him again in late October 2008, Sorosky told them Blagojevich would invoke his Fifth Amendment rights. The attorney didn't know it then, but the request was an apparent attempt to lock Blagojevich into statements that would contradict what agents were hearing on their recordings.

With the investigation all around him, Blagojevich was unlikely to be in the state's political mix beyond 2010. And longtime nemesis House Speaker Michael Madigan had called for a committee to begin studying impeachment. The newspaper editorial boards were also starting to think it was a good idea, casting Blagojevich in an increasingly negative light. An end to his political career would leave him with almost no options to continue giving his family the kind of life they had enjoyed. Money was going to be a problem after he left office, and Blagojevich didn't have the kind of reputation that sometimes led to high-paying jobs for ex-politicians. He was damaged goods. No law firm would pay to put his name on the door, using him as a trophy. No major corporation would want him as its figurehead. And no one was going to pay to see him on the lecture circuit. In short, he needed an escape hatch.

And he would find one, at just the wrong time. The recipe crystallized just as the feds flipped the switch on their recordings. In Blagojevich's delusional mind, the one good thing about Obama's election was that it left him with the ability to choose the president-elect's replacement in the Senate, and he was determined to try to maximize it for his own benefit. It was a final trump card that he could play to end many of his problems at once. Get him money and a job prospect after he left office. End the threat of impeachment. He could even pull the rip cord on a golden parachute and name himself. Get him out of Illinois. Get him to Washington.

The final ingredient in the explosive cocktail came from the incoming president. As was his prerogative, Obama also had thoughts about who might replace him. He wanted someone he knew and could work with, and someone who could hold the seat for the Democrats and maintain the balance of power in Washington that he was enjoying at the beginning of his first term. So Obama had reached out through intermediaries to communicate his wishes at the same time Blagojevich was turning things over in his mind and imagining what his best strategy would be. With Obama invested in the pick, Blagojevich thought he had all but won the lottery. All of his enemies—Madigan, the newspapers, and even the feds—Blagojevich dreamed, were about to see that he could still outsmart them all.

＝＝＝

The morning after the wiretapping began, Blagojevich was at home on Sunnyside Avenue, talking with his newest deputy governor, a young analyst named Robert Greenlee, who was part Blagojevich sounding board and part toady. He had been promoted months earlier and quickly earned the governor's trust. It was October 30, and the presidential election was just days away. There were polls circulating on Obama and his opponent, John McCain, on everything from the economy, to who was most ready for the job, to who would do a better job on national security issues. Blagojevich, the Democrat, felt Republicans would do a better job keeping the nation safe.

"Don't get me wrong, the second time I voted for Clinton, the first time I voted for Bush senior. If you ever repeat this, Greenlee, first I'll deny it, secondly I'll wait a little bit, then I'll fire you. I'll give it a month or something, and then we'll come up with some charges, and you'll be out," Blagojevich said.

Greenlee laughed. By the way, he said, the *Washington Post* had a story on the Senate seat. Lots of names were in the air. Jesse Jackson Jr., Tammy Duckworth, Jan Schakowsky, Valerie Jarrett, Emil Jones. At least Jackson and Jones were African Americans and congressmen, and either would give Blagojevich a political boost in the black community. Maybe even Bobby Rush, another US representative, could be tossed into the mix, Greenlee said.

"Black Panther," answered Blagojevich. But let's not get ahead of ourselves, he told Greenlee, maybe the election was tightening up some. Maybe

Obama could still lose. Blagojevich sounded hopeful describing the issues that might still produce a McCain win. Patti had her own criteria in deciding which man would get her vote, Blagojevich said.

"Who's more likely to fire Pat Fitzgerald," the US attorney in Chicago, Blagojevich told Greenlee. "That's who she's voting for."

"Probably go with Obama," Greenlee said.

Later the same morning, an early call was captured between Blagojevich and his chief of staff, John Harris. It was an intelligence call of the type the men had on a regular basis. The governor and his top staffer would often bounce off each other things they had seen in the media and ideas they had for strategy. Harris was a former army intelligence officer and judge advocate general who had risen through the ranks of city government under Mayor Richard Daley to become his budget director. He had worked in Daley's campaign and held big jobs in the Department of Aviation and the Chicago Police Department. He joined the governor in 2005 and often discovered he had the task of reeling his boss in from each particular day's bizarro idea, so much so that Blagojevich often called him the Prince of Darkness. But on this day, it was just idle chatter about the election and anything else that might come up. What did Harris know? Blagojevich asked.

The presidential race shouldn't even be as close as it seemed to be, the men agreed. With the housing market crashing and some of the frustrations of the Bush White House, there should have been a more sweeping push for change. Blagojevich sounded resigned to an Obama win but still somewhat hopeful he could trip at the finish line.

Agents listening to Robert Blagojevich's cell phone recorded a call between Robert and the governor's general counsel, lawyer William Quinlan. On October 30, Quinlan was reviewing a newly released indictment against Bill Cellini and trolled through it looking for links to Blagojevich. Robert was most interested in mentions of Illinois road builders, since it was a group the Blagojeviches were pressing for campaign cash. The builders and the tollway were mentioned in the document, but not in any way that should have an impact on what they were doing. "None of it says Rod had anything to do with it," Quinlan said.

And there were calls about fund-raisers past and future. Rod called once to report State Senator Jimmy DeLeo had raised $50,000. "Fucking A," Robert answered. And there was a return call from Bedi, discussing a fund-raiser in the Indian community for the next day, which was Halloween. A number of guests were expected, said Bedi, hoping to show he was doing what he could to bring out a crowd. Something like thirty people were headed for the India House restaurant in Schaumburg, a northwest suburb. Nayak was one of the hosts.

"And, uh, each one has allocated about five to six people," Bedi reported. "And Rod knows about all of them because, uh, each one of them has done a fund-raiser for him."

The next morning, news that Bill Cellini had been indicted in the Operation Board Games investigation for his role in an attempted extortion at TRS was in both papers, and Blagojevich was reacting early. The FBI tracked calls from his home as he spoke to his press agent, Lucio Guerrero, about how the coverage had turned out. The *Sun-Times* had used a dramatic "Shakedown" headline and Blagojevich's picture. Cellini had been accused in the attempt to get a finder's fee or a Blagojevich campaign donation from movie producer Tom Rosenberg in order for his firm to get investment money from the Teachers' Retirement System, which had been part of the Rezko case as well. Having it back in the papers, along with photos of him, was making Blagojevich uncomfortable. In a call with Greenlee that morning, Blagojevich insisted no one had done anything on his behalf. He sometimes claimed he had only a vague idea of what TRS even was. Cellini had been recorded saying Rosenberg meant nothing to "the big guy," meaning Blagojevich, and signaling that Blagojevich apparently knew what was going on.

"I don't believe that's true either," Blagojevich told Greenlee. "Nobody ever talked to me about him."

Blagojevich was due at India House around midday, so he had plenty of time that morning to digest the Cellini coverage. One call was with DeLeo, who was sympathetic, not surprisingly. *Tribune* columnist John Kass had put DeLeo himself in a column about Cellini that day. DeLeo had read both papers, and the men agreed it sounded like Rezko was probably helping the government. DeLeo said he knew that Cellini's health was OK, though he had dealt with cancer, and he and Blagojevich agreed he might actually have a shot at beating the case.

"I'm trying to figure out how they could bring a charge like that against him when that was a 'not guilty' at trial on Tony, and then Tony's talking to them. That's my read," Blagojevich said, noting that one count Rezko hadn't been convicted on was the Rosenberg charge.

"Well they weren't going to indict him, and then after Tony started talking to 'em now they have somebody saying here's a tape that he says this, and now they got Tony sayin' well yeah he was there and he was, you know, layin' out the blueprint how to do it," DeLeo answered.

It was true that Rezko had used Cellini for his knowledge of how to use the state system, DeLeo went on, remembering how he had told Cellini to stay away from Rezko. There was nothing Rezko could do for him at the stage of life the older and established Cellini was in, DeLeo recalled saying.

"Yeah, I had that conversation with 'em years ago," he said. "But, ya know, he just liked the art of politics."

At the heart of the matter was the spat between Rosenberg and Stuart Levine. "North Shore Jew competitiveness" had developed when Rosenberg was trying to sell a company, DeLeo explained.

"And, ya know, a friend of mine once told me he said that uh, Jews have been chased out of every country in the world," DeLeo said, laughing. "They're just terrible people whether they're Highland Park North Shore Jews or, or from Israel or wherever part of the world they're from."

Ironically, DeLeo had just spoken to Rahm Emanuel, one of the city's most powerful Jewish politicians. Still a congressman but headed to the Obama White House, Emanuel wanted to know if Rod would listen to him about appointing someone to replace Obama in the US Senate. It was the first time the government had caught any kind of message coming back to Blagojevich about the wishes of anyone in Obama's circle. And it didn't go over very well.

"What a fuckin' piece of shit," Blagojevich barked to DeLeo. He still blamed Emanuel for campaign ads that year run by the Democratic Congressional Campagin Committee. The ads aimed to boost Democratic state senator Debbie Halvorson by pointing out donations by Republican Marty Ozinga to Blagojevich. "He's got a right to do that, but he wants me to listen to him on his Senate appointment?"

Blagojevich was supposed to be in Schaumburg in an hour, but he finished jogging and got on a call with Harris. He had a development to talk to him about. Tom Balanoff and Andy Stern of the Service Employees International Union wanted to come see him the following Monday and Tuesday, which was Election Day, presumably about the Senate seat. That was fine, but Blagojevich and Harris wanted to have a long talk first. They needed to strategize about what they would say publicly about the supposed process to name a new senator.

"We're not giving up on McCain though, right?" Blagojevich slipped in.

There was already momentum in the African American community to consider Obama's Senate seat a black position, the men agreed. Harris likened the situation to his time in the Daley administration, when the job of police superintendent was considered by some to be a "black spot." Still, Daley had broken that mold when he named Phil Cline, who was white, to replace Terry Hillard, who was black.

"What [Daley] does is he tries to put a black somewhere else then, so like he puts a black in charge of the fire department," Harris said. The men were only half serious, but the thought that whoever replaced Obama should be African American came to be a regular theme for Blagojevich.

Right then, however, Blagojevich was still fixated on the Cellini coverage and how the case was being linked to him. Though he was upset the *Sun-Times* had used his photo, he conceded he actually liked how he looked.

"I actually like the picture," he said, urging Harris to agree he looked handsome. "The picture's more important than the article."

After the Indian fund-raiser was over, Blagojevich and Harris would talk again, ruminating on which politicians might support which possible picks for the Senate and whether Obama would have a preference. If he did, it would be good to know exactly who that was early in the process, they agreed. Maybe they should ask David Axelrod, who had become Obama's top adviser, if they have a horse in the race, Harris said.

Blagojevich was against the idea of an Obama victory, but his duty to appoint a replacement if it happened was very quickly filling up his work-day hours. Even into the evenings, it was on his mind. Still on Halloween, when it was almost dark enough for trick-or-treaters to be circulating in his neighborhood, Blagojevich was back on the phone with Greenlee, who had prepared a list of potential qualifications for the Senate seat that the governor would announce publicly. The paper had been sent to Washington for a look by one of Blagojevich's advisers there, Bill Knapp.

Calls about the seat were coming to Blagojevich at home.

"Got some lady calling my house for Jesse Jr. here a little while ago," Blagojevich told Greenlee, who called Jackson shameless. "Unbelievable, isn't it? Then I, we were approached pay to play. That, ya know, he'd raise me five hundred grand, an emissary came. Then the other guy would raise a million if I made him a senator."

"I'm, ah, you know I'm not surprised by him at all," Greenlee answered.

It was a watershed moment for prosecutors, as they heard Blagojevich in his own words describe a criminal offer and potentially implicate a US congressman. The governor had even used the term *pay to play*, showing he was more than aware the kind of territory he was getting into. Agents noted among themselves that the so-called ethics governor certainly didn't turn around and call them to report such an outrageous effort to give him cash.

The money offer had come from Nayak at the fundraiser, and there was a mixup on the number. Robert Blagojevich had thought Nayak meant he would raise $1.5 million when Nayak held up one finger on one hand and five fingers on the other, when Nayak actually had meant $6 million would be raised. From then on, the governor continued to think the offer was a quarter of the real amount Jackson's friends were contemplating.

If Obama did win, another intriguing idea was simply appointing himself, Blagojevich said, asking Greenlee if he thought that was a good idea. Maybe he could just appoint a placeholder now, someone who would step aside if Blagojevich ran for the office in 2010. It was hard to know which would be the better play, since the economy was bad and the party in power, the Democrats, could pay the price that year. If he waited until 2010, he might not win anyway, he told Greenlee, and if he appointed himself now, there could be so much backlash, he wouldn't be able to hold it.

The following morning, Robert was back on his cell phone, thanking Rajinder Bedi and his brother for the Indian event the day before. Another fund-raiser was being planned for December 6 in the western suburb of Oak Brook. Members of the community were looking for a hall that might seat one thousand people. An excited Robert turned around and called the governor, informing him there were already twenty-five commitments for tables that ran $2,500 each.

Even before 9:00 AM, Blagojevich was back on the Senate appointment. He had formed a few key options in his mind. One was a political deal with Michael Madigan to send his daughter, Lisa, the state's attorney general since 2003, to the Senate in exchange for the House Speaker backing Blagojevich's legislative agenda: a balanced budget, no tax increases, expanded health care. If he wanted to stay governor and be able to do great things, that was the way to go. But Blagojevich wasn't sure he wanted to be governor, so there were other things to think about. He could appoint himself or appoint a placeholder like Illinois Senate President Emil Jones and then run for the seat in 2010. Or he could bow to the wishes of other powerful politicians, most notably Obama. It was possible Obama might want his friend, Chicago businesswoman and civic leader Valerie Jarrett, to be appointed—that name was in all the papers—but that was only a good option if Obama really wanted her and was willing to give him things right up front, Blagojevich said. None of the options really looked perfect. Send Jones, and Madigan comes after you even harder, Blagojevich told Greenlee. As for sending himself, the Democrats would want to hold the seat and might back him, the governor said, unless his problems with US Attorney Fitzgerald got worse.

"If the Fitzgerald stuff gets worse," Greenlee answered, "you're fucked either way."

Later that morning, Blagojevich was back on the phone with his brother, checking in on fund-raising activity. Monk had updated Robert on another fund-raising plan. The governor was considering a bill that would divert casino revenue to the state's struggling horseracing industry, and Blagojevich was seeking a campaign donation from track owner John Johnston and his family. Monk had told Robert that effort was going fine and that he was still waiting to hear from Krozel on his donation. Blagojevich told his brother Monk should also be tapped to call and ask for $100,000 from Blair Hull, who had lost the Senate primary in 2004 to Obama, spending millions of his own dollars. To Blagojevich, Hull was a known sap, a man who had paid for private jets for the governor in the past in a bid for influence. Now Hull was interested in replacing the man who had beaten him in 2004.

"Blair Hull actually thinks he can be senator. You believe this guy?" Blagojevich said. "He's an idiot."

Jesse Jackson Jr. thought he could be the pick, too, Robert answered. Right, said Blagojevich.

———

November 2 was a Sunday, and pro football provided at least a momentary distraction. Robert was on his cell phone teasing Blagojevich about his team, the Cowboys. "America's Team" had been annihilated by the New York Giants, and Blagojevich was trying to tell his brother they hadn't been expected to win anyway.

After the fun, it was right back to talk of fund-raising. Lon Monk was calling Hull and the Indians. Blagojevich said with an Obama win, he was going to have to get serious about deciding on the Senate seat.

"Do I just finish out my term as governor?" Blagojevich said. "You know, do I try to run again as governor? I can't see me, I don't want to be governor again."

"Look man, that's, that's your gut check right there," his brother answered. "So no one needs to tell you anything."

"There's just a bunch of shit that I got to, you know, divorce from myself when I'm making these decisions, this decision," Blagojevich told Robert. "And I got this, you know, unbelievable thing in front of me. I can appoint the next senator, including myself."

Blagojevich said his model was Mitt Romney, a former Massachusetts governor who had managed to put together a national network of supporters and be relevant on a national stage. Well, Romney had wealth, Robert answered. That wasn't something the governor had managed. Right, said Blagojevich, but it could be possible to figure both out contemporaneously. Maybe spending a little time in Washington as a senator was the best way to emulate what Romney had done, Blagojevich said, but he was clearly skeptical of his own thoughts.

"Don't you think I'd be Carol Moseley Braun if I make myself a senator?" Blagojevich asked, referencing the one-term Illinoisan whose time in the senate was marked by controversy and virtually no accomplishments.

There might be other routes, he said out loud, like getting a TV show. Sending himself to Washington meant sending himself into instability and the unknown. There were no guarantees. Nineteen seventy-two had been a Republican landslide, for example, he said, and then Watergate had changed the landscape almost overnight. He could get washed out by any number of variables.

What he wanted to do most was run for president.

"The moment when it first hit me was when I saw Obama, when I was there when he announced. And I said this guy is seriously running for president, and I've worked with him. Now I know I can do it. You know what I mean?"

Maybe in eight years, Robert said. Blagojevich would be sixty then.

"Reagan's my model," Blagojevich said. "Obama's model would be John Kennedy, but mine would be Reagan."

The next day was November 3, just a day before the election. It was a key day for Blagojevich, as Obama's wishes for the Senate seat he was about to vacate were going to get much clearer. The first official messenger had in fact been Emanuel. He had called Harris when Harris was at a shoe store. The governor's chief of staff had taken the call and learned that Obama did in fact have a specific preference for who would succeed him.

Harris told Blagojevich about his talk with Emanuel on a call that started normally enough. Harris and his boss chatted about the imminent presidential vote and Halloween a couple of nights before. There had been two

Sarah Palin costumes in Blagojevich's neighborhood. Then Harris began to recount what he had been told. If someone were to believe Rahm, Obama very much cared about his replacement and wanted that to be Valerie Jarrett. It was like a switch was thrown in Blagojevich's mind.

"OK, now we should get something for that, couldn't I?" he said, with Harris responding that there would need to be more talks. "How about Health and Human Services, can I get that?" Blagojevich asked.

If Obama really cared, maybe, Harris answered. What Blagojevich might realistically expect to get in return might depend on what his perceived alternatives were. The better the alternatives, the more bargaining power the governor had. Bill Daley was one.

"Lisa Madigan," Blagojevich said. "That's right. It's Lisa Madigan."

If he fronted Lisa Madigan as a very good option for him, the price for Obama to get what he wanted would go up accordingly. Blagojevich immediately thought of leaking an item saying he was very interested in Madigan to *Sun-Times* gossip columnist Michael Sneed. His press representative, Lucio Guerrero, had told him he often wrote things for Sneed in her own voice and e-mailed them over to her for consideration in her column. That was doable now as well. Do me a favor, Blagojevich said to Harris, look up who had been secretary of health and human services. Former Wisconsin governor Tommy Thompson was an obvious one who had made the kind of move Blagojevich was now pondering. Maybe there was another cabinet position that wouldn't be stupid, he said. How about UN ambassador—ridiculous?

"Shit, that'd be cool, huh?" the governor said. The potential trades were seemingly endless. Blagojevich called his wife and brother to tell them about the possibilities.

Back at the FBI's Lisle office, agents were fairly ecstatic. There was a feeling among supervisors that they finally had the governor of Illinois where they wanted him. They had caught him in illicit deals in the making, and it had taken just a few days of wiretapping to do it. Agents were working long days, sitting on the phone lines with earphones listening to what was unfolding, periodically letting Cullen and other bureau bosses listen to the calls on a speaker. Many couldn't believe what they were hearing. Wiretap investigations usually involved long periods of sitting and waiting for a particular phone to ring, but this was a veritable explosion of phone traffic and information. It was Cullen's job to give daily briefings at a meeting with Chicago's FBI boss, Rob Grant, and other bosses. It became a joke that no one wanted to follow Cullen's Blagojevich update because it was so good.

At the US attorney's office, the reaction was nearly the same. The office was getting daily briefings on the ongoing taping and copies of the discs that were being burned of the calls. There was a distinct feeling of, "You've got to be kidding me."

Rod Blagojevich, the governor of the state, was turning his ability to appoint someone to the US Senate into an auctionable item. Prosecutors knew Blagojevich was occasionally into some very sketchy and probably illegal fund-raising, and their taping effort had started down that trail. Now they had something that was off the charts in terms of expectations. One likened it to targeting someone who was suspected of dealing guns and drugs and learning "Oh, by the way, he's trying to kill the president of the United States."

=====

Blagojevich had his November 3 meeting with Balanoff and Stern, after getting hints they had been tapped by Obama and those around him to get Blagojevich the message that Valerie Jarrett was the preferred candidate to replace Obama. The meeting took place downtown at the Thompson Center at Blagojevich's state offices, outside the bounds of the federal taping operation. What was caught on tape were calls the governor had with Harris and Greenlee prior to sitting down with the union bosses. "War-gaming" was what he called it, deciding how to make a play to be named secretary of health and human services in exchange for appointing Jarrett as Obama wished. He agreed with his advisers that he wouldn't come on too strong and make a direct request just yet. He would sit back, act confused, and mention he had other good options on the table, such as Lisa Madigan. That would placate her father and break the Springfield logjam. "There is a carrot and stick thing," is how Blagojevich described it to Harris. "Do they think that I would just appoint Valerie Jarrett for nothing? Just to make him happy?" His bid to take the HHS post shouldn't be dismissed out of hand, he said. He had done more with health care as a governor than Tommy Thompson had. And there were still other possibilities that were being worked out, such as asking Emil Jones to empty his Illinois campaign war chest and give it to Blagojevich in exchange for becoming a senator.

That evening, after the meeting, Blagojevich was at home, digesting what had happened in a pair of calls with Greenlee. Balanoff and Stern weren't pushing him, Blagojevich said, and seemed most interested in him not appointing Jesse Jackson Jr. The drive for Jarrett had not been that explicit, and Blagojevich wasn't that impressed. The pair had been coy about why they were there and suggested they weren't speaking for Obama.

"And if they treat me without, you know, any real, that they, they don't have any great interest in the Senate seat and they're not gonna offer anything of any value, then I might just take it. You know what I'm saying, Bob?" Blagojevich said.

If impeachment proceedings against him became a reality, the governor would be kicking himself for naming some senator and leaving himself no advocates in Illinois. Blagojevich and Greenlee agreed, it was better that the knock on Blagojevich be that he appointed himself a senator than that he was impeached. The media was getting behind the idea of Blagojevich's removal. Greenlee hung up to look up a *Tribune* editorial and called right back. The paper had in fact said it was time to have an Illinois House committee study impeachment. Blagojevich could be heard on the call leaving his conversation with Greenlee for a moment to tell Patti what his aide was saying. The *Tribune* had thrown a line in about studying impeachment in an endorsement of Michael Madigan.

"Tell him to hold up that fucking Cubs shit," Patti said angrily. "Fuck them. Fuck them! Why should you do anything for those assholes? Sam Zell. What kind of bullshit is that?"

Patti was telling her husband he should forget about an arrangement he was trying to set up with the Tribune Company, which still owned the Cubs, offering state assistance for the renovation of Wrigley Field. Maybe Patti was right, Greenlee said, Tribune Company owner Sam Zell would say he had nothing to do with the editorial board, but maybe he should be told to step in if he wanted to get the Cubs thing done.

"Or just fire 'em. He owns the paper. I mean what would, ah, William, William Randolph Hearst do?" Patti asked. "Say, 'Oh, I can't interfere with my editorial board?'"

The governor said someone should pool every negative thing the paper had written about him and then go to Tribune Company officials with it. Harris could do that. Zell could be told the paper's editorial decision was making it hard for him to make the kinds of decisions he needed to, Blagojevich said. Someone should tell Zell to get rid of those people.

There were many factors that needed to go into his Senate choice, he told another adviser, Doug Scofield, a short time later. Scofield was a political consultant for, among others, the SEIU and was passing back-channel

messages to Blagojevich's staff on what Balanoff had been hearing. Blagojevich launched into a rant with Scofield as well, saying the Senate seat was
too valuable to give away or give away on some vague promise of fund-
raising support down the road from Obama supporters. It needed to be way
more concrete than that.

"It could be, you know, billions of dollars for the State of Illinois and
deal with my budget and some sort of mechanism to ensure the Democrats
protect me and don't impeach me. I don't know how you do that, but it's got
to be something like that, you know? The fucking idea that I fucking should
give this fucker a US Senator and he has got Tony Rezko up his ass more
than me. Fuck them. Fuck them," Blagojevich said of Obama.

"Fucking Tony, you know, don't get me started. I wear the jacket because
fucking, you know, I trusted Tony and he fucking, you know, he went off
and did his thing in my administration, OK? But I didn't ask him to fucking
buy me a house. After the news got out that there were issues about him,
after the word got out that there were issues about him, you know we made
adjustments. Hear what I am saying?"

Blagojevich told Scofield he had clearly stated he had a political deal with
the Madigans as a possibility, and Scofield agreed Balanoff would probably
take that back to the incoming president. The governor was wondering how
to follow up with Balanoff or whether to just call David Axelrod. His preference, Blagojevich said, was to wait and let them come to him. Rahm had
opened up a channel, too. Overall, he was in the catbird seat.

"Not everybody gets . . . to have a one-vote US Senate election."

The next morning was Election Day, and Blagojevich read a report on the
Politico website reporting that he had met with Stern and Balanoff about
Obama's choice to replace him. Blagojevich was somewhat encouraged
because he figured the leak had come from Stern, suggesting Stern actually was visiting him on Obama's behalf. His calls early that morning were
a whirlwind of speculation about how he might be approached and how
he could play his hand. The options were numerous, and Blagojevich was
eager to see things play out. The governor wouldn't come to know it until
later, but Balanoff would get a direct call from Obama on Jarrett that day,
and Balanoff would reach back out to Blagojevich for yet another meeting.
The Health and Human Services post was still foremost on Blagojevich's
mind, and he kept coming back to it even though he told Greenlee in a call
that morning that he figured the request would be laughed at and then dismissed because of Blagojevich's Rezko connection.

"Fuck you. Rezko didn't stop you from being president," Blagojevich said. There should be a list of possible things he could get for the seat, he said to Greenlee, just don't write it down. Maybe he could be ambassador to Canada? Greenlee should look up who past ambassadors had been and what their qualifications were. Look at Germany. Look at England. Look at France. Look at Italy.

When Blagojevich got on the phone with Harris that morning, he likened the coming negotiations to a sports agent wheeling and dealing.

"My free agent wants to play for the Cowboys, he wants to play for the Eagles. OK. How much you offering, Obama?" Blagojevich said. "What are you offering Madigan? You know what, we can always go to the, we can always go the Forty-Niners with Emil, you know what I mean? We can always end up there. Or me."

And the reality was sinking in that he really could send himself. Agents caught him on phone calls with Patti, discussing how much senators make. Everyone was trying to guess the election's outcome by reading into reports on turnout at the polls. The winds were blowing for Obama.

"So all of this, I didn't let you down, did I? I feel like I let you down," Blagojevich said, his own presidential dream bubbling to the surface again.

"Oh, forget it," Patti said. "Are you crazy?"

"There was no room to run. There was no room to move," Blagojevich answered. "I couldn't do it. Right?"

"Yeah. Don't worry. Don't worry."

A little while later, in another call, Patti had decided Blagojevich should pursue an ambassadorship to India. That was the best choice. Their daughters would find it very enriching. "How are the running routes around there?" Blagojevich asked, as Patti was on a computer looking up the embassy. And speaking of their daughter Amy, Patti's sister had said she should go that night to Obama's rally in Grant Park after the vote.

"Like it's history," she said.

"Yeah, so what," her husband answered.

Obama's apparent election was making Blagojevich very unhappy, and in calls captured and uncaptured, he was spending more time with the thought of just sending himself to the Senate, on to something new in his career that would give him more of an upward trajectory. The advisers who were telling him that was a bad idea were starting to catch the bull's horns. Scofield was one who often said that was a bad idea, and Blagojevich told Greenlee in a call that he was getting sick of it. Scofield's constant naysaying

was getting highly annoying. He had told Scofield how he really felt, he told Greenlee.

"Then, you know, now is the time for me to put my fucking children and my wife first, for a change," Blagojevich remembered telling Scofield. Fuck all of the consultants who had told him to choose a career path at his family's expense. To say Blagojevich was getting wound up would be a major understatement.

"And then I, I started venting, you know, part of my vent was, 'Yeah, and what have I gotten for—? Oh, the people are gonna fucking be mad and the fucking newspapers are gonna rip me for this? OK? I fucking busted my ass and pissed people off and gave your grandmother a free fucking ride on a bus. OK? I gave your fucking baby a chance to have health care. I fought every one of those assholes including every special interest out there, who can make my life easier and better, because they wanna raise taxes on you and I won't. I, I fight them and keep them from doing it. And what do I get for that? Only 13 percent of you all out there think I'm doing a good job. So fuck all of you.'"

14

"I've got this thing . . ."

Barack Obama won the election that day, becoming the nation's first African American president. He held a historic rally in Chicago's Grant Park as millions watched on television. Blagojevich was there, shaking hands and putting a good face on things. He spent time at a party thrown by Emil Jones at a hotel across the street and hung out near Obama's stage. Among those he ran into were the Reverend Jesse Jackson, who wanted to talk with him about his son, and Tom Balanoff, who told Blagojevich he needed to see him again.

The next morning, Blagojevich was back on the phone with Greenlee, talking again about ambassadorships he could get for the seat but also talking about the public face being put on the search. There would be a 1:00 PM press conference where Blagojevich would discuss his supposed process for finding a worthy senator. And he talked to Harris about calling a special election to replace Emanuel in the Fifth Congressional District. Obama had asked Emanuel the night before to be his chief of staff, was what the media was reporting. One other thing Harris should know, Blagojevich said, was that Balanoff was coming in again to talk about the Senate appointment.

"He was very explicit with me. 'I talked to Barack about the Senate seat. Can I come and see you? Can I do it tomorrow?'" Blagojevich told Harris. "I said, 'Sure.'"

The governor wanted advice on how to make his approach when he had Balanoff to himself again. Harris said it was likely Balanoff would say

Obama had Jarrett as a preference, but the president-elect didn't want it to be known publicly that he was asking that someone be chosen for him.

"Hold it, let's talk about this now. So do I say, how bad does he want it? I don't think so," Blagojevich said, trying to play out how an exchange might go. "Maybe I say instead, I, I say, 'Listen, he's the president-elect, he obviously has a lot of weight. You know, with, with his intere-, his interests in what he would like. You know, I, I, I, I clearly, I definitely respect that, and, and certainly value it.'"

But the message back for Obama would be that Blagojevich had other pressures as well. Emil Jones, an old Obama mentor, thought he might get the seat, Blagojevich said he would say, and there was Lisa Madigan. He had Mike Madigan screwing him, and he was under federal scrutiny because of his and Obama's mutual friend Tony Rezko. Blagojevich should say he had to give serious consideration to a Madigan play, Harris advised. The real trick was subtly bringing up the other end—the possibility that Blagojevich could find a place in Obama's administration. One way would be to say that the new senator, Jarrett, and Blagojevich could go to Washington together and repeat the kind of health programs Blagojevich had pushed in Illinois on a national scale. The question was whether to specifically say he wanted to be secretary of health and human services.

That's where it would be difficult. Maybe ease into it, Harris said. "How do we take care of the president-elect's wishes while at the same time taking care of the people of Illinois?"

"Yeah. And, and, and my, and me, do I say me?" Blagojevich asked.

"Right, by, by keeping me strong," Harris answered.

"But I don't want that," Blagojevich said. "I'm not looking for that. I'd like to get out, the fuck outta here."

The objective was to get a good gig in Washington, Blagojevich said. He was being left behind in Illinois while everyone else was seemingly about to make history. And if he didn't appoint Lisa Madigan, her father would make his political life even more hellish. So, he could appoint Jarrett, and the two of them would leave town together.

Well, if that was his mind, then Blagojevich should go ahead and lay that out there in the meeting, Harris said.

Blagojevich said he knew getting something like UN ambassador was extremely unlikely. How much would Rezko be in Obama's mind before agreeing to any kind of job for Blagojevich? the governor wondered. Obama had to be nervous about Rezko. There was a story that Blagojevich had heard that he believed, he told Harris. Rezko had given $25,000 cash to a man named Bruce Washington, who came from the Cook County political organization of John Stroger but had been working for Blagojevich.

"The cash was for Obama. Not for me," Blagojevich said.

"Right."

"You understand?" the governor asked.

When Blagojevich sometimes mentioned Obama having bigger Rezko issues than he did, it was often this story he was thinking of. His mentioning that much detail about the matter would continue to perk up the ears of the investigators listening to the call. Bruce Washington was interviewed, as was Rezko, but not enough detail was gathered to make much of it. Rezko had talked about giving money to a number of politicians, but often that kind of off-the-books cash was almost indistinguishable from what was called "walking around money" on the South Side of Chicago. In campaign season this money was used for extra little expenses, and on voting day it provided cabs for elderly voters and bought lunch for people in the neighborhood if that's what it took to get them to the polls. The Obama-Rezko story stemmed from the 2004 election. Still, Blagojevich was signaling he thought his convicted fund-raiser, Rezko, had indirectly given $25,000 cash to the man who had just been elected president of the United States, and Blagojevich didn't think Obama ever disclosed it.

———

Before he met with Balanoff, Blagojevich spoke to both Harris and Greenlee again. He was dreaming big. What was more important, Commerce Secretary or ambassador to India? He was CEO of a $58 billion corporation—the state of Illinois; why couldn't he be ambassador to India?

"If he makes me secretary of state, do you think a pundit or two would say, 'Man, he sure must have something on Obama when it comes to Rezko?'" Blagojevich said to Harris as both men laughed. "Holy shit."

Maybe there was something in the private sector that Obama could influence. He could get Blagojevich on a good corporate board or two or make him head of something like Families USA, the Kaiser Foundation, or the Red Cross. Elizabeth Dole had that job. CEO positions would pay, so the men decided to patch Greenlee in to tell him to do the research.

With Greenlee on the phone, Harris outlined what he and the governor were just talking about. He should research organizations that were heavily dependent on federal aid, making them more vulnerable to being influenced by Obama's wishes. Greenlee understood. There were all kinds of foundations out there that fit the bill and pushed a progressive agenda for the middle class.

"Something like that would be great," Blagojevich said. "What does that pay?"

Could be between $300,000 and $500,000, Harris said. It was all interesting. Greenlee should consider them all, including the Red Cross. How about the Salvation Army? Greenlee tossed out.

"Oh, that would be huge," Blagojevich said. "But do you have to wear a uniform? Forget that."

Meanwhile, Balanoff had reached out to Scofield to pass a message to Blagojevich that it would take another day before he could meet with him, giving Blagojevich more hours to throw around scores of ideas of what he could ask for. It also gave him time to field a call from one of the men he looked up to in politics, Dennis Hastert, a former Speaker of the US House from the far western suburbs. Hastert was a longtime Republican, but it didn't matter. They had much in common. Blagojevich had voted for Reagan twice, he reminded Hastert. The men talked about the Senate seat and what Blagojevich should do. In Hastert's opinion, the best move was a "double swap." Appoint someone like Lisa Madigan and get something for it, and then Blagojevich would have to appoint someone attorney general to replace her.

"So that is a two-fer," Hastert said. He liked the idea of a deal with Madigan that let bygones be bygones. Lisa would go to the Senate, and her father would agree to get a group of things going in Illinois. "That has to be the quid pro quo."

Blagojevich also spoke with his nephew, Alex, Robert's son. It was his twenty-sixth birthday. And that was too bad, Blagojevich joked. Just four years older and he could have made Alex a US senator for his birthday.

Doug Scofield was next. Blagojevich told him he was still getting used to the idea that Obama was president.

"It's a big deal. OK, it's Joe Louis and Jackie Robinson and, right?" Blagojevich said, before devolving into a slight depression. "That's a good thing. It's uh, eh, forget it, it is what it is and we've gotta deal with it."

Not exactly a ringing endorsement, but it did mean Blagojevich was picking a new senator. Scofield was still acting as a back channel between the governor and the leaders of SEIU, including Balanoff, who was still coming in the next day. SEIU was the biggest funder of Families USA, an advocacy group dealing with health care. OK, Blagojevich said, so Obama could move out whoever was there so Blagojevich could have it.

Blagojevich told Scofield he had done some television news shows the prior night after Obama's win. His least favorite had been with Chicago television journalist Carol Marin, who reminded him there had been presidential swirl around him in 2002, but the FBI had blown that up. It was a bitter pill for Blagojevich to swallow at that moment. "I hate her," he said.

But back to the real subject at hand. Health and Human Services was a spot he really wanted. If that were offered, he'd jump at it, he told Scofield. UN ambassador, he would take that, too.

"You Russian motherfuckers," Blagojevich imagined. "Can you see me?"

It was a lot to think about. Everything was in the air. "You know what I mean," he said. Something in his head was messed up, he said later in the call, and he was afraid he could still wind up delivering pizzas somewhere. He needed something else to reach for.

"I mean, I, I've got this thing and it's fucking—*golden*," Blagojevich said with a slight pause, as if he was fully relishing the opportunity he now had in front of him. "And I, I'm just not giving it up for fucking nothing."

═══

Blagojevich would spend most of the next two days trying to decipher the new lay of the land. He often described his meeting with Balanoff as "good." It was a good meeting or a good discussion. His message had been received. "They know that I could do it for [Jarrett]," Blagojevich told Greenlee.

Not long before the meeting, there had been a new wrinkle, as Harris thought maybe Blagojevich could wind up leading Change to Win, a national labor organization affiliated with SEIU. That might make his ask even more direct and something Balanoff and Stern could presumably control. It might give Blagojevich the profile he needed to stay on the national stage for eight years and wait out Obama's presidency. The feds had captured Blagojevich and Patti talking about it, as Patti used the Internet to try to figure out how much a position like that might pay. Patti flipped through foundations and saw one tied to Tippi Hedren, the actress.

"Bird lover," Blagojevich deadpanned.

But when Patti found Change to Win, there was a problem. Oops, she finally said, it didn't look from the website like anyone was being paid. That set Blagojevich off. Don't worry about it. He would negotiate an annual salary of a million dollars, and Obama would just give the organization more money if it was a problem.

"All of this gets fuckin' created, you understand. It doesn't mean a fuckin' thing who gets paid or doesn't get paid over there. 'Cause none of it is— fuckin', we're makin' it up."

Blagojevich explained that the beauty of the situation was SEIU was the intermediary. They could easily be part of the arrangement. But Patti was put out.

"I tried to be helpful, and you jumped down my fuckin' throat," she said.

Now, as Blagojevich told Greenlee and Harris how things had gone with Balanoff, he said the key was that the Obama people now knew a Jarrett pick was a real possibility if the governor of Illinois could be thrown a bone.

"They also know I want something," Blagojevich told his deputy governor. He had stressed that the "Madigoon" play was an option but had also hinted enough to Balanoff that if something could be done for him, that favor would supersede any alternatives.

To Greenlee, the biggest obstacle was probably still the Rezko situation. The Obama camp was unnaturally afraid of it. For example, they hadn't even officially invited Blagojevich to the Grant Park rally.

"You honestly think they'd snub me? No way," Blagojevich said, in disbelief. That was news to him.

The governor's staff had gone back and forth in e-mail to Obama's people without telling Blagojevich because they were scared of his reaction. In retrospect, it might have been a good thing for Blagojevich to know Obama's mind. He was all about severing all ties to Illinois.

Blagojevich thought that the height of Obama's ascendence should make Rezko meaningless but probably wouldn't. The thing he had asked for, a post in the administration, probably wouldn't happen, and Rezko was the reason. The governor said he mentioned the Bruce Washington story to Balanoff, just to let him know he knew it. At least the Obama people would know he was serious about things. He had done as well as he could that day, he said.

"It was a good, good discussion, executed well," is how Blagojevich described it to Harris.

And it wouldn't take long to get a response. It would come the next morning, November 7, the Friday after Obama had been elected. Word came in the form of a call with Scofield, who said the message had been received, and word was the Obama people weren't sure what they could offer, but there could be more talking.

"They're not quite sure what to make of it," Scofield said.

It seemed Blagojevich might have overplayed his Madigan problem, as part of the response was that maybe Lisa Madigan could be offered something in the new administration, getting her out of Springfield and maybe the Madigans out of Blagojevich's hair. Blagojevich wasn't exactly sure how that solved anything for him, but ever the optimist, Blagojevich said he thought that at least meant the other side was willing to deal.

It seemed whoever on the Obama side was fielding the information understood the Madigan problem, but something else had come back. The president-elect wanted to be done with Illinois politics. Bringing Blagojevich to Washington to be in the cabinet was definitely contrary to that desire. Health and Human Services was a very big ask.

"I think they are surprised and don't quite know how to respond," Scofield repeated.

Blagojevich turned around minutes later and let Harris know on a call what was happening.

"Doug called on behalf of Balanoff. He would like to see me again as soon as, you know, at my earliest convenience," said Blagojevich. He had been told they didn't really know what to make of the request, but Obama wanted Jarrett and was going to resign his Senate seat within days. "Barack really wants to get away from Illinois politics," he added, as both men laughed.

Blagojevich explained what Scofield had said about Lisa Madigan. The message had been received, but the response back had been the idea of moving Lisa Madigan to Washington, not as a senator but in the kind of post Blagojevich might want. That seemed to do nothing for Blagojevich on any front, they agreed.

"Tell them to put Mike Madigan in the cabinet," Patti said in the background.

Anyway, things were in motion. There was no reason to rush, and in fact Blagojevich wanted to run some clock. Other potential emissaries were coming at him with the same Obama-Jarrett information. One of them was Obama friend Alexi Giannoulias, the Illinois treasurer. The governor decided he was going to dodge Giannoulias that day, and Balanoff, too, for that matter. He was going to let things cook. They hadn't known what to make of his request, but that was a natural reaction. They weren't just going to appear and say OK to making him HHS secretary immediately.

Eventually he would have another conversation with the union boss, and maybe someone would eventually deal more directly with Jarrett herself.

"She has also been told now that I would do it if I got this," Blagojevich said. "So now she knows I can get this Senate seat if my friend would give him this."

Obama wanted out of Chicago politics. That was just another term for Rezko, Blagojevich said. Harris said all in all, he was feeling a little better than neutral. Things seemed to be about where Blagojevich wanted them. The governor thought HHS was "an unlikely long shot," but at least people on the Obama side were churning over his request. A short time later, he would go back over things with Scofield yet again. No one on the president-elect's side had immediately said his ask was ludicrous. If Obama had a problem with Blagojevich's plan, the reason was Rezko.

"He may want to get out of Chicago politics, but I subscribe to the view misery loves company," Blagojevich said. Jarrett had a lot of influence with Obama, and the seat was hers to win or lose.

"So she's holding Health and Human Services, and I'm holding a US Senate seat. OK?" Blagojevich said. "She's holding hers with two hands, just kinda clinging to, you know, little pieces of it. Me, I've got the whole thing wrapped around my arms, mine, OK? I'm willing to trade the thing I got tightly held, to her for something she doesn't hold quite as tightly."

Again, prosecutors noted the gravity of what Blagojevich had said. They were aware of the Balanoff meeting but had not recorded it. What they captured in the call was Blagojevich summarizing for them what had taken place and reporting that he had in fact told Balanoff that he would trade the Senate seat if he could be named to a cabinet post. It was self-dealing, and the remark escalated the situation. No more were they recording Blagojevich theorizing about what he should ask for or what he could get. He had done it. He had passed the message to someone he believed was speaking for Obama.

———

Late in the afternoon of November 7, Blagojevich had a long talk with Harris and another of his Washington, DC, advisers, Democratic pollster Fred Yang. Blagojevich and Harris brought Yang up to date with what was going on. The governor had delivered the message that Jarrett could be a senator if he could be given HHS, he said, and had also told Balanoff that if he were cornered and felt he had "no other option" for filling the seat, he would just send himself. Blagojevich had even had things checked out and learned that some senators had their wives become lobbyists in Washington while they served.

Exactly what having "no other option" meant was unclear, but Blago-jevich tried to explain. It seemed to mean not having an option that would mean something good for him. The idea was to solve his family's financial issues and get something that would give him a political future. Leading something like Change to Win would pay him a handsome salary and give him a national platform on an issue. Something that didn't pay well was relatively useless to him. "I wanna make money," he said. Men like Ronald Reagan and Richard Nixon had done work in the private sector during their "wilderness years," Blagojevich said, and later returned to the national stage.

Harris liked the plan to work a deal with Obama that would see him get Jarrett as a senator and land Blagojevich at Change to Win through the union in a position that might even be created just for him. It wasn't a direct trade that could put pressure on Obama, the men agreed, likening it to a three-way baseball trade.

"It gives Barack the ability to stay out of Illinois politics," Harris explained to Yang. It was easier for Obama to do something indirect. "'Cause he's got a buffer. So there's no obvious quid pro quo for Valerie."

On November 10, a few days later, there was another long conference call on the situation, where this time Blagojevich and Yang were joined by Blagojevich's other adviser in the capital, Bill Knapp, as well as Quinlan, strategist Doug Sosnik, and Patti. Blagojevich told the group he had done a lot in politics but it was time to think about his future. Obama had made it tough for him to make another quantum leap up, so it might be time to take a step back and make some money. He had college to consider for Amy in a few years. Knapp warned that making himself a senator would turn him into a national joke. That wasn't the kind of launching pad Blagojevich was thinking of for the next stage of his life, throwing him directly into the history books for all the wrong reasons.

"Don't worry about it. I hear ya," Blagojevich said. "Fuck."

The storyline on CNN and everywhere else was that Obama wanted Jarrett in the Senate, Knapp said, and it would probably be in Blagojevich's best interests, now and in the future, to fall in line and make that happen. That's where the momentum was going, so it probably wasn't smart to do anything other than fulfill Obama's wishes, unless there was some major reason in Blagojevich's self-interest not to. And that simply hadn't emerged in any clear way. What he could do, Knapp said, was use the Madigan problem and possible Lisa Madigan solution as a "stalking horse" to get as much consideration as possible from Obama.

"Well, that's right," Blagojevich said. "That's what we're doing."

So that left the question of what to get. Blagojevich said he had made his HHS request but knew that was likely to be a nonstarter. Knapp agreed the post was highly unlikely.

"You don't believe I can be ambassador to India?" Blagojevich asked.

"No," said Knapp. And ambassador to Russia, same answer. "The Rezko thing is this cloud that's gonna prevent this. I mean he's not gonna trade Valerie for his reputation. Presidents don't do that. You know what I'm saying?"

Quinlan piped up that maybe Obama could get Patti installed on some corporate boards somewhere, you know, so it wouldn't really look like one thing for the other. But Knapp wasn't super excited about that either. With Patti not really being a known business person, it could look weird.

Patti noted she had been a realtor and appraiser, and she thought there was a congressman's or ex-governor's wife on the board of Fannie Mae or Freddie Mac. The housing crisis didn't make that the place to be, though, and Knapp noted it also made it a place of intense scrutiny.

To Knapp, the question was what Obama could do to help Blagojevich out in a couple of years when his term as governor expired. But for Blagojevich, that just wasn't good enough. They were struggling now, he said.

"It's no good. I gotta get moving. The whole world's passing me by, and I'm stuck in this fucking job as governor now," Blagojevich said. Factors like the *Tribune* writing about all of Patti's real estate clients were making it harder and harder for the family to earn a living.

"I mean, you guys are telling me I just gotta suck it up for two years and do nothing," Blagojevich said. "Give this motherfucker his senator. Fuck him. For nothing? Fuck him."

Obama wasn't just going to get to publicly pretend he didn't want anyone in particular, while Blagojevich made a pick that would do nothing for him—even politically—or worse yet make people upset with him. Maybe he would just appoint Jesse Jackson Jr., which seemed to be the one thing no one around Obama wanted.

"That would be revenge," Knapp agreed, laughing.

There had to be a way to figure something out. Michelle Obama was on corporate boards. Patti was qualified. Maybe she should have just gone into nonprofit work from the beginning. Then she wouldn't be dealing with what was happening to her now.

"And then I have a personal issue, which is, I feel like I'm fucking my children," Blagojevich said. "That's what I feel like. The whole world's passing me by, I'm stuck in this fucking gridlock for two more fucking years, OK, and nasty fucking shitty fucking press and everything, you know, and every asshole out there. We know few friends."

The advisers—Yang, Knapp, and Sosnik—seemed to mostly agree. The best play was probably to just appoint the person Obama wanted, Jarrett. Blagojevich would get the benefit of boosting his legacy by naming a qualified African American woman to the Senate and would build up good will with a popular president who was from his home state. The move could somehow pay off down the road. Don't stick your finger in the eye of the next president, is how Sosnik put it. Wait and see what could come for you later if you do what Obama wants.

But it was Patti who said the Blagojeviches were already past the good-will-for-nothing point. They'd already asked. The governor had sent the message that he wanted to be the next Tommy Thompson.

"I don't think you live your life hoping that somebody's gonna help you down the line," Patti said. "That's a bunch of baloney."

At the FBI's listening room, there continued to be a mixture of thrilled disbelief and newfound resolve at what was being caught on the recordings. Agents believed they were capturing the sitting governor in incriminating conversations, and they played the calls for supervisors.

At one point, the FBI's national director, Robert Mueller, was in town for a Chicago event. Having heard about the success of the Blagojevich operation, Mueller wanted to hear some of the recordings for himself. He stopped at the FBI's Chicago headquarters on Roosevelt Road on the West Side near Ogden Avenue and took a seat in Rob Grant's office. Agents had put together a disc of some of their favorite snippets for Mueller to hear.

Who was the guy dropping the F-bombs? Mueller asked.

Well, that was the governor of Illinois, agents explained.

"You've got to be kidding me," Mueller said, shaking his head, clearly pleased with how investigators were doing.

=====

Blagojevich, of course, was juggling multiple issues throughout the fall of 2008. Not only the Senate seat and his own fund-raising attempts, but also other fallout from Obama's election. Rahm Emanuel was leaving his seat in

Congress to be White House chief of staff. But Emanuel wanted to leave his future options open as well, including coming back to his seat in the Fifth Congressional District. He didn't know then that Chicago's Mayor Richard Daley would be announcing his retirement in less than two years, opening up the way for Emanuel to take a dream job and lead the city as its new mayor.

Emanuel began putting out feelers to talk directly with the governor, with Blagojevich imagining one topic for Emanuel would have been to try to discourage the governor's sister-in-law, Deb Mell, from making a run for the seat. What Emanuel wanted was someone who could be named to the seat with the understanding of it being temporary. Someone could be a placeholder and step back out of the way if Emanuel wanted to go back to Congress. The Constitution called for a special election to be held for a replacement, but Emanuel was looking for a loophole.

Emanuel and Blagojevich finally spoke on November 8. Blagojevich was at home when he made the call and got connected, asking Emanuel how he was.

"All right, buddy," Emanuel said. "How you doing?"

After the pleasantries, Emanuel cut to the chase.

"My guys are looking at this, and I got to get the final legal document, but in the meantime you should know, bizarrely, in my interest of, uh, you know, having somebody there that doesn't want to make it a lifetime commitment," he said.

And Emanuel had someone in mind. Cook County Commissioner Forrest Claypool was interested in serving for one or two terms and then going to the cabinet. That seemed fine, but the problem, Blagojevich said, was he didn't have the power to appoint anyone.

Emanuel said that was wrong. It had been researched. If he stepped down in mid-December, just weeks before the swearing in of the next Congress, it would be too fast to have a special election called. It wouldn't make Claypool a US representative for good, but it would give him a three-week head start on the special election that would have to follow. Claypool had a name already, so the appointment would give him both that head start "and a presumption," Emanuel said. This conversation should stay between them.

"And I will not forget this. And I appreciate it," Emanuel said. "And that's all I am going to say. You and I shouldn't go farther."

Was Daley going to help Emanuel with this situation? Blagojevich wanted to know. The congressman and the mayor had a long history together.

Emanuel had been a Daley fund-raiser, and Daley's political muscle had been called into action to help Emanuel get elected to Congress. Rich, as Emanuel called him, wasn't crazy about Forrest, but it would work out.

"So what are you doing on this Senate thing?" Emanuel said. "Are you really playing with Lisa?"

They would have to talk more in the future, but yes, Blagojevich said. It was something that might make sense politically.

Well, let him say one thing about Valerie Jarrett, Emanuel answered, bringing up that name, as both men seemed to dance around the topic. There was a housing crisis in America, and Jarrett, aside from being an African American woman, knew something about the housing market. She had been CEO of a real estate development firm.

A few more names were batted back and forth, such as US Representative Luis Gutierrez and Jesse Jackson Jr. One person Blagojevich should not name was Emil Jones, Emanuel said, who would be an embarrassment in Washington. It was clear Emanuel and Blagojevich would have more to say about the topic. But meanwhile, Emanuel would get him the legal papers on the possible Claypool appointment.

Good, said Blagojevich, he'd take care of it.

———

As the days wore on, Blagojevich would have dozens more calls about the seat and what to do with it. Among them, on November 10, was a call with Scofield, where the governor for the first time wanted it communicated to Balanoff that maybe he had oversold the idea that he would never, ever, appoint Jackson Jr. It was an idea that was creeping back into his head. Obama probably wasn't going to touch Blagojevich because of Rezko, he had said, meaning he could even "get ambassador to Macedonia," he told Bill Knapp.

Also on November 10, Blagojevich was speaking on recordings for the first time about the establishment of a 501(c)4 organization, a nonprofit that could be politically active. Blagojevich imagined one could be established as a vehicle for him. Someone wealthy, like J. B. Pritzker of one of Chicago's preeminent business families, could pump millions of dollars into one. Pritzker had already expressed interest in the Senate seat.

In additional calls with Scofield, Blagojevich talked about getting a leak into the *Sun-Times* through Michael Sneed that he had been in long talks with Jackson Jr. about the seat, hoping to stoke the Obama people. There was no Jackson meeting, but Blagojevich wanted to try to leverage the idea of one. Things weren't moving as quickly as he wanted toward a trade for a Jarrett appointment. The truth was he could gain good will with the public by appointing any of a number of African Americans, not just Jarrett. A Jackson leak might be just the jolt he needed.

Rod and Patti Blagojevich were on the phone one more time late in the day. Jarrett just wasn't going to happen for nothing when there were other plays out there. The Obama camp wasn't giving him the respect he thought he deserved when it came to Jarrett. Now Obama was on the top of the world, and the impatient Blagojevich didn't think the president-elect was playing ball. "How can we help you?" Blagojevich said. "There is none of that coming back."

Blagojevich didn't care if the president of the United States was upset with him. What was he going to do, Blagojevich said, make US Attorney Pat Fitzgerald come after him more?

"How about Rita Rezko for the Senate?" Blagojevich spouted, speaking of Tony Rezko's wife. "Don't they realize I can fucking do that?"

How about the president's alleged bagman, Bruce Washington? Blagojevich went on. The guy who had taken $25,000 from Rezko's office, supposedly for the man now headed for the White House. "How about I make him the fucking senator?"

Blagojevich was losing patience, and November 11 wouldn't start much better. Harris was on the phone with the governor shortly after 9:00 AM, talking about Wyma probing on behalf of Emanuel about the Senate pick. Anyway, Harris had spoken to Wyma, who had told him he was passing a message from Emanuel.

"Rahm asked him to deliver the message that the president-elect would be very pleased if you appointed Valerie and he would be, ah, 'thankful and appreciative,'" Harris repeated. "Those are the operative words."

"Uh huh," Blagojevich answered. Harris hadn't gone further or described behind-the-scenes dealing, he told the governor.

"Grateful and appreciative, huh," Blagojevich repeated, almost to himself.

"Thankful and appreciative," Harris said, correcting him slightly. But it didn't matter. The message from Obama—which seemed to be that there would be no trade at all—didn't really sink in.

"I think a 501(c)4," the governor said. "Can we get his friend Warren Buffet or some of those guys to help us on somethin' like that?"

One thing to think about was possibly naming Louanner Peters, another Blagojevich deputy governor, to the seat. She had always been loyal to him and was an African American. She was so loyal, Blagojevich believed he could appoint her now, and she could possibly be asked to step down at any point if Blagojevich faced impeachment. When she resigned, then he could name himself in a pinch and go through a trap door, out of Illinois.

"Well, OK, so we know he wants [Jarrett]," Blagojevich said. At least he knew that, though he seemed somewhat taken aback. "They're not willing to give me anything except appreciation. Fuck them. You know what I mean? Right now Louanner's the front runner."

The men hadn't heard back from Balanoff and speculated that maybe the Obama camp had switched messengers because they didn't like what the union boss had come back with or how the talks had gone. Maybe now it was Wyma from Emanuel. Wyma as the waterboy, Blagojevich said, which the governor found ironic since Wyma sometimes alleged that Emanuel hit on his girlfriend. At any rate, they couldn't be sure what Emanuel's motives were. The confirmed emissary was Balanoff, and they would do nothing before hearing back from him. Meanwhile, Blagojevich would put out word that Jesse Jackson Jr.'s star was rising.

Minutes later, Blagojevich was talking to Scofield and repeating the new message. But Scofield also had not heard from Balanoff or anyone else at SEIU. That's what he was waiting for now. The governor wanted to know if, when Scofield did talk to them, he could ask about a 501(c)4, the kind of organization that money could flow into and he could lead. "It's gotta be legal, obviously," he said. If he got nothing from Obama, he was going to have to go in another direction, Blagojevich said. He could very well appoint an African American woman, but it would be Peters. Thanks and appreciation was nice, but Blagojevich and Scofield agreed Obama needed to offer something more tangible than that.

"I get to take a ride on Air Force One," Blagojevich joked. "You know I get to maybe, maybe spend the night in the Lincoln bedroom."

The governor was left wondering what other career path he might have taken. What if he had never run for governor and stayed in Congress? Maybe he could have run for Senate in 2004, when Obama did. Where would that have taken him? He might have beaten most contenders in the primary, but Obama probably would have nosed Blagojevich out, they agreed.

He would have lost his seat in the House, but he wouldn't have any federal investigations to worry about. He would never have had any falling-out with his father-in-law. Yeah, Scofield answered, but if he had never been governor, a lot fewer people would have health care.

"I hope they're sittin' on the jury," Blagojevich joked. "I hope those people with health care are sitting on the jury."

=====

Just after 7:30 AM the next day, November 12, Blagojevich was on the phone with his press agent, Lucio Guerrero, for a morning briefing. Blagojevich instructed Guerrero to work with Doug Scofield about what to say in a Sneed item about Jackson Jr. and the idea that his stock was rising with the governor.

OK, Guerrero said, but what about Valerie Jarrett?

What about her? said Blagojevich.

There were reports on CNN late the prior day reporting that sources were saying Jarrett was no longer interested in taking the Senate seat. She was probably going to be joining Obama in the White House instead. Hmmm, Blagojevich said, that was odd since he had gotten such continued hints that Jarrett wanted the seat—and that Obama wanted her there.

The information would set off a daylong flurry of calls, beginning a few minutes later with Harris, who thought the information could be a tactic. The Obama camp could be downplaying her desire to save face in case Jarrett didn't get the appointment. Or, he said, they could be firing a shot across Blagojevich's bow that the pick wasn't that important to them. Either way, it was best not to overreact, they agreed. Blagojevich should wait to hear from Balanoff or maybe send Scofield to reach back out to him. The governor was still fixated on his newest plan, to get wealthy Obama friends to find money for his issue-advocacy organization. As much as $20 million could be funneled into it. Bill Gates and people like that could each throw in a couple of million, and a board could be put together that Blagojevich liked. "Let's fund it to the level that he's asked for and then we'll get Valerie Jarrett," Blagojevich said Obama could think, in full denial that a Jarrett pick was moving off the table.

But what if he did get the final push off? What was his next move then? Peters?

"I don't have one. I mean Jesse Jr., it's a repugnant thought to me," Blagojevich said. "I can't believe anything he says, wh-what he's got third parties saying to me is a heck of a lot more substantial than what we're getting from the Obama people, OK?"

Some of Blagojevich's other business that day dealt with his fund-raising. He heard from Robert, who said he had left three messages for Magoon, the leader of Children's Memorial Hospital from whom Blagojevich was looking for a donation. Blagojevich said he would go ahead and call himself. It was a few hours later when Blagojevich called Greenlee and asked about the status of the rate increase that would affect Children's Memorial. It was due to go into effect on January 1, but Blagojevich wanted to know if they still had total discretion over it and if it could be pulled back. "Budgetary concerns, right?" the governor said.

Blagojevich also had calls with advisers Yang and Knapp, with Knapp saying he had heard a stronger version of the Jarrett rumor. It was impossible to know exactly what the truth was, Knapp told the governor, suggesting it could even be that Emanuel wanted Jarrett in the Senate because he didn't want to have to deal with someone who was that close to Obama in the White House, where Emanuel was headed. At any rate, a transition team was meeting in Chicago over the midday hours to go over a bunch of things, so they agreed more might be known later. Blagojevich was still talking up the idea of the issue-advocacy group, but Knapp was trying to persuade him to possibly tough out his time leading the state. If the investigation dried up and he got things done in Illinois, he would be a lot more valuable in the private sector than he would now if he just fled the governor's office.

Well, the drying up could in fact be the outcome, Blagojevich said, as he had heard that Rezko was not cooperating. He was getting sick and tired of everyone throwing Rezko back on him, anyway.

"You know Rezko was actually, almost had Patti do the real estate deal for Obama's house," Blagojevich said. "How do you like that?"

"Say that again?" Knapp said, seemingly stunned.

"Uh, Rezko, uh, was talking to Patti about a property, a friend of his, who was buying a house in Hyde Park," Blagojevich said, convinced his wife had almost wound up in the arrangement.

What Blagojevich was talking about, of course, was the controversial private real estate dealings between the Obamas and Rezkos in 2005, after Obama had become a US senator. Barack and Michelle had closed on a mansion in the Kenwood neighborhood for $1.65 million, which was well under asking price, on the same day Tony and Rita Rezko paid the full $625,000 listed price for a next-door parcel. The Rezkos then transferred a strip of their land to the Obamas for $104,500 and arranged for a $14,000 wrought iron fence on the line between the properties. The cozy deal put together while Rezko was known to be under federal investigation would haunt Obama, who called it "boneheaded," throughout the 2008 presidential campaign, when he was also busy donating to charity tens of thousands of dollars linked to his onetime friend and political patron.

At 10:26 AM the same day came a call from Harris, who had heard from Rahm Emanuel. Jarrett was in fact out of the running. She was going to the White House, so there would be no trading for anything for her appointment. Obama supposedly had four names he would find acceptable from that point, in no particular order, Emanuel had said. They were Jackson Jr.; Jan Schakowsky; Tammy Duckworth, a disabled Iraq War veteran who was born in Bangkok, Thailand, and had made a losing bid for Congress; and Dan Hynes, Illinois's comptroller who lost to Obama in the Senate primary in 2004. That was it, and Emanuel said he was to be the only go-between on the issue, meaning Balanoff was out of the picture, too.

As the two men digested the new information, Blagojevich remained interested in money going to an issue-advocacy group for him and said maybe someone could approach Emanuel with that idea. Harris didn't rule it out but said to him that the value of the ask had clearly been diluted. The incoming administration had offered an array of options including a white man, a white woman, an Asian woman, and one African American man who had previously been unpalatable. The only person they seemingly did not want was Emil Jones.

Blagojevich's next call was to his secretary, Mary Stewart, asking her to find Tom Balanoff for him.

The governor got him, but it quickly became obvious that Blagojevich was well ahead of him on the negotiating front. When he told Balanoff that Emanuel had called him that day, Balanoff still assumed it was about Valerie Jarrett. And it was the governor who told Balanoff the four new names, not the other way around. At any rate, Blagojevich said he was going to sit back and try to make the right choice. He had much to think about, and Balanoff said he would reach out to Jarrett himself and mention the 501(c)4.

"Nothing's changed," Blagojevich said, even though Obama had thrown him four names.

"You know and I think, you know, you have another candidate for a whole lot of reasons that, uh, is obviously valid so . . ." Balanoff said.

"Which one is that, Tom?"

"Well, the whole question of Lisa," replied Balanoff.

"I got that one, right," answered Blagojevich, who had seemingly forgotten all about it.

━━━

Robert Blagojevich's phones were busy, too, both his own cell phone and at the Friends of Blagojevich. Lon Monk gave him updates about dealing with racetrack owner John Johnston's family for money and waiting to hear from others. Johnston promised constantly that he was "good for it," or at least that's what Monk said, and the money was coming. On November 12, Robert was doing cleanup from a Serbian event and seeing whose checks had cleared. He asked one organizer if a check from Chris Kelly had gone through. Yes, the man said, that motherfucker's check had made it. They agreed Kelly was a loser, but be careful, Robert said. The man apparently didn't fully know who Kelly was.

"You've got to check Google."

Among Robert's other conversations was with Roland Burris, who also was interested in the Senate seat. In a conversation about fund-raising and ways to get Burris engaged, in a remark that would haunt him later, the politician who had previously run against Rod for governor said he thought he could personally do something to get money to the campaign fund. "Tell Rod to keep me in mind for that seat, would ya?" Burris said.

"And God knows number one, I, I wanna help Rod," Burris said. "Number two, I also wanna, you know hope I get a consideration to get that appointment."

The governor also continued to use his brother as a sounding board. Round and round he would go on every name in the air and even some that were new. Robert liked Gery Chico, for example. He found him a man of good character. Fine, Blagojevich said, but Chico wasn't black.

The next week or so provided no more clarity for the governor, as he bounced from adviser to adviser searching for direction. It started with Scofield and a way to salvage his dealing with the Obama administration. He wanted it "in Rahm's head" sooner rather than later that he would still make a pick in exchange for Obama's friends funding an issue-advocacy group. Someone should go and say that was something Blagojevich wanted help with, but not in connection with the Senate seat. Maybe Wyma could do it. Blagojevich wasn't thrilled with Emanuel anyway. "All a one-way street with that little asshole," the governor said to Scofield. "Fuck him."

Not in connection with anything else, Scofield repeated, apparently seeking some clarification.

"It's unsaid," Blagojevich said, adding it would be up to the messenger to communicate that. "Well, you know what I am saying."

Maybe Scofield could talk to Wyma and ask him to pass the message on the governor's behalf.

"I'm a little reluctant myself to talk to Wyma. Between you and me I just feel like, I just feel like, ah, I don't know if I can, I don't know. I feel like, I can't completely trust him with Rahm. I don't know why. Why do I feel that way?" said Blagojevich, who would later directly ask Scofield to go to Emanuel. The governor later confided in Harris that another reason he didn't want to make the call was that he figured Wyma might someday be questioned about things Rezko might know. He didn't want the conversation to come up. He wouldn't have guessed in a million years that Wyma had already been in meetings with prosecutors and investigators were already listening to him.

Blagojevich stayed mostly fixated on appointing an African American, but on many calls he sounded more desperate. He seemed to be losing his grip on normal reasoning or was at the very least saying things he never would have said in public.

"Oh yeah. Yeah, here, look, you want a black US senator. Louanner is black, OK. Has a little bit of an Afro-centric look to her but not anything that is threatening," Blagojevich said on a call to Fred Yang. "You know what I'm saying?"

Yang answered that someone like Dan Seals, who was of a mixed racial background, would be good.

"See Dan Seals and Obama and Valerie Jarrett and everyone," Blagojevich said, "too much white blood in them."

Louanner Peters was not from Hyde Park, Blagojevich said to Greenlee in another call, with its "light-skinned, black fucking elite."

Maybe he would just send himself after all. As a senator, he would demand Special Forces training and then go hunt down Osama bin Laden by himself. "You gotta give me all the best intelligence you have," Blagojevich said. "The Obama people say, yeah, fine, give it to him, good, here, send him, good, maybe he'll get killed. Then we don't have to worry about this guy anymore, and the Rezko shit dies there."

Or maybe he would write his own book like Obama did, but it would be a parody. "*The Audacity of Hopelessness,*" he said.

But his scattered look for some nameless African American hero may have peaked on November 21. Among the names he had thrown out in recent days were Oprah Winfrey and Cubs great Ernie Banks. Blagojevich was apparently lifting weights that morning, as the clanking could be heard while he spoke to Harris and plowed through a workout. Had Harris gotten any names of black military personnel from the adjutant general he was planning to call?

Harris had gotten two, but he wasn't that impressed. They were African American, all right, but they were both Air National Guard and not exactly war heroes. One was now an anesthesiologist, and neither was especially compelling.

And about that Oprah thing, Harris said. That was crazy.

"Yeah, see that's where you're wrong," the governor said.

It's true the Oprah pick would be way out there, but Blagojevich said he could do it. She was a Democrat for Obama, and she was a kingmaker. She had endorsed the man who became president. She had made him. It wasn't just that he wanted a celebrity friend, the governor said.

"This one, she's so up there, so high, that nobody can assail this pick," he said. "This would be huge."

There was also Melody Spann-Cooper, president of the African American owned WVON Radio in Chicago. Patti liked her, Blagojevich said. And there was still Louanner Peters. The truth was they were now stuck in the mud, Blagojevich said. No one was coming up with new names.

How about Arnold Schwarzenegger? said Blagojevich. Not black and not from Illinois, but the governor asked Harris to find out what the residency requirement might be, even though that would be a long shot. Someone might only have to spend one day in Illinois to be eligible to serve as a senator.

"But, you know, you got like a black Albert Einstein or somethin'?" Blagojevich asked.

The governor wanted Harris to be writing this stuff down. Did he have Spann-Cooper? "Is there a Mother Theresa type out there?" he said. Maybe Jackie Collins, the state senator, Blagojevich said. He was leaning away from Jackson Jr. and toward Peters.

"This thing's a whole fuckin'—it's a mess because there's so much nega-tivity in me," Blagojevich said, as he gasped for air from his reps. "It's not healthy."

Who else in the field was potentially Valerie Jarrett–like? Blagojevich said. It was as if he was back to square one, but square one didn't even exist anymore. Harris just sat at times, saying "mm-hmm" and then pausing. All he could add was that he would start growing the list.

You know what was good about Oprah? Blagojevich asked.

"There's nothing affirmative action about her," he told Harris. "She's a huge success. A mega success in her own right." Not like some of these other names he was throwing around, Blagojevich complained, who weren't as qualified.

"How 'bout Halle Berry," Blagojevich said. "Get her to move to Illinois and make ya a senator, and then have a shot to fuck her."

Maybe he could get that—the whole deal, Blagojevich joked as Harris laughed.

"Imagine doing something like that?" the governor said.

———

At the end of November, Blagojevich had calls with Lon Monk attempting to tie up loose ends on the fund-raising front before the end of the year. Monk described his efforts to get the wanted contributions from both John Johnston, who was waiting for Blagojevich to sign the recapture bill to route casino funds to his horse tracks, and Krozel, the road builders representa-tive. Both men were promising to come through, is what Monk told the governor. In truth, Monk wasn't having nearly as much success as he was letting on, and his reason for talking to Blagojevich was twofold. He was nominally helping the governor, but also Monk was being paid as a lobbyist for Johnston, and he was trying to get a read on when the governor might sign the racetrack bill so he could report back to the man who was paying him.

Most of the pressure on Blagojevich was political, but there was also a call from an old friend with a stake in what was happening. On Thanksgiv-ing Day, Chris Kelly called out of the blue. After having been largely out of touch for many months, the men caught up with each other for more than an hour and spoke about how Kelly's personal life was in shambles: his rela-tionship with his wife, Carmen, was falling apart and his business was all but ruined. He did have a girlfriend, he said, and he had secretly invested in a nightclub.

Soon, their talk transitioned to the "nightmare" that the federal investigation had been and how Kelly was getting ready to go to prison after pleading guilty in his own cases, before circling back to politics. Obama had reached the presidency by stealing Blagojevich's story, they agreed.

"I've never done more good for more people and never had so many people mad at me," Blagojevich lamented.

Kelly asked what Blagojevich thought of Rezko and then gave an opinion of his own.

"I got one word," Kelly said.

"Bad guy." Blagojevich answered.

"That's two words." Kelly said. He had been thinking of the word *operator*.

"Just an operator," Kelly said. "You know, his operation is good for you, then he's a good guy. His operation hurts you, then he's a bad guy. He's an operator. That's all he is."

When it came to prison, Kelly knew it was going to be ugly, he said, but he had an ace in the hole. It was a friend he knew in Florida, Bernie Kosar, the former NFL quarterback. Kosar had asked Kelly if he wanted him to talk to Florida's governor, Jeb Bush, and ask him to bring up a pardon for Kelly with his brother, President George Bush. It was a long shot, but it just might work.

Bush was going to do some high-level pardons and some lower-level ones, which Kelly might be, the governor replied. It was only later that Blagojevich began to think Kelly might have been feeling him out for other reasons. Kelly also had connections to the Johnstons, who had their own big-time Florida connections, and Blagojevich thought maybe they'd had Kelly call him to try to push on the horse racing bill.

But the Senate seat was really still the top priority on Blagojevich's mind as the month was drawing to a close. Everyone from Oprah Winfrey to Obama friend Eric Whitaker—who had once been a Blagojevich appointee as director of public health—was still being tossed around by Illinois's indecisive leader.

One string of Blagojevich's efforts did involve the supposed deal for Lisa Madigan. He had ordered Greenlee to sketch out ideas for what he could get in a Madigan deal, going over making a list of what concessions to seek from her father. "I would call it arguably the second biggest deal in American history next to the Louisiana Purchase," he told Greenlee, and told Patti he might very well wind up going that way.

But he remained clearly disgusted with the idea of handing "that princess" a Senate seat. He planned to require a special session of the General Assembly to get the things he wanted passed if Michael Madigan accepted the offer and to go public with his overture if Madigan wound up rejecting it. He told seemingly everyone he spoke to about it that it made him sick to his stomach even thinking about it, but nonetheless, "the flavor of the month is Lisa Madigan," he told Yang. One moment he seemed resigned to the idea and the next he was back in the weeds. "Nobody is in. Nobody is out," he told his adviser on the same call.

———

On Monday, December 1, Blagojevich headed for Philadelphia and a national governors' conference. President-elect Barack Obama was there to set out his economic recovery plan and greet chief executives from states across the country. Among those traveling with Blagojevich that day was Quinlan, who was on the phone with the governor that morning telling him about a recent trip to the Reagan library.

"Shit, Obama is gonna get a library, and I'm just gonna fucking fade away," Blagojevich said. "Hopefully that's the worst of what happens to me, and I don't go to prison."

The good news, Quinlan said, was that Rezko was back in the news, this time asking for a sentencing date, which would be a good indicator that he wasn't cooperating with the government or at least that they weren't getting along. Rezko was making a public show that he had told the government everything he could and he wanted to end the limbo of being held in solitary confinement in the Metropolitan Correctional Center.

On the phone with Harris a short time later, Blagojevich told him to quietly line up names of people to fill remaining open appointed slots in state government and to have grant action ready, just in case he wound up appointing himself to the Senate in short order. His first option was to deal with the Madigans, he told Harris, though he didn't trust them. If he appointed Lisa, he could make Quinlan the new Illinois attorney general. But if it didn't work out, the leading fallback that morning was himself. And among his questions was what investigative powers a senator had. Could he subpoena people himself or force federal agencies to answer to him?

Just after 3:00 PM that day, Harris was on the phone with Rahm Emanuel, who was also headed to Philadelphia, but wanted to know where Blagojevich was on the Senate seat pick. Well first of all, Harris said, there was some disappointment in Jarrett withdrawing her name.

"I think that was doable, and I could have worked on my guy in terms of vantaging his expectations, but before we could do that, before you gave me a chance to work on him, it was gone," Harris told Emanuel.

"No, I know," Emanuel said. "The thing was on that one you should have moved."

"No, no, I understood, and I got your message loud and clear about 'thankful and grateful' and ..." Harris answered, as Emanuel said, "Right."

Emanuel said he understood there was a Lisa Madigan movement in the air, but he seemed to be mostly withdrawing from specifically influencing the governor.

=====

For most of two days, it was quiet in Blagojevich's political circles in Chicago with Blagojevich in Philadelphia. But it was anything but quiet in the offices of US Attorney Patrick Fitzgerald at the Dirksen US Courthouse. With the taping essentially on pause with Blagojevich out of town, Fitzgerald held a meeting with Grant of the FBI and top people from both the bureau and the US attorney's office. What were they going to do? The original shock and anger at some of what they had heard on the recordings had given way to figuring out how to end things.

Fitzgerald had grown concerned that they had a sitting governor who had yet to make an appointment after working for weeks to see what he could get for himself in a deal for the Senate seat. They could let things go a little further, but it was starting to get risky that Blagojevich would actually make a choice. Schar said it would be derelict of those in the room to allow Blagojevich to make a decision. Everyone in the meeting believed the process had been corrupted, no matter how Blagojevich finally acted. To do something before he made a pick and out the investigation would at least make that corruption known, and the political world could react to any pick by the governor.

In the end, there was agreement. Very soon, they would act, and likely on the morning of December 9, a Tuesday, the day before Blagojevich's birthday and after a possible meeting the governor had been talking about with Jesse Jackson Jr. The governor could do whatever he wanted after prosecutors charged him, but at least it would no longer be on them. One worst-case scenario would be to have the governor make an unexpected choice and then be charged, leaving the US attorney's office to explain to the public why nothing had been done to stop him. No one wanted to have to tell the people why they had let that happen.

So with that decided, there was only one major decision left. Would the office just issue a criminal complaint and allow the governor to appear in court as so often happened in major public corruption cases? Again, there was agreement, and the answer was no. Blagojevich would be arrested, treated no differently than anyone else who might face charges this heavy. Besides, an arrest would stamp the situation with the appropriate seriousness, the group decided. The meeting adjourned, and planning began to take the governor of Illinois into custody.

Blagojevich was back in Chicago on December 3 and gave Harris a phone update on how things had gone. He had met with Yang and Knapp, who was very against the idea of Blagojevich ultimately choosing to send himself to the Senate. But first, the governor wanted to know how his idea of getting Cubs general manager Jim Hendry a street sign was going. Fine, Harris answered, they were being fabricated and should be up by Christmas. Blagojevich was pleased, and the men started talking about another idea Blagojevich cared a lot about. It was trying to get even more state money to the Cubs. Not in the Wrigley redevelopment plan the governor was already thinking about, but a grant for millions from the state in funds that were supposed to be set aside for science and technology spending. Maybe they could come up with something like solar panels for the ballpark.

On the Senate seat, if there was consensus, it seemed to be for the Madigan play, Blagojevich told Harris. As painful as it was, he could appoint Lisa Madigan and expect a list of things in return. The problem would come if the overture to her father were rejected out of hand. The governor seemed barely able to handle the thought of having to go back around in circles trying to decide what to do. That was the main reason Blagojevich was keeping the thought of sending himself to Washington alive. It would be the best way to head off the most extreme situation, he told Harris.

That was "the double-I," Blagojevich said. Indictment and impeachment. Unlikely, the men thought, but still something to consider.

Just after 1:00 PM, investigators picked up a call on Monk's cell phone. It was Chris Kelly, still looking for information on whether the horse racing bill was going to be signed. Kelly thought he had basically asked Blagojevich to do it, but there was still no action. The governor's pal, who had been all but ostracized due to his own federal cases, was getting angrier.

"Un-fucking-real. Jesus," Kelly cursed. "Selfish motherfucker. Huh. Everything is a goddamn game."

About an hour later, Monk was sitting at the Friends of Blagojevich, and the bill was on the agenda. The microphones in the room captured the conversation. There had been no contribution, and there had been no bill signing. Monk was going to see about visiting Johnston at one of his racetracks that afternoon, and the two could be heard going over what Monk might say.

He was going to ask for the campaign cash, with the signing hanging in the balance.

Monk told Blagojevich he was prepared to have a more pointed conversation on the matter. The message was going to be that Blagojevich was going to sign all of the pending bills on his desk at once, right after the first of the year. So for perception reasons, it was good to have the money right now, to have some separation.

"Look, I wanna go to him without crossing the line and say, 'Give us the fuckin' money,'" Monk said.

"Right," answered the governor.

"'Give us the money, and one has nothing to do with the other, but give us the fuckin' money,'" Monk went on. Stop screwing around, he would say, and besides, Blagojevich was concerned Johnston would get skittish on a donation if the governor signed right then. "I'm going to use the word *skittish*," Monk said.

And with that, Monk headed for a meeting with John Johnston, later calling from his cell phone to say the message was delivered. Meanwhile Blagojevich handled important phone calls on a tapped phone at the campaign office. One was with Senate Majority Leader Harry Reid, and a second with Senator Robert Menendez.

Reid told the governor there was one truth in the Senate situation. Only one person was going to be happy, the person Blagojevich picked. All in all, Reid said, he had no dog in the fight and only wanted to see someone chosen who could get reelected. The last thing Reid said he wanted was a placeholder, because he would have to figure out a way to help the next candidate raise money while that person wasn't in the Senate.

"But listen, whoever . . . you choose I will do my utmost to make him feel comfortable and do the best we can with him," Reid said.

Blagojevich described his ability to name a senator as a mixed blessing, and really not much of a blessing at all. And then he dropped a name into the conversation. He had a "very active" Jesse Jackson Jr. wanting the seat, Blagojevich told Reid.

"Yeah, I don't have to say more on that, do I?" Reid said, indicating both men considered the idea a nonstarter.

Right, said Blagojevich. But things were delicate. African Americans were an important base for him. At least there were other ideas in the air, Blagojevich said, without mentioning Madigan. But he had been in touch with Senator Durbin, and maybe when the time came, Reid could help get behind Blagojevich's plans. Reid said he would do that, and in moments the conversation was over.

Three minutes later, Blagojevich was on the phone with Menendez, the Democratic Senatorial Campaign Committee chairman. It was the same message. Menendez said he realized all the pressure Blagojevich was under, but what was most important was maintaining the party's majority in the Senate. The most thought should be given to who could hold the seat. Again, Blagojevich said, there were a lot of dynamics at work in Illinois, but he would do what he could. And again, Blagojevich asked if Menendez might at some point step in to help him push an idea across the finish line.

"I don't know if it's going to happen or if it's possible. Maybe at the appropriate time as this unfolds you guys might be able to, you know, close it," Blagojevich said. "And as this unfolds I think Dick Durbin will play a big role, but we will see."

"Hmmm," said Menendez. "That sounds like a Madigan thing."

"Yeah," said the governor. "Well that's it."

Most of Blagojevich's calls were trending in that direction. The governor seemed to be settling in on making his nemesis happy in a bid to do something political in exchange for the seat. Among his conversations captured by the feds was one with White Sox chairman Jerry Reinsdorf and another with Chicago Teamsters boss John Coli.

"And she's got a name that probably can hang on to that seat beyond two years," Coli said.

"Yeah, oh yeah," Blagojevich said. "And the downside is they turn me down and then, OK, fine, you guys will all know I have gone the extra mile man to try to get you a capital bill."

"Absolutely."

"OK, sleep on this," said the governor. "I haven't gotten my head yet completely in this place yet."

"I will," Coli told him. "It's just between the two of us, and we will chat a little privately on Tuesday. . . . If you can make it on the ninth to our party that would be great."

———

On December 4, Blagojevich spoke again to Monk, who was heading out of town. They agreed it made sense for the governor to follow up with Johnston by phone, "from a pressure point of view." Blagojevich said it was good Monk had gotten in his face.

Early in the day, Blagojevich seemed to be sewing up his push for the Madigan deal, asking Greenlee to prepare a more finalized, simplified list of demands to make in exchange for making Lisa Madigan the new senator. He was only dealing with brief flashes of anger about her, questioning why he would make life so easy for her but then quickly talking himself down.

He told Harris how upset the thought was making him.

There was no mercy or compassion about her, Blagojevich said. She was "the anti-Portia," he went on.

Who? said Harris.

"Portia in fucking Shakespeare's *Merchant of Venice*. She gave that, you know, the soliloquy, er, on mercy, on the quality of mercy speech," Blagojevich explained. "There is no mercy, man. And this fucking bitch wants to be senator, and I'm going to hand her a Senate seat. Fuck these people. These are bad people, man. Bad people!"

He spat at Greenlee to find workable solutions he could ask for on issues like taxes, something meaningful. If he was going to name Lisa Madigan, there was going to have to be a significant payout for the people. Greenlee agreed and promised to make focused asks on things that people knew about and lived with. People in Cook County were certainly feeling sales tax increases. "Yeah," Blagojevich said. "Fucking right!"

In the news that day was talk of a clemency bid for former governor George Ryan, who had been sent to prison for more than six years in the license-for-bribes scandal. It was upsetting Blagojevich that people had thrown around his name with Ryan's for so long, he told Greenlee.

"George Ryan's a fucking crook. It is so fucking galling to me that, you know, I'm being linked to George Ryan in some respect, you know, that I'm being scrutinized like this because I'm so not like that guy. Don't you think? I'm anything but a buddy down there," Blagojevich said of Springfield. "He was pals with everybody. What do you want? Take care of this. Take care of that. He was a total inside guy."

Blagojevich said the same thing to Yang in another call that morning. George Ryan was a crook and a hack and nothing like him, but he was seventy-four and had an ailing wife. Maybe it was time for an ounce of mercy. Lisa Madigan—the merciless one—had of course stripped Ryan of his pension and had come out against clemency for him. Now Blagojevich was going to just hand her a seat in the Senate, he said, again, but at least it would be part of a megadeal.

But during the course of the day, Jesse Jackson Jr.'s name began to creep back into the conversation, first in a call the governor had with Patti and then in one with Harris when Blagojevich told his chief of staff to float the name again with Rahm Emanuel. Blagojevich thought he had promised too many people that he would never name Jackson, and he needed to communicate that a Jackson choice was still possible. If people like Durbin, Reid, and Menendez wanted Lisa Madigan, they needed to get going and help him make it happen. And whether the goal with Jackson was indeed a head fake or becoming a more substantial possibility, Blagojevich scheduled a meeting with him for Monday, December 8.

He told Yang in a call late that morning that he planned to sit down with Jackson, as repugnant as the idea was. Maybe it was something he needed to open his mind to. By the way, the Jackson camp had offered a whole bunch of things to him, Blagojevich told Yang. "You know, fund-raising."

It was all supposed to be an elaborate ploy, but Blagojevich continued to bolster the idea that to him, maybe it wasn't. After Yang, the governor was back on the phone again with Harris.

"I'm honestly going to objectively look at the value of putting Jesse Jr. there," he told Harris. "As ridiculous as it is and as painful and offensive as it is and as, uh, I'm going to think about—I mean if I am prepared to put Lisa Madigan there and that doesn't work out the fallback is OK, well, what's your next play."

Jackson was the "uber African American," Blagojevich reminded Harris. He would consider what it would mean in black politics and how it would strengthen him, Blagojevich said, and don't forget, third parties had offered him $1.5 million in fund-raising help. "They're throwing numbers around," the governor said. He could repair the damage with other allies, like Balanoff, who had been told Jackson would never be picked. Blagojevich said he could just tell Balanoff "the Obama people were pigs" who didn't give up anything.

The conversation with Harris was followed by several with Lucio Guerrero. Blagojevich wanted it planted in the *Sun-Times* that he was considering Jackson. Someone like the paper's Washington writer Lynn Sweet could possibly be given a story. Remind her that Blagojevich and Jackson's father, the Reverend Jesse Jackson, had traveled to Yugoslavia together to negotiate the release of US soldiers. There was an old relationship there that people had forgotten about, the governor said, and don't forget that Obama would support the pick. The president-elect had passed four names to him after Jarrett withdrew, and one was the younger Jackson.

At 2:09 PM, Blagojevich was back on the phone with Yang discussing a poll that was positive on Jackson, which was timely since that's the way Blagojevich said he was then leaning. Greenlee was on the call too, and he was not amused with the idea. He had made it clear on past calls that he was no fan of Jackson Jr.

"I'm not joking," Greenlee said. "If you do Jesse Jackson, I can't promise I'm staying here."

"Yeah, well don't give up on—look, Greenlee, I'd love to keep you, but at some point, man, I mean, you're asking me to do Lisa Madigan," Blagojevich answered.

Madigan had zero support from African Americans, so that should give him pause, the governor said. Greenlee said to him, Jackson was simply untrustworthy. Whatever deal could be struck with him—which Blagojevich had said might possibly include keeping black candidates from running against him in the future—would seemingly have to be taken with a grain of salt. Fair enough, Blagojevich said, but there were tangible things for the Jacksons he could get up front this time.

"Is this, is essentially the deal with Jesse Jr. will be that the Jacksons will support you for reelection?" Yang asked.

"No, there's more to it," Blagojevich answered.

"What else?"

"There's tangible, concrete, tangible stuff from supporters," Blagojevich said, as Yang pressed for more detail. "Well like, you know. You know what I'm talking about," the governor finally told him. "Specific amounts and everything."

Well, said Yang, he would have to rely on the governor's judgment as to what was being offered and whether "there's enough candy for you."

"Two equally repugnant picks, on a personal level," Blagojevich said later in the call. "However, I must say, having ex-, some experience with both of them, if they were both drowning and I could save one, I really think I'd save Jesse. Just so you, so that means, from a personal standpoint, he's less objectionable to me than she is."

Only minutes after the three hung up, Greenlee called the governor back. They had barely said hello before Blagojevich chastised him for how he had spoken up on the call with Yang. Don't talk too much out of turn, Blagojevich said, because Greenlee didn't fully know what was going on. He was just trying to further leverage Jackson Jr. with the "national people," like Yang, who was in Washington.

"I see what your play is," a skeptical Greenlee answered; he got it. Blagojevich said he wanted Washington Democrats to say "holy fuck" and really think it could be Jesse. It was all a play, said Blagojevich, who had said so many times he would never, ever appoint Jackson. But it was clear to Greenlee that the dam was cracked, and Blagojevich quickly undercut himself yet again.

"And by the way, you know, who knows, it could be," the governor said of a Jackson pick, seemingly trying to get his deputy governor to warm to the idea. "I'm not gonna completely rule it out."

When prosecutors heard Blagojevich make the "tangible" remark, they believed the Jackson proposal was in fact the way the governor was going to go. They did not believe the Madigan plan was realistic, and they were operating under the belief that Blagojevich knew that as well. The governor had said so on many calls, guessing that Madigan was probably going to reject him. Prosecutors and the FBI knew that when Blagojevich was floating his Madigan idea, he was thinking of asking the Speaker of the House for billions in programs with no reasonable funding source, and he was supposedly going to ask for it to be accomplished in days or weeks. Blagojevich had been recorded saying that if and when Madigan said no, he would at least get the political benefit of having it look like he was trying to do something for the people.

And Blagojevich wasn't done making phone calls. Moments after talking to Greenlee and trying to assure him Jackson was at least mostly a mirage, he was talking to his brother, his chief fund-raiser who had fielded most of the offers from the Jackson camp. Raghu Nayak had sent Robert faxed letters of support for Jackson and had told Bedi and others about the fund-raising offer. Robert Blagojevich didn't have Harry Reid's ear or that of anyone in the game, but the governor was giving him directions now. And the direction was to go and see Nayak about the Jesse Jackson Jr. appointment. Blagojevich was no longer completely ruling out naming Jackson, he told his brother. Jackson was being elevated, and Washington was freaking out. Why should it be necessary that he appoint Madigan and get nothing? "Fuck you, Harry Reid," Blagojevich said.

Go and talk to Nayak in person, Blagojevich said, and tell him the Jackson pick was realistic. But about those promises of help, some of that stuff had to start happening immediately.

"Right now. And we've gotta see it," Blagojevich said. "You understand? Now you gotta be careful how you express that. And assume everybody's listening, the whole world's listening."

———

Robert followed his brother's direction and called Nayak, setting up a meeting that would take place the next day, December 5, "someplace quiet that we can just sit and talk." The men chose a coffee shop where they would plan to meet at about one o'clock.

But it was a meeting that never happened.

The governor would never have known it, but the newsroom of the Tribune Tower was active well into the evening of December 4. The paper had written about John Wyma receiving a subpoena weeks earlier after confronting him outside the Friends of Blagojevich but had not yet written about any help he was giving the federal government. Now that was about to change. After receiving information that the federal net was rapidly coming down on Blagojevich, the newspaper was pushing to publish a story that Wyma's cooperation had led to recordings being made by investigators. The newspaper also had information about a planned arrest date and that the investigation had spread to whether Blagojevich had corrupted the process of choosing a new senator to replace Barack Obama. A decision by top editors led to the paper holding off on reporting about the Senate seat allegations, at least temporarily, but the choice was made to go forward with a story on Wyma and the recordings of the governor. Reporter John Chase, who had covered Blagojevich for years, was chosen to contact the governor's press team and try to get some kind of comment.

Federal agents were still listening in as the information reached Blagojevich's ears through Lucio Guerrero. It was nearly 10:30 PM.

"Little late," Guerrero said sheepishly as Patti picked up the phone at Blagojevich's North Side home. "Is the governor around?"

Blagojevich got on the call.

"Ah, Scofield and I got a call from John Chase about ten minutes ago. Uh, he said they're writing a story for tomorrow's paper that says as part of a federal investigation they have recordings of you, and also, John Wyma's cooperating with the feds. Uh, I've got calls out to Quinlan, waiting to hear back," Guerrero said. Chase hadn't said what was on the recordings and was looking for comment. It was running the next day.

There was a pause as Blagojevich seemed to be digesting the information.

"Recordings of me?" he finally said.

"Correct," said Guerrero.

Three minutes later, Blagojevich was on the phone with Quinlan. The attorney was doubtful that the information was right but didn't know exactly what to say. "Lon is adamant there is no way John Wyma is cooperating," Quinlan said.

At about 10:40 PM, Blagojevich, Guerrero, and Quinlan had another call. The governor was searching his memory for things he might have said to Wyma, thinking he had been acting strangely, and remembering that Chase had been outside the fund-raising meeting on October 22.

"You know, I was pressing [Wyma] on a fund-raiser from Vondra," Blagojevich recalled. "You know, I said Vondra wants something. I may have said that. I don't know."

Don't worry, said Quinlan, but there was more.

"OK, and then I'm thinking Magoon, call Magoon see if he can do a fund-raiser because, um, you know, one was not for the other, but Dusty Baker called me and said they're behind payments on children pediatric doctors."

Blagojevich would spend a restless hour on the phone with his lawyers, including Sheldon Sorosky, speculating on what the information meant and whether Blagojevich could be in trouble. Blagojevich repeatedly went back to the October 22 meeting, trying to remember whether he had crossed any lines and saying he didn't believe he had. There was a flurry of calls as Blagojevich representatives tried to find Wyma, and the governor got hold of his brother. He shared what was said in the call from the *Tribune* and asked Robert to remember the last time they sat with Wyma.

"Assume he was wearing a wire in there," Blagojevich said. "Was there anything that I said that could have been—"

"Ah, Jesus, I don't know," Robert answered. "You know, uh, you know I, Jesus, I'd have to really think."

After midnight, Robert was checking for the story online and was back on the phone with Blagojevich and Patti. The speculation continued about what the information could mean, with Blagojevich wondering out loud if Wyma "would fuck me like that." Over and over he mentioned his discussion about Vondra, fearing that had been taped and saying he didn't think he had done anything wrong.

It would be nearly 1:00 AM before Blagojevich would get off the phone, after a final call with Sorosky, Quinlan, and Patti. They were rehashing the scenario, trying to figure out how much jeopardy the governor could be in. The speculation remained on fund-raising and on conversations with Wyma. Their thoughts didn't turn to the Senate seat and to whether what Blagojevich had been doing for weeks could be an issue for him. What was certain, Blagojevich said, was that he could be facing another disappointing situation where someone who had been close to him had turned away. Blagojevich had often complained that his faithful circle of friends was shrinking, and he was afraid he would have to add another name to that list.

―――――

"Feds taped Blagojevich" was the *Tribune*'s banner headline the next morning, and the appearance of the story set the governor off on yet another cycle of calling lawyers and advisers about what to do next. Blagojevich insisted he never knowingly did anything wrong but remained concerned that he could have unwittingly done something that the feds now had on tape.

One of his calls was with his brother.

"What you're likely to be hit with, it would seem to me, is just nothing concrete but they would say an allusion to, uh, some type of improper behavior. Just because this, this organization, the Children's Memorial, um, got something positive and now let's go talk to them about doing a fundraiser," Robert said.

"Yeah," Blagojevich answered. "That's not a crime."

In other calls that day, including with Quinlan, the governor agreed the worst he might have done was say something confusing. Robert checked his calendar for October 22, and while he had made notes about calls, there was nothing unusual. The governor could not remember anything as blatant as pulling Wyma aside and saying some state action would come from one of his clients making a large donation, but Patti still thought whatever money was left in the Friends of Blagojevich coffers should be moved to one of the governor's lawyers.

Some of his attorneys and advisers were a little more concerned than they were otherwise letting on.

"So where are you and I moving to?" Quinlan joked on a call to Harris. "Because the whole idea of us not being part of anything, if they're taping him, I mean holy fuck."

In fact, Quinlan and Harris thought the information was probably right. Blagojevich had been taped. The only question was when and how often, and Quinlan expected recently. Harris said he wasn't personally worried, just more concerned for people like Lon Monk and even Chris Kelly. He was doing more joking with Quinlan than actually sweating it out.

"What a dysfunctional family we are," he said.

Blagojevich began to feel better himself later in the day when Wyma's attorney, Zachary Fardon, issued a flat denial that Wyma ever wore a wire. That was correct, and it wasn't what the *Tribune* had reported, but the talk on the calls from that day went from Blagojevich thinking about what he might have said to talk about whether Wyma could sue the paper. The story that *Tribune* reporters had carefully crafted only said that Wyma had cooperated and that his help led to federal recordings. Blagojevich still at that point didn't imagine that his phones—including those at his home—had been tapped by the government.

And the taping would continue throughout that day and into the weekend, including catching the Blagojevich brothers scrapping the meeting that Robert had set up with Nayak.

"Go ahead and just call him and say, 'Well, it's too obvious now because of this story,'" Blagojevich said.

The governor would slowly ease back toward his normal business. He hadn't forgotten about the *Tribune* and the effort to see certain editorial board members cut loose before he agreed to help the Cubs get state money for Wrigley. There had been a round of layoffs at the paper, but writer John McCormick was still very much in place. Blagojevich wanted to know what was going on from Harris, who'd had conversations with Tribune Company executive Nils Larsen, one of Sam Zell's right-hand men. Harris said there was no word McCormick had been dismissed, but there were more cuts coming.

"I wanna sue the *Tribune*," Blagojevich said, turning his attention back to Wyma. "I mean, I'm bein' harmed by these stories. At some point I'm gonna sue 'em. I mean, I might have a lawsuit on this if this isn't true."

Harris pointed out that the story didn't say what had been recorded. There was nothing negative beyond the idea that Blagojevich was taped. "You could be ordering a cheese and mushroom pizza," he said.

Blagojevich's brother was even more encouraging.

"You've been going through the gauntlet here," he told Blagojevich. "And just remember you are going to come out of this stronger. That's the way you got to think."

"No, that's right."

"That's the way you fucking got to think."

———

Blagojevich was confident enough to attend a December 6 fund-raiser with his Indian allies in Elmhurst. It was not well-attended, leaving Robert to describe it as a "goat fuck" on one call, but those who did appear included Jesse Jackson Jr.'s brother, Jonathan.

Meanwhile, Blagojevich continued to speak freely on his phones, including about the Senate seat and how he would proceed. And the widespread media reports repeating the *Tribune* story didn't keep Rahm Emanuel from reaching out to Harris to find out what was happening and make another pitch. Emanuel said he saw three good picks: Lisa Madigan, Tammy Duckworth, or someone from the black business community. Harris threw out Jackson's name, to see if that was still acceptable, and there was no immediate yes or no. Emanuel said he was on a plane and didn't want to have a long conversation about it. He would get two or three names from the business world together and get back to Harris, he said.

That happened the next day, December 7. Emanuel offered up Cheryle Jackson (no relation to Jesse Jr.), who had been the governor's first press agent but rubbed coworkers and reporters the wrong way with inept leadership. She left Blagojevich to head the Urban League, but Emanuel didn't know she'd also had a falling-out with the governor because she once bounced a campaign donation check to him.

"He has got to do something that big, otherwise he is going to get killed here," Emanuel said. "It's a statement about him now."

Cheryle Jackson seemed to fit everyone's criteria, he said. She would be an example of the governor promoting an up-and-coming African American. If he were the governor, Emanuel said, he would just name Madigan and get it over with, believing there would be an implicit but not explicit deal with her father. But otherwise, he understood why a black candidate would be in Blagojevich's interests. And in his opinion, this new idea was the best move.

"I am more than willing to talk to him after you broach it," Emanuel said.

As for Blagojevich, he had a long talk with Scofield about what it would mean if he were recorded and whether any of his friends could be trusted. He had been invited to come talk to the *Tribune* editorial board, which he was declining, and he was trying to come up with things to say when he made his first extended public remarks on the *Tribune* story.

"Where do you put Wyma on an integrity scale?" Blagojevich said. "One being Stuart Levine, and ten being Jesus?"

"Ahhh, where would I put John?" Scofield eventually said. "Uh, you know, I don't know, eight or nine."

"That high, huh?"

"Absolutely. I've never had any reason to feel otherwise," Scofield said.

A moment later, it was more names. "Where do you put Lon?" said the governor.

"Same place."

"Where do you put, uh, John Harris?" Blagojevich continued.

"Same place," Scofield answered again.

"Chris Kelly?"

"Uhhh, this conversation stays between us?" Scofield said. "Four."

"Whoa! Four, huh?" said the governor. "Where do you put Rezko?"

With Levine being one, Rezko was a three, Scofield replied.

"Where do you put Mell?" Blagojevich asked, meaning his own father-in-law.

"Three," said Scofield, and, "I'm kickin Chris up to five."

It was a funny, frank talk, Blagojevich said. And it was just the kind of thing that people would hear if he ever actually was recorded, the governor said. That's what he was going to say tomorrow, when he finally addressed the press. Anyone could record him. They wouldn't like the blue language, but they'd hear nothing criminal. Right, said Scofield.

"Yeah, I don't think so either," said the governor. "I mean with those Nixon tapes, Jesus! They're funny. When you hear Nixon say 'cocksucker,' it's fuckin' funny, in a Nixonian way, right?"

During a break in a Golden Gloves bout (he lost), eighteen-year-old Rod Blagojevich winks for a photographer.
RICHARD YOUNKER

An early family photo of the Blagojeviches circa 1970.
TRIAL EXHIBIT

Patricia Mell-I that this too too solid flesh would melt, thaw and resolve itself into a dew! -Hamlet

Patti's photo and quote from her senior yearbook at St. Scholastica High School in Chicago.
ST. SCHOLASTICA HIGH SCHOOL YEARBOOK

(right) Blagojevich's first political patron, Chicago Alderman Edward Vrdolyak.

ASSOCIATED PRESS

(below) Alderman Dick Mell (right), Blagojevich's father-in-law, speaks on the floor of the Chicago City Council with fellow Chicago Alderman Eugene Schulter.

ASSOCIATED PRESS

Governor Blagojevich announces his All Kids health-care plan in 2005 at a location for many of his political events, A. Finkl & Sons Co., where his father once worked.

ILLINOIS DIVISION OF MEDIA SERVICES

(above) At a party for his first inauguration in 2003, Blagojevich speaks to powerful Speaker of the House Michael Madigan as Blagojevich fund-raiser Antoin "Tony" Rezko listens in.

ILLINOIS DIVISION OF MEDIA SERVICES

(left) Alonzo "Lon" Monk introduces his friend Rod Blagojevich as the newly elected governor of Illinois.

ILLINOIS DIVISION OF MEDIA SERVICES

Governor Blagojevich talks to Doug Scofield on a state plane in the early days of the Blagojevich administration.

ILLINOIS DIVISION OF MEDIA SERVICES

(right) Governor Blagojevich speaks with Bradley Tusk following a speech to members of the Illinois General Assembly.
ILLINOIS DIVISION OF MEDIA SERVICES

(below right) Governor Blagojevich, Patti, and their two daughters, Amy and Annie, at one of Blagojevich's favorite places—Wrigley Field.
ILLINOIS DIVISION OF MEDIA SERVICES

(below left) Chief of Staff John Harris.
ILLINOIS DIVISION OF MEDIA SERVICES

Tom Balanoff, a longtime political supporter of Blagojevich and president of the SEIU, at Blagojevich's All Kids announcement.
ILLINOIS DIVISION OF MEDIA SERVICES

Governor Blagojevich marches in the 2003 India Independence Parade with three major supporters in the Chicago-area Indian community: Harish Bhatt (left), Raghu Nayak (right), and Rajinder Bedi (far right).

(above) Governor Blagojevich, then–US senator and presidential hopeful Barack Obama, and Mayor Richard Daley attend a 2007 rally to push for the 2016 Olympics to come to Chicago.

ILLINOIS DIVISION OF MEDIA SERVICES

(left) Governor Blagojevich talks with US Representative Jesse Jackson Jr.

ILLINOIS DIVISION OF MEDIA SERVICES

(left) Longtime Blagojevich adviser and lobbyist John Wyma leaves Blagojevich's campaign headquarters on October 22, 2008, after a meeting that was recorded by federal agents.

(right) Stuart Levine is dogged by the media leaving federal court.
ASSOCIATED PRESS

(below) Governor Blagojevich is swarmed by the media on December 7, 2008, outside the site of a union dispute. He declared he had nothing to hide from any federal effort to tape him.
ILLINOIS DIVISION OF MEDIA SERVICES

(above) Governor Blagojevich announces he's appointing Roland Burris to replace Barack Obama in the US Senate.

ILLINOIS DIVISION OF MEDIA SERVICES

(left) Rod Blagojevich's mug shot, taken the morning of his arrest.

TRIAL EXHIBIT

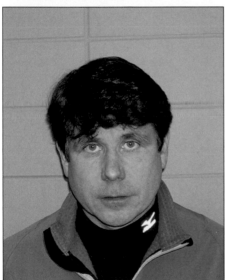

Blagojevich lawyers Sheldon Sorosky (left) and Sam Adam Jr. hold a press conference discussing the case.

ILLINOIS DIVISION OF MEDIA SERVICES

(right) A nervous and sweating Chris Kelly in the lobby of the Dirksen US Courthouse, the same day he first attempted suicide.

(below left) Robert Blagojevich at the federal courthouse.

(below right) The prosecution team (from left): Carrie Hamilton, US Attorney Patrick Fitzgerald, Reid Schar, and Chris Niewoehner

A court sketch of Blagojevich testifying under cross-examination by Reid Schar, as US District Judge James Zagel looks on.

Blagojevich gave the public a version of that sentiment the next day: taping him was not a problem. It was December 8, and the governor of Illinois thought he was dealing with just another media crisis and potentially with a tentacle of a federal probe that had dogged him for years. There was nothing but sunshine on him, he told reporters. Any covert recording would catch some colorful language, but nothing more. And he met with Jesse Jackson Jr. that day at his state offices downtown, where there was no federal microphone. That night, while showing up for a taping on CNN at the Tribune Tower, Blagojevich ran into the *Tribune*'s Rick Pearson, the paper's chief political reporter, and said maybe he'd make him senator.

The next morning Blagojevich was scheduled to wake up early and head downtown for a 6:10 AM remote taping of the *Today* show to discuss a sit-in by laid-off workers at a Chicago window factory. But late that night, word came that he got bumped from the show, which Blagojevich said he was actually relieved about. "I don't have to get up that early," he said.

Listening in, though, were federal agents who were deciding to move forward with their plan. Had there been no *Tribune* story, the federal government might have run their recording effort longer, hoping to see if they could somehow net an actual bad deal for the seat with someone in the Jackson camp. Instead, they decided they had enough. They would arrest a sitting governor in the early morning hours of December 9. They would take him into custody at his home, the blond-brick bungalow he had run the state from for six years.

PART V

The Trials

15

Arrested

The state police cruisers idled in front of the Blagojeviches' home much as they had every day for nearly six years.

It was a chilly Tuesday morning on December 9, 2008, and before dawn broke a steady early winter rain began to fall across the city. A car alarm went off briefly in the gloom nearby, but none of the troopers stirred.

It was nearly 6:00 AM when a pair of dark sedans and an SUV raced north on Richmond Street and turned left on Sunnyside Avenue, stopping in front of the house of the governor of the state of Illinois. It was an FBI arrest team, and a man jumped out of one of the vehicles and knocked on the window of one of the state police cars. Rod Blagojevich was going to be taken into custody.

The phone rang inside the dark home, startling Blagojevich, who was half asleep while contemplating an early run. On the phone was Rob Grant, head of the FBI in Chicago, who was part of the arrest team outside. Grant had come because of the gravity of the situation and in case the troopers guarding the governor's home needed to be confronted with an authority figure. Also present were a pair of female agents, as the Bureau knew someone might need to sit with the governor's daughters and Patti. The idea had been to make the arrest as low-key as possible, under the circumstances.

Two agents were outside the house, Grant told the governor, and they had a warrant for his arrest. He needed to get ready to leave.

"Is this a joke?" a shocked Blagojevich answered, thinking maybe his pal Jimmy DeLeo was pulling his leg.

Of course it wasn't a prank. Grant and his team were really there, and the FBI boss put Blagojevich on the phone with the leader of his security detail, who confirmed the situation.

Blagojevich hung up and called his assistant, Mary Stewart. The governor was being placed under arrest, but the wiretap of his home phone was still running and caught the ensuing panic inside.

"Who do we call?" Blagojevich said. "They have agents outside."

"Hello," Stewart said, confused. "Hello. Hello."

"Hey, get me Quinlan right away and Shelly right away," asking for his lawyers.

"Oh my God," Stewart answered.

"Right away," the governor said again with urgency.

It would take a minute or two, but soon Quinlan, the governor's counsel, was on the phone with him.

"Hey, what's up?" Quinlan said.

"The FBI is here arresting me."

"Really?"

"Yeah," said Blagojevich. "Here, they're at the house."

"Honest to God?"

"I swear to God."

"Who told you that?"

"They're here," the governor said. "They're at the door. They called. Head of the FBI called."

"And said we're here?"

Right, said Blagojevich, apparently turning to greet agents who were coming in. "Yeah. Hi. Yeah. Hi."

"Did you call Shelly?"

Blagojevich had but was still having trouble getting through.

"Yeah, call him. We got a call into him."

Patti got Stewart back on the phone as her husband was being taken out. He had put on his running gear and was preparing to go with the agents.

"I've got to go right now," one of the women on the arrest team could be heard saying in the background. "Door closed?"

"Uh, yeah, they just took my husband away," Patti said desperately to Stewart. "I need to talk to *fucking* somebody."

Outside the FBI vehicles could be seen moving around on the Blagojevi-ches' street. The governor was cuffed and led out the back door to the SUV, which had pulled around into the alley.

A few minutes later, it was Quinlan on the phone again. He had seen the *Tribune*, he said, which had run another story about the investigation. The paper was on the street with an article saying the investigation had spread to Blagojevich's selection of a new senator.

"They're saying—let me finish—they're saying that the investigation is about Rod and the Senate seat and somebody recorded him," said Quinlan, who told Patti his first thought was Jackson Jr., the day before. Patti was upset. She had a subpoena for documents related to the Senate selection. What do we do now? she asked. "They took him in his running clothes."

———

Patti finally reached Sorosky, who quickly drove to the FBI building near Ogden Avenue on the city's West Side. The sometimes late-rising Sorosky just happened to have had an early hearing at the DuPage County court-house that morning, so he had been up and dressed when he got the call.

As he waited for his lawyer, Blagojevich was being held in a corridor just off the FBI building's sally port. The long hallway provides access to a series of secure rooms, but for most of his time there, Blagojevich was allowed to walk the hallway. At times he half jogged in the corridor and stopped to lean up against a wall and stretch, as if he were actually going to get that run in after all. But any running now would be a big problem, and Agent Daniel Cain, standing nearby, joked that he didn't want to have to make a tackle before the governor appeared before a judge.

When Sorosky arrived, agents had a few things to say to the stunned governor, hinting he might still be able to help himself. There were people above him he could possibly talk about, they said, people in higher offices than even he was in. Sorosky interjected that Blagojevich didn't even really know Mayor Daley, drawing a chuckle from agents who joked Sorosky was a provincial Chicagoan.

But they didn't clarify just whom they were talking about. There was no specific mention of Obama or his fund-raising with Rezko or the calls where Blagojevich mentioned Bruce Washington and the $25,000. In real-ity, investigators never viewed the governor as a potential witness against anyone above him but were hoping to gather information about anyone on the calls or not captured on tape that he had dealt with. The FBI statement to him was more of an opener to what might have been a conversation if Sorosky had not shut things down. If Blagojevich had spontaneously admitted he had done something wrong, he could have at least described dealings with others that federal authorities were interested in making cases against. Never was Blagojevich seen as a credible threat to the incoming president.

Meanwhile, *Tribune* reporters who had been camped out at the governor's house for days saw the activity and were working to confirm the arrest. The paper was aware of the possible arrest date for the governor but had grown concerned that publishing the story about the taping days before could alter the FBI plan. After confirming that Blagojevich and also John Harris had been taken into custody, the paper sent out an e-mail bulletin that rocked the state. It had been little more than a month since Barack Obama had stood in Grant Park as the country's incoming president. It was possibly the all-time height of Illinois politics, only to be followed by an epic embarrassment.

What transpired next was one of the odder arraignments in the history of the Dirksen US Courthouse. There was the governor, standing in court in a dark blue track suit with a turtleneck underneath, his mop of hair shifting from side to side as he looked back at a crowded courtroom full of people who could hardly believe what they were seeing.

Harris was there, too, and was leaning toward helping the government immediately in a bid for leniency. He was talking with his attorney, Terry Ekl, about how he could help himself. Prosecutor Reid Schar had whispered to Ekl that they should talk right away to reach the best arrangement for Harris, who wasn't who the government was really after. Ekl knew the score immediately and was blunt with his client.

"John, if you're ever going to cooperate with the government, do it now," he told him. The last thing Harris wanted to do was sit before a jury next to Blagojevich and go down with the ship, so the governor's chief of staff took his lawyer's advice, offering a proffer of his testimony within two weeks of his arrest. He would eventually meet with prosecutors more than thirty times. Ekl would go on to give a presentation of what he thought Harris could offer to US Attorney Fitzgerald, his first assistant Gary Shapiro, the Blagojevich investigation team, and other supervisors. The government made Harris a witness and told Ekl he was free to argue for whatever punishment a judge thought was fair, with a cap of thirty-five months in prison.

As for Blagojevich, he would leave court on his own recognizance. He was still the governor and still had the ability to name Obama's replacement, although it was quickly clear that was a far different prospect than it had been just twenty-four hours earlier. In Springfield, the war parties were forming. Legislators were quickly plotting impeachment proceedings in the event Blagojevich did not step down, and they considered what they could do to take away the governor's ability to name a senator.

In Chicago at the Thompson Center, where Blagojevich had met Jackson the day before, state employees joined others across the city huddling around televisions to watch Fitzgerald hold a press conference on the charges.

"Governor Blagojevich has been arrested in the middle of what we can only describe as a political corruption crime spree," Fitzgerald told a room jammed with reporters and news cameras. "We acted to stop that crime spree."

Thinking about the environment of eight weeks earlier would put things in context, the top prosecutor said.

"There was a known investigation of the Blagojevich administration that had been going on for years involving allegations of pay-to-play conduct and corruption," Fitzgerald said. "There had been a recent trial of an associate of Governor Blagojevich in which allegations were aired."

In addition, there was a new ethics law going into effect on January 1, 2009, that would bar contributions to the governor from those doing business with Illinois. Maybe that would be expected to slow pay to play in state government down, Fitzgerald said, but guess again. The opposite had happened. Blagojevich had tried to shake down a roadbuilding executive for $100,000 in contributions while a $1.8 billion tollway project was being announced. He had tried to get a $50,000 contribution from the chief executive of Children's Memorial Hospital while offering to boost state funding for the facility. He had tried to get money from a horse racing executive in exchange for signing a bill that still sat on his desk aiding the racing industry. And he had tried to extort the *Chicago Tribune* and force the paper to fire editorial writers in exchange for a state deal.

"But the most cynical behavior in all this, the most appalling, is the fact that Governor Blagojevich tried to sell the appointment to the Senate seat vacated by President-elect Obama," Fitzgerald said. "The conduct would make Lincoln roll over in his grave."

Blagojevich had described the seat as "bleeping golden," Fitzgerald said. He wasn't giving it up for nothing. "Those are his words, not our characterization, other than with regard to the bleep."

The governor had sought a number of things for the seat, the prosecutor said, including a cabinet post, an ambassadorship, or a job heading a foundation. In another scheme, Blagojevich had considered a bid to trade the seat for $1.5 million in campaign money. He had been recorded not being offended by the offer but worrying about whether it would be paid. "He wasn't against the corrupt deal; he was against being stiffed in the corrupt deal," said Fitzgerald. Blagojevich had told an intermediary to be careful when reaching out to the person who had made the offer. "That's the governor of Illinois," he said.

And Fitzgerald would go on to thank the *Tribune*, noting the paper had delayed reporting on some aspects of the investigation, allowing the taping to get off the ground. The newspaper's editor, Gerould Kern, later answered by explaining that prosecutors at times had asserted that disclosing some information would have jeopardized the probe. "In isolated instances, we granted the requests, but other requests were refused." Some blamed the newspaper for forcing authorities to arrest the governor when they did. But that was not the case. Blagojevich's arrest date was chosen at least a week before he was taken into custody.

FBI boss Grant was also at the press conference, reminding reporters that George Ryan had been convicted less than three years earlier. The federal authorities involved in that effort had hoped it had sent a clear signal that no one could sell their office, but apparently that message hadn't been received. Grant had seen a lot since arriving in Chicago about four years before. "A lot of you were in the audience, asked me the question of whether or not Illinois is the most corrupt state in the United States," Grant said. "But I can tell you one thing: if it isn't the most corrupt state in the United States, it's certainly one hell of a competitor."

———

On December 10, both Obama and Jackson Jr. denied knowledge of Blagojevich's alleged bid to barter with them over the Senate seat. Obama said he had never had direct talks with Blagojevich, told investigators he wasn't aware of the governor's schemes, and issued a report later in the month on his staff's contact with the governor. Emanuel had been the president's point person on the matter, and Obama acknowledged he had given four names to his new chief of staff to deliver to Blagojevich for consideration. But Obama and those around him said they were satisfied no one on their side of the ball had done anything inappropriate with Blagojevich. It was more about monitoring the erratic governor of Illinois and trying to influence him—as much as that was even possible—to choose someone who could hold on to the seat. Blagojevich was wound up over who would be the next senator from Illinois, but that didn't mean Obama was thinking about it night and day, too.

"There was so much on his plate then, and he was not fixated on that particular issue," Axelrod recalled later. Obama was an incoming president choosing a cabinet and getting ready to take over a country that was engaged in two foreign wars and facing a growing financial crisis. "That was not one of the top things on his mind."

As for Jackson, he said he didn't know about any offer of cash for his appointment.

"I thought mistakenly I had a chance and was being considered because I had earned it. Despite what he may have been looking for, that's all I had to offer," Jackson said. And he would keep up his denials, despite Raghu Nayak later telling federal authorities that the congressman was present for talks on offering Blagojevich up to $6 million in fund-raising. But the biggest fallout for Jackson would come from something else Nayak said. The *Sun Times* was first to report the Indian businessman told authorities he had twice paid to fly a Jackson mistress from Washington to Chicago, a hostess at a cigar and martini bar. The news story would derail thoughts Jackson had of running for Chicago mayor in 2011.

With the criminal case promising to be unique in state history, Sorosky was going to need a defense team, and one of Chicago's legendary lawyers was soon in the mix. Ed Genson had been a top defense lawyer in the city seemingly from the dawn of time and had represented a wide spectrum of white collar criminals. But Blagojevich didn't stop there. He and Sorosky remembered the performance of a young lawyer named Sam Adam Jr. at the criminal trial of R & B superstar R. Kelly, who had been accused in a child porn case. Genson had been part of that team also and had credited the young Adam with winning the case. If the governor ever got into real trouble, the men had agreed, Adam would be the way to go. The funny, brassy, and bombastic young lawyer had grown up in the halls of the city's Criminal Courts Building at Twenty-Sixth Street and California, as his father, Sam Adam Sr., prowled the halls as one of the city's best-known criminal defense lawyers. The governor knew him as well. Many years earlier, when Blagojevich was a lawyer working for Sorosky, he was sometimes excited when he got a chance to do a criminal case. But in one instance he was turned away when a client told him no thanks, "I hired the best lawyer in town—Sam Adam."

By 2008, the older Adam's best years probably were behind him, but he still had a quick legal mind and a likable air. He was eclectic to say the least, with sport coats that were sometimes a bit frayed, Masters green or rose colored, and too tight, but he had a great gift for reading people and the ability to force a chuckle even from his opponents in court—never mind that he would be a vicious adversary once a jury got in the box. And it was the same with witnesses. He charmed them at first, and then left them a quivering pile of ash by the time he was done. Many in the city remembered him for defending US Representative Mel Reynolds in a high-profile sexual assault case.

Adam and his son were masters of the street fight and would have been perfectly at home in the era of capers, crooks, and gamesmanship depicted in the musical *Chicago*. Adam Jr. had played checkers as a boy with courtroom deputies and watched his father stomp around courtrooms like a thespian. He was born to follow in his father's footsteps, though one of his first legal stops had been as a green state's attorney in Wisconsin, where he went to school. But that didn't last, as he apologized to one of the first women he got a conviction on in traffic court. Back in Chicago, he hit the ground running, piling up clients and walking the courtroom halls like an outgoing, good-looking teen who just discovered high school. He couldn't walk three feet in the building without running into someone he knew, giving an overemphasized handshake to judges, reporters, and even some cops. "Twenty-Sixth and Cal" was a world unto itself, with its own rules and mores, where lawyers were often paid in wads of cash by their clients two seconds before court began. The younger Adam was once paid with a Cadillac by a client, complete with spokes.

Adam Jr. was a quick study, milking every bit of his humor in court, sometimes just believing the jury would know what he meant even if few legal observers would. He would often just scream, "Come on!" to make a point and had defended R. Kelly by telling jurors the singer wouldn't have carried around illicit videotapes like "the porno Santa Claus." At a bond hearing for a man accused of murder after his wife disappeared, Adam showed up with missing posters with the woman's image on them, passing them out to reporters and putting on a show for news cameras.

Genson and the older Adam had worked together for decades and had usually agreed on legal strategy, but that wasn't to be the case when it came to Blagojevich. In an early meeting with all the lawyers involved in defending the governor, Genson was the one who was adamant about stepping down and beginning to quietly angle a way out of the case—or at least toward an outcome that was OK for the rest of Blagojevich's life. It was more the federal way. Lie low. Don't do anything to poke the government in the eye.

But Adam Sr. didn't like it.

"Wait a minute. He doesn't have to resign," he said. "Why should he resign?"

To Adam, it made Blagojevich look guiltier in the open court of public opinion. Some in the case would come to believe that Genson had a long-standing relationship with Illinois Senate President John Cullerton and that he had promised Cullerton he would get Blagojevich to step down and not appoint a senator. Genson would deny the charge, but legislators already were pressing a deal that Blagojevich give up his detail and continue to get paid by the state, while giving up his powers. Adam wanted to tap into Blagojevich's fiery energy and willingness to fight. The governor had never quietly backed away from a challenge before; why should he now? He should continue to be the governor, Adam thought, and that included appointing a senator.

Genson thought that was ridiculous. Blagojevich should never appoint someone, he argued, in part because the Senate would probably consider it a tainted pick and not seat the person anyway. Adam thought the seat once held by Carol Moseley Braun and Obama should go to an African American, and Adam did not believe the Senate would have the guts to keep that person from being seated.

The first choice of Blagojevich and his lawyers was Eric Whitaker, who was among the names Blagojevich had thrown around during the fall, but the defense team was hampered from reaching him that December because he was on vacation with the Obamas. State Senator Rickey Hendon was also on the list, but the team ultimately decided on US Representative Danny Davis just before Christmas. Davis said he would think about it but came back a couple of days later to say he still had work to do in his district and would decline.

It was Adam Jr. who had the next idea—Roland Burris, a former comptroller and Illinois attorney general.

The politician had already expressed some interest in the fall, speaking with Robert about fund-raising and indicating he'd like to be considered for the seat. But Burris hadn't been hopeful about raising anything, and Robert hadn't gone into detail about their exchange with the governor, who in turn didn't raise a flag with his lawyers. It was Adam Jr. who went to Burris, because he had known his children for years. "If the governor wants me, have him call me," Burris answered.

When Genson found out, he was unequivocal; if Blagojevich appointed someone, he would resign from the defense team. It was Genson's stern position that Blagojevich still shouldn't be taking a hostile stance. The attorney was bouncing between hearings in Chicago and an impeachment trial that was under way in Springfield, where Genson argued he was fighting shadows because he wasn't allowed to call witnesses. Meanwhile, the feds were turning over to state lawmakers snippets from their tapes that they thought could be used to make a case for Blagojevich to be removed from office.

It was after a court hearing on the release of tapes in federal court in Chicago that Genson was asked whether he knew that the governor was giving a press conference promising to fight every step of the way through court.

"The heart and soul of this has been a struggle of me against the system," Blagojevich said. He was planning to do a series of national TV appearances to state his case: *Good Morning America, Larry King Live*, anywhere that would have him.

And that was it for Genson. He never insisted a client obey him, but they at least had to listen, he told reporters. "I wish the governor good luck and Godspeed," he said, before leaving a voicemail for his onetime friend and partner, Adam Sr., breaking ties for good.

After Sam Adam Jr. left his house, Roland Burris called Fred Lebed, his close friend and adviser. It was around six o'clock in the evening on a Friday, but Burris had exciting news.

"Blagojevich just offered me the Senate seat," Burris said. "They said, 'If asked by Rod would you consider the offer?' What do you think I should do?"

Lebed's first advice was to not talk about it with anybody unless they both agreed. This was huge news, and while Burris had been angling for this Senate seat since even before Obama was elected president, it was important to keep this sort of information contained. Blagojevich was toxic, and there was also no guarantee the appointee would get seated by the remaining senators.

"Just keep it between us," Lebed told Burris.

The next afternoon, though, Burris couldn't keep his mouth shut. Attending an event at the Ramada Inn in the South Side neighborhood of Hyde Park, an ebullient Burris encountered dozens of friends and occasional supporters, including several ministers, activists, and political consultants. Burris told many of them about the proposal and asked them what they thought he should do. By the end of the event, nearly all of the two hundred people there had heard about it.

Lebed visited Burris the following day at his South Side home. He knew Burris badly wanted to take the job, but the real question was whether he could endure the media onslaught for accepting a Senate seat from an embattled governor accused of selling that seat for money.

"Can we stand it?" Lebed asked Burris.

"Yeah," Burris responded.

The formal pitch from Blagojevich and the Adams came soon after, and the plan they hatched when Burris accepted was fairly simple: try to get out in front of the story as much as possible. As soon as the governor's press conference announcing the pick was over, Burris would do every national media television show he could.

The decision was set to make the announcement at the Thompson Center on Tuesday.

Word was leaking to the press that Burris was going to accept the appointment and that he was on the phone with Illinois members of Congress and their staffs. Senator Dick Durbin told Burris not to accept the appointment. But Burris was unconvinced. This was his opportunity, and he wasn't going to waste it. He, Lebed, and his friend and attorney, Tim Wright, walked out a side door of their fifth floor offices and down the hallway. Secretaries and staffers saw him leaving and applauded.

"Good luck, Mr. Burris! You make us so proud," one said. Burris stopped, hugged the woman, and quickly proceeded toward a freight elevator where they could get into an awaiting car to make the short drive over to the Thompson Center without being seen by the media and photographers waiting for him outside.

After Burris and his entourage took a quick ride up the governor's elevator to the governor's offices on the sixteenth floor, Blagojevich greeted Burris with a wide smile and a warm handshake. The governor seemed amazingly relaxed. Naming Burris to the post was a smart political move. With Obama gone, there were no African Americans in the Senate and those who tried to stand in Burris's way would face criticism of being racist.

In an effort to pound home that point, US Representative Bobby Rush, a leader in Chicago's African American community, arrived for support.

In the governor's office minutes before the press conference was about to start one floor below, Blagojevich crossed the room like a man who had retaken the high ground.

"You just wait. Just watch," he said, spitefully predicting the senators in Washington would eventually fold and accept Burris. "Those racist bastards. Those racist motherfuckers."

Burris would be appointed, promising he was a "tool of the people of Illinois" and not of Blagojevich. But it would be a rocky road to taking the seat. Senators first planned to have armed officers ban him from the Capitol and then turned him away claiming the paperwork to install him was not in order. It would be mid-January before he was finally sworn in as Obama's replacement, and he would quickly face an ethics probe into his dealings with Blagojevich. When he testified at the Blagojevich impeachment proceedings, he minimized his contacts with the Blagojevich camp on the Senate seat. After he was sworn in, he sent in a written affidavit amending what he had said to the impeachment panel, and the *Sun-Times* made the discrepancy public. It was later revealed that Burris had been taped talking to Robert Blagojevich and promising to make a campaign donation, though he was nervous about the timing of being chosen as the senator and giving the governor money. "And if I do get appointed, that means I bought it," he had said on the tape, guessing at the public reaction. Burris eventually was able to weather the publicity storm, pushing aside calls for his resignation, and served in the Senate until the next regular election was held in 2010.

———

Blagojevich made good on his promises to tour the country claiming he was innocent and fighting the impeachment process in the court of public opinion. For days he was seemingly omnipresent, making it difficult to walk near a television without seeing him complaining about being railroaded in Springfield.

The strategy of Sam Adam Sr. and Jr. was to let their client talk, though not specifically about the details of the tapes. The idea was to make Blagojevich a celebrity, believing the bar would then be higher for getting a conviction. American history showed time and time again that convicting a famous person was simply more difficult. O. J. Simpson, Michael Jackson, R.

Kelly, Robert Blake. The list went on and on. "Beyond a reasonable doubt" seemed to become "beyond a shadow of a doubt" with a celebrity defendant. The Adams wanted to make Blagojevich larger than life and raise the bar for a starstruck jury. Most of the TV appearances went about as planned, until Joy Behar on *The View* asked Blagojevich to do an impression of Richard Nixon promising, "I am not a crook." The governor declined, but it was close. To some, including Sam Adam Jr., who was waiting just off stage, it seemed for a second that Blagojevich might take the bait. Adam later said he had serious thoughts about charging the set and knocking Blagojevich out of his chair if he started doing his best Nixon. Other times the governor didn't show as much restraint. He told the *Today* show he had some interesting thoughts when he was taken into custody. "I thought about Mandela, Dr. King, Gandhi, and trying to put some perspective in all of this," he spouted.

After one TV appearance, Blagojevich had just arrived at the Trump Tower in New York when he spotted former New York City mayor Ed Koch. Like a shot, Blagojevich left Adam Jr. and ran right up to Koch, telling him he was his favorite mayor. A somewhat startled Koch gave him a concerned, fatherly look in return.

"Are you listening to your lawyer?" Koch asked.

———

Blagojevich broke from his PR tour long enough to head to Springfield for the impeachment proceedings and make an emotional closing argument on his own behalf on January 29. Before giving his speech to the state senate, Blagojevich sat quietly in his ornamented office, bopping his leg up and down and tweaking his speech, making notes in longhand. With *New York Times* reporter Monica Davey and a photographer accompanying him throughout the day, Blagojevich called Patti several times and combed his hair once. Then, minutes before he was supposed to speak, he stood up and told an aide, "Let's go home. Screw it. It won't matter."

But Blagojevich was nothing if not indecisive and ultimately chose not to listen to himself. He went ahead with the speech, pointing his finger and promising he had not let the state down. He spoke for forty-seven minutes but didn't stick around long enough to see the result. He slipped out of the Capitol through a private tunnel and made his way to the state's nine-seat airplane. He took his usual spot, a front-facing seat on the left side, and headed back to Chicago.

As the plane soared thousands of feet above Illinois, the telephone on board rang. Blagojevich ordered everyone not to answer it. If it was the news that the Senate had removed him from office, he didn't want to hear it. "I'll tell you what," he laughed. "I'm not jumping out. Not for those people, no way. I don't like heights."

He landed in Chicago before 2:00 PM. The senators still hadn't voted, so his security detail, still intact, took him home. A short time later, though, they were gone. For the first time in Illinois history, an Illinois governor had been convicted in an impeachment trial. Rod Blagojevich was no longer governor and was forbidden to hold a public post ever again in Illinois. The vote was 59–0, and Lieutenant Governor Pat Quinn was sworn in as the state's forty-first chief executive.

Reporters, television crews, and even a few supporters gathered at Sunnyside and Richmond. Blagojevich stepped onto the front stoop of his home, where he made a brief statement before wading into the crowd. He grabbed a boy who asked if he wanted to play basketball in the summer. Then he oddly grinned as he demanded photographers take pictures of him with the child.

Choking back emotion, he said: "I love the people of Illinois today now more than I ever did before." He continued, "The fight goes on."

And so it did, in public. Blagojevich went back on the talk show circuit, giving shortened versions of his impeachment speech about how he had been cheated out of a fair process and taken from the people of Illinois. He was right back in New York, doing more appearances and hoping to turn the tide in his favor.

One of his appearances was on *The Late Show with David Letterman*. It was probably the show he had wanted to do the most, and he all but gushed over its legendary host.

"Well, you know, I've been wanting to be on your show in the worst way for the longest time," he told Letterman, setting himself up perfectly.

"Well, you're on in the worst way," Letterman answered. "Believe me."

———

Two months later, Blagojevich was formally indicted on sweeping corruption charges that essentially accused him of running the state of Illnois as a criminal racket. Lon Monk, who was by then talking with the government himself and planning to plead guilty, was named as a defendant, as were

John Harris, Robert Blagojevich, and Chris Kelly, who already had been charged in two federal cases of his own. Using the version of events provided by Monk and Rezko, prosecutors claimed that Blagojevich was interested in corruption before he was even sworn in for the first time in 2002. He and his closest advisers had plotted to make as much money as they could through state business and split it up when the governor left office. There were sixteen counts in all, ranging from broad racketeering charges to specific counts of fraud and extortion tied to instances when Blagojevich had allegedly cheated the state. Included were accusations the governor had tried to sell the Senate seat, shaken people down for campaign contributions, tried to get *Tribune* editorial writers fired, and attempted to hold up the funding for a North Side school so he could get another fund-raiser. Prosecutors dubbed the governor's illegal ring the Blagojevich Enterprise.

"The primary purpose of the Blagojevich Enterprise was to exercise and preserve power over the government of the State of Illinois for the financial and political benefit of Rod Blagojevich," the indictment stated, "both directly and through Friends of Blagojevich, and for the benefit of his family members and associates."

Meanwhile, there was a housecleaning of sorts under way in Springfield. Blagojevich appointees all over state government saw the writing on the wall and either stepped down or were dismissed. Christopher Corcoran, who had handled Blagojevich's account at the high-end Oxxford Clothes suit store, was fired from the state job the governor had helped him get, and Rajinder Bedi resigned from the Illinois Department of Commerce and Economic Opportunity. Historic sites that Blagojevich had ordered closed in the face of tough economic times were reopened, and there was talk of overturning some of his signature programs—such as giving seniors free access to public transportation.

But even with much of what he had done in state government being unraveled, it's no stretch to say Rod Blagojevich had never been such a household name. He was a comedy stage show—"Rod Blagojevich Superstar"—and a shampoo. He was fielding a variety of offers for work, including as an ambassador of sorts at Nevada's infamous Bunny Ranch, and as a contestant on the reality TV show *I'm a Celebrity, Get Me out of Here!* The show paid $80,000 a week (about half Blagojevich's yearly salary as governor), which made it attractive to Blagojevich despite the fact he would have to slog through a jungle location and participate in gross challenges on TV. The only problem was the show's producers planned to shoot it in Costa

Rica, and US District Judge James Zagel refused to let Blagojevich leave the country before his trial.

That left Patti to take over the duty of heading to the rain forest for America's entertainment, featured along with the likes of reality-star-turned-singer Heidi Montag, former Detroit Piston John Salley, and actor Stephen Baldwin. Before long Patti was eating a tarantula to stay on the show and talking to her fellow contestants about her husband being a good person and about his many campaign travails. One had been his run against veteran Illinois politician Judy Baar Topinka, Patti told John Salley.

"And he thought of her as like a crazy old aunt," Patti said. "That he had to kind of like suffer and just kind of like roll your eyes at. Like she's the kooky old aunt that, you know, you have to be respectful to her because she's your old aunt."

And like most people who find themselves on *Survivor* or a similar show, Patti got a chance to talk to her family while she was still in the wild. Rod and her daughters told her how proud they were of her over a video phone.

"They're clean. They're reading," Blagojevich said of the couple's daughters as Patti looked on. She would spend more than three weeks in the jungle and afterward credited it with restoring her faith in people and introducing her to a new diet of rice and beans. But she failed to win; that honor went to actor Lou Diamond Phillips.

———

As Blagojevich and his wife were becoming D-grade celebrities, those left back in Chicago were dealing with the fallout of the criminal case. Among them was Chris Kelly.

On Tuesday, September 8, 2009, Kelly's phone rang. It was his attorney, Michael Monico. He told Kelly, who was headed to prison soon on a tax conviction, that he had to show up in court later that day because federal prosecutors wanted to revoke his bond. Kelly quickly realized why.

In the two years since he had first been indicted, Kelly's once whirlwind life had folded into a downward spiral of despair and chaos. His relationship with Blagojevich was obliterated. His roofing company, which once thrived due to business at O'Hare Airport, was all but done since City of Chicago officials banned him from ever doing business with them again after he was charged in yet another federal fraud case related to a contract for roofing work at hangars. Lenders had moved to foreclose on his Burr Ridge mansion. And the fifty-one-year-old had separated from his wife, Carmen, and was now living in a downtown Chicago condominium near Millennium Park with a thirty-year-old Latina divorcee who worked in a Logan Square nightclub. Kelly had invested tens of thousands of dollars in the club, Vlive, and he had recently stormed down there to talk with the owner about why he wasn't seeing much return on his investment. He demanded to see the financial books. The exchange quickly turned heated, and Kelly, screaming and yelling, was turned away. Federal prosecutors had caught wind of the quarrel and went to court to revoke Kelly's bond, a move that could have forced him to jail immediately.

Kelly told Monico he would be there and was true to his word. He appeared before US District Judge Charles Norgle, who decided not to revoke Kelly's bond, instead allowing him to enter prison days later, as planned. But the judge listened as Kelly pleaded guilty in the O'Hare case, admitting he was part of a kickback scheme to illegally get $8.5 million in work at the airport.

The normally brash and confident Kelly was unusually subdued, even given the circumstances. Standing before the judge was a broken man sweating through a blue shirt and shifting from one foot to the other. At times he spoke so softly it was impossible to hear him.

Out in the hallway before the hearing began, the desperation on his face was clear.

"I know my life is over," Kelly told a pair of reporters. The federal government had put enormous pressure on him, charging him three times in all, including in the Blagojevich case. And while there had been talks about what kind of break he would get to plead guilty to all the cases at once and then testify against his former friend, Kelly had said no. What he thought about was not his time on earth, Kelly said, but the next life.

"That's why you stay true to who you are," he said. "I've never changed that. Never."

After court, Kelly told his girlfriend, Clarissa Flores-Buhelos, he planned to see his daughters. But at 7:30 PM, he called her to say he had fallen asleep at the "yard." Flores-Buhelos knew exactly where Kelly was talking about. For the last five months, he had rented a storage yard near an old True Value at 173rd and Cicero in south suburban Country Club Hills to stockpile some of his roofing equipment. It was nothing to look at, a gravel lot loaded with weeds and a small trailer. But Kelly had been hanging out there a lot recently, fumbling about in the trailer for hours at a time. He kept a sleeping bag in the trailer.

Kelly then conceded he hadn't just fallen asleep. He had taken some pills. Flores-Buhelos headed down to the yard immediately, a trip that could take more than a half hour from downtown. When she arrived, the gate was locked. A five-foot-eight-inch former Northwestern University basketball star, Flores-Buhelos quickly jumped the fence and spotted Kelly stumbling around with a flashlight. She took Kelly to her car, where the two sat and talked for a few minutes. Flores-Buhelos didn't like how Kelly was acting and told him she was taking him to the hospital. Kelly said he didn't want to go, but she insisted. She called one of Kelly's friends, who also called Monico and Kelly's brother, Charles.

Flores-Buhelos took Kelly to nearby Oak Forest Hospital and parked near the ER. Kelly was still groggy but seemed better. His friend Carlo Buonavolanto showed up, and after about thirty minutes outside the two decided not to take him into the hospital but instead to drive him back home to the downtown condo. But first, they returned to the yard to find out what kind of pills he had taken.

Inside the trailer, Flores-Buhelos saw a bottle of Aleve and a box of Tylenol Cold medicine. She also noticed a smell she thought was carbon monoxide. When she asked Kelly about it, he acknowledged he had left one of his trucks running outside of the trailer, connected a hose from the tailpipe, and dragged the other end of the hose into the trailer in a bid to kill himself.

By the time all three got to the condo, Kelly was in better spirits, but Flores-Buhelos and Buonavolanto talked about getting Kelly a psychiatrist. When Flores-Buhelos went into her bedroom, she found tucked between her pillows a letter inside an envelope with Kelly's handwriting on it. She knew what it was and didn't want to read it. She placed it a drawer. She and Kelly then talked before going to sleep. Kelly promised he would never do anything like that again.

———

Three days later, on Friday, September 11, Kelly and Buonavolanto met at Monico's office in downtown Chicago to talk about getting Kelly some help. The meeting lasted two and a half hours. Flores-Buhelos went to work, and by 2:20 PM, Kelly had made his way out to Country Club Hills. Wearing a white baseball cap, a short-sleeve T-shirt, and blue jeans, he walked the aisles of a Wal-Mart. He purchased several items, including bread, 2 percent milk, and a box of D-con rat poison. He loaded the items into his 2007 black Cadillac Escalade and took off.

Less than an hour later, Kelly sent Flores-Buhelos a text. "I LOVE 46." 46 was their code for the day they met. Just after 5:30 PM, Flores-Buhelos texted Kelly her work schedule, trying to arrange a day to make dinner reservations. Kelly didn't respond. A few more hours passed, and Flores-Buhelos texted Kelly again, telling him she was leaving work soon. A half-hour later, at 10:15 PM, Kelly finally texted back.

"Come get me asap yard."

———

Depression had enveloped Kelly once again.

He had been at the trailer, positioned his sleeping bag near photographs of his three daughters, and chugged the milk. More bottles of aspirin and Tylenol were opened. So was the box of rat poison. He had vomited inside the trailer and stumbled outside, holding the Wal-Mart bag filled with more blue and white pills. He had vomited again right in front of trailer where numerous pebbles of the rat poison were later found.

After getting the text, Flores-Buhelos called Kelly, but he didn't pick up. She texted him, "call me pls." When she eventually got him, Kelly sounded groggy. On the way to the yard, she kept texting him. "I need u!!!!!!" At 10:40 PM, she texted again: "Almost there!"

When she pulled up to the lot, she found Kelly's 2007 black Cadillac Escalade parked nearby. Kelly was hunched over the wheel. He had defecated and thrown up all over himself. He wasn't wearing any shoes. She pulled him out of the SUV and got him into the backseat before she took the wheel and headed back to Oak Forest Hospital. On the way there, Kelly kept yelling for Flores-Buhelos to slow down because he felt sick. He told her he had taken aspirin, Tylenol, and rat poison.

This time, Flores-Buhelos didn't hesitate to go inside the ER. She contacted friends, including Buonavolanto. Initially, a doctor said Kelly was OK "but just needed to rest." Kelly was coherent and talking, but Buonavolanto feared for his friend's life. Physicians later told Flores-Buhelos they wanted to move Kelly to Stroger Hospital, the county-run hospital that was better equipped to treat him. Oak Forest focused more on rehabilitation services and acute care than general emergency room procedures. It took several hours for an ambulance to arrive to transport Kelly to Stroger, and when hospital and ambulance staffers went to strap Kelly down for the move, he became aggressive.

"No, C," he said to Flores-Buhelos, "it's my life. Tell them they won. Tell them they won."

Hospital staffers gave Kelly a sedative and moved him to Stroger. When Flores-Buhelos arrived, she waited for an update with Buonavolanto and another of Kelly's friends from college, Mike Allen. While at the hospital, the three decided to call Carmen Kelly, who arrived at Stroger a short time later. Doctors worked on Kelly at Stroger, but his condition continued to deteriorate. Shortly, despite their best efforts, Kelly was dead.

For two hours after Kelly's death, Flores-Buhelos, Buonavolanto, Allen, Carmen Kelly, and Kelly's sister Gertrude remained with the body until they were told it had to be taken to the Cook County Medical Examiner's Office.

Allen went back to the yard, looking for a suicide note. When he arrived, he found the Wal-Mart bag outside the trailer with the blue and white pills still inside, along with opened bottles and opened and empty boxes of the rat poison. Inside the trailer, he found the empty milk jug, the sleeping bag, and the pictures of his daughters. He sat on the stairs outside the trailer for several minutes before collecting the Wal-Mart bag and the pills. He didn't want Kelly's family hearing about the details. He then tried to get Kelly's Escalade at Oak Forest, but hospital security stopped him.

———

In just hours, the news of Kelly's death broke on a bright Saturday morning. Kelly's comments to reporters at the Dirksen courthouse just days earlier had been prophetic.

Some bloggers instantly began speculating that maybe Kelly was murdered, comparing the death to that of Vince Foster. The mindless conjecture wasn't helped by a press conference held that weekend by the Country Club Hills Mayor Dwight Welch, who flashed Flores-Buhelos's ID on TV and said she had "lawyered up" and wasn't talking to investigators. Flores-Buhelos's attorney, Terry Gillespie, fired back, "The mayor's a jackass. The girl's best friend in life just died hours before." The mayor also described Allen as a "mystery man" who was trying to take the Escalade away from the scene of an ongoing criminal investigation. Allen's decision to hide evidence didn't help matters either.

the Internet. It was TV host and native Chicagoan Bonnie Hunt that probably gave Blagojevich the toughest time.

"At some point, even for your own children, don't you want to be accountable?" she asked. "Sometimes you make bad choices."

For once, Blagojevich seemed rattled and raised his voice.

"These are false accusations, and there are taped conversations that will
set the record straight," he said. "That's the truth. I'm the one that wants you
all to hear them. My accusers don't. Now what does that tell you?"

"You went to law school. I didn't," Hunt answered. "I'm only a nurse, but
I might inject you with something just to get you to quiet down."

On Howard Stern's radio show, Blagojevich was a little more in his
element.

The shock jock said he was pulling for the former governor. In New York,
Eliot Spitzer had resigned as the state's governor months before Blagojevich's arrest, and Stern wanted to know if Blagojevich felt any empathy for
him. Sure, said Blagojevich, but he mostly felt bad for Spitzer's wife, because
Spitzer had been embroiled in scandal as the client of a call girl. As for
the two former governors, there wasn't much of a comparison in Blagojevich's mind. Spitzer had done what he was accused of, while Blagojevich was
innocent.

"He got a blow job, and I got fucked," Blagojevich said.

Stern's sidekick, Artie Lange, couldn't hold his tongue.

"I thought he got fucked, too," he said.

———

In court, both Monk and Harris pleaded guilty, and Blagojevich repeatedly
made the playing of as many tapes as possible his top priority when a jury
heard his case. Like seemingly everything else that pertained to Blagojevich, it was an upside-down scenario. Most defendants fight to keep as many
secret recordings as they can out of their trial, while Blagojevich wanted
just the opposite. If a jury heard every tape in context, the governor said
repeatedly, it would see his point that he was just bouncing ideas around
and looking to come up with the best options, not plotting to do something
illegal. It was a message Blagojevich trumpeted when he finally got his own
slot on a national reality show, *Celebrity Apprentice*, before he was "fired"
by Donald Trump. He worked hard to paint himself as innocent, even as
viewers across the country got to see that the former Illinois governor could

But in a matter of days, Flores-Buhelos talked to police and Allen came forward and handed over the Wal-Mart bag full of pills. The medical examiner's office later determined Kelly overdosed on salicylate, an ingredient found in aspirin, and acetaminophen, Tylenol's main ingredient. He also had Benadryl in his body.

═══

The day after Kelly died, Rod Blagojevich was on the radio, hosting a weekly program on WLS. He all but blamed Kelly's death on the stress prosecutors placed on him to testify against the former governor. In New York to promote his new book, *The Governor*, about his view of his life and the criminal case against him, Blagojevich still took to the airwaves in Chicago, saying, "Chris Kelly took his life because of the pressure he was under."

"He refused to make it easier on himself to lie about someone else," Blagojevich said. "My friend Chris Kelly's death will not be in vain."

Without directly discussing Kelly's problems with addiction, Blagojevich said, "Chris was a person with big appetites. He had some vices, but he also had virtues . . . and so, now for my friend Chris, all his trials are now over."

Four days after his death, on a warm morning in the middle of September, about two hundred gathered at St. John of the Cross Catholic Church in Western Springs. News cameras and reporters gathered on the sidewalks around the modest structure in the upper-middle-class suburb west of the city. Quinlan was there, as were Chicago Alderman Ed Burke and all four members of the Blagojevich family. The Blagojeviches sat noticeably right behind Kelly's family and wiped away tears throughout the ceremony, Rod hugging Amy when she appeared upset.

The eulogy was given by Kelly's brother, Charles, who confided that when he spoke to Chris about his funeral plans he wanted to make sure they were brief and simple. A former federal prosecutor and attorney working in Las Vegas, Charles Kelly never mentioned Blagojevich in the eulogy.

"Christopher Kelly is at peace," he said. "Nothing more. Nothing less."

═══

Blagojevich's second national publicity tour was similar to his first, a whirlwind of appearances on shows to tout his innocence. On *Jimmy Kimmel Live* he autographed the chair he sat in, and Kimmel then "sold the seat" on barely operate a computer. And that wasn't the first time his message to the world was blurred by distractions. In its February 2010 issue, *Esquire* magazine carried a long, mostly positive, feature about him where an out-of-town author questioned Fitzgerald's prosecution and Blagojevich contended he had been stolen from the people. He had the truth on his side, and unlike most politicians, he told the magazine, he was a real person.

"I'm blacker than Barack Obama. I shined shoes. I grew up in a five-room apartment," he was quoted as saying, a sentiment that required him to issue an apology.

In the spring of 2010, his push reached a fever pitch just weeks before his trial was to begin. Nothing had worked to publicly shame prosecutors into allowing all of the tapes into the case. To them, many of the recordings were off-point. And all told, there were hundreds of them. It was the prosecutors' burden to prove Blagojevich guilty, and they got to pick and choose the tapes they thought were relevant to that end. Blagojevich's defense could argue to have more tapes played, but it was clear to most observers that Judge James Zagel, who was overseeing the case, wasn't simply going to open the flood gates to any tape at any time. The trial would have taken months to complete.

But Blagojevich wasn't going to give up. He called a press conference on the street outside the Adams' law office on the South Side and all but challenged Fitzgerald to a duel. He summoned the media just in time for the evening Chicago newscasts to take his tirade live. There was a court hearing the next day, fittingly set for high noon, and Blagojevich wanted a commitment to be able to play the tapes he wanted to prove his innocence.

Fitzgerald had lied to the public when he accused Blagojevich of engaging in a crime spree, Blagojevich said, and now Fitzgerald was keeping tapes out of the case that would show the ex-governor hadn't done things the way prosecutors said he had. His anger was apparent even under several layers of pancake TV makeup.

"I challenge Mr. Fitzgerald. Why don't you show up in court tomorrow and explain to everybody, say to the whole world why you don't want those tapes that you made played in court?" Blagojevich spat. "I'll be in court tomorrow. I hope you're man enough to be there tomorrow too."

Well, Fitzgerald wasn't, and Zagel didn't take kindly to the ploy. Instead of starting a serious hearing on the former governor's plea to let a jury hear everything, the judge scolded him like a child. You don't get to have whatever you want, was the message from the bench. Knowing Blagojevich's personal history, Zagel explained that it was just like boxing. There are rules that everyone has to follow. Blagojevich was left to nod along as the judge sounded like a parent explaining something for the one millionth time.

"Those rules are enforced by the referee, not by the boxers. I am that referee, no one else," the judge said. "I will not permit the legal equivalent of head butts."

And no punching below the belt, probably, but it didn't seem like the defense got the message. Unable to have the jury hear what they wanted it to hear, a major defense motion appeared on the public docket, asking to be able to call President Obama as a witness. Obama could discuss what role certain messengers to Blagojevich played in the situation and possibly rebut the testimony of witnesses like Rezko, who might take the stand and slam both the president and Blagojevich over his past dealings with them. Many of the motions filed by both sides to that point included redacted sections that were blacked out if they covered sensitive topics, but this one had come in without its key sections censored. Defense lawyers would swear they didn't do it on purpose, and that one among them had simply made a mistake when filing the document electronically in court records. But nonetheless, the damage was done, and the information was out in the jury pool.

The defense motion showed that in a closed session with a judge, prosecutors had revealed some of what Rezko told them. The information included that Rezko had sought to influence the man who became president with illegal campaign money and that he used a lobbyist to hold a fund-raiser for Obama in exchange for favorable governmental action.

Obama always denied Rezko ever asked him to do anything illegal and said he had never done anything in that category. But in the end, that didn't matter, Judge Zagel would later rule. The defense fell "very short" of showing Obama's testimony was needed. Nothing Zagel saw, including notes from an FBI interview of Obama, showed that the president was aware of the specifics of Blagojevich's attempts to illegally bargain with him. Obama had maintained enough distance from the governor to keep himself removed from what was going to play out in court. And Obama's role didn't really matter anyway, Zagel said; it was Blagojevich's belief about what was happening—his perception of events—that really counted.

16

His Day in Court

Picking a jury to hear Blagojevich's trial was something Sam Adam Jr. had joked about before.

One day in the courthouse lobby after a pretrial hearing, an older and fairly deranged looking African American woman wandered past a gaggle of reporters Adam was chatting up about the case. One reporter elbowed him and whispered that maybe she would make a good juror. Everyone around the courthouse had been making jokes that the defense was looking for alternative personalities to try to convince that the ex-governor, featured on scores of tapes talking about crimes, was not guilty.

Adam didn't miss a beat.

"Foreman," he had said out loud that day, referring to the scraggly woman, throwing his head back with a belly laugh.

For Blagojevich, the first day of jury selection—June 3, 2010—must have felt eerily familiar for him as he arrived at the Dirksen US Courthouse. He was dressed in a dark, sharp suit as he stepped from a car and made his way toward a rope line at the front of the building. Seemingly physically unable to walk past without working the crowd, he moved toward onlookers waiting for his arrival and began shaking hands as news cameras swarmed him. It looked very much like he was on the campaign trail and not headed for a courtroom.

People calling themselves supporters carried signs. "If a man can't talk crap in his own home, take my husband please!" one read. Steps inside the courthouse lobby, Patti Blagojevich stopped to say it was a good day.

"The well wishes, e-mails, and rosaries left on our doorstep . . . have helped us through a rough time. But today is a good day because today is the day that begins the process to correct a terrible injustice that has been done to my husband, our family, and to the people of Illinois," she said.

Upstairs it was more of the same. Blagojevich got off the elevator and swept around the corner toward the courtroom. He quickly walked by the head of a line of people getting ready to go into the room and again stopped to shake hands.

It took Patti to literally pull him away, leaving him walking sideways toward Zagel's room as Patti yanked on his arm. He nodded and gave a "hey" to a line of reporters near the door, while nearby, a woman shouted at him that she was having custody problems with her children and asked him to investigate.

"Catch me after court," he called over his shoulder.

Once inside, Blagojevich sat with his hands folded, chuckling with his lawyers and looking like a ball of nervous energy. At one point with everyone still milling around and getting ready, Patti sat at the head of the table making some kind of point and rapping her fingers on the table. From a distance it appeared as if she were probably the one running the show.

In the courtroom gallery, reporters needled one another to pass the time. Zagel was a notorious slow-starter, and this was no different. Some in the press gallery passed around a *Tribune* editorial cartoon from the day. It was a silhouette of a circus scene, with clowns and jugglers, and carried the caption: "I see the defense is ready."

Adam Jr. loped over, always one to laugh with reporters when the chance was available. "At this rate we'll start in July," he said. Nearby, Assistant US Attorney Reid Schar sat as still as a stone, resting his head in one hand with his eyes closed, looking like he was trying to shut out what was happening around him and meditate on what he had to do.

Suddenly the potential jurors were in the room. They filed in a row at a time. Blagojevich looked up briefly but seemed afraid to nod or raise a hand. He quickly looked down at the defense table and then partially turned his back toward the group to say something to Adam Jr. Zagel greeted the group with a message about how important what they were doing was in a democratic system. It was a message not unlike what would-be jurors receive in courtrooms all over the country every day, but it had that extra Zagel flair.

"We fought a revolution so you could sit here today," he told them. The colonists had been subjected to kings but had taken it upon themselves to change that and deliver something new to the earth. "Your presence in this courtroom is a living symbol of the birth of our nation."

Blagojevich took notes with a silver pen, sometimes underlining things emphatically as if it were really, really important, and sometimes glanced around the room.

"The defendant, Rod Blagojevich, while governor of Illinois, engaged in various criminal acts," Zagel said by way of introduction, stating the prosecutors' accusation. The jurors by then knew what case they had been called to potentially serve on, but now it was really sinking in.

And it was registering with others, too. Patti sat in the first row looking around with a frown, with her heavy bangs hanging in her eyes. As she blinked, they moved.

The first prospective juror questioned was a CPA in her sixties. As he would each time he questioned a new juror, Zagel asked about her habits when it came to reading and watching the news media. It was important to weed out some who may have been too immersed in Blagojevich news and who had formed their own firm opinions. As it turned out for number one, the CPA said she didn't watch much TV news.

"Smart woman," a TV reporter in the gallery mumbled.

The next woman recalled something about bugs—an apparent reference to Patti's jungle adventure on television.

The panel of six men and six women eventually would include a Japanese American born in 1944 in a California detention camp. He had become a marine who served in Vietnam and had worked as a videotape librarian. One man was college-aged, working at a Best Buy and trying to figure out his life. Another was another former marine who suffered a bad hip injury while serving in Lebanon. He had already had one hip replacement and was concerned about how long he might have to sit while listening to evidence.

One woman was a graphic designer who did direct mail work. Zagel had asked her about a pet she had mentioned on her form, a hybrid Yorkiepoo. "She's awesome," the woman had said.

Few had really paid attention to one of the older women who was selected. She was prospective juror number 106. She was in her sixties and a retired official for the Illinois Department of Public Health. She had once been director of teen counseling for the Chicago Urban League and said she had once handed out campaign literature for a relative who ran for public office. Liberal talk shows were her favorite thing to listen to. Nothing in what she said had sounded any alarm bells for prosecutors, who did not save one of their challenges to have her struck from the jury. Like all the rest, she had promised that she could be fair and had said that nothing in her background would prevent her from making her own choices and reaching a verdict based on the evidence alone.

=====

Rod Blagojevich arrived for the real start of his trial to the normal throng of onlookers at the federal courthouse, waving and nodding his way toward one of the metal detectors. He fumbled for an ID to show security—not that he wasn't instantly recognizable—and piled through the checkpoint with an entourage of attorneys, Patti, and notable New York author Jimmy Breslin, who was following him around for a book project and described accompanying the governor as an "honor." Patti was accompanied by her brother, Richard, who often showed up as a sign of support, as did Patti's sister, Deb. Missing, of course, was her father, who stayed away from the proceedings entirely and wouldn't discuss it with reporters at city hall. Dozens of people in the lobby stopped what they were doing and watched as the state's former leader flipped his tie over his shoulder to put his belt back on. It wasn't exactly a low-key entrance, and Blagojevich went right up to reporters waiting for him in the lobby.

"I'm not the governor anymore, so I actually have to be on time," he said.

Not that Blagojevich ever seemed to be lacking energy, but on this morning he seemed especially electric. He was doing his best to amp himself up, to put a good face on a day that had been bearing down on him for months. Blagojevich said that frankly he felt like the trial was a new beginning and that the truth had been kept for too long in a "lock box."

"Finally you'll get to hear the things I've been dying to tell you for a year and a half," he said, as Patti nodded behind him.

Well, there were a few things that prosecutors had been dying to say as well, and the task fell to Carrie Hamilton. She was tough and direct and had led off the Rezko trial in sharp fashion two years earlier. Hamilton, Niewoehner, and Schar, the three-member team from that case, were going ahead against the governor in the same order. Hamilton, the group felt, was the best person to deliver the opening statement. She was a female face talking to the jury about one part of the case that was among Blagojevich's least favorite: the alleged shakedown of Children's Memorial Hospital, with the governor withholding state money from the storied facility because its leader hadn't given him a campaign donation. If you were a politician, that went into the category of very, very bad public relations. The hospital helped children "without considering where they come from and if they can pay."

Rod Blagojevich. Stealing from sick kids.

And that was just one scheme in the case, Hamilton said. Another involved a plan for the state to borrow $10 billion to deal with its budget, and another whether a school would get a state grant. The governor had the power to decide if tollways were built and who would sit on state boards.

"With all of this power came responsibility," Hamilton said. "And when he made those decisions, he was not supposed to do so because of how much money went into his campaign fund.

"Instead of asking, 'What about the people of Illinois?' he was asking, 'What about me?'"

The pattern started early in Blagojevich's first administration, when a ring of men around the governor found a way to extract $500,000 from a plan to borrow $10 billion and give it to state pension funds to invest, Hamilton said. The conspirators found an investment company willing to pay a secret kickback for the state business, and Blagojevich, Rezko, Kelly, and the then-governor's chief of staff, Alonzo "Lon" Monk, agreed to split the money once Blagojevich left office. Blagojevich knew full well what was happening when inside deals were put together by stacking state boards and commissions with loyal members who would do the administation's bidding, Hamilton said.

Hamilton painted the picture of an increasingly desperate Blagojevich who had swept into office but saw his inner circle dissolve over time. Rezko and Kelly had faced federal charges and had been taken away from Blago-jevich's fund-raising machine. In his first campaign and the early stage of his administration, Blagojevich rarely had found himself having to com-municate directly with donors, but that was changing by the fall of 2008. He had been reduced to speaking with some people directly, and his list of middlemen had shrunk to Monk, Wyma, and his brother, Robert.

In 2004, when Rezko was still able to get money to Rod and Patti Blago-jevich by attaching Patti to real estate deals and paying her $12,000 a month as a bogus "consultant," their family was financially stable. Detailing what they had learned years earlier, Hamilton said Rezmar took in a $40,000 com-mission, and that same amount was paid to Patti Blagojevich's company, River Realty, the very next day. The $40,000 was then paid to Patti herself from River Realty another day later. That kind of arrangement, Hamilton said, was a clear example of pay-to-play funds winding up in the pockets of the state's first couple. It had meant that the Blagojeviches' income that year was more than $300,000 and their debt was under $100,000.

But by 2008, with Rezko gone, the Blagojeviches subsisted on the governor's salary of $170,000, and their debt more than doubled.

Financial disaster was looming, Hamilton said, until . . .

"His golden ticket arrived on November 4, 2008," she said. Barack Obama was elected president, and that meant Blagojevich had to appoint a replacement. It was a significant official act, and Blagojevich had decided to cash in, she told the jury. To appoint Obama's friend, Valerie Jarrett, Blagojevich had demanded a cabinet position or millions of dollars being put into a charitable organization that Blagojevich would head when he left office. US Representative Jesse Jackson Jr. had been considered as well, but not because of what Jackson might be able to accomplish for people in the Senate, but "because of what Blagojevich thought could be done again, for him."

<hr />

Robert Blagojevich's lawyer, a veteran Chicago attorney named Michael Ettinger, would address the jury next. He introduced his client as "retired Lieutenant Colonel Robert Blagojevich."

The government didn't have the evidence to convict him, Ettinger promised. He was an outsider and someone who had shown up in the case only toward the end, promising to come to Chicago to help his brother when he was needed. Robert Blagojevich was no politician. He was a businessman.

"Until they shut me up, he's innocent," Ettinger bellowed. "He's an innocent man. A great man."

The Blagojeviches' father was an artillery man in the Yugoslavian army, Ettinger said, and Robert had followed in his footsteps. He had been in the ROTC in college, and that had become his life. He had been successful in the US Army. That was a point Ettinger would try to drill home every chance he could, with two veterans on the jury. He wanted the panel left with the idea that Robert was a public servant and that he had been on the outside looking in when his brother really got down and dirty in the fund-raising arena. Rod Blagojevich was the politician and the professional fund-raiser, and Robert Blagojevich was the defender of American freedom who had been in charge of three nuclear warheads while in Europe. He had the same top secret clearance as the Joint Chiefs of Staff, Ettinger trumpeted.

"He debriefed sixteen NATO generals," he said.

As Ettinger wrapped up his opening statement, Adam could be seen rubbing his hands and furrowing his brow. He looked down at the defense table in concentration one moment and smiled at people sitting near him the next. You could almost see him mentally hopping up and down like a prizefighter who can't wait for the bell, and there was a buzz in the room just before he finally stood up. The jury had a feeling, Adam told them as he began. They had heard all kinds of allegations that Blagojevich had demanded money, and it just wasn't true.

"I'm telling you, that man there is as honest as the day is long, and you will know it in your gut," Adam predicted. There was a way they could tell, he said. Where was the money? Hamilton had just put up a chart showing the heavy financial pressure the Blagojevich family was under.

How well were the schemes working if there was no money for the alleged kingpin?

"This is the biggest public corruption case in the state of Illinois and the country," Adam shouted. "And what did they tell you? He's broke. He didn't take a dime."

Scores of federal agents had certainly looked for money in the Blagojevich case, he said. They had pulled no punches and left no stones unturned. "This is the federal government," Adam said. "The same people chasing bin Laden are chasing him. And how many illegal checks were made out to him? None."

At the defense table, Blagojevich was suddenly looking more relaxed. He had a look of satisfaction on his face, like he was relieved that his side of things could finally be aired and no one could quiet it. He nodded as Adam promised that Blagojevich would testify himself and explain to the jury what he was really thinking.

"He's not gonna let some four-eyed, chubby, yelling lawyer tell ya," Adam said.

There had been a plan to sell $10 billion in bonds, Adam said, but Blagojevich had no role in which firm to pick to lead the sale. John Filan had, "a guy who ain't corrupt," and the plan had saved the state millions.

"Follow the money," Adam said. "We've got four months here."

Rezko had taken the kickback from the bond deal and had used it to pay off his own business debts. These things happened under Blagojevich's nose, Adam said, his voice jumping from a near whisper as he stood just before the jury to a full bellow as he roamed around the courtroom like a gospel preacher. This was what Rezko did, he borrowed—or stole—from Peter to pay Paul. And he did it over and over again.

"Rezko is the Bernie Madoff of Chicago," Adam yelled. "He had pyramid scheme after pyramid scheme. He fooled everyone. And he fooled—with all due deference, governor—you."

And with that, Adam pointed toward Blagojevich, who sat with pursed lips like he was humbly accepting Adam's allegation that he had been duped.

Rezko was the real villain in the case, Adam claimed. He had risen from the gritty streets of Chicago and pounded out a living in the cutthroat real estate world and had been just as tough in the political arena. He had pushed for influence where he could, donating money to everyone from Illinois Senator Dick Durbin to President George Bush.

"If I'm in an elevator with him, I'm hiding my purse," Adam joked. Rezko was good at scheming, getting an award as the area's Arab American businessman of the decade, Adam said, and he had been friendly even with an up-and-coming politician named Barack Obama.

"Obama had no idea that what was happening to Tony was implosion," Adam said. Rezko's business began to fall like a house of cards once money began to run out and he could no longer afford to pass cash from business entity to business entity to keep things afloat.

He had wagered much of his business on a massive project at Roosevelt and Clark in the South Loop, but his legal problems arose just at the wrong time. Debt piled up in his fast food empire and in his real estate ventures, and instead of being public and facing his issues, Rezko sought to pull his way out of things by borrowing from people he wasn't being honest with.

Adam called the allegations involving Jackson and the Senate seat "upside down" and suggested Blagojevich was only floating the idea of a Jackson appointment because he thought it would help sell Washington power brokers who hated Jackson on the idea of the appointment of Illinois Attorney General Lisa Madigan. If Madigan were named to the seat, Blagojevich supposedly theorized, it would placate his main political nemesis in Springfield, powerful House Speaker Michael Madigan, Lisa's father, who was challenging the governor's initiatives at every turn.

The main concern of Obama and other Democratic leaders was that the seat be held in the election of 2010, and it was Washington's opinion that Jackson couldn't do it. Adam said the leadership was asking that someone be sent to them, "just not Jesse Jackson Jr.," he said. "Lord, please."

That left some on the jury laughing, and the giggles continued when Adam said he didn't think Jackson would have held up his end of the supposed deal anyway.

"Jesse Jackson Jr. ain't giving anybody no money," Adam said, as if tapping into some kind of South Side knowledge stream unavailable to most. The entire idea was a clever ploy that worked, he said, because just before Blagojevich's arrest, Emanuel called and said he would fly to Chicago to broker the Madigan arrangement. All the pieces were falling into place for a legal trade, Adam contended, just as the FBI pulled up to the governor's front door.

———

When Lon Monk walked into the courtroom for the first time to testify, Blagojevich looked up and stared, shooting daggers at the man who had been such a close friend. Monk was now fifty-one years old and had the trim, athletic build of the runner that he was. Blagojevich looked like he had been planning how to react when Monk appeared and decided, as he almost always did, to look like he was ready to fight. Monk simply looked straight ahead at the witness stand, where he was headed. Step by step, passing spectators and the press, he never even glanced at Blagojevich, occasionally looking down at the courtroom's brown and white dotted carpeting. As Monk passed the gallery and the front bench where Patti Blagojevich was sitting, she began staring at the back of his head, joining her husband's glare.

Monk said he was currently unemployed and living in Decatur with his wife. He had gone to law school, he said, had been a sports agent, worked in government, and was a consultant and lobbyist in 2008. Monk appeared very businesslike, in a sharp suit. He had a short haircut and spoke directly and clearly with no noticeable accent of any kind. His appearance suggested he could just as easily have wound up sitting at the government table as a federal prosecutor had the track of his life been different.

He had been approached about cooperating as long ago as 2007, Monk said, but he had refused. It hadn't been until the taping in 2008 had become public that Monk realized he had to try to save himself. He had pleaded guilty to conspiring to solicit a bribe, and in return a possible five-year prison sentence would be reduced to two. He said he understood he wasn't going to be prosecuted for anything else he had done as long as he was truthful in his testimony.

"It's the two years I'm focused on," he said.

Monk told the jury that when Blagojevich was in Congress in 2000, Monk was in Washington working as an agent when his friend told him he was going to run for Illinois governor in 2002. Monk said he was interested in helping, and Blagojevich put him on his congressional payroll as general counsel before Monk became Blagojevich's campaign manager in the summer of 2001.

Among Monk's duties was to make sure campaign money wasn't spent too quickly, he said.

FBI Agent Daniel Cain had testified before Monk. Cain showed the jury charts of Blagojevich's fund-raising totals rocketing upward during the 2002 and 2006 gubernatorial campaigns, suggesting his machinery for pulling in contributions was in overdrive. They showed how he demolished Vallas, Burris, and Jim Ryan in fund-raising in 2002.

Fund-raising was always a priority in the Blagojevich camp, Monk explained. He said the campaign set goals for "bundlers," and Monk's job was to call them up to make sure their promises were being met.

When Monk began talking about what bundlers were, Rod dropped his pen almost in disgust, leaned back in his chair, and exhaled deeply. Then he picked the pen up and began taking notes again.

Three or four times a week, key members of the campaign met to hash out fund-raising strategies, Monk said, and Blagojevich would often be there. Niewoehner asked how knowledgeable Blagojevich was about the people and organizations the campaign was targeting for donations.

"Very knowledgeable," Monk replied.

Among Blagojevich's biggest bundlers were Rezko and Kelly, the roofer from Burr Ridge who wound up on Monk's radar because of his numbers, Monk told the jury. Kelly donated hundreds of thousands of dollars himself, Monk recalled, and just had a knack for getting others to raise money too. When bundlers in the campaign had goals, Kelly knew how to stay on them and demand that they be met. As for Kelly himself, no one even bothered to come up with a mark for him to hit.

"He was involved in so many aspects of fund-raising it just didn't make sense for him to set a goal," Monk remembered. Prosecutors had put up a photo of Kelly, and Blagojevich looked up at it almost admiringly.

Money was power when it came to politics and campaigning. Blagojevich had realized that cash was key early on in his political life, and Kelly knew how to badger would-be contributors to get it. As a strategist, Monk, too, knew that having a formidable war chest was a signal to supporters and enemies alike. It would lend weight to a candidate and suggest to the party that he could win, Monk said, thereby leading to even more money coming in. These big dollars in the campaign fund could have a chilling effect on anyone wanting to challenge the candidate. In Blagojevich's first campaign for governor, having a lot of campaign dollars was especially important. Vallas had a lot of support in Chicago, so Blagojevich would need to confront him on the airwaves there. The other part of his campaign strategy was to try to neutralize Vallas's Chicago support by concentrating on downstate voters, and Blagojevich would have to spend his way to name recognition there. And once Blagojevich faced Ryan in the general election, having lots of money allowed him to run political ads sooner and get a jump on his opponent.

The brusque Kelly and the energetic Blagojevich were like-minded and became close, Monk said, and Kelly found his way in to more than just fund-raising meetings. When Blagojevich gathered with advisers to discuss media plans, Kelly was there. And Rezko also wound up more plugged in than might otherwise be expected for someone with no official state title. Once Blagojevich was elected and sworn in to office in January 2003, the two fund-raisers constantly made recommendations to fill top posts in the new administration "and in some cases [sat] in on the interviews," Monk said, and they often submitted their picks for who should be named to dozens of Illinois boards and commissions. Rezko and Kelly traveled with the governor, too, Monk said, taking fund-raising trips with him and bringing their families to Springfield to stay at the governor's mansion on the rare occasions when Blagojevich was there. As chief of staff, Monk said he spoke to the pair regularly, often when they were recommending some company or firm to get a state contract. Monk told the jury he was well aware the pair made their recommendations either to reward campaign contributors or to have the ability to ask for cash. And what did Monk routinely do for them? Niewoehner wanted to know.

"Whatever they asked," Monk said.

===

It was Kelly who had first brought up the topic of making money illegally through state business, Monk recalled. Even before the election in 2002, Kelly had said something to him when they were alone in the parking garage of the building that housed Blagojevich's campaign office, he said, evoking images of meetings with Deep Throat in *All the President's Men*. The Republicans had done it for years, Kelly told him, and in fact men like Cellini were Republicans in name only. It wouldn't be hard to direct business to their friends and themselves and bring in cash.

"This was something that we were going to be able to do now that we were close to Rod and he was going to be governor," Monk recalled Kelly telling him. "I was intrigued by the topic and wanted to make money."

The following summer, after Blagojevich was in office, things became a bit more organized, Monk said. He told Niewoehner he remembered a meeting at the Rezmar offices where he, Rezko, Kelly, and Blagojevich met to discuss ways they themselves could profit. They sat around a long conference table. and Rezko sketched out eight or nine proposals on an easel, or maybe a blackboard, Monk said, and put an estimated dollar amount by each. In all, there were hundreds of thousands of dollars in corruption plans. And there was a definite sense that what they were talking about was to be top secret, for obvious reasons. The four didn't even use their names, he said, referring to one another as "1, 2, 3, and 4." Kelly would later get into the habit of just showing four fingers when referring to how the group could profit from one scheme or another, Monk said. First on Rezko's list was a plan to set up or buy an insurance company that could get state contracts. Levine certainly had proven there was money in that. But the four wouldn't have to bribe anyone. Blagojevich had allowed Rezko and Kelly to name loyalists to key state posts. When some of the plans worked, Rezko would hold the money in a secret account until Blagojevich left office.

Blagojevich had been moving toward selling the $10 billion in pension obligation bonds to address budget problems and needed an investment firm to head the deal up. This was when Rezko and Kelly had become very interested in having Bear Stearns sell the first chunk, despite a number of big firms being on the list. And they got even more excited when just before the first sale, state budget staff floated the idea of selling all at once because interest rates were so favorable, Monk said. Kelly, with no experience, advised Blagojevich on the massive bond deal, Monk recalled, and he remembered thinking the situation was probably going to help with fundraising somehow or that "we were gonna make money." He even recalled the meeting at the Thompson Center before Blagojevich pulled the trigger on selling all the bonds at once. Monk testified he saw Rezko and Kelly huddled together in the back of Blagojevich's office and that Kelly at one point pulled the governor aside. Shortly thereafter, Blagojevich told his staff to do the big sale and abandon the idea of a group of smaller outlays.

In a later conversation, Monk said Kelly bragged about having persuaded Blagojevich to go ahead. But it was Rezko who really filled him in later, Monk said.

"As a result of Bear Stearns being able to sell all $10 billion [in bonds], Bob Kjellander, who was a lobbyist for Bear Stearns, had given Tony, in an effort for getting this done, $500,000" from the total he received, Monk told the jury. "And that Tony was putting that in a separate account for the four of us."

Kjellander would always deny any wrongdoing. He classified the money he gave to Rezko as a loan.

Rezko would in fact hold the cash, Monk said, though he confessed to never getting any of it directly or knowing where it went. There was one hiccup when Kelly heard that Rezko had taken out $100,000 to help with a business situation. Monk said Kelly had been angered because he was afraid the withdrawal of such a large sum could somehow alert authorities to the presence of the illicit account, and he had demanded Rezko put it back.

And with that, Monk's first day on the witness stand came to a close. At the defense table, Blagojevich had continued to watch with disgust. He scribbled notes and looked into the gallery at Patti, who sometimes rubbed her neck and looked around the courtroom herself in amazement. It was like they had never actually considered what Monk would say, and they were genuinely surprised by how bad it was. Blagojevich's reactions were so pronounced, prosecutors later asked Judge Zagel to tell him to cut it out because he was distracting the jury.

The next morning, Blagojevich arrived and was his usual chipper self, shaking hands and saying hello to anyone who stopped to look at him for longer than two seconds. One person who shouted support from a line of spectators getting ready to enter the courtroom was Derrick Mosley, a former community activist who was sent to prison for trying to extort $20,000 from gospel singer DeLeon Richards and her husband, baseball player Gary Sheffield.

"Superstar!" Mosley then shouted at Sam Adam Jr. "We want some cross-examination today!"

But that would have to wait. Monk wasn't quite through answering questions from Niewoehner, who started again by asking about Rezko and Monk and their interest in getting appointments pushed through for their own benefit. Monk said they were more interested in the more important positions that had real sway over contracts and state business and cared much less about many of the less important spots in the administration. Niewoehner put an image of a memo up on an overhead screen for the jury to see. It was a list of candidates that Rezko had given to the administration for "consideration." Doctors Malek and Massuda were there, two of the people who had helped Levine carry off the odd vote at the IHFPB, and so was Daniel Mahru, Rezko's business partner.

"A lot of them were donors, yeah," Monk acknowledged for the jury, while Blagojevich did his best to keep a poker face at the defense table.

Blagojevich had had a large fund-raising event the summer after he was elected, in 2003, and there was a lot of planning and discussion about bringing in money ahead of it, Monk remembered. There was direct talk about linking fund-raising to state positions. Rezko was very opinionated about how it should work when someone wanted a spot.

"At a minimum, some of these people should have been donating $25,000," Monk recalled him saying. One who would show up at the fund-raiser was Rezko business associate Ali Ata, who would hand a check directly to Blagojevich and later be named head of the Illinois Finance Authority. He had testified about it at Rezko's trial and was expected to do the same at Blagojevich's. Niewoehner showed Monk the board minutes from the January 2004 IFA board meeting where Ata had been hired over a sham candidate. Rezko had quickly sought a loan with the help of the IFA under Ata to help support his pizza business, which Monk said caused a little bit of worry in the administration because of how it looked. Ata eventually had signed a document on IFA letterhead that made it look like an investor was getting assistance from the IFA, which helped Rezko's business bring in $10 million from General Electric Capital Corporation. In reality, Rezko had set up a straw purchaser, and he, Ata, and Rezko associate Al Chaib had been charged separately with that fraud.

Monk also remembered Levine's reappointment to TRS and the hospital board. Governor George Ryan had appointed him, but Levine had no trouble making an impression on Rezko and Kelly and sticking around with Blagojevich. Monk told Niewoehner he remembered talking to Kelly after Kelly had come back from a meeting at Rezko's offices with Levine.

"[Kelly] said [Levine] knew how to get things done at TRS, in terms of influencing board members and having things voted on that he was in favor of," Monk said. "He referred to him as an operator."

Kelly realized Levine could steer approvals to certain companies that were willing to give something back. Levine had filled Rezko in on it as a way to make money.

"He was kind of enthusiastic about it and said this is something he or we should be doing, the four of us," Monk said, meaning 1, 2, 3, and 4.

Monk and Rezko had a decent relationship of their own, one that included Rezko occasionally slipping Monk $10,000 in overnight mail envelopes. Monk said it had happened up to nine times, the first coming when Monk had asked Rezko about buying a luxury car and the weathy real estate developer turned political godfather had offered to pay for it. There was another envelope just before Monk got married in September 2004, and others just because. Monk used the extra cash for things like gas and food and clothes, too nervous to deposit the funds into a bank account, though he then worried that someone investigating him would wonder why he had suddenly stopped using ATMs. Rezko also had paid for the basement to be refinished at Monk's Park Ridge home, sending contractors there and charging him nothing.

Payments to Monk were payments to Monk, but this was Blagojevich's trial. Monk also told what he knew about Rezko hiring Patti Blagojevich to a $12,000-a-month job, for which prosecutors said she did nothing. Monk recalled everyone deciding it was better for her to go on a retainer rather than being paid on commission, which would require actual properties to be sold for her to be paid. Showing up at the office also was an issue, because Patti was a busy mother to two young girls. Still, the Blagojevich lawyers advised, it was a good idea for her to at least appear at Rezko's offices every now and again.

Niewoehner went back to the "1, 2, 3, 4" code. It had been Kelly's idea, but the governor had used it too, Monk said. Once in 2007 or even 2008, Monk recalled, in the campaign office, Blagojevich had put his hand up in front of him.

"If you're ever asked about this," Monk said, quoting Blagojevich and holding up one, two, three, and then four fingers, "don't say anything."

And then Blagojevich had made a slashing motion across his throat. Nearby, the ex-governor was shaking his head again.

———

Monk said Blagojevich was regularly getting shut out in his last-ditch bids to bring in cash before the legislation took effect January 1, 2009. One attempt focused on the head of a roadbuilder's organization, Jerry Krozel, and Blagojevich's planned announcement of state funds for tollway construction.

Monk said in the fall of 2008, the then-governor hoped the tollway plan would "incentivize" Krozel to make a large contribution. Blagojevich planned to announce a $1.8 billion tollway program and held out a possible $5 billion infusion as a carrot with the thought it would make Krozel and his organization very happy, Monk said.

"We need to get $500,000 from him," Monk recalled Blagojevich saying. Monk said he checked in with Krozel a few times about a possible donation but didn't come out and ask for that much because he "didn't feel like it" and didn't think it was reasonable with the economy in the tank.

Blagojevich said he was willing to announce the smaller outlay for the tollway, which he eventually did, but wanted to wait and see what kind of money came in from concrete and roadbuilding groups before making the $5 billion plan public. If he wasn't satisfied with the fund-raising result, "fuck 'em," Monk recalled Blagojevich saying.

Monk also described increasing paranoia surrounding Blagojevich's closest circle as the federal investigation closed in. Fund-raiser Christopher Kelly had started speaking in code to Monk, Rezko, and Blagojevich, Monk remembered. The use of the numbers was common, including by Blagojevich.

Before Monk left the stand, Niewoehner asked about the December 3, 2008, conversation that had been recorded by bugs in the Friends of Blagojevich offices. Prosecutors had played for the jury the tape on which Blagojevich and Monk appeared to be rehearsing what Monk would say to John Johnston, the owner of a pair of horse tracks that Blagojevich allegedly shook down.

Monk said meetings at the office started with a general fund-raising discussion among himself, Blagojevich, and Robert in the conference room, but the governor then took him aside into his private office to talk to him about his "issue." That issue was Johnston, and Blagojevich allegedly pushing the track owner for a donation by the end of the year.

Early in the tape, Monk told Blagojevich he was headed to Oklahoma for his dad's "army reunion." That wasn't actually true, as what Monk was planning to do was go play golf with some pals. He just didn't want the governor to know that, he said, because Blagojevich had previously flipped out on him when he took golf trips late in the year when fund-raising was critical.

The ploy was to make it sound like the signing of the bill and the donation weren't related, even though they were, but there could be a perception problem if the governor signed the bill helping the horse tracks and suddenly a donation appeared on the books. Johnston should be told to make a donation right then, the men agreed, and he could be assured that the signing would come in short order.

"Look, I want to go to him without crossing the line and say, 'Give us the fucking money,'" Monk said on the tape. "'Give us the money, and one has nothing to do with the other, but give us the fuckin' money.'"

It was all preparation for the conversation that Monk would shortly have with Johnston, he testified. Eventually it was decided that Monk would say Blagojevich was concerned that Johnston would get "skittish" about the donation if Blagojevich signed the bill, as the feds had recorded. Make the donation now, Johnston would be told. Blagojevich was going to sign a large group of bills together within weeks, so it would look better if a donation came in soon and the horse track bill were signed with the other bundle later.

Niewoehner wanted to make the point crystal clear for the jury. Was Monk actually telling Johnston that the two were not linked? No, Monk answered, they were confident Johnston would read between the lines and figure it out.

"I wouldn't have to say that if they weren't linked," Monk said.

A few days later, Johnston himself would tell the jury about the conversation he had with Monk. Johnston had wispy, sandy-colored hair and the somewhat weathered look of a man who had spent his share of time outside around horses. Companies associated with his family had given the governor hundreds of thousands of dollars over the years, though they hadn't donated anything in 2007 while the governor was using most of his incoming campaign dollars to pay lawyers defending him from the ongoing federal probe. Johnston had hired Monk that spring to be a liaison to the governor's office, but it seemed like Monk often turned around and asked for money on Blagojevich's behalf. He remembered the racetrack bill had passed in November 2008 and was sent to the governor's desk for a signature. Johnston called on a regular basis to see if Blagojevich would sign it, he said, because he was losing money daily. He remembered the December 3, 2008, meeting, saying he figured Monk might have some news about the bill but would also ask for more campaign cash. To deflect the request, Johnston said he had his dad, Billy, come to the meeting, calling him an "ornery SOB" who had rattled Monk's cage in the past. And it worked, until Monk got John Johnston in the stairwell alone.

"He turned to me and he said, 'One more thing. The governor is concerned if he signed the bill, you might not be forthcoming with a contribution,'" Johnston recalled. "I said, 'I thought that's what the governor might be thinking.' I said, 'Your suggestion of a contribution at this time is inappropriate.'"

But Monk wasn't deterred. "He said, 'OK, different subject matter. I need you to get a contribution in by the end of the year.'"

Johnston said he knew his donation was tied to the bill's signing, and he felt some pressure, even though he knew he would never be writing a check. He was angry, he testified, and it would just look wrong. Besides, Monk was supposed to be his lobbyist. "My lobbyist," he said with a wry smile. "I showed him the door, and I never spoke to him again," Johnston said. "And I never wrote the check."

Blagojevich was arrested days later, and he signed the horse track bill December 15—nearly a week after his arrest.

=====

Adam Jr. started slowly when he finally got to cross-examine Monk, seemingly channeling the anger of his client behind him. Monk had accused Blagojevich of plotting to divide up the state of Illinois.

Monk had to have known the penalty would be severe if they were ever caught. And speaking of being caught, they would have had to be very careful. That would mean at the very least knowing what the corrupt deals were that they were going to do so they could work to cover them up, right?

"Yeah," Monk acknowledged almost sheepishly.

"And you can't remember the first one?" Adam said, raising his voice in mock exasperation.

"They were just ideas," Monk answered.

"And you can't tell us the first one?" Adam said again.

"I don't remember," Monk said. Adam was doing a good job of using Monk's lack of memory of the details of the meetings to make the whole thing sound preposterous. Monk tried to make it sound like the corrupt ideas were in such an embryonic state that they didn't make any difference to him at the time. It was more like a corruption brainstorming session to him. He made it sound like Rezko was kind of talking off the top of his head while he and Blagojevich sat there and nodded. But Adam kept at it, pointing out that Monk didn't even know where all the money was supposed to go.

"There wasn't any specificity," Monk insisted again. "They were concepts and ideas."

Adam asked him to name the second item on Rezko's list. Then the third. And when Adam asked if the governor did anything to make items on the board come to fruition, Niewoehner objected.

When the prosecutor had questioned him, Monk said he thought maybe the pension-obligation bond deal was on the list, but Adam circled back to poke holes in that, too. Monk had said the meeting between the four was in late summer, even September. But Adam told him the POB deal was completed in June 2003, trying for a Perry Mason moment. You could tell from the expression on Monk's face that he realized what Adam was getting at as he was asking.

"It couldn't have been one of those ideas, could it?" Adam said loudly. The deal was over by the time of the supposed meeting.

"But it could have been on the board," Monk insisted.

"Was it?" Adam said angrily.

"I don't remember."

Adam received essentially the same answer regarding a supposed second meeting at a Los Angeles hotel that Monk had talked about. Monk couldn't remember the details. Rezko was at a board, Kelly was often piping up with thoughts, and there was a buffet this time. But Monk still couldn't recall any of the plans on the list. Monk didn't know where the money was going to be held, and, as it turned out, he never got a dime from the ideas anyway.

But, reminded Adam, Monk did say he got some money from Rezko. Not in the form of dividends from state corruption but money in the form of good old-fashioned cash stuffed into envelopes. Adam suggested maybe it was hush money. Word went out that spring of 2004 that the feds were turning up the heat. Levine had been visited by the FBI, and they had played Levine tapes of himself talking to players in the scheming, including Rezko. Was it a coincidence? Adam asked, as the former governor at the table nearby, for once, stopped taking notes and seemed to relax as he leaned back in his chair to watch.

"The only cash in this entire scenario you're aware of is the cash Rezko gave you," Adam said as if it were the definitive statement on the matter.

Monk was facing ten years or more in prison, and a person seemingly would say just about anything to avoid that. And for Monk, Adam said often, that meant saying what the prosecutors wanted to hear. Monk said he had to tell the truth, but wasn't it really that he had to tell the government's version of the truth?

Adam wanted the jury to know he thought that assertion applied to the last subject area he wanted to get to, the Children's Memorial Hospital deal. Monk had testified about a meeting at the campaign office in 2008, when Blagojevich had heard from his brother that Pat Magoon of CMH wasn't paying up in return for the governor agreeing to boost the facility's state payback. Blagojevich had supposedly gotten mad almost instantly and got on the phone with a secretary demanding to talk to Bob Greenlee and telling the deputy governor to either hold up the plan or slow it down.

But Adam had notes of a conversation Monk had with the government where his version of events had been different. He had said Wyma was at the meeting, and it was Wyma who had set Blagojevich off. And furthermore, the campaign office was bugged and its phones were tapped, and no one ever had played that call for Monk during his cooperation. The jury wouldn't be hearing it either, because the government didn't have it. Adam threw that in Monk's face as yet another challenge on whether Monk was just making things up.

"You've never heard that phone call, have you? Because it doesn't exist," Adam said, raising his voice again. "It doesn't exist, does it?"

An uncomfortable-looking Monk shrugged and tried to say he didn't know for sure, as Adam moved toward him. Niewoehner later had Monk say he didn't know which line the governor pressed or whether the conversation had happened in a part of the office where the microphones weren't really picking things up. But for right then, Adam demanded to know what Monk was trying to get the jury to believe.

"You're putting it on his back, aren't you, Mr. Greenlee?" Adam said, muffing the kill shot. But in typical fashion, he shook his head and half laughed and corrected it. "Mr. Monk, sorry."

The defense later came to believe that Adam's cross of Monk was a turning point in the first trial. Zagel kept a much tighter leash on them from there forward, and particularly on Adam Jr. It was as if the judge had wanted to see how far the Adams might take things and, having found out, was not about to let it continue. As the defense tried to bore in on future witnesses, even about some topics they believed the government had gotten into, Zagel told them to call the witness back themselves if they wanted a thorough exploration. The defense often chafed, thinking it was a ridiculous interpretation of the law to block them from aggressively cross-examining witnesses.

———

Joseph Aramanda had the look of a successful if somewhat world-beaten businessman when he took the stand about a week into the trial. He had met Rezko in 1996, and they became close friends. Their families had traveled together to places like Italy and Dubai. In fact, Rezko had been on a trip to the Middle East with Aramanda at the time he was indicted in 2006, making authorities wonder whether he would return to face the charges. Aramanda had been an executive in Rezko's businesses, serving as chief operating officer for the more than one hundred Papa John's pizza franchises that Rezko owned, until he bought a collection of the restaurants from him. Rezko had offered him spots in the Blagojevich administration, Aramanda said, but he turned down a post in the Department of Aging to pay attention to the pizza business in 2003. Things weren't going well, Aramanda recalled, and it made more sense for him to try to save his struggling franchises than to take on something new in government. That same year, Aramanda said, he went to Rezko looking for someone to loan him money to help prop things up.

As it turned out, Aramanda said his friend had someone in mind. It was Robert Kjellander, and Rezko set up a meeting. Aramanda had spoken to the political insider before, including at a fund-raiser at Rezko's home for Blagojevich and Barack Obama. And after just one discussion, Aramanda remembered Kjellander agreeing to loan him $600,000. He hadn't been that interested in what the money was being used for, Aramanda said of his creditor, and he didn't really ask for any paperwork or collateral. The money would go a long way toward helping Aramanda settle some debts and keep things afloat, and he had hoped to spend perhaps half of the money to build a new restaurant that might generate some better income.

But just days after Aramanda signed for the loan and got his money, there was a bit of a nasty surprise. Rezko suddenly brought up that Aramanda owed him more than $400,000 from their own transaction involving Aramanda buying some of the pizza restaurants. So Rezko wanted Aramanda to use much of the money to pay some of Rezko's own outstanding debts. Aramanda protested, but Rezko said he didn't have anywhere else to go at the moment, so asking for the favor had been unavoidable.

So Aramanda unwittingly became a pass-through for Rezko to get funds out of the POB deal. Kjellander had collected the $809,000 in payments for his consulting arrangement, and Rezko had worked things so that some $475,000 went from Kjellander, through Aramanda, to his own creditors. Thousands went to Al Chaib and others. Aramanda testified that he called Rezko's secretary and was given a list of names and amounts and wiring instructions, which he followed.

Kjellander considered the $600,000 a loan, which Aramanda was expected to pay within a year, and he was on the hook for it despite getting to pump about $125,000 into his pizza franchises. When the bill came due, Rezko hooked Aramanda up with his friend Jay Wilton from the tollway rest stop arrangement, who loaned Aramanda more money to pay Kjellander and who eventually purchased some of the restaurants himself.

But as he questioned Aramanda, Niewoehner was just as interested in having him talk about another proposal Rezko had made to him. Aramanda remembered Rezko saying it could mean more than a million dollars annually. The businessman might be able to start a consulting firm that could act as a middleman on deals with state pension funds. Aramanda could get to know people at the firms and others who dealt with them and then use Rezko's connections to get the firms' state approvals. There was someone already involved in such "work," Aramanda was told, and perhaps they could get connected and form a partnership. It was Sheldon Pekin, who Aramanda understood was already in line to collect $750,000 as a finder's fee on a deal to bring Glencoe Capital an allocation from TRS.

The two did meet, and Aramanda agreed to accept $250,000 from Pekin, which Aramanda thought could be the beginning of a business they might be in together. But as soon as Aramanda had the money in hand, Rezko was again directing that the money go to his own associates. Aramanda testified that he gave $40,000 to a Rezko creditor. He went along, Aramanda told Niewoehner, because he felt somewhat obligated to Rezko for introducing him to the new opportunity in the first place. Aramanda never testified that he felt like a tool that Rezko used to funnel money out of state contracts.

To bolster what Aramanda was saying, prosecutors went to tapes from the Rezko and Levine investigation, which had been played to the jury that convicted Rezko in 2008. There was Stuart Levine's voice in a courtroom again, stammering and stuttering through the speakers. Levine was chastising Pekin for asking whether Christmas was coming early and warning that if more money didn't go to Rezko soon, "Tony's not gonna do business any more like that."

Ultimately, Aramanda said, he decided the "business" wasn't for him.

Instead of the million dollars or so a year, Aramanda would be placed on a much lower salary, with the opportunity to do better if there were more finder's fees to go around. In other words, Rezko was altering the deal. Because of the size of some of the transactions that were going to come together, "[Rezko] would be sharing in the transactions along with others," Aramanda told Niewoehner, and said Rezko mentioned three other people who would have their fingers in the pie as well.

"Ton, Chris, and Rod," Aramanda said. "I understood he must have some arrangement with the three others he mentioned, and some way of splitting the fees."

———

Former national Democratic fund-raiser Joseph Cari looked a bit like Dustin Hoffman as he took the witness stand. He had dyed, mussed hair and wore an expensive-looking suit.

Assistant US Attorney Reid Schar walked him through ground he had covered during Rezko's trial, as he explained how he got tied up with the Blagojevich camp. Cari was a Democrat but actually had supported Blagojevich's opponent, Jim Ryan, in 2002, because his wife was battling cancer and so was the Republican candidate. But after the election was over, David Wilhelm, a close friend of Cari's, came off a campaign job with Blagojevich to take a position leading the transition team.

"David wanted me to meet the people around the governor," Cari said, adding that meant mostly Rezko and Kelly. Team Blagojevich was still pumped from his win, and Blagojevich had the White House on his mind.

Cari said he eventually met with Kelly and then with Levine to talk about what it took to put together a national fund-raising organization. Cari had led fund-raising for Al Gore and remembered the weeks he spent in Florida "counting chads," in reference to the disputed 2000 presidential election.

Cari said Levine took notes throughout their meeting and promised he would be sharing them with Rezko. But the witness was there to mention one episode in particular. It was his recollection of the October 2003 fund-raiser in New York that he agreed to help set up with his friend Carl McCall, the former New York comptroller.

Cari said he went to O'Hare International Airport to fly to New York on Levine's private jet, and those on the flight included Kelly, Levine, and Blagojevich. Cari said he found himself in a conversation with Blagojevich that centered on politics, shifted to the craziness of Florida in 2000, and segued from there into national fund-raising. Blagojevich told him he wanted to run for president and pointed to former president Bill Clinton as a success story he could model himself after. Clinton had run as governor of Arkansas, and that was way better than using something like Congress as a platform.

"As a sitting governor he had an ability to raise a lot more money than a sitting US senator," Cari said.

Blagojevich saw the same chances for himself coming out of Illinois. "As a sitting governor you're giving out contracts and legal work and consulting work, and you can go back to those people and ask for money," Cari said the governor told him.

What was Blagojevich saying? Schar asked.

"That he would be giving out state business and would go back to those people for contributions," Cari said.

Cari went on to say he had a number of conversations with Levine, Rezko, and Kelly and that all hinted the administration would reward him richly if he would get involved in the Blagojevich fund-raising machine. Cari was a leader at a Chicago law firm at the time and was a partner in the insurance investor Healthpoint, so he had ways to be rewarded.

"Mr. Levine explained to me that the governor, Mr. Kelly, and Mr. Rezko were going to put together a mechanism where they were going to be appointing people to boards and giving out legal work, accounting work, consulting work," Cari said. "And then they would go back to these people for campaign contributions."

In one conversation, Rezko made it very clear Cari's firm would get state work or Healthpoint would find itself with a bounty of pension funds to manage. His response?

"No," Cari said, rather emphatically. It was for personal reasons, he said. His wife had passed away, and he felt like he was in no condition to take on something of that magnitude. Indeed, in 2010, eight years after his wife died, Cari had told Niewoehner he still was on medication for depression.

His answer to Rezko wasn't accepted, apparently, Cari said, as the offers just kept coming. Cari agreed to meet once again, this time with Chris Kelly, who had roughly the same pitch. If Cari would raise money for them on a national scale, there would be plenty of cash thrown his way in Illinois. And there was a flip side of the message, he recalled. Say no, and it was clear Healthpoint would never get a fair hearing in the state.

"It was startling to me," Cari said, still looking fairly wide-eyed on the witness stand. "I went back to my law office."

Still, it wasn't startling enough to get Cari to sprint away from Levine. Believing he could keep some good will for Healthpoint and knowing it was important to his partner McCall because of who was leading the firm, Cari worked to try to link JER to TRS resources. Niewoehner played for Cari the tape of him talking to a nervous Levine about convincing JER to pay a fee to someone Rezko had selected. One of the calls was from the spring of 2004, when Levine threatened to "undo things" for JER if the contract hiring the bogus finder wasn't signed. There was $80 million in TRS funds at stake if it didn't get done. The jury listened to the call as Levine said it was exactly the kind of thing that upsets the "political powers that be."

When Cari was cross-examined, he was asked about his party affiliation and how he had moved from supporting Jim Ryan to Blagojevich. He was very much a Democrat, Cari said, and had only supported Ryan for personal reasons related to a friendship Ryan had with Cari's wife over their health. Levine was Ryan's finance chairman, so Cari had gotten to know him then, and the relationship continued after Cari's partner, McCall, reached out to Levine to connect friends he had at JER to TRS funds. Once the JER extortion got going, Cari was asked, wasn't it Levine who was pushing Cari to get the firm to sign for the mystery consultant, not Blagojevich?

Sure, Cari said, agreeing that he did what he could to keep Levine pleased with him. But it wasn't just so Healthpoint could continue to get Illinois funds.

"It was very clear to me based on conversations I had with Rezko, Kelly, and the governor that if you don't play ball their way, there would be repercussions," Cari said, telling the jury his law firm was on his mind. "We had a lot of clients before the state."

With Cari finished, prosecutors next called to the stand Jill Hayden, who was director of boards and commissions under Blagojevich. She wouldn't be on the stand for long, but as she had at Rezko's trial in 2008, Hayden testified that among everyone making recommendations to fill state posts after Blagojevich was elected, Rezko and Kelly had the most success. After he had submitted a name for "consideration," Rezko would often call her to check on the status of key people he was placing on boards, Hayden said. Once he sort of laughed at her when he checked on someone and she said she just had to get it approved by Monk, as if that were some kind of obstacle. Prosecutors were most interested in the Illinois Finance Authority, pointing out that by January 2004, Hayden's records showed that either Rezko or Kelly had nominated five of the nine members of the panel—a majority. And Rezko was behind the IFA's candidate for executive director, his associate Ali Ata, who was cruising toward being approved until it was discovered that state statutes required that the governor submit two names for consideration. So to address the formality, state paperwork showed that the name of another man, Michael Horst, also had been recommended as a candidate for the job. But there was just one problem. Horst himself didn't even know he had supposedly been tapped to possibly lead the state organization. He was an accountant who worked in the office building where Chris Kelly sometimes worked, and Kelly had seen him at Christmas parties. Hayden acknowledged it was her job to run the vetting process for candidates for state positions, but she said she didn't review Horst's background.

"He wasn't a serious candidate," Hayden said, stating the obvious.

The jury wouldn't have to wait long to hear from Ata himself. He was on the stand next, walking up to be sworn in wearing a suit jacket over an open shirt. He told the jury he was fifty-eight and living in the leafy suburb of Lemont.

Ata said he had known Alderman Mell for years, and it was through him that he eventually met Blagojevich. He had been a financial supporter of Mell's, and that bridged into Ata supporting Blagojevich in 2002. He recalled holding a pair of fund-raisers and said he had contributed thousands of dollars personally as well. One of those checks was from August 2002, and it was for $25,000. Ata said he remembered the circumstances of when he had given it to the campaign. Rezko had him come to his offices on Elston.

When he arrived, he found Rezko with the governor, Lon Monk, Chris Kelly, and state legislator Jay Hoffman. He recalled being led into the conference room.

"Mr. Rezko indicated that I continued to be a team player," Ata testified. "And I had expressed interest in joining the administration."

And with that, Rezko took his check for $25,000 and put it on the table in front of Blagojevich. Ata had relayed the story at the earlier trial also, and it had left many with the impression that Ata would one day be telling it again at a trial of the governor himself. Now, here he was, with Blagojevich seated nearby taking more notes on a legal pad.

"Mr. Blagojevich thanked me for my support, and he had asked Mr. Rezko whether we had discussed opportunities in the new administration," Ata said deliberately in a bit of a nasally monotone. There was very little emotion in his voice at all.

Ata said Rezko had first offered him a spot leading the state's Capital Development Board, but that went away when Hoffman loudly protested that the position traditionally was reserved for someone from downstate.

Later, at the big Blagojevich fund-raiser at Navy Pier in 2003, Ata said he had a second conversation with the governor about working in the administration. He said he had a one-on-one talk with Blagojevich in which the governor again thanked him for being such a loyal supporter and brought up that he knew Ata was interested in a state post.

"He said it better be a job where I can make some money," Ata recalled.

An investor in Rezko real estate, Ata said he was at his political godfather's office about twice a month, and it was easy to get the message about doing what Rezko wanted after Ata became head of the IFA. He said once, while waiting for an audience with Rezko, he saw Kelly King Dibble, head of the Housing Development Authority and a onetime Rezko employee, leaving his office, upset. Rezko had sent her a message to follow up on some state action, and she had apparently ignored the order. Rezko had gotten her a message through the chairman of the authority's board congratulating her on her new assignment.

"She was very concerned about that, because she did not have a new assignment," Ata testified, saying Dibble wasn't being a team player. "She thought she was going to be fired."

It was clear through Ata's testimony that he definitely was part of Team Rezko, saying he lent Rezko tens of thousands of dollars he never got back and didn't seem too upset about. There was the sham loan for the pizza business. And in another instance, when a building Ata owned that was being leased to the state was in danger of losing that lease, Rezko stepped in to help. All it took to have Rezko keep the lease from being terminated was giving him 25 percent of its ownership.

Throughout the earliest parts of the Blagojevich trial, it was clear Rezko seemed to be the chief among schemers in the case. In every scenario discussed, it appeared that Rezko worked to have the best angle, and it was not hard to imagine him worming into lots of places that Blagojevich may not even have been specifically aware of. Monk had made it clear the governor had essentially given his blessing to Rezko and Kelly to set up what they needed to as they tried to bring in money for the secret group of four. But Ata testified that he had seen cracks in Rezko's normally stoic and in-control facade. Ata had been shown equipment that had been placed in Rezko's offices to alert him to the presence of any federal recording devices. And Ata said he received calls from Rezko friends urging him not to cooperate. Once, in a car, Rezko himself asked Ata if the FBI had approached him, Ata remembered, and Rezko had mouthed "FBI" as he said it. And on another occasion, Ata said he had been told that Rezko was planning a nuclear option of sorts. He was working through Kjellander, a Republican and long-time friend of Bush White House adviser Karl Rove, to get then-president George Bush to replace Chicago's US Attorney Patrick Fitzgerald, thereby derailing the federal probe that was closing in on him.

Ata's testimony had been fairly uneventful during his direct examination. He had stayed about on script, telling the jury essentially the same things he had said when he testified against Rezko in 2008. But during that trial, he had been cross-examined by Joseph Duffy, a seasoned veteran of the federal court who picked through Ata's complicated financial picture to try to show the jury what Ata stood to gain by testifying against Rezko and avoiding further prosecution himself. Questioning Ata for the Blagojevich defense would be Sam Adam Jr., who had last stood up to question Monk and had scored some points with his freewheeling and confrontational style. But Zagel had become increasingly agitated with the defense since, stopping questioning at times to give advice about proper questions, sometimes in front of the jury. His fuse was clearly shortening quite a bit, and it would not take long for Adam Jr. to light it.

"You're a proud American, aren't you?" Adam started, making it immediately clear where he was going. "It was the FBI that came to your company in 2001 and intimated that you were not a good American?"

Ata said that wasn't quite right. But the government was already objecting. Adam told Zagel he wasn't trying to get too close to a sensitive topic.

"Yes, you are. Don't do it," the judge said sternly.

Adam may be a lot of things, but timid is not one of them. So he simply went right back at it, asking Ata whether the truth of the matter was that he shared only a name with someone who took part in the 9/11 attacks.

That was it for Zagel, who didn't appreciate Adam's attempts to suggest the FBI might have picked on Ata in some way, thus drawing the jury's sympathy and hinting Blagojevich was in the same category. He stopped things and asked the jury to leave the room while Adam retreated toward the defense table. With the jury gone, Zagel insisted to know what Adam's independent knowledge was of what the FBI had said to Ata. Adam tried to talk up an answer, but Zagel stopped him and told him to answer the question. Finally, Adam said he had no independent knowledge.

"That's the end of it unless you have concrete evidence other than what he thought about what the FBI did," Zagel said, flashing more anger than he had at any point during the trial. "Usually if I sustain an objection, that means you don't repeat the question."

The jury was brought back in, and Adam tried to get his feet back under him as quickly as he could. He started asking about Ata's fund-raising for Mell and Blagojevich.

"You would agree that hosting fund-raisers had nothing to do with you getting a job?" Adam asked.

"I don't know how to answer that question," Ata replied.

Adam's point was that no one, not even Rezko and definitely not Blagojevich, had told Ata he'd better have a fund-raiser if he wanted to work for the state. But the questions were coming quickly, and through and over government objections. Adam said Ata was going to tell the truth about what had happened, right?

"Don't do that," Zagel said, sounding like he was trying to keep his exasperation in check. Adam had come from the school that said it didn't matter how many objections came during cross-examination, the point was to talk to the jurors and plant seeds in their minds while getting the witness disoriented. Zagel was clearly tiring of it. Adam was trying to ask whether anything about the fund-raising was an explicit quid pro quo, but the judge didn't want Ata being forced to give a legal conclusion he wasn't qualified for.

"It was not a job for the money," Adam declared, apparently trying a statement that would have the combined effect of telling the jury that and getting Ata to agree in some way. But Zagel cut it off.

"It's a nice argument and feel free to make it in closing arguments," Zagel said. "But it's not a question."

———

Prosecutors moved next to the alleged shakedown of Rahm Emanuel over a grant for Chicago Academy High School. The school's leader, Dr. Donald Feinstein, was called to the stand to tell the jury how his worries nearly turned to panic when, in September 2006, some of the crews that had been at work on the fields prepared to walk off the job for lack of payment. Feinstein frantically called the governor's office but to no avail. Staff there didn't even know where the money was supposed to be coming from.

"I felt that it consumed me," Feinstein told the jury about his search for the money. The cost of the project would skyrocket without the cash. Athletic seasons would be lost and the headaches of a partially finished project would only increase as the site sat through the winter. Finally, Feinstein said, he went back to Emanuel's office before money eventually started to trickle to the project. Only as bills came due would money be released from the state. It didn't come all at once as most grants would.

Prosecutors called Bradley Tusk to the stand to tell the jury what was happening on the other side of the curtain. He was introduced as a bit of a wunderkind. In addition to his years in DC and New York, he had joined the Blagojevich administration as a deputy governor in 2003, before age thirty. Tusk said he remembered Kelly seemed to be everywhere all the time, appearing with Rezko in key strategy sessions, even though the two men had no formal role. And while they seemed to be around too much, Tusk said the governor wasn't around enough. He talked about how his boss often couldn't be found, even when bills were sitting on his desk for weeks waiting for his signature. Tusk said he was often left to seek authorization to sign bills for Blagojevich, making key decisions in state government even though he was only twenty-nine when he started with the office.

But Reid Schar didn't waste much time getting to the real reason Tusk was called. He asked about the time Tusk had spoken to Emanuel and Emanuel had been upset about money for a school. Tusk recalled it immediately, the Chicago Academy. He said he had spoken to Emanuel and then to Blagojevich, who told Tusk why the grant was slow in coming.

"He said that before the grant could be released, he wanted Congressman Emanuel's brother to hold a fund-raiser for him," said Tusk, who told the jury he remembered wanting off the call as fast as possible. The demand was both "illegal and unethical," Tusk said, and he wanted no part of it. Ari Emanuel was a wealthy Hollywood agent and the inspiration for the Ari Gold character on HBO's *Entourage*.

The call so rattled Tusk, he said, he quickly worked to give a warning to other staff members that Blagojevich might ask them to make a similar pitch, starting with Wyma. And he remembered calling Quinlan, the governor's general counsel, to tell him, "You need to get your client under control."

On cross-examination, Sheldon Sorosky asked whether Tusk had been hired because the Blagojevich administration wanted "an independent, intelligent young man." It was in keeping with the defense idea that Blagojevich was surrounded by smart, law-abiding people, many of them lawyers who would do nothing illegal themselves and, while they would listen to Blagojevich spout off, would do their best to keep him from crossing lines.

Blagojevich was much more of a "big picture guy," Sorosky said, right? He didn't much care for the nitty-gritty parts of running the state. Would that be accurate?

"It would," Tusk said, in a tone that made it clear that was a fairly monumental understatement. Is that why you were hired? Sorosky asked, drawing an objection from Schar.

"No mind reading," said Zagel, whose law enforcement background included leading the state police and time in the Cook County state's attorney's office, where he had been a veteran when Sorosky was a junior prosecutor.

Very well. Wasn't it true that Blagojevich also was just a hothead? He would say whatever came into his mind?

"Once in a while, he says things and blows off a lot of steam?" Sorosky asked.

"Yes," Tusk answered.

Sorosky suggested that maybe Tusk had never even explained that there was a problem to Blagojevich, who was normally at home and maybe not fully engaged. Was such a fund-raiser really what the governor was concentrating on? But the judge sustained a government objection.

"They were in different places, so now we have mind reading over the telephone," said Zagel.

Fine, Sorosky said. But if this was so bad, when did Tusk quit his job? Certainly not right away. He hadn't rushed off to the FBI or the US attorney's office to report the supposed shakedown.

"I took a lot of reasonable steps to deal with it," Tusk said.

When Schar questioned Tusk again, he asked about Sorosky's claim that the governor was just expressing himself in some fiery way, asking about a fund-raiser in some half-joking rant instead of being serious about connecting the school grant to Ari Emanuel hosting some swanky fund-raiser in Los Angeles. Tusk had taken things seriously enough to attempt to stop Blagojevich.

But Sorosky wouldn't drop the point about Blagojevich maybe just bursting out with something a single time in one conversation that never was followed up on.

"Just because he said that once, that's why we're here on this issue?" Sorosky said, prompting Zagel to sustain an objection from Schar even as the prosecutor was still getting out of his chair.

"Now we're into mind reading of the prosecution," the judge said.

=====

In many ways, John Harris's life was ruined by crossing paths with Blagojevich. He had attended Northwestern University and Loyola Law School. He had been a US Army officer, including working as a judge advocate general. While working for Mayor Daley, Congressman Lipinski recommended him for secretary of transportation, and he first came into contact with the Blagojevich crew while interviewing for the job with Lon Monk, Chris Kelly, and Tony Rezko. He was also approached about being the executive director of the Illinois State Toll Highway Authority, but neither state post panned out. It wasn't until 2005 that the Blagojevich administration tapped him for a job he took. With Monk leaving to join Blagojevich's reelection campaign, Kelly came to Harris about the chief of staff spot. He dangled the fact that Blagojevich was considering a White House run and suggested Harris could go along for the ride. Harris would only commit to two years at first, meeting with Blagojevich and Bradley Tusk about coming on to replace the outgoing Monk. He would spend more than three years with the governor, who came to rely on him heavily for advice.

Carrie Hamilton wanted to make one thing very clear.

"Did Blagojevich count on you for legal advice?" she asked.

"No," Harris told her.

But it seemed clear the governor counted on him for virtually all other aid. Harris was one of a close ring of people Blagojevich felt comfortable calling almost around the clock to bounce his thoughts off. The topic could be anything that popped into the governor's head, from strategy to policy to Blagojevich just wanting to spout off and complain. And Blagojevich was a real talker. The conversations could ramble for an hour or more, with Harris suffering along as Blagojevich spoke in circles about the topic of the moment. It was what Harris was dealing with throughout the fall of 2008, until he was arrested the same December morning as his boss. So many of the tapes the government planned to introduce in its case would be played for the jury while Harris was on the stand, which he first took June 21, 2010. He was forty-eight and living on the Northwest Side, trying to support a wife and three sons. With government work no longer an option for him, Harris was looking to make a respectable salary by studying to be an electrician on power lines. It was a job that could bring in a good paycheck because not many people had the nerve to try it.

Harris's intelligence and disciplined background were obvious immediately as he started his testimony. He gave sharp answers and barely needed to be led, as he clearly knew what was really being asked of him as he was being questioned. Sitting up straight and focusing on the questioner, Harris didn't seem to wear down as his testimony went on for hours. His hair was trimmed neatly, and he wore glasses, and when he spoke in a slightly nasally voice, he seemed not unlike a straight version of *Simpsons* character Waylon Smithers, top assistant to the evil and powerful Mr. Burns.

One of his first tasks was to corroborate Tusk's description of what was going on behind the scenes on the Chicago Academy grant and the dispute with Emanuel. He told Hamilton that Tusk had told him about the situation and that Blagojevich had held up the funds. Whatever the "discrepancy" was, Harris said he told the governor, it was going to become problematic on several fronts to continue to hold Emanuel to the fire. The real victim was the school, which was counting on the money and had a torn up parking lot to show for it. Blagojevich relented, Harris said, but would only allow the grant money to trickle out as the school actually received its bills.

Blagojevich's apparent obsession with using his post to make extra money—mostly through his wife, Patti—was apparent early on, Harris said. Blagojevich had come to him asking about positions in the governor's office that could be created just for Patti.

"I told him I didn't think that it was a good idea," Harris said. As a realist, Harris said it was often his job to throw cold water on the governor's plans. Still, Harris said he felt like he went along with many ideas more than he should have, giving the impression that he was a very smart guy with a very crazy boss who did what he could to keep Blagojevich under control. Sometimes he directed the governor toward ideas that were just slightly off base, hoping to keep him from going down paths that were completely insane or dangerous.

Blagojevich talked about appointing Patti to the Illinois Pollution Control Board, Harris recalled, but that, too, seemed like a bad plan. It was one

of the few appointed posts in the state that had a list of minimum qualifications, which Patti didn't have. But Blagojevich said others had used the
board that way in the past; he knew a seat on that board paid more than
$100,000. The main problem for the first lady, Harris pointed out, was that
the board post wasn't really a spot where one could just float along. There
were almost weekly meetings and quite a bit of required reading on fairly
complex issues the board would address. It wasn't something Harris said he
understood the governor was looking for in terms of a job for Patti. What
was he looking for? Hamilton asked.

"Something that paid but didn't require a lot of work or a lot of time,"
Harris answered.

The governor already had used Harris to reach out to leaders of Chicago
financial firms hoping to get his wife hired somewhere. Patti had obtained
what is known as a Series 7 license, allowing her to sell securities. Harris
said he reached out to some he knew in the business, including John Rogers
at Arial Financial and Ray Kilic at Citibank, where he got Patti a meeting.
But it was more bad news. Kilic told the governor's wife that it was a tough
business to get into and the picture was bleak. Younger people who had
just graduated with MBAs were pouring into the field, and they were willing to work long hours seven days a week to be successful. Again, not what
the governor and his wife were looking for, though Harris said the couple
seemed to think the meeting meant that Patti should get hired anyway.
Their noses were bent out of shape when Kilic didn't call back, though Harris said the Citibank exec just thought he was meeting Patti as a courtesy
and answering some questions for her. Kilic received an e-mail from Patti
that had given him the impression that Patti was offended, so Harris said he
would go to the governor and smooth out the situation.

It came up during a car ride a short time later, Harris recalled, and it was
clear Blagojevich's feathers were ruffled.

"He told me to make sure Citibank doesn't get any more state work,"
Harris said, and that went for Rogers and Ariel Financial, too. "He didn't
think they had done enough to help Patti."

Hamilton moved to the meat of what Harris would tell the jury by first
asking about the tollway funding plans. Blagojevich in 2008 was considering the small, medium, and large funding plans for the tollway, which the
governor knew would be a boon for everyone from road builders to laborers
and engineers. The road builders cared little about political parties and made
donations regularly to anyone in power or anyone who looked like they might

come to power, as Cellini, a Republican, had shown years earlier by hosting a large fund-raiser for Blagojevich. "The road builders just want to keep building" is how Harris explained it. So the governor approved the smallest plan on the table, a $1.8 billion option, so they wouldn't be satiated. Everyone involved knew there was a much larger funding option that could be forthcoming, so the governor's requests for cash would have a much better carrot attached to them and the road builders would stay interested in Blagojevich's attempts to push a capital bill past House Speaker Michael Madigan. It was early fall when the small funding plan was approved, but Harris said Blagojevich was keenly aware of the deadline closing in at the end of the year in the form of the ethics bill. He wanted to know how quickly his administration could "get contracts out on the street," so he could bring in campaign money for them.

===

At the time Obama won the Iowa Caucuses, Blagojevich hadn't thought it was possible that the former Illinois state legislator had a realistic shot to be elected president. And even by the summer of 2008, Harris had pointed out that when the governor spoke about making a Senate pick, the talk didn't really advance beyond naming himself or using the promise of the appointment to keep Jones in his corner on the ethics bill. The first time Harris said he remembered that changing was on October 6, 2008, when he was in a car with the governor on a ride to Northwestern University for an event. Blagojevich had been pretty blunt.

"So, what do you think I can get for this Senate seat?" Blagojevich asked, with Harris responding by asking if the governor meant, "For you?"

"I said, 'Well, you can get a new ally or reward an ally. That's what you can get,'" Harris remembered, with Blagojevich saying they would just talk about it later. And later that month, Blagojevich did bring it up again, Harris said. It was in a meeting with his general counsel, William Quinlan, at the Thompson Center. The governor again talked about what he could get for making the pick, brainstorming about getting a wealthy businessman like J. B. Pritzker to make a large donation to a private foundation.

"He was talking about money for his campaign fund or some not-for-profit," Harris told the jury. "Both Bill Quinlan and I told him, 'You can't get money for the Senate seat. You shouldn't even consider that as an option.'"

Harris said Quinlan was later even straighter with the governor, telling him flat out that whether he was serious or just joking, he shouldn't even say things like that out loud. But of course Blagojevich would, having dozens of conversations that federal investigators would capture on tape beginning later that month and into November and December as Blagojevich rambled on and on about strategies for getting something for himself for the seat. Harris said Blagojevich had a very small ring of advisers who gave him ideas on how to go about making a pick in conversations that often devolved into "war-gaming" about how he could be rewarded for his choice, particularly by Barack Obama. Meanwhile, the governor's administration gave the public appearance that a very cautious and responsible process was being set up to establish search criteria and weigh possible candidates.

"I will embark on fulfilling my duties under the United States Constitution and Illinois law to appoint [Obama's] replacement," one talking point prepared by Harris read. "I will follow a thoughtful and deliberative process. It will be orderly and timely.

"I will not turn this into a public spectacle."

======

The first call played for the jury with Harris on the stand was one from November 3, 2008, where Harris told the governor about getting the call from Emanuel while he was at the shoe store. He could be heard telling Blagojevich that it was obvious Obama was very interested in who replaced him, a remark that appeared to put a renewed charge in Blagojevich's thoughts about getting something for himself in the arrangement.

"We could get something for that, couldn't we?" Blagojevich said on the tape. He had gone on to talk about maybe being appointed secretary of health and human services under Obama. Hamilton didn't want the jury to miss the obvious point, so she asked if, when Blagojevich said that, he meant he wanted to make sure he got something for himself.

"Yes, it would be for him," Harris answered. Emanuel had told Blagojevich that Obama cared, opening up some possibilities in Blagojevich's mind. Obama caring meant there was a list of political things Obama could help Illinois with, but there were also things the governor thought he could get just for himself. A cabinet appointment was one thing on the governor's mind. "That was something that was in Barack Obama's power to give if that was something the governor asked for."

Harris and Blagojevich discussed candidates that could be thrown into the mix to enhance the governor's bargaining position. One of those was

Illinois Attorney General Lisa Madigan. Blagojevich's defense had suggested Madigan was really the person Blagojevich was going to appoint all along. It would be a political deal with her powerful father designed to break the Springfield logjam, is how the defense suggested it would go. But when it came up on the tape, Harris said Lisa Madigan's name was only meant to be used to make it look like Blagojevich had good political options, thereby boosting the value of the seat and bettering the governor's standing in the pursuit of something that would personally benefit him.

To get Madigan's name out there, Harris agreed the idea that she could be the pick should be leaked to Michael Sneed at the *Sun-Times*. But it was all still hypothetical, Harris said, and designed just to give the Obama camp something to think about going forward.

"He was adding meat to the bones of this concept of pushing Lisa Madigan as a credible alternative," Harris said. The resulting Sneed item said there had been talks, when really neither side had reached out to the other. "He's beginning to articulate the storyline."

———

It was clear from the tapes that to Blagojevich, the options he was throwing around were absolutely real. The incoming president of the United States would surely deal with him and give him something significant in exchange for Blagojevich nominating Valerie Jarrett or another Obama pick to the Senate. It was just about playing his cards right, Blagojevich thought. The call from Emanuel to Harris was a trigger of sorts. It let Blagojevich know that Obama really cared about who would replace him, though the situation seemed to have been greatly exaggerated in the mind of the governor. Before the call, Blagojevich thought either about appointing himself or about what he could do with the pick to help himself in the state, such as appointing Emil Jones to defeat the ethics bill. But after the call, his thinking expanded. Now he imagined a golden parachute that could secure his future after he left office. Obama cared, and Blagojevich thought that meant he had a great deal of currency. He would spend weeks strategizing about how to use the situation for his own benefit.

The jury heard a recording of the November 5 call between Blagojevich and Harris. The governor started by asking, "How do we play this?" The administration was planning a press conference in a few hours to talk about how the search for Obama's replacement would be conducted. Blagojevich's question and Harris's actions with the governor in the fall of 2008 would become central to the case against Harris. It wasn't hard to see why Harris had been charged. In a number of instances he went beyond just telling the governor yes to every wild fantasy and scheme and sounded much more like a coconspirator helping the governor plan the next move in Blagojevich's perceived chess match with the Obama circle. Harris thought of it as doing his job, advising his boss on something he cared about. But to prosecutors it was aiding and abetting a politician who had crossed the line into the criminal realm.

The jury listened as Blagojevich asked what he should do next about Balanoff. He already had met with him and Andy Stern once and then had a chance encounter with him at Obama's victory rally in Grant Park, after Balanoff had gotten a call from Obama. And the union boss had told the governor the same thing Harris had gotten from Emanuel. Obama was interested in seeing Jarrett named to the seat.

Balanoff was called to the stand to tell the jury how he had gotten that message from the president-elect himself.

His union was involved in the Obama campaign, providing manpower mostly in Northern Indiana, because Illinois was seen as an obvious lock. Early in the fall of 2008, Balanoff's own preference for the Senate seat was US Representative Jan Schakowsky, a union ally. But he later had a conversation with the union's national leader, Andy Stern, who said he had spoken with Valerie Jarrett, and she was interested in the position. Stern wanted a meeting with Blagojevich about the pick, so Balanoff used their political consultant, Doug Scofield, to set it up. It was the day before the election, November 3, 2008, when they got their first audience with the governor. They met him at the Thompson Center, and Balanoff recalled starting out the conversation by talking up Schakowsky. The names of a number of possible candidates were tossed around, including US Representative Jesse Jackson Jr., though no one thought that was a particularly good idea. Lisa Madigan's name was in the air, too, with Blagojevich saying it would be a smart political decision that could help him move his legislative agenda. As for Jarrett, Blagojevich just listened, Balanoff said.

The governor thought he would hear from President Obama directly if Jarrett was his desire, but as it turned out, that wasn't going to happen. Obama was going to make his preference known, but Blagojevich wasn't going to get any kind of direct phone call. Balanoff was at dinner that night when his cell phone rang. He looked down and saw "unknown" on the screen, so he didn't pick it up.

"Tom, this is Barack, give me a call," a waiting message said. But Balanoff testified that he didn't have the number. A short time later, though, while Balanoff was pumping gas at a station at Congress and Dearborn, Obama called again. They exchanged greetings, and Balanoff remembered saying, "We're going to bring Indiana home."

That would depend on turnout, Obama said, but that wasn't what he was calling about. Obama knew Balanoff was in contact with Blagojevich about the Senate seat and wanted to pass on his own preference. Obama told Balanoff he had two criteria, the union leader remembered. One was that the pick be good for the people of the state, and the second was that the person would be strong enough to be reelected when the seat came back open for a vote two years later, in the fall of 2010. Several people filled the bill, Obama said, telling Balanoff he had decided not to support anyone publicly. As for Valerie Jarrett, Obama said he really wanted her in the White House even though she had expressed interest in the Senate seat. Balanoff took it as another signal he could go ahead and make it known that Obama would support the naming of his friend to the seat. Even though Obama wanted his friend in the White House, he appeared to be fine with her name being tossed around for the Senate seat.

———

Doug Scofield was among the witnesses to describe how Blagojevich's past and his vision of that future merged. Scofield remembered how incredibly jealous Blagojevich was of Obama and how he thought the new president had taken the path he had hoped to walk himself. Scofield had dealt with the governor and his instabilities for years and was there to hold his hand at the end as he tried to find someone for the Senate seat and plotted to use a pick to brighten his prospects. Blagojevich had an "in and out view of world," Scofield said, meaning he often perceived that you were either for him or against him, and there was no in between. It led to many people walking on eggshells around the governor and telling him what they thought he wanted to hear. It was normally an annoying situation, but it became dangerous for Blagojevich when there was no one to talk him away from some of his ideas in 2008.

Describing exactly how bad Blagojevich's finances were was the job of IRS agent Shari Schindler, who testified that by August 2008, the governor and his wife had piled up some $90,000 in credit card debt and were down $220,000 on a home-equity loan. Everyone knew the governor really liked his suits, but Schindler's testimony suggested his years in office were one long spending spree. Schindler had taken apart the family's financial picture and showed where all of the governor's cash was going. He had spent about $400,000 on clothes while leading the state, including more than half of that figure at Oxxford. One day alone in December 2006, Blagojevich had dropped $20,000 there.

The testimony wasn't doing much for Blagojevich's image, and it shed new light on his taped complaints about poverty in 2008. There was a month Schindler reviewed when Blagojevich spent $12,000 on clothes and just $81 on toys for his girls.

And Blagojevich didn't seem to have a great handle on his campaign finances either, though just enough to get himself into trouble. Prosecutors called Agent Murphy to the stand to talk about his interview with the governor at Blagojevich's lawyer's office in March 2005. It was the meeting when Blagojevich claimed to have a firewall between himself and specific knowledge of who was donating how much money to his campaign.

Prosecutors hoped to erode that claim by bringing Kelly Glynn back to the stand. She had last appeared at the Rezko trial, discussing how Friends of Blagojevich tracked incoming money and how cash was credited to certain contributors. It just wasn't true that Blagojevich didn't know what was going on, she said. Right from the time he was inaugurated in 2003, he was always in the fund-raising meetings, even when individual contributors were discussed. What she described sounded a lot like what was on tape in the case, with Blagojevich holding meetings where he was intimately involved in knowing how specific people would be approached, what they could be asked for, and what the results would be.

"We would be going through a list of people who had made commitments or not made commitments," Glynn testified, and Blagojevich was right there. He was happy when he got good news about cash coming in and mad when people stiffed him. He always wanted to know what person X or Y had donated or failed to give. Glynn said there were certain people who were approached, promised something, and never delivered. The campaign office called them "repeat offenders," and Blagojevich would react strongly when their names came up in his fund-raising meetings. Blair Hull was one whose name got Blagojevich riled up, Glynn said.

"That's what the governor would chime out with: 'Bullshitter!'" she yelled. It was a little too specific a memory and sounded a little too much like Blagojevich to be dismissed as just an overeager witness doing the government's bidding.

———

After Jerry Krozel was called to testify and described his dealings with Blagojevich in 2008, including how he felt he was being pressured to come up with money for the governor if he wanted to see the larger tollway expansion project announced, prosecutors called Rajinder Bedi to the witness stand.

He testified in a thick accent, wearing a Sikh turban, and told the jury he had taken a job as editor of the *Indian Reporter and World News* in Chicago and that he was still doing consulting on trade matters after leaving his state economic development post. Bedi described himself as very close to Raghu Nayak, who had made the cash offer over the Jackson appointment. The two attended the 2008 Democratic National Convention together and were so close, in fact, that they had committed tax fraud together. Nayak issued large checks to a company Bedi was running, and Bedi gave him cash in return that Nayak could pocket. Bedi knew Nayak to be a fund-raiser for both Blagojevich and Jackson and said he had seen the politicians together at a fund-raiser at India House in May 2008, where they talked about one of Jackson's favorite pet projects, the proposed third Chicago airport at Peotone.

The October 31 fund-raiser at India House was intended to support a Jackson Jr. bid for the Senate, and just days before it, Bedi said he was at a breakfast meeting with both the congressman and Nayak. But just as Bedi was about to describe what had happened there, Zagel asked the jury to leave the room and wanted to hear from Niewoehner how things would be described. And from the sound of it, it was no good for Jesse Jackson Jr., whose excuses about the meeting would later include that he never heard what Nayak and Bedi were talking about even while they sat at the same table.

The conversation over breakfast had also included talk about Peotone but then swung to Jackson wanting to be the senator, Niewoehner told Zagel.

"Nayak says to Jackson in Bedi's presence, 'I will raise a million if he appoints you to the Senate seat,'" Niewoehner said. That conversation had led Bedi to tell Robert Blagojevich the same day that Nayak would fund-raise and wanted Jackson to be appointed.

The judge decided the jury should hear a softer version of that account and brought the panel back into the room to let Bedi finish up. He told the jury there had been talk about both fund-raising and the Senate at his meeting with Jackson and Nayak and that he told Robert that Nayak was close to Jackson and was "very interested" in seeing him appointed.

"I mentioned Raghu Nayak can raise a lot of money," Bedi said, but Robert answered that he didn't think his brother's relationship with Jackson was nearly good enough to get that idea off the ground.

———

Robert Greenlee was seemingly the kind of guy Rod Blagojevich wanted around him in government. He was smart, very capable, and willing to do what the governor said almost to the point of being a mindless drone. He sat on the stand looking the part of a somewhat doughy wonk, obviously intelligent but seeming more than a little nervous. During his closing argument, Sam Adam Jr. said Greenlee looked like "Tom Arnold and Buddy Holly had a kid."

He had a degree from Yale, had gone to law school with Tusk at the University of Chicago, graduating in 1999, and since his odyssey with Blagojevich had returned there to study religious history. He had only ever used his law degree working in mergers and acquisitions, and he worked his way out of the state budget office to become a deputy chief of staff for Blagojevich in 2007 and finally a deputy governor in 2008. Like Tusk, he was young and bright and eager to take on government challenges. So he wound up being the administration's point person handling legislative matters and policy.

Greenlee told the jury his responsibility was to figure out how to take a legislative idea through the system, from determining how to pay for it and get it passed by the General Assembly to seeing it was implemented. Like the other former aides who testified before him, Greenlee described a fairly dysfunctional office where Blagojevich was most often missing or not wanting to be engaged on the day-to-day activities of running Illinois. He told the jury the governor once hid in the bathroom to avoid having a budget discussion with John Filan and said from his perspective, Blagojevich was either nowhere to be found or calling constantly on things that didn't really affect him. But Greenlee knew to keep his boss happy and take the phone calls when they came and bend over backward to agree with his boss while he was on them. As he explained it, he just didn't have the luxury of getting Blagojevich too bent out of shape at him. Being too contradictory could get you cut off, and Greenlee needed to be able to get Blagojevich to talk to him when there was an emergency.

And there often was, Greenlee said. After sixty days, legislation that had been sent to the governor's desk for a signature would automatically become law if it went unaddressed. There were times when bills the administration was opposed to were about to go into effect without Blagojevich imposing an amendatory veto, so Greenlee said he would have to "capture" the governor in a plane or a car and push the legislation under his nose to get his attention.

"When he had nothing else to do," Greenlee said with an affected tone that made it clear he had often been really annoyed with his boss and was relishing that he got to call him out publicly for being a jerk.

Once Greenlee said he was forced to catch up with the governor during a Blagojevich family dinner at Southport Lanes on the North Side. As the governor ate with his wife and daughters, Greenlee said he went over some twenty pending pieces of legislation that had piled up awaiting Blagojevich's attention.

"Southport Lanes," Reid Schar said snidely, "isn't that a bowling alley?"

"It's a bowling alley, bar, and grill," Greenlee answered, as if that somehow made a difference.

One of the stretches when Blagojevich had been hard to shake was late October and early November 2008. The governor was fixating on the Senate seat that Obama was giving up, and Greenlee was among the people being pulled into the orbit of the schizophrenic governor. Ambassadorships. Secretary of health and human services. Appointing himself senator. All of it swirled in the governor's mind as Greenlee sat on the phone and agreed the ideas sounded good. He remembered one talk when he was going to work out at Crunch Gym. Instead he sat in his car and talked to Blagojevich for an hour. His boss carried on and on about the Senate seat "and how the choices he could make regarding the seat could place him in a position to be relevant on the larger stage," which Greenlee took to mean coming up with a way to launch a bid to be elected president in 2016.

Blagojevich had a laundry list of ways he could rebuild his political future and boost his fortunes through making the appointment. They were the familiar moves the jury had heard a number of times by that point. The entire process was moving around those imagined options and how Blago- jevich could help himself out, Greenlee said. But still, the governor ordered what amounted to a sham selection process set up. There was much talk about a search team for weighing the qualifications of candidates. And there were meetings in which there were discussions about the priorities the pick should have. They should have an interest in health care, the thinking went, and they should care about things like infrastructure improvements and eco- nomic development in Illinois. They should have "exceptional skills" and an affinity for the people of the state. But in the end, none of it really mattered.

"In name we picked a search team, but there was no process," Greenlee told the jury. "We never actually had any meetings or conducted any search activities."

With Greenlee on the stand, prosecutors played a series of tapes that set up both the Senate seat shenanigans and Blagojevich's alleged attempt to force the *Tribune* to fire negative editorial writers if the company wanted state involvement in the sale of Wrigley Field. The jury heard the record- ing where Blagojevich was on the phone telling his brother they had been approached to "pay to play" by Jesse Jackson Jr. supporters. On one call from November 3, 2008, Blagojevich could be heard telling Greenlee to put together a list of ambassadorships the governor might seek in exchange for the Senate pick. Greenlee said he did organize a sheet of posts Blagojevich could use as a cheat sheet, going to Wikipedia before work and printing out sheets for countries such as United Kingdom, France, and Italy. Each entry showed who the current ambassador was and what their qualifications were, as well as lists of notable people who had held each post. For example, the United Kingdom entry noted that five men who would go on to be presi- dent had held the position. That was the kind of information Blagojevich wanted to hear.

―――

The government had been presenting evidence to the jury for more than five weeks before they called to the stand the man who had propelled the investigative endgame in the fall of 2008. John Wyma was boyish and blond, telling the jury he was forty-three. He described his job as a lobbyist in Washington in the simplest of terms, saying he represented corporations and entities, "helping them with the federal government."

corrupted from the inside out. Wyma said he never took the information to his clients, believing it was "obviously wrong."

When it came to the specific charges against Blagojevich, prosecutors first had Wyma discuss the school grant Blagojevich allegedly sat on in 2006 to try to get Rahm Emanuel's LA brother to hold a fund-raiser for him. Emanuel was someone Wyma was close to, he testified, saying he remembered getting a call from the then-congressman who was wondering if Wyma knew anything about why the school was missing its money and if anything could be done about it. Wyma said he spoke to Bradley Tusk, another friend, who told him what the problem was. Wyma's testimony corroborated Tusk's version of events.

"He believed the money was being held by the governor because he wanted Emanuel or his brother to hold a fund-raiser," Wyma recalled. Once Blagojevich dug in on something—as he clearly did on the school—nothing could change his mind. "The timing was horrible," he said. While Wyma knew Emanuel was looking for some help from the state for the school, he said he was not going to go to him and ask for the fund-raiser, calling it "poor judgment."

Even so, Wyma said he stayed in the regular fund-raising meetings into 2008 and would sometimes advise his clients to make donations to the governor. By that summer, he said, the change in state ethics law was bearing down.

"We had to get as much as we could as quickly as we could," Wyma said, telling Carrie Hamilton it was fair to say there was pressure on him and the others who were close to Blagojevich. One of his clients in October 2008 was Michael Vondra, a wealthy construction executive who also ran waste management facilities. Vondra had Wyma set up the October 6 meeting with the governor to talk about possible state incentives to offer to BP to lure the oil giant to bring a project to Illinois. The meeting seemed to go fine, and afterward, Wyma stayed behind and said he spoke to Blagojevich about what they had just heard.

"He said he liked Vondra a lot, and he wanted to get $100,000 from him by the end of the year," said Wyma, who remembered reminding Blagojevich that Vondra had held a fund-raiser for him just a month or so earlier. And regardless, Wyma said he told the governor, the six-figure request was totally unrealistic.

But fund-raising and the year-end deadline that the ethics legislation represented were on Blagojevich's mind, apparently, as Wyma said he next

He had been Blagojevich's chief of staff for more than three years Blagojevich was in Congress, and when Blagojevich first ran for goverr. Illinois, Wyma had the title of political director. That meant he traveled \ Blagojevich on the campaign trail and was the liaison between him and campaign staff. He recalled that Lon Monk was running the campaign, wi the help of Blagojevich's Washington advisers, Bill Knapp and Fred Yang.

As they had with many of the other witnesses who had come before him, prosecutors had Wyma talk about the roles that Chris Kelly and Tony Rezko played in the governor's transition to power. Kelly was among those with instant, direct access to Blagojevich, Wyma said, and Kelly and Rezko came to be important after the election, having a say in who was named to boards and commissions. As for Wyma, he took on a less formal role, working as a very successful lobbyist who had the governor's ear and sat in on regular fund-raising meetings from 2003 all the way up until 2008. A core group close to Blagojevich that included Kelly, Monk, and others would look at lists of past donors and fund-raising targets and make decisions about who was best to reach out to them about contributing to the campaign. Wyma said he was typically pointed toward people he knew.

"Either a client of mine or it was an individual I had a historic relationship with from working with Rod," he said.

Blagojevich was engaged in the meetings and asked questions about particular people, Wyma said, and would sometimes provide the fund-raisers with amounts he thought should come in from those individuals.

Wyma kept his official residency in Washington, DC, but opened a lobbying office in Chicago. He had a group of heavyweight clients, including AT&T, Nicor, and Philip Morris, as well as governmental clients such as the Chicago Transit Authority, and made $1 million his first year. By 2004, Wyma was looking to hook up companies with investment funds from Illinois organizations such as the Teachers' Retirement System, which of course pulled Wyma into the orbit of Stuart Levine, who by then was seizing control of TRS and handing the reins to Rezko. Wyma said what he came to learn was that there was a list of companies that would be considered for getting investment funds. He reached out to Chris Kelly, who told him Rezko was involved in the situation.

"It was $50,000 to get on this list," Wyma said Kelly eventually told him, meaning a $50,000 campaign contribution to Blagojevich in order for a state board controlled by Rezko to even have a company looked at for state investment. Once again, it was an example of state government being bridged into trade association president Gerry Krozel and the tollway plan. Wyma said the governor filled him in on his planned announcement of the $1.8 billion expansion and that Monk was going to Krozel for half a million dollars. Blagojevich had the power to announce a much broader package but told Wyma he was going to wait and see how Krozel and his roadbuilder contacts did on the fund-raising front.

"If they don't perform, fuck 'em," Wyma remembered the governor telling him, telling Schar he wasn't confused about whether the governor was saying he was in effect holding back money to see if campaign contributions would come in.

At the same meeting, another of Wyma's clients, Children's Memorial Hospital, was among the topics of conversation. Blagojevich mentioned that Dusty Baker had called about the reimbursement rate, and the governor said he was going to listen to the hospital's request and do something about it.

"He was going to give them eight million bucks," Wyma remembered Blagojevich telling him, "and he wanted to get Magoon for fifty."

That was $50,000. As in a campaign contribution from the leader of a children's hospital who had come to the governor's attention because he was seeking an increase in the amount of money the state gave for the treatment of ill children who couldn't pay for their medical care. Wyma said he pointed out that CMH was a nonprofit and that the $50,000 goal was "way out of balance anyway." And furthermore, the deadline at the end of the year related to businesses and companies that made state donations. It didn't even apply to the hospital. So Wyma said he told the governor he should go ahead with the reimbursement plan and wait and possibly come back to the fund-raising idea later.

"What do you mean, wait?" Wyma repeated to the jury what the governor asked. Ten days?

As ridiculous as that was, Wyma said he left the meeting with the hospital and the fund-raising from Magoon on his to-do list. But he did nothing. He said it was way too uncomfortable for him to directly approach a client who had a pending state action and ask for money. Robert Blagojevich called the next day and left a voicemail that prosecutors played for the jury next. The governor's brother teased Wyma a little bit by saying he was calling to make sure Wyma would get his job done.

Whatever. Wyma said he had no intention of following up with Magoon, because the message the hospital official was going to take away from the effort was that "the fund-raising ask" was going to be tied to the state reimbursement.

"I thought they would feel pressure," Wyma testified, using language that was similar to how he had described what happened when Tusk had tried to get him in the middle of the school grant for Emanuel. "I was increasingly alarmed by the level of aggressiveness the fund-raising had taken on."

So, Wyma said, he withdrew from fund-raising altogether. He already had the subpoena on Provena Health to deal with. And when he went to see the FBI about it on October 13, Wyma decided to fill agents in on what was going on at the campaign, he told the jury. He was uncomfortable and decided he wasn't going to be dragged into a larger problem. He told the FBI about the fund-raising push and gave them the voicemail that Robert Blagojevich left him about going forward with pushing Magoon to fund-raise for the governor. With a meeting coming up at the Friends of Blagojevich on October 22, investigators wanted Wyma to attend, and they had asked him to wear a wire and capture the conversation that would unfold there. But Wyma had refused. He told the jury he just didn't feel comfortable becoming a tool of the government. When he received the subpoena, he said he felt a duty of sorts to tell the truth about what was going on, including in the two meetings he had just been to.

"I didn't feel I had a responsibility to go out and proactively record," Wyma explained from the stand.

Still, Wyma had been helpful enough to propel the endgame for the feds. With his refusal, they had simply gone around him, taking the information he provided about fund-raising that crossed the line into extortion to a federal judge to get permission to place the recording devices in two rooms at the Friends of Blagojevich. Wyma said even though he wouldn't wear a hidden microphone, investigators pushed him to go to the meeting as planned.

"They didn't want the investigation to be impeded or disrupted," he said, telling the jury that he did attend. Lon Monk, the governor, and the governor's brother were there discussing which of them would be the best one to approach Magoon for cash. Rod didn't want to explicitly mix government and fund-raising, Wyma said, and ultimately Robert was chosen to "make the ask."

Prosecutors next moved Wyma to discussions about the Senate seat swap that fall. Wyma had continued acting as if nothing unusual were going on with him, while reporting to federal authorities on his contacts with the Blagojevich administration. His friend Rahm Emanuel called him in

November 2008 about the Senate pick, he told the jury, asking him to be a messenger on his behalf with Blagojevich. Emanuel had a fairly simple message for the governor.

"He expressed to me the president-elect wanted Valerie Jarrett in the Senate and asked if I could relay that message" to Blagojevich, Wyma said. The rest of the communication was that Obama would "value and appreciate it." Wyma agreed to relay the information and tried to reach the governor first, he told the jury. When he wasn't able to, he connected with John Harris to deliver the message. Wyma said he told Harris it made sense to him to listen to what Emanuel was saying. If growing his relationship with Obama, who was riding into office on a wave of popular support, was something that was part of the governor's "decision matrix," Wyma said he told Harris, "it would make sense to have Valerie as the pick."

But Wyma recalled that Harris had an answer for that. "His decision matrix and my decision matrix were not the same as the governor's," Wyma testified that Harris told him. Regardless, Harris said he would deliver the message unedited and unabridged. There was no promise for when there would be an answer, but Wyma testified that he had expected someone would be getting back to Emanuel in fairly short order. Instead, Wyma again found himself as a conduit for negotiations between Blagojevich and the team that would soon occupy the White House. Lobbyist Doug Scofield, in his unofficial role as an adviser to Blagojevich, called Wyma back.

"He said he was calling on behalf of the governor," Wyma testified. He thought that was odd enough, since he typically just talked to Blagojevich directly and didn't need a go-between. Scofield told him the pick was still open, Wyma recalled, and that the Blagojevich camp "wanted to get into Rahm's head" the notion of a nonprofit organization dedicated to addressing health-care issues nationwide. Wyma said it sounded to him like Blagojevich was essentially asking for a job, and Scofield had answered that that was basically right.

"He said, 'Yes, Rod would be interested in being executive director of this,'" Wyma told the jury. The plan was to plant that seed while at the same time make it not look like one thing was linked to the other. Blagojevich thought Emanuel and people close to Obama would have the ability to have people raise money for such an organization, was the thinking, Wyma said, but it didn't make much sense to him to expect to talk about Obama's wishes for the Senate seat and then throw in an "oh by the way" about Blagojevich's desires to be paid to head a charitable organization funded by the new president's friends. "Very transparent" is how Wyma described it for the jury. So he decided to ask Scofield how he would have such a conversation, in which Blagojevich's job request and the Senate pick would be brought up in nearly the same breath. Scofield's idea was to try to front it, Wyma recalled.

"He suggested I say upfront this has nothing to do with the Senate seat," Wyma said. So in other words, make it look like an honest request on a different topic when essentially the opposite was true. Wyma was supposed to state there was no connection but say that when the governor got out of office he would want such an organization set up that Emanuel and others could find money for.

Hamilton asked Wyma what he took away from that suggestion.

"That was the most artful way you could express a really bad idea," Wyma answered, saying he ultimately decided not to be the one to deliver it.

Cross-examining Wyma was Sorosky, who tottered forward from the defense table in one of his extra long ties. Things started amicably enough. The lawyer wanted to know if he could call Wyma by his first name, John.

"Do you mind if I call you Shelly?" Wyma answered, sending a signal that he wasn't going to be lulled by Sorosky's goofy charm.

So Sorosky started to walk Wyma through his background. He had been Blagojevich's chief of staff in Congress, and he had left on good terms. He had gone on to work for Senator Chuck Schumer, who Sorosky called "the distinguished New York senator," drawing an objection from Hamilton, who sounded like she was out of patience just minutes into the questioning. Sorosky said he didn't think the senator would mind being called that.

"No," Judge Zagel answered. "But Senator Schumer is not in this courtroom."

As always when the judge rebuked him, Sorosky, like Adam before, moved on like he hadn't even heard it. And the objections kept coming, such as when Sorosky asked Wyma whether Rod Blagojevich was his "political godfather in Illinois" and whether "the best person you knew in Illinois happened to be the governor." Zagel tried to give Sorosky another chance to formulate a proper version of the question, but Sorosky came right back and asked if Blagojevich was "the person you knew best in Illinois."

"If that was the question, I should have sustained the objection," Zagel said as people in the full courtroom gallery chuckled.

Sorosky nevertheless seemed to be moving toward a point. One of Wyma's many clients was Provena Health, and he said he was paid $10,000 a month to help them navigate the choppy political waters of Illinois and assist them in getting a certificate of need from the Illinois Health Facilities Planning Board that would allow the hospital group to build a cardiac center. Sorosky wanted to know what role Rezko had played in helping that approval and whether Wyma had spoken to Michael Malek, a member of the IHFPB whom Rezko had placed there. There was just enough to it that Zagel asked the jury to leave the room momentarily so he could ask Sorosky where he was going with the line of questioning.

With the jury gone, Sorosky said Wyma's subsequent actions amounted to a bribe. He expected Wyma to say that he had helped set up a backroom meeting between Malek and Provena, where Malek worked as a physician. Zagel told the defense lawyer he could ask about it, but without the explosive language accusing Wyma, who already had told the jury he was testifying under a grant of immunity, of something specifically illegal. Once the jury returned, Sorosky asked if Rezko had communicated something about Malek and Provena.

"He told me Dr. Malek had issues [with Provena] and he would appreciate it if I would hear Dr. Malek out," Wyma said. There were essentially three issues, he said. Malek wanted to be paid more, wanted to do spinal work, and wanted a dispute over labor act violations ended. Malek and Provena met, and Provena wound up getting its certificate of need, but, Wyma said, he could only get credit for arranging the talks, and nothing more. He hadn't negotiated anything, he told Sorosky, and the topic was dropped after Wyma acknowledged again that the subpoena over Provena had helped lead him to cooperate, suggesting maybe there was more to it.

In fact, Rezko had told authorities that he had told Wyma that the price of the Provena approval would be that the hospital make good with Malek and donate $25,000 to the Blagojevich campaign. A $25,000 contribution had been made just weeks later, a fact that was available in public records and that the *Tribune* had even reported in its article that ran on the Wyma subpoena just after his meeting at Blagojevich's campaign office October 22, 2008. But neither side asked about it, as both wanted a degree of separation from Rezko, leaving the jury with just the version Wyma gave.

———

The last witness prosecutors would call was Magoon, the Children's Memorial Hospital CEO, to tell what the play had looked like from his side of things. Magoon said the facility lost $20 million caring for children through Illinois Medicaid in 2007, so increasing the state reimbursement rate had been a priority in 2008. After Dusty Baker was good enough to call Blagojevich on the hospital's behalf, Magoon said Blagojevich spoke to him and promised a rate change that would mean around $10 million more per year. It was a big relief to Magoon, who said he asked whether there was anything he could do to be of assistance. Blagojevich just said that the increase wouldn't go into effect until the following January 1, so he asked Magoon not to make anything public before then.

"He suggested we continue to work with his staff," Magoon said. "But he wanted absolutely no attention drawn to the fact the decision had been made."

Blagojevich didn't explain why, but things became clearer to Magoon just days later. Robert Blagojevich left him a message at work. When they finally connected, Magoon was asked for money.

"He had asked if I would be willing to raise $25,000 for the governor from my business associates and board members, and he asked if I would do that by the end of the year," Magoon told the jury.

Magoon said he told Robert Blagojevich that he didn't think he should be getting a call like that at work, but feeling like he was walking on eggshells with the promised reimbursement rate change, he told Robert that the governor had been very supportive on a number of issues that were important to the hospital and he would have to think about the request.

Magoon said he was left with no doubt about what was going on. He had been asked to keep quiet about the reimbursement decision until January, which had been coupled with a fund-raising request for the same timeframe. And Magoon said he was aware of the changing ethics law that also just happened to coincide with the same date. Without promising to increase the rate publicly, Blagojevich wasn't really on the hook to do it at all.

"It caused me great concern," said Magoon, telling the jury he was most worried that Blagojevich would just change his mind about doing more to help the hospital. "On the one hand I felt threatened and I felt at risk and I felt a little angry."

Instead of contacting his associates and friends about pulling money together for Blagojevich, Magoon said he contacted the hospital's attorney and told his staff to record any further phone calls from Robert Blagojevich.

Defense lawyers tried to soften the blow by having Magoon say that nothing overt was said by anyone connecting the fund-raising to the promise of financial help for Children's Memorial. Robert Blagojevich hadn't threatened him, he agreed. The lawyers also pointed out that the hospital eventually got its rate increase, although it was after the governor was arrested.

The testimony had hit at one of the core values Blagojevich always trumpeted at public appearances and during his campaigns—health care for children. Apparently, not even that was sacred when it came to Blagojevich's desire to stuff his campaign coffers. But he was in a good mood as he left the Dirksen US Courthouse that day. It was July 13, just six weeks after the trial had started. Prosecutors had rested their case a month earlier than some estimates and had done so without calling to the stand key players in the alleged corruption, such as Stuart Levine or Tony Rezko.

But that wasn't on the former governor's mind as he waved to TV cameras and shook his hands on his way to a waiting car.

"I can't wait to testify," he said.

Julie and Robert Blagojevich went together like jelly and peanut butter. She was the sweet, supportive wife who was the perfect accent to her steadfast husband, the center of their family. Robert was a well-spoken military veteran who wore his pride on his sleeve, certainly smart enough to run a real estate investing business and have enough success to be able to take a few months to go to Chicago from Nashville to help his brother's campaign operation in a pinch. He had a calm, reasoned demeanor. Rod's sane brother, in other words.

Julie testified first, looking wide-eyed and seemingly wishing she could be just about anywhere else on earth. It was her job to help tell the jury Robert wasn't some power-hungry moneygrabber who just wanted to capitalize on his brother being governor.

It was the summer of 2008 when the request came. Julie said she remembered spending the Fourth of July holiday at the home of her brother-in-law, the governor, who took her husband aside during a backyard party and asked him to lead his campaign fund for a while, or at least until the end of that year.

"He was reluctant to do it," she said. "His life was in Nashville. His business was elsewhere."

But Julie said she thought it was important for her husband to fully consider it. The brothers' mother, before she died, had told them to always help each other. Robert's main source of income was the ownership of rental apartment buildings in Tennessee, so he didn't necessarily have to stay home. The brothers were living busy lives in separate cities, so Julie said she saw the post as a chance for them to grow closer.

"I told him I thought he should do it," Julie said, with more than a hint of regret in her voice. Her timidity made her seem genuine about the situation, like she realized it probably had been her wifely nudge that had brought this situation on her family.

Julie said it was her view that her husband shouldn't take a salary, because taking money for the job would create the air of nepotism about it and could reflect poorly on Rod in the Chicago press. It was no secret that Rod Blago-jevich and his wife had investigations swirling around them, and Julie told the jury that was her one concern before giving her final blessing to a job that would see her husband working for his high-profile brother and com-ing home to Nashville every ten days or so to see her. She said she and her husband had dinner with Rod and Patti to talk things out, and when it was through, everyone was comfortable.

"To the best of their knowledge, the federal investigation was behind them," Julie said.

———

Robert sat on the witness stand like he had a broomstick up the back of his shirt. He had spent months preparing to testify, and right away it seemed to pay off. He was clearly ready to go through his story with his lawyer, Ettinger, and explain how he had gone from a respected businessman in Nashville to federal defendant in Chicago in just five months in 2008. He rattled off the details of his college and army careers in a calm, clear voice and, not surprisingly, agreed with his wife about how he and his brother, who had once been "tied at the hip," had been pushed apart by their separate lives. "He was legal, political. I was military, business," he said. "We drifted."

And the fund-raising job was seen as a possible way for him and his brother to get to spend some significant time together. He wasn't even a Democrat; he was a hardcore Republican whose only fund-raising experience was in the charitable world, Robert explained. He had raised money for the likes of the Red Cross, but trying to stuff a campaign coffer would be a completely new experience, he remembered, and he knew he would be a novice going in. His only prior experience in the arena had been during the runup to his brother's reelection in 2006, but that had just been helping place campaign signs and calling a few people who already had donated in 2002. Robert worked a few months, his brother won reelection, and he went home to Tennessee.

In 2008, it was different. The governor's close ring had been chipped away by the federal government, and Blagojevich had few people he believed he could trust. One of them was Robert, so he asked his brother to come and run his campaign fund. Flattered, Robert accepted, and he told the jury that to him, the rules were always clear. You were never to tie a fund-raising request to official state action, and Robert was convinced he never had. He had made calls to people like Magoon, from Children's Memorial Hospital, but those requests were not linked in his mind to the fact they had something pending that the governor was considering. Robert said his brother's talks about the rate increase for the hospital were outside his presence, so he didn't even know about the proposal when he spoke to Magoon that fall.

Likewise, Robert said his conscience was clear when it came to more questionable conversations he'd had with his brother. It was Robert who had been told to reach out to Nayak in December 2008 when Blagojevich was thinking about increasing Jesse Jackson Jr.'s chances. Robert said he thought his brother was most interested in Lisa Madigan's appointment and his ability to possibly break the logjam in Springfield in a deal with her father. The Jackson choice, and the offer of money, had been viewed by the brothers as an outrageous joke, Robert said.

When Rod sent him to see Nayak, he wasn't even exactly sure what he was going to say.

"I'm not sure other than to talk to Raghu Nayak about the elevation of Jesse Jackson Jr.," Robert said, adding he wasn't going to bring up fund-raising. "I wasn't following exactly what he wanted me to do."

The governor had told him to be careful about how he approached the discussion, but Robert had an innocent answer for that, too. It just meant to be careful not to mix fund-raising and the seat. But how about when the governor had talked about getting something tangible and getting it up front from the Jackson people? Robert simply said he wasn't exactly sure what that was about.

"But I know it had nothing to do with that [fund-raising] approach because that was a dead issue," Robert said. He had killed that already. There were tapes of Robert telling members of the Indian community that money wouldn't be a factor and that his brother would do what was good for the state.

It was the same thing Robert told Chris Niewoehner, who cross-examined him. But Niewoehner was armed with tapes that made it sound like Robert had been right there when his brother was considering what he could get for a Senate appointment.

"So the question is what horse trading do you do?" Robert said on one call. Blagojevich was thinking of naming Jarrett to the seat, so, what did Robert think his brother could get for that?

"I used it in the context of just what politicians do," Robert said. He was just talking as a concerned brother.

That didn't mean Obama would illegally kill the criminal probe, Robert said. The president might stop the investigation "if it were proper," Robert said. "He's got laywers and advisers around him. I'm not telling him to go one off and do something illegal."

That led Niewoehner to ask another hypothetical question. What about if someone put a bag of money in front of Blagojevich and asked for a favor, like the situation Ata had described? Robert was playing a guy who clung to the straight and narrow, so how about that question?

"He'd tell that guy to pick up the money and walk right out with it," Robert said, not backing down. Nearby, Rod was looking on with admiration as his brother defended him.

When Niewoehner began playing tapes of the brothers talking about this or that job Blagojevich might get for the Senate seat, Robert did well. He was calm enough that he could have passed a lie-detector test on some answers and sternly resistant on others. Tapes of Rod talking about getting appointed to the Health and Human Services post were innocent enough to him.

"If he had said he wanted to be secretary of defense, I would have laughed at him," Robert said. "Call it what you like. It's two politicians or their representatives trying to work up a political deal."

When Blagojevich was taped talking about politician Blair Hull being named to the Senate, the governor had talked about a $100,000 campaign contribution being sought from him. Niewoehner asked whether that was a conversation about power and reward. That was no political deal.

"If John McCain won, your brother wouldn't have had an appointment to make, would he?" Niewoehner asked.

"No. I wish that would have happened," Robert answered.

Robert repeatedly said that in his view, offers of money from Jackson's supporters in the Indian community were completely wrong. He had done what he could to insulate his brother from some of those offers, he said, finally acknowledging that yes, at times he did pass on the information. But it was more like "field operations" and less like telling the governor something that he might jump to take. "I didn't want him stepping on land mines," Robert said. "I wanted him to be aware there were people who had these objectives. He needed to know that there was a danger there."

Robert testified that he thought the Indian community was clumsy in its approach on behalf of Jackson. One of the early attempts came during the Halloween fund-raiser, when Nayak made an offer of up to $6 million if Jackson could get the seat. Robert said he simply told Nayak that wasn't happening and didn't bother to pass on the amount that was higher than the $1.5 million that had been floating around. It was another land mine, Robert agreed, but one from a likable exaggerator that didn't merit bothering the governor over. Robert said he had made it loud and clear that no offer like that would be accepted, and he had moved on. Nayak's boasting often fell short of the promised marks, Robert said. For example, he promised to bring a friend who was a billionaire to the fund-raiser the weekend before Blagojevich's arrest. And despite all the big talk, the friend had written a check for about $10,000. Not small potatoes, but not exactly a check of the caliber Nayak had hinted at.

"I know it wasn't for $6 million," Robert said.

———

Rumors swirled about what was going on when court ended for the day after Robert's testimony, and the ex-governor wasn't called to the stand. Despite Adam Jr. promising Blagojevich would defend himself, and despite Blagojevich promising on seemingly every television show in the country that he couldn't wait to testify, he decided in the end that he would not address the jury. The Adams made it look like they were fighting over the choice, with the younger Adam wanting Blagojevich to answer questions and his father being more conservative, but they were in fact in agreement. The public rift was just another example of Twenty-Sixth Street fakery, designed to give Adam Jr. a little cover. In reality, the defense team was confident in the choice to keep Blagojevich back. When he had practiced being cross-examined, it had not gone well. Blagojevich had spent time prepping with Adam Jr. and Sr. and lawyer and friend Jay Wallace, going to a local park to rehearse his answers for fear of continued government bugging. Then, as

Adam Sr. took a final day of getting ready himself, he made what he later called a big mistake. Lawyer and legal team member Michael Gillespie had told him that his father, Terry Gillespie, would work on a mock cross with Blagojevich. The Adams said yes, not knowing that Genson, away from the case for so long, also would be present. Genson had appeared and given the opinion that Blagojevich wasn't ready. It had shaken the governor and became a self-fulfilling prophecy. "Genson said I better not go on," Blagojevich told his other lawyers.

His client's lack of confidence weighed on Adam Sr., as did the belief that despite promises from Zagel that Blagojevich would be allowed fairly free rein to testify as he pleased in his own defense, the judge would not live up to that bargain. He recalled the Family Secrets mob case, when Zagel had told lawyers he would allow mobster Frank Calabrese Sr. room to talk about his view of the case, only to repeatedly cut him off. Adam sensed a trap. "He's a copper. That's it," he later recalled saying about Zagel.

The decision to keep Blagojevich off the stand was iced when the father and son attorneys talked and came to the opinion that the government had held back some of what it might bring against Blagojevich, believing they would use it when he took the stand, and it turned out that Schar had in fact been preparing for the cross one day each weekend for more than six months. The lawyers also feared Rezko could be called in rebuttal if he testified. And finally, Robert's testimony had gone remarkably well, and they hoped it had rubbed off on their client. If Robert acted as the de facto spokesman for the brothers before the jury, that was a situation they were inclined to accept.

"It is my decision, under the advice of my attorneys," Blagojevich told Zagel the next day when he officially said he would not take the stand. "I make the decision fully and voluntarily."

He had still been sitting at the defense table as the announcement was made, but he turned slightly and gave a wink to Patti. Afterward, he would try to explain what had happened, citing the "dispute" between Adam Jr. and Adam Sr., with the younger Adam wanting him to defend himself as the lawyer had promised he would and the older Adam taking a different tack.

"Sam Adam Sr.'s most compelling argument and ultimately the one that swayed me was that the government in their case proved my innocence," Blagojevich told the press. "They proved I did nothing illegal and that there was nothing further for us to add.

"In fact they proved that I sought the advice of my lawyers and my advisers," he continued. "They proved that I was on the phone talking to them, brainstorming about ideas. Yes, they proved some of those ideas were stupid, but they also proved some of the ideas were good."

If he had learned one thing from his ordeal, it was that he talked too much, Blagojevich said. So he took Patti by the hand and turned toward the door, waving over his shoulder as he walked out onto busy Dearborn Street.

17

A Second Trial

The first note from the jury was nothing abnormal. As many juries do, the panel asked for a transcript of one of the closing arguments. This jury wanted a copy of Niewoehner's final remarks, which had come with a focused presentation on the overhead projector about how the evidence and testimony could be processed if Blagojevich were to be convicted. It wasn't a great sign for the defense, as they would rather have had the jury request the argument of Adam Jr., who had called his client a victim of sorts. "Think about who they're telling you he extorted," he had said. "The president of the United States. Give me a break!"

No one on either side had panicked at first, but that turned out to be the wrong reaction, as the wheels quickly came off the wagon. The jury members seemed to be having a hard time agreeing on anything, including lunch. One day they ordered eight different kinds of pizza, including taco. The next substantive jury note was more ominous.

"Is it permissible to obtain a transcript of the testimony?" read the note, signed by the jury's foreman, James Matsumoto. "It would be helpful."

It was unclear if the jury was asking if it could get transcripts of the testimony of particular witnesses or if it was essentially asking for a transcript of the entire trial. If it was the second one, it wasn't hard to imagine the jury setting a new record for length of deliberations. In the end the request wasn't clear, but Zagel certainly wasn't going to send back hundreds of pages. Time dragged, and it was more than three weeks before the note that signaled very serious discord on the panel. A note came out asking for the oath the group had taken as jurors to deliberate with an open mind and so on. At least one person was apparently holding out and possibly refusing to engage the rest of the jury.

It was no surprise when the panel finally filed in to deliver its split verdict. They were divided on every count but one, and Blagojevich's head dropped when he learned he had been convicted of lying to the FBI about fund-raising. The jury had decided he had been untruthful when he told Agent Murphy that he kept politics and fund-raising separated by a firewall.

Matsumoto, the foreman, was the veteran with the family links to the Japanese internment camps. That he would be selected the leader was no surprise, as he had been seen in the jury box drawing his own detailed maps and charts of the evidence that were so intricate they almost seemed suitable for framing. More mysterious was the identity of the holdout. While the group had been more evenly divided on some of the alleged shakedowns in the case, they had fallen 11–1 on the alleged Senate seat sale. Someone had held steadfast under the weight of the entire case and the wishes and beliefs of the rest of the jury panel. It was Juror 106, a grandmother and retired state official, and the first to interview her was the *Tribune*'s Stacy St. Clair.

JoAnn Chiakulas had ridden the train each morning to hear the evidence and finally the arguments and had developed stomach pains and insomnia under the stress of knowing that she would not bend from her own finding on the evidence in the case. She was not convinced Blagojevich was guilty, and no amount of pushing and prodding by her fellow jurors was going to move her from that opinion.

"I could never live with myself if I went along with the rest of the jury," Chiakulas told St. Clair. "I didn't believe it was the correct vote for me."

It was a pretty straightforward explanation. Her former state job had nothing to do with her choice, Chiakulas swore. Besides, she had retired before he even took office. Her ex-husband had donated to Blagojevich, but it was decades after they had divorced. She wasn't a fan of the former governor, either. She said she had all but ignored his television "shenanigans" before the trial.

The Blagojevich Chiakulas said she heard on the tapes was practically incapable of having the focus of thought to organize a criminal conspiracy. There was no decipherable plan, she said, telling St. Clair that while she had voted "not guilty," she had not meant it as a vote for "innocent." In fact, there didn't seem to be much about Blagojevich that she actually liked, calling him narcissistic and essentially scatterbrained.

But whatever the reasons, Chiakulas and the division on the jury had left twenty-three counts on the table and forced the case to a crossroads. Schar wasted no time answering for the government. Blagojevich would be tried again, preferably as soon as possible. Prosecutors were ready to pick a new jury immediately.

Luckier was Robert Blagojevich. The jury had been unable to decide his case either, and the government had a different message for him. He would no longer be pursued. Robert's prosecution was dropped "in the interest of justice" as prosecutors tried to clean up their case and focus on the ex-governor. Even jurors who had voted to convict Blagojevich had been quoted in the press saying they were confused by the massive amount of evidence, the minute detail in the criminal circuitry prosecutors had asked them to consider, and the dozens of pages of instructions. Losing Robert Blagojevich would remove his testimony from the case and streamline things. The ordeal that had begun for Robert when he agreed to come to Chicago to help run his brother's campaign fund was finally over. He planned to return to Tennessee after having dinner in Chicago with a son who was living there.

"We're going to have steaks," he said.

———

Sam Adam Jr. had immediately hung his head after the split verdict was read. He had given the case his all and knew he could most likely not improve on that result. The case had worn on the ebullient Adam emotionally and financially, and the last thing he wanted was to have to do it all over again.

"I can't. I'm not kidding," he said just after the verdict. "I'll go to jail. I can't do it again."

With little haranguing, Zagel let the father-and-son team off the case, probably as happy to see them go as they were to be hitting the exit. There was very little for Adam Jr. to gain by staying. His practice had taken a financial hit, and there was a real sense in Chicago legal circles that he had taken the case about as far as he could. He was the guy who had run the government to a tie on many of the major counts, and that was going to be hard to repeat a second time. Getting out when he did, he preserved what many saw as a win for him personally and professionally. In addition, Adam Jr. didn't expect that his act would play twice in federal court. He was emotionally exhausted and had depleted whatever currency he had with Judge Zagel. He felt he had been shut down at every turn by the judge late in the trial, leaving him feeling ineffective. In short, Zagel was trying to force him to adhere to a stricter set of rules than he was used to.

———

The verdict sent the case into a holding pattern, leaving both sides to consider how to get a different result the next time around. In addition to jettisoning Robert Blagojevich from the case, prosecutors dropped the sweeping conspiracy counts that had led the prior case. The counts were good because the government could use them to connect the dots between lots of alleged acts, but they could feel amorphous when it came time to argue before a jury. Some jurors seemed to think that Blagojevich had done *something* wrong, but they didn't exactly know how that belief corresponded with the actual criminal statutes the government was trying to use.

For a second trial, prosecutors thought they could make the case more direct. The strategy became to present what Blagojevich had done, play the tapes, underscore specific fraud counts, and ask for a conviction.

Blagojevich, meanwhile, was keeping a lower profile than he had the first time around. He would occasionally pop up on a talk show or pistachio commercial. As the second trial neared, he invited a few reporters into his tidy brick home to complain about his treatment and admit that he really was fearful of what could happen to him.

He allowed two *Tribune* reporters in on the same day a second pool of 150 possible jurors arrived at the Dirksen courthouse to fill out questionnaires and begin the process of selecting a panel to hear his retrial. It was April 20, 2011, some eight months after the first jury had ended its work mostly deadlocked. The TV news trucks were back idling on the family's street by then, with cameramen standing around hoping to get some quick B-roll of Blagojevich coming or going. Patti opened the front door for the *Tribune* reporters and quickly complained about the media. She basically woke up when they pulled up out front for the morning broadcasts, sometimes before 5:00 AM, she said, adding that she felt the worst for her neighbors, who had done nothing to bring the media scourge upon them.

After offering something to drink, Patti showed the way to her husband's office. He appeared looking every bit like a politician dressed to do a fireside chat, wearing neat jeans and a collared shirt under a blue V-neck sweater. He shook hands warmly and made sure his interviewers were comfortable.

Right off the bat, the ex-governor said he had mixed emotions about having to go through a trial again, especially, he said, when he was falsely accused. He hadn't put on a defense, and he insisted the government had failed to prove the allegations it had so dramatically leveled against him more than two years earlier at Fitzgerald's fiery press conference. He wouldn't wish what he was going through on anyone, Blagojevich said.

"I will make a confession here: there's some trepidation," he said. "There's fear of course when you have to face something like this."

Blagojevich moved through the talking points he had used with other reporters, about being profoundly amazed at having to face another jury and being unable to sleep late at night when there were still hours to go before dawn. The mind races and fears creep in, Blagojevich said, the biggest one being that he would not be around to protect his two daughters and watch them grow up. He might wind up unable to work and make a better life for the girls. But at the same time, he said, he was eager to get things going again, sounding much more like a man who planned to defend himself by not only calling witnesses but also speaking directly to the jury. He hadn't gotten any of the vindication he believed he deserved, he said, as the family dog, Skittles, ran around his legs.

"I'll never give this up, because they're lying about me," he said, his back stiffening. "I'm an innocent man with honest intentions, who . . . was trying to end up in the right place on the decision with regard to the US Senate seat. And those other allegations are just trumped-up lies."

The investigation of him had always been on his mind, Blagojevich said. Word had been spreading in the fall of 2008 that the feds were stepping up their pursuit of him. Rezko had changed his mind and begun helping prosecutors. New subpoenas were flying to people who were close to him. His own lawyers, including Bill Quinlan, had told him that defense attorneys representing others in Blagojevich's circle were telling him they had never seen the US attorney's office so determined to get someone.

So why be on any phone talking about anything that federal investigators might, according to Blagojevich, "misinterpret?" As was his way, Blagojevich turned that question on its head.

"That's why you have five hundred hours of telephone conversations with me," he said. "Just the opposite in fact was the case. You have all these conversations and this talk in large part because . . . I want to be sure that whatever

I do, whatever I think about doing, whatever other people have suggested I think about doing, that I talk about them over and over and over again. With my legal counsel Bill Quinlan; with my chief of staff John Harris, who was a former prosecutor in the military; with my deputy governor Greenlee, who was a federal judge's law clerk; with my political consultants, who are world-class Washington, DC–based political consultants who do presidential races."

Blagojevich hinted strongly that he would take the stand the second time around and defend himself. He suggested he was not above calling a number of politicians to the stand to talk about their dealings with him. He was going to be aggressive and was determined to win, though he had been preparing his family for any result.

Patti didn't like it when he told this story, Blagojevich said, but he had told his daughters everything would be OK, one way or another. He had said something to his daughters. "I said something like, 'Worst-case scenario—which I don't expect will happen—you can get another dog and call him Daddy,'" he said.

———

The second trial in the summer of 2011 lacked some of the buzz of the first, but "Blagojevich 2.0" still brought crowds to the Dirksen courthouse. And it was quickly evident during jury selection that the pool of people who would hear the case was even more saturated with Blagojevich coverage and TV appearances than the first group had been. One man had downloaded a government recording of Blagojevich blowing his stack and swearing as the ringtone for his cell phone. Others used words like *nutcase* to describe him.

"If you take that literally, it does not mean 'guilty,'" Zagel argued to keep the jury pool larger, possibly only half joking.

There was an art teacher, a doctor, and a truck driver for the city. One woman said she was president of a suburban school board, and Zagel asked if she could set aside what she had heard about Blagojevich and reach a verdict based just on evidence in court. "I've been working on that mentally ever since I got the summons," she answered.

Much of the media coverage of the second jury's selection seemed to revolve around a woman who asked out of jury duty because she had tickets to *The Oprah Winfrey Show*. Oprah, who had not been named to the US Senate in 2008 after all, was still doing her show in Chicago. The woman was eventually let go.

Blagojevich seemed fairly relaxed as the second panel came together. In the hall outside Zagel's room one day, he ran into none other than Matsumoto, the foreman of the first jury, who planned to watch much of the second trial, feeling as if he had unfinished business with the case. Blagojevich spotted him and quickly walked up to shake his hand.

"I'm glad you're not on this one," he said.

The lawyers eventually whittled their way through a group with clear feelings against the former governor, before settling on a group of eleven women and only one man.

———

For their case, prosecutors would switch up their order of delivery, starting the second time with Niewoehner, who said Illinoisans had trusted Blagojevich by electing him twice.

"And he sold out that trust," Niewoehner said, speaking in a loud, earnest voice, pacing before the jury. Blagojevich stared at the prosecutor as he pointed in Blagojevich's direction.

As they had during their opening statement at the first trial, prosecutors said Blagojevich in 2008 viewed Barack Obama's election to the presidency—and Blagojevich's ability to appoint someone to the US Senate to replace Obama—as his ticket to getting out of the financial difficulties he was sinking into that year. Blagojevich tried to use his ability to name a senator to get a post in the new administration or to get campaign cash, Niewoehner said. The power he had was corrupted for his own benefit and to help him get out of debt, he said.

"He decided to sell the US Senate seat to solve his problem" by making criminal demands, the prosecutor said.

His opening statement was something like "Blagojevich for Dummies" as Niewoehner used an overhead to boil the case down to just five specific crimes. And each was much more focused than in the first trial. Instead of building a pyramid with "the Blagojevich Enterprise" at its base, prosecutors presented narrow episodes of what had happened in the fall of 2008.

On the Senate seat, Blagojevich first wanted a cabinet post in exchange for naming Jarrett and let an intermediary know.

"And right there, the crime is complete," said Niewoehner, emphasizing that just asking was wrong. The prosecutor made similar small-bore statements about the attempts against Magoon, Krozel, and Johnston and about Blagojevich's alleged attempt to get a fund-raiser to help a North Side school on Emanuel's behalf.

"Right there, when the defendant ordered that demand to be sent, the crime was committed," Niewoehner said again.

There was no mention of any alleged crime taking place before 2006, as prosecutors focused on the fall of 2008. Much of Operation Board Games was being left on the table in a further attempt at simplicity. Also pared down was the allegation that Blagojevich had tried to extort the *Tribune* and force the firing of editorial board members.

With Adam Jr. not in court, the opening defense statement was left to attorney Aaron Goldstein, who had been part of the first trial but more of a sideline player. Still, Blagojevich had great faith in him, in part because he tapped into Blagojevich's natural love of the underdog. The prosecution of Rod Blagojevich is "a tale of sound and fury, signifying nothing," Goldstein said, sometimes channeling Adam Jr. by raising and lowering his voice. "Do you think they found a big bag of cash hidden somewhere?" he said. "No, they found nothing, because in fact there is nothing."

The defense flashed images of Blagojevich on an overhead screen, including one of a young Blagojevich with his parents and one of Monk at his wedding. Monk betrayed his friend, Goldstein stressed. And as for other men in the case who portrayed themselves as victims, they were millionaires and not victims at all. That group included leaders of horse tracks who stood to make money from casinos if Blagojevich signed a bill authorizing them. The supposed victims didn't come to any understanding that they were being shaken down "until they come a-knockin'," Goldstein said, meaning the feds.

Blagojevich simply listened to overtures about the Senate seat, Goldstein said, including from Obama. He wasn't extorting or bribing anyone, the lawyer told the jury. Blagojevich was thinking about his own future, even thinking out loud about naming himself to the seat. "He was talking about his dreams," he said.

＝＝＝

Harris was back as an early witness in round two, as the government reshuffled the deck in an attempt to hit the Senate seat hard, early, and often. *Tribune* reporter Bob Secter blogged for the paper that it was like the Ultra Slim-Fast version of the Blagojevich case. Harris was going over testimony that the first jury hadn't heard until week four of the first trial, and he completely skipped over his testimony on Patti trying to get jobs with Blagojevich's influence.

Tom Balanoff also was called to the stand again, repeating his story about taking the call from Obama at the gas station and how he had set up meetings with the governor.

On Election Day, Balanoff and his wife had been at the Hilton and Towers on Grant Park and walked across toward Obama's stage to hear the speech. Balanoff saw Blagojevich with Emil Jones as he was walking into the park, he said, and had a short private conversation with him. Balanoff referred to the conversation they'd had just prior to the election and said there was more to say now. Blagojevich had said great and to give him a call, and the two men parted. Scofield was used to set up the second meeting, and it turned into a one-on-one between Balanoff and the governor.

"I said, 'I'm close to President Obama, and I'm close to you,'" Balanoff recalled for the jury. He had spoken to someone, and he was there to advocate for Valerie Jarrett.

Blagojevich was supposed to get it. Balanoff didn't want to specifically spell it out, but he wanted to communicate that he had talked to the incoming president without specifically saying it. Obama had wanted at least the appearance that he was staying out of the situation. So Balanoff simply parroted what Obama had said. Jarrett would be good for the state and, as it turned out, a good political decision for Blagojevich. Jarrett was African American, a woman, a sharp Chicago business leader, and a friend to organized labor.

"He agreed, politically it would be smart," Balanoff remembered.

But the governor also tried to throw up a smoke screen for the union boss. He told Balanoff he was in "active discussions" with the Madigans to send Lisa to the Senate.

Did Balanoff know whether there were really any "active discussions" between Blagojevich and the Madigans? Schar asked.

"I didn't," Balanoff answered.

Regardless, both men knew it would take months to get that kind of deal off the ground, especially if Blagojevich wanted to see some legislative results from Michael Madigan before appointing Lisa. There was no way Jarrett had that kind of time, especially with Obama wanting her help in his new administration.

So with the idea in the air that Jarrett had some competition, Blagojevich tossed out his real message. If he could be appointed secretary of health and human services under Obama, he could live out his passion. Balanoff said he got it.

"I understood that if he could be appointed to that position, then Valerie Jarrett could be appointed to the Senate seat," Balanoff said. "If I took that back and if that could happen, then he would appoint Valerie Jarrett to the Senate."

Schar asked Balanoff what his response had been. Balanoff testified that it was instant, with Balanoff telling Blagojevich that simply wasn't going to happen. Why? Blagojevich said in return. Was it because of the ongoing federal investigation against him? Well, yes, Balanoff had said, wasn't Blagojevich worried about that?

"He said no," Balanoff told the jury.

At any rate, Balanoff was trying to be the advocate that Obama wanted, so he told the governor he would in fact reach out to Jarrett and keep the ball in the air. He would make a call and throw some of the things Blagojevich had said to her, and then maybe he and Blagojevich could meet again for coffee that Saturday.

The coffee meeting never did happen. Balanoff said he did talk to Jarrett, who agreed she didn't have time for Blagojevich to figure himself out or weigh whatever he thought he could do with the Madigans. And Balanoff remembered telling Jarrett the governor had said some "goofy stuff" to him about a cabinet post.

It was November 12, about a week later, Balanoff confirmed, before Balanoff would again be heavily used by Blagojevich in his negotiations. It was just after Emanuel had delivered a message from Obama through John Wyma, who had called Harris with it. It was the "thankful and appreciative" message that hadn't sat so well with the governor.

Schar wanted to make one point clear with the jury. It was obvious on the phone call that Blagojevich had all but scrapped whatever the Madigan "negotiations" had been. The governor had barely mentioned the supposed idea of a deal, and Balanoff said he concluded there hadn't been any real talks. Blagojevich had talked about money being funneled into a group that he would of course be paid to lead and said "and then we could help our new senator, Valerie Jarrett," push the organization's agenda.

Balanoff said he got the message.

"It was clear that he was—at least in my mind—that if this would be set up, he would make Valerie Jarrett a senator," Balanoff testified. "I believe he thought I was going to take it back to Valerie Jarrett."

But it hadn't mattered, as news quickly broke that Jarrett was taking a job at the White House after all.

The cross-examination of Balanoff was mostly unremarkable, except for Judge Zagel's reaction to it. Goldstein asked for details about what Blagojevich had said at the November 3 meeting about Lisa Madigan, hoping to emphasize to the jury that the governor had been relaying a very real option. Balanoff said again that Blagojevich had told him he would be getting rid of a political rival by sending Madigan to Washington and could get going with some of his stalled legislative plans. Goldstein stressed that it was Balanoff who had called Blagojevich to set up a meeting where he would tell the governor what Obama wanted, not the other way around. Balanoff had sought out the governor and forwarded messages from the man who would become president. Blagojevich had never explicitly said he would trade one thing for another. And as far as the "active discussions" with the Madigans, Balanoff had no independent knowledge of whether that was real or not.

"That's correct," Balanoff said.

It was the next few questions that would get Goldstein into hot water with the judge. The lawyer asked if when he told Blagojevich "that's not going to happen" in response to the HHS idea, he had told the governor to stop because he was doing something wrong. It brought a strong objection from Schar, who already was objecting every few moments. The judge already had warned the defense that they were not to raise a "legal advice" defense— the defense that Blagojevich shouldn't be convicted of any crimes because lawyers and others around him had never warned him he was crossing into illegal areas. To make that defense takes a finding by the judge that the defendant had raised issues with a lawyer who had specifically advised that what wound up being the charged conduct was not a crime.

Moments later, Goldstein was at it again, asking whether Balanoff passed along Blagojevich's "goofy" ideas, or if he and Jarrett had stopped and decided to call authorities. It wasn't until after court that Zagel told Goldstein that if he wanted to try that again, he should save it for the very end of his cross-examination. Otherwise, he might get cut short and not get to ask other questions he might still have that could be helpful to his client.

"I will sit you down," the judge warned. The normally stoic Zagel had an intensity in his voice that he didn't flash often. Patti later said the entire day had made her want to cry in court because she felt like prosecutors were objecting so often, and Zagel in turn sustaining them, that the truth was being buried. It was all continuing to point to the former governor himself needing to testify to be able to tell the jury everything he wanted it to know.

———

In the wreckage of the Blagojevich matter, Doug Scofield's reputation had suffered a hit but not been devastated. In 2011, he was the senior partner of his own business, the Scofield Company, which dealt in public affairs and government relations. It was easy to see why he was good at what he did. He projected just the right amount of book and street smarts. He was affable and put off the kind of easygoing vibe that seemed to allow people to trust him quickly. He had an impressive resume, working as chief of staff to US Representative Luis Gutierrez for ten years. He had been a communications consultant for the likes of the Salvation Army and the Regional Transportation Authority.

And if you were to click on his biography on his company's website in the spring of 2011, you would have thought that these had been his most notable work experiences. The materials made no mention that he had been Blagojevich's deputy campaign manager or policy and communications director when Blagojevich first ran for governor in 2002 or that he had been the first deputy governor for him. There was also no mention that Scofield hadn't liked the fact that Rezko and Chris Kelly had so much influence in the new administration and that he had left. Nor did it recount how he had stayed in contact with many of the players in Blagojevich's world, and with the governor himself, returning to assist the governor's reelection campaign in 2006. And in 2008, Scofield had found himself talking with the governor more and more, as another major client, the SEIU, was trying to influence Blagojevich's choice to replace Barack Obama in the US Senate. It was that experience that had led to multiple interviews with the FBI and the US attorney's office and two trips to the witness stand at a high-profile federal trial.

When Balanoff and Andy Stern had wanted to see Blagojevich in early November, they had asked Scofield to contact Blagojevich and set it up. When the men went to see Blagojevich on November 3 at the Thompson Center, Scofield was in tow. Schar asked about the sit-down, and as he had at the first trial, Scofield walked jurors through his involvement. He recalled the first meeting Balanoff had with the governor just as his client did. There was talk about what Obama might want Blagojevich to do with the seat and talk about Valerie Jarrett. Blagojevich just seemed interested in knowing anything that sounded like inside information about Obama's preference. And he, too, recalled Blagojevich suggesting he was talking to the Madigans. The speaker was blocking whatever he was trying to do, Scofield recalled Blagojevich saying, so maybe he could break the logjam by appointing Lisa.

Scofield had walked Balanoff and Stern back to their nearby office afterward but then had returned to the Thompson Center. He had met again with the governor, as well as Harris, Bill Quinlan, and Greenlee, the deputy governor. What ensued was a clear discussion of what the governor thought he could get in return for making the pick Obama wanted, Scofield remembered.

The governor was intrigued that Obama wanted someone in particular, Scofield said, and saw it as an opportunity that he could make an appointment and exchange it "for something for himself."

After Balanoff heard from Obama directly later that night, it was Scofield who again set up a meeting with the governor. The second meeting would be November 6, and the day before it, Scofield and Blagojevich were on the phone just after 11:00 AM. It was then that Scofield would become the answer to the trivia question, who was Rod Blagojevich talking to when he described Obama's old Senate seat as "fucking golden"?

"Right," Scofield had responded and then listened to Blagojevich carry on about how he could just parachute himself to Washington if no one would give him anything that he found to be satisfactory for the appointment.

Schar asked just what Scofield really thought the governor was saying when he said that infamous line.

Scofield gave a very straightforward answer, telling the prosecutor he had taken Blagojevich quite literally. The "thing" was his ability to appoint a senator, Scofield testified, without any hint in his voice that this was particularly memorable for him or that it had grown to be the bizarre, signature catchphrase of the entire case. The thing was golden, the governor had said, Scofield said.

"It's valuable to him," he said. "He's not giving it up for nothing in return."

Scofield wasn't at Balanoff's second meeting with the governor, but he had stopped by afterward to see how things went. He found himself talking to Blagojevich and Harris about it and learned that Blagojevich had gone ahead and conveyed his interest in a cabinet spot. The governor thought things had been generally positive and was pleased he had gotten his message across.

"If the president-elect was interested in Valerie Jarrett for the Senate seat, the governor was willing to appoint her," he recalled. "In return for that, the governor was interested in being appointed to the cabinet and was particularly interested in health and human services."

Before Scofield left, he said Harris had wanted to know what Balanoff's salary was at SEIU or just in general what his compensation package was. Scofield said he had told them he didn't know for certain but thought it was something like $125,000 to $150,000.

"They seemed surprised the figure was not higher," he remembered.

———

Just two weeks into testimony at the second trial, it was very apparent that prosecutors were aiming a much leaner and meaner case right at the governor and his machinations over the Senate pick in 2008. Their sprawling original case had wound through Operation Board Games toward the Senate, while the second round *started* there and concentrated on major witnesses and key recordings. It took just three weeks total for prosecutors to present their case the second time—or about half the time it took in 2010. Many of the off-point details that had made headlines in the first trial were dropped, like that Blagojevich hid in the bathroom when he didn't want to see his budget director, that he loved expensive suits, and that Obama's team didn't want him at Obama's Grant Park victory rally.

But before the government would rest its case, Rajinder Bedi returned to the stand, again recounting how he had wound up as a go-between telling Robert Blagojevich about the plans of Raghu Nayak and an offer of campaign money if Jesse Jackson Jr. were made the senator. Bedi testified without much detail of the Jackson meeting where he said decisions were made to offer money, seemingly leaving it up in the air whether the jury would think Jackson was behind the offer.

Greenlee testified again about the last few calls he had with Blagojevich and how he didn't believe Blagojevich when the governor told him to relax about what he had heard him say to Fred Yang and that he was just trying to leverage a Jackson Jr. pick with the national people. And Wyma was back as well, telling the jury about his decision to flip, again describing how the fundraising inside the Friends of Blagojevich had grown too aggressive for him to stomach just as he had gotten a federal subpoena for his own dealings representing hospitals before the corrupt Illinois Health Facilities Planning Board.

"To hear him lie like he is lying is like a dagger in my heart," Blagojevich said as he left court after listening to Wyma testify against him for a second time. "But tomorrow is another day and next week is another week as we get closer and closer to sorting it all out."

Blagojevich would continue to come and go from the trial on most days carrying a large black briefcase, looking like he was doing more than just sitting idly by as his lawyers ran the case. But that didn't stop him from greeting people who were waiting to get into court on any given day. He often headed down the hall to the men's room just before the trial began and stopped to chat with people lined up outside the room. He would happily give an autograph to anyone who asked, signing notebooks, loose slips of paper, and copies of his book. "Birds always sing after the storm," he wrote in one note. Another day just outside the building, he tried and failed to sign an orange.

———

The week of May 16, 2011, was historic in the city of Chicago. Rahm Emanuel was sworn in as the city's forty-sixth mayor in a chilly ceremony at the Frank Gehry–designed band shell in Millennium Park. Chicago's first Jewish mayor had won the office in a landslide and promised change that would sweep the city away from financial disaster and from the "old way of doing things." Emanuel acted like he was a million miles from his entanglement with Blagojevich, even though he was just blocks from where Blagojevich was sitting in court. And he was not yet free of the case's gravitational pull. More and more, as Zagel sustained government objections and told the defense to recall witnesses in its own case, it became clear Blagojevich's lawyers would call witnesses of their own and that Emanuel would be near the top of their list.

Obama's name came up at the start of that week as well, though not in the way Blagojevich wanted. His lawyers again asked Judge Zagel for access to the FBI report of an interview agents had with Obama in February 2009. They were looking for any indication Obama was aware of Blagojevich's alleged "asks."

Zagel said no but offered a few clues to the report, which he had read closely. The interview suggested Obama—who was fairly busy at the time—didn't know to any useful degree what Blagojevich was doing.

"The premise [Obama] was aware of the asks is not supported," the judge said, reminding the defense that it didn't really matter anyway whether the incoming president knew or didn't know of Blagojevich's ideas.

"There is a longstanding rule of law that a planned victim does not have to know he was the target of an attempt," he said. "You don't get to argue that you should be acquitted because your plan to rob a bank was unknown to any teller."

Also back on the stand that week repeating his testimony was Patrick Magoon of Children's Memorial Hospital. The defense asked to be able to cross-examine him on his history of giving money personally to politicians and to point out he had a post on the board of the Illinois Hospital Association, a lobbying group that contributed generously to Friends of Blagojevich in the past.

With the jury out of the room, Goldstein questioned Magoon about that history but didn't draw out anything the judge found useful. Nice try, Zagel said, but he thought the defense had "cratered" in the effort to show they should be allowed to get into that area with Magoon. It was a term that confused at least Goldstein.

"That's like crashing into the ground and making a crater," Zagel explained, dryly.

So, which would the defense team be to Zagel, Goldstein said, the meteor or the crater?

"Either one," the judge said.

The blocking of the defense from getting into such background quickly became a theme. There were three witnesses that Blagojevich's lawyers wanted to paint as political creatures who were familiar with the fund-raising world: Magoon; Gerald Krozel, the road builders representative; and John Johnston, the horse racing executive. None of them were babes in the woods who would have been shocked by any outreach from the Blagojevich camp about fund-raising, even while they had items in front of the governor that they wanted action on. The defense wanted to show that Magoon and the others should have known where the fund-raising line was and that Blagojevich was walking right up to it without going over it. Without the context of the men's histories, they were in essence testifying in a vacuum, with the jury thinking Blagojevich came out of nowhere and just asked for cash. It just wasn't credible that they would now be feeling some extraordinary pressure from the governor or his operatives, the defense argued.

Krozel was the next to take the witness stand. Goldstein questioned him outside the presence of the jury, too, asking whether he had been a chairman of the Illinois concrete pavers' group and vice chairman of the American Concrete Paving Association. Krozel said he had been politically active since the 1980s, back to when Jim Thompson was governor. Krozel recounted how he had heard from Thompson that he should become more "politically involved," which he took to mean more active in fund-raising. He did so, Krozel said, and Thompson agreed to a repaving project on the Eisenhower Expressway that would benefit Krozel's organizations. It was an odd story about a Republican governor who was the former US attorney who had put Governor Otto Kerner behind bars.

Regardless, Zagel again said the defense couldn't go there during cross-examination, upsetting Goldstein. Much of the case was based on the understanding of three men who were used to fund-raising for others when they stood to gain something from state action, he said.

"The only difference in the level of uncomfortableness is we have now a man on trial," Goldstein said. "They have a bias and motive to give an understanding. How do we test what someone's understanding is? We look at their personal experiences because it's a very subjective thing."

These were men who had played the game, and now just because the government was telling them to say something, they were doing so, he said.

"Nine hundred times before it was no problem," Goldstein said. "Now it's, 'Oh, I felt all this pressure.'"

The jury hadn't been there to hear Goldstein explain, but many in the press corps looked at one another and thought the argument was about the most cogent vision of the defense case that they'd yet heard, at least at the retrial. To get at it, the defense was going to have to call its own witnesses and probably even the former governor himself.

But the jury heard only what Krozel was allowed to tell them. He was seventy-one and basically retired and had been dealing in recent years with a very ill wife who had an undiagnosed mental condition that left her bedridden. He had last worked fulltime for Prairie Materials, a large construction-related firm. He had been summoned to a meeting with Monk and Blagojevich on September 18, 2008, and didn't really want to go. It was obvious he was going to be asked for money again, and it was a terrible time to have to turn around and try to raise money for Blagojevich. The economy was steadily worsening, and the shadow of federal investigations had tainted the governor. Niewoehner asked why he had gone, then.

"He was the governor," Krozel said.

Blagojevich had talked about the progressive tollway program, Krozel recalled, which would start with a $1.8 billion expansion plan. There could later be a follow-up plan as large as $6 billion, which perked Krozel's ears.

The industry was down, and that amount of work would have meant a lot. At the very least it would have saved dozens of jobs at a concrete plant in Dixon, Illinois, that was slated for closure. As he had at the first trial, Krozel then described how Blagojevich floated the idea of a campaign donation, seemingly linking the tollway program to whether Krozel would contribute.

Krozel said he was still in the meeting with the governor and Monk when Blagojevich had started talking about the ethics law that was going to make it illegal to collect campaign cash from companies doing business with Illinois. So, good news, Blagojevich said sarcastically, he wouldn't be able to ask Krozel for money any longer after January 1. So this was it, Krozel recalled; Blagojevich wanted him to fund-raise before then.

He got the message, Krozel said. Only the governor had discretion over the tollway proposals, and Blagojevich had mentioned them almost in the same breath as asking Krozel to raise campaign money. In politics, something like that wasn't happening by accident.

"I felt there was a connection between the amount I was going to raise and the project itself," Krozel said. "I thought if I couldn't raise any money then there wouldn't be a tollway bill."

———

At the first trial, Lon Monk had been the first key prosecution witness, and he had been the voice to tell jurors about the early years of the Blagojevich administration. At the second trial, he wasn't quite an afterthought, but he was called after Krozel and seemed to be relegated to the abbreviated role of backing up the accounts of others.

Cross-examination was a slog right out of the first trial, with Sorosky offering lines of questioning that seemed partly designed to plant ideas in the jury's heads and partly intended as a filibuster to ensure the defense wouldn't have to start putting on evidence before a weekend that was approaching. It started off with the classic attempt at making a cooperating witness look like a weasel who was a serial liar. Monk agreed he'd had no experience with campaigns before Blagojevich hired him as his campaign manager in 2002 and then his chief of staff. The new governor had simply trusted him because they had a solid friendship that went back decades.

"Yeah, he trusted me," Monk said.

Sorosky also thought he could score some points on the Rezko front. It was becoming clear Operation Board Games and Rezko were taking a back seat at the second trial and Rezko wasn't going to be called, so there was little risk dragging his name around. Monk again testified that he took cash from Rezko when he was chief of staff and that he hadn't told Blagojevich. That was one thing, but with news swirling of investigations, couldn't Monk have at least warned his "friend" to steer clear of the fund-raiser?

"This would clearly be a time when Rod would want your advice and counsel," Sorosky said, drawing one of more than one hundred objections that flew as he questioned Monk. The point was, that advice had never come as Monk just kept pocketing money. Didn't he go to law school? Wasn't he an intelligent person?

"Sometimes," Monk answered.

When Monk answered that his getting cash hadn't done anything to alter his attitude toward Rezko, Sorosky reacted with mock surprise, asking whether Monk knew he was under oath. Objection again.

"Don't do it again, Mr. Sorosky," Zagel said, growing more agitated.

The objections continued, for compound questions and irrelevant questions but mostly for argumentative questions. Sometimes minutes would go by without Monk's voice even being heard in the room as Sorosky tried to formulate questions that the judge might actually let Monk answer, and then Niewoehner repeatedly stood to object. Monk sat and stared at times with his chin resting on his hand.

Sorosky did work through some of the tapes with Monk, pointing out times when he had lied to John Johnston about having talked to Blagojevich on his behalf and then turning around and lying to Blagojevich about how soon a campaign contribution might be coming from Johnston. At one point Monk had lied about going to play golf, Sorosky pointed out, telling Blagojevich he was taking his father to a military reunion.

"You wouldn't even tell that truthful statement to your old friend, would you?" he asked. Objection yet again.

———

More than two years after his arrest, and after prosecutors twice had presented their evidence that the onetime governor of Illinois had abused the powers of his office and turned his decision on naming a US Senator into an illicit auction, it was again Blagojevich's turn to put on a case. And this time, he wasn't going to let the opportunity float by without making some noise.

Team Blagojevich came out of the gate with both guns blazing, dragging into court both a sitting congressman and the new mayor of Chicago. The star power was surely an attempt at distracting the jury after it had heard the government's abbreviated but still confident case. But Blagojevich hoped to challenge the very allegation that anything had been offered for the Senate seat by anyone at all. Not only had the alleged swap never been consummated, but if there wasn't even anyone on the other end of the bargaining table, what had Blagojevich really been doing? Wasn't that almost the same thing as standing out on the sidewalk and mumbling to yourself?

First up was US Representative Jesse Jackson Jr., who strode into court in a dark suit and a silvery tie. Federal court surely was one of the last places he wanted to spend the day, but the charismatic politician swore to tell the truth and looked relatively comfortable as he took a seat on the witness stand. He described his congressional district as running from around the Museum of Science and Industry to University Park in the south suburbs, and then he was asked if he knew the defendant.

"I know Governor—former governor Blagojevich," Jackson said, motioning toward the defense table. "The guy sitting over there in the corner with the gray suit."

Blagojevich gave a little knowing wave back to Jackson with a look on his face that suggested, if nothing else, he was going to get some satisfaction from pulling another politician back into the fray. Jackson said that in the fall of 2008, he knew Blagojevich had the responsibility of naming a senator to replace Obama and that he wanted that post for himself—and badly. He said his strategy was to basically run a public campaign for the seat. He had been vocal and unapologetic about pursuing it. He had visited the editorial boards of newspapers and enlisted the help of other politicians to support him. He had asked prominent people to write letters on his behalf and done national TV shows talking about it, all in the hope of generating a groundswell of support that might push Blagojevich to recognize a public demand to have Jackson installed in the Senate.

Jackson acknowledged that yes, in fact, he had met with Nayak and Bedi on October 28, 2008.

"I talked with scores of people about the US Senate seat," Jackson said.

At that meeting or anytime that fall, Sorosky asked, had Jackson ever requested the Senate seat in exchange for fund-raising?

"No, sir, I did not," Jackson said in a definitive tone, answering a moment later that he hadn't ordered it, either.

Jackson eventually had gotten an audience with Blagojevich, just the day before the governor's arrest. He said he had organized a binder of his accomplishments to bring along and rely on, not a cash bid. The congressman slipped on some reading glasses as he leafed through it on the stand, telling Sorosky that it appeared to be the notebook he had put together. He had met with Blagojevich for some ninety minutes that day, Jackson remembered, and the topic of fund-raising had not come up. Never had he offered campaign cash if he were named to the seat, he said again.

"Absolutely not," Jackson said with an earnest look on his face.

Niewoehner cross-examined Jackson, who again described how he had taken his push for the Senate seat to the people of the state. His relationship with Blagojevich in the fall of 2008 was "frosty at best," he acknowledged, saying he wasn't then on speaking terms with the governor.

The prosecutor then asked about Nayak, who Jackson described as close to him. Nayak was "a likable guy," Jackson told the jury. "The kind of gentleman you would welcome into your house."

There was no mention of the scandal that had effectively ended thoughts of another of Jackson's political ambitions the year before. Nayak had told federal authorities that Jackson directed him to make the cash offer for the seat but also asked him to fly a female "social acquaintance" from Washington to Chicago to visit him. Jackson had again denied the cash offer but apologized for the news of the other woman, saying it was a private matter that he and his wife were dealing with. The story had broken just as the race to replace the retiring Richard Daley as Chicago mayor was beginning to take shape, essentially derailing any idea Jackson had to angle for that post and clearing another hurdle for Rahm Emanuel.

The problems between Blagojevich and Jackson went back to Blagojevich's first campaign for governor, when Jackson had decided not to endorse his fellow congressman in the 2002 Democratic primary. Blagojevich had never forgotten it. Jackson also had been asked for $25,000 for Blagojevich by then-congressman Bill Lipinski, he said, though Lipinski would later deny it in a brief appearance of his own on the witness stand. Jackson said Lipinski reminded him that Illinois Republicans had enjoyed a stranglehold on the governor's mansion in the state for decades, and Blagojevich was a chance to break their string of wins. Jackson hadn't exactly jumped at the suggestion.

"No chance," he said.

And as it turned out, Blagojevich wouldn't forget that either.

After he was elected, Blagojevich had traveled to Washington with Mayor Daley in 2003 for a visit by Illinois leaders. Jackson told Blagojevich that his wife, Sandi, a lawyer who would go on to become a Chicago alderman, was interested in a position in his administration. What she should do, Jackson recalled Blagojevich saying, was get his wife's resume and biography to Rezko, who by then was controlling significant state post picks. Jackson said he wound up hand-delivering them to Rezko himself, and Rezko had told him that his wife was being considered for director of the Illinois Lottery. That was encouraging, but it wasn't to be. Sometime later, Jackson said he was watching the news and saw a story about Blagojevich naming a lottery director. Needless to say, "It wasn't my wife," Jackson told the jury.

Months later, Blagojevich was back in Washington for another Illinois visit, Jackson said as Blagojevich sat at the defense table with his head resting on his chin. The two were in the same meeting room, Jackson remembered, but there was a bit of a chill in the air. Jackson said he got the sense right away that Blagojevich wasn't going to do anything for Sandi. And as he was leaving, Blagojevich had said as much, telling Jackson he was sorry nothing had worked out. And Blagojevich apparently couldn't resist rubbing it in a little. Jackson told the jury that as the Illinois governor was leaving the meeting, he had turned and "in classic Elvis Presley form" snapped both of his fingers and delivered a message in the King's voice.

"'You should've given me that $25,000,'" Jackson said, quoting the governor and wiggling slightly in the witness stand like he was doing Elvis himself. The congressman said he was sure Blagojevich was referring to the money that had been asked for during the 2002 campaign.

The defense was aware of Jackson's story, and it was one reason the Adams weren't really eager to call him to the stand during the first trial. The second team had thought it was worth having Jackson talk about not being behind any Nayak cash offer for the seat and had hoped to object and keep it out. Once Jackson was on the stand, it had slipped in after he described his relationship with Blagojevich as frosty. Goldstein sought to blunt it when he questioned Jackson again, asking about the snapping while pointing out that he wasn't really a big Elvis fan.

"You work for one," Jackson shot back and then repeated how Blagojevich had snapped at him. Many in the courtroom laughed as a sitting congressman again imitated the former governor of Illinois imitating Elvis Presley. You know, Jackson said of how Blagojevich spoke to him, like, "Thank ya veruh much."

Moments after Jackson walked out of court, the next witness came through the doors of the courtroom. Jurors were about as wide-eyed as they had been when they first came into court and saw Blagojevich sitting at the defense table in front of them. Rahm Emanuel walked up the aisle of the court-room in a crisp suit, his back straight in his normal gait. He didn't glance toward Blagojevich as he made his way to the front of the courtroom to be sworn in by Zagel. As he sat on the witness stand and looked toward Shel-don Sorosky, he had a slight smile on his face that seemed to be somewhere between irritation and amusement. He offered only a quick "fine" when the defense attorney asked how he was but cracked a wider smile when Sorosky asked him for his current occupation.

"Thank you, mayor of the city of Chicago," Emanuel answered.

Was it fair to say that was sort of a new job? Sorosky asked.

"Unless your subscription to the newspaper ended recently, yes," Eman-uel said.

From there, the questions the defense was allowed to ask were pretty tightly controlled. The judge wasn't going to allow a fishing expedition into what Emanuel had or hadn't done or decided to do in connection with Blagojevich's offers on the Senate seat. As Sorosky spoke to Emanuel, the mayor leaned in toward the microphone as if he already knew exactly what he was going to say.

Sorosky asked if anyone had come to him in 2006 to say Blagojevich was holding up the grant for Chicago Academy until Emanuel's brother held a fund-raiser.

"No," Emanuel said, drawing his lips tightly together after he spoke the word.

He answered only "yes" when asked if Obama was elected president in 2008 and whether he was a key player on the subsequent transition team that fall. "Yes," Valerie Jarrett was a potential candidate for the Senate seat, and "yes" he knew her, and "yes" he had advocated for her.

So, Sorosky said, winding up just a little bit, had anyone come to him and said, Mr. Emanuel, Valerie Jarrett can be appointed a senator by Governor Blagojevich, but in order for that to happen, you have to use your influence to see that an advocacy group be established and funded for Blagojevich to lead?

"No," Emanuel said.

The defense hadn't been allowed to get into whether Emanuel really was interested in helping Blagojevich any further with any other plan he might have had for the seat. Zagel already had barred the defense from getting into a meeting Emanuel had with US Senator Dick Durbin and Obama political czar David Axelrod just the day before Blagojevich's arrest in which the Blagojevich idea of appointing Lisa Madigan to the seat in a political deal had come up. Blagojevich himself would have to talk about discussions he had with Emanuel about him agreeing to talk to Obama about the possibility of brokering such a deal if the jury was to hear about it. And the defense hadn't wandered into Emanuel's knowledge of earlier trade offers Blagojevich had made, including being named secretary of health and human services.

Emanuel stepped from the witness stand in less than five minutes and walked right back out of the courtroom. He left from a parking lot underneath the courthouse so he didn't have to pass through the lobby where a bank of news cameras was in place that might have captured shots for the evening news. It was only later that Emanuel had spoken dismissively of finally making an appearance at the Blagojevich trial. It had taken longer for him to get there from city hall a few blocks away, he said, than it had for him to testify.

18

"My Words"

If Blagojevich really was "running for innocent," as reporters liked to joke, he was about to give the campaign speech of his life. Many thought as soon as he was charged he was destined to take things on himself. There was little chance he wouldn't eventually get up from a defense table, straighten his suit jacket, give Patti a peck on the cheek, and walk up to the witness stand to try to talk his way out of it.

As he stood and glanced over the room, he appeared to make eye contact with a few people, giving sharp nods of his head like a politician giving last-second greetings to people he knew before a speech and making it look like the room was his.

The idea of Blagojevich not trying to explain to a jury what he was doing on all of those wiretaps was so contrary to his personality, it was almost unthinkable. Blagojevich not testifying was like a trained greyhound deciding not to chase a lure or a great actor passing on a chance to perform. It was in his nature to take the stand, to speak his mind. Blagojevich had spent months leading up to his first trial promising to do it, which only added to the surprise when he had passed on the chance to talk to the 2010 jury. He had taken the advice of his lawyers during round one, had stayed silent, and later thought it was a big mistake.

Many thought that Blagojevich was driven to the witness stand during the second trial by Judge Zagel, and in many ways he was. During the first trial, Zagel had given the defense more leeway, beliving Schar would get

407

to clean it all up during a cross-examination of the ex-governor, which of course never occurred. So because of the switcheroo the first time, Zagel had kept a much tighter leash on Blagojevich and his lawyers during the second trial, effectively increasing Blagojevich's need to testify. Many of the explanations that Blagojevich wanted to give were only going to come from him. But the truth of the matter is, very little of that meant anything to Blagojevich by 2011. The look on his face when asked if he would testify at the second trial made it obvious: his eyes would narrow slightly, his jaw would clench, and he would nod his head, even while saying he wouldn't make any promises.

When he finally did walk to the front of the courtroom, he had a head bob for the jury, too, and then another to the court security officer standing near the witness stand. There was no hesitation when he turned to the judge and raised his right hand. He sat and looked forward determinedly, seated upright with his hands in front of him as if it were a debate and the format called for him to be seated at a table with his opponents. He told the jury his name, that he used to be their governor, and that he was there that day to tell them the truth.

There were many benefits to Blagojevich testifying on his own behalf, despite the risk of opening himself up to cross-examination. First, to the defense, the case was really about intent. His lawyers wanted the jury to think Blagojevich had never really meant to cross any legal lines, even if by listening to the tapes they thought he had. Maybe they could forgive any accidental transgression, if they got to know Blagojevich. His version of the case was that he could barely control his mouth, from his free-flowing profanity to discussions of what to do with a US Senate seat. Blagojevich claimed his idea of a strategy session was to throw out any and every thought that entered his head and then sift through dozens of them to find a good one, like some kind of prospector panning for mental gold. What better way to demonstrate that than having Blagojevich babble on right there in court?

And of course the other benefit was that after meeting and hearing Blagojevich and spending time with him, most people tended to find themselves liking him even if they didn't want to. He was so goofy and seemingly loopy, many people found him to be an engaging guy who probably would be pretty fun to hit a bar with or sit next to at a ballgame. There could be no harm in having jurors thinking, "This sort of crazy guy with the hair who's spouting poetry and historical facts is the criminal mastermind we've been hearing about for weeks?"

So Blagojevich's last attempt to show that he wasn't a devious cheat who had brought the Illinois governor's office to new levels of corruption began with his life story. There was the growing up in Chicago and the little league baseball. There was the remembering of long ago jobs and school days, the struggles and the meeting of the love of his life. As with anyone else, there were failures and victories, partings and meetings, setbacks and the strength to keep going. Blagojevich had gone from shoeshine boy to governor of Illinois. One of his loves and great fixations was US history, and he had longed to see his story end with him as the kind of figure that others might study. He did believe that anyone in America could be president, up to and including Serbian kids from Chicago's Northwest Side who like Elvis and memorize encyclopedias.

"You know, you hear these tapes and these conversations—and I'll have a chance to talk about a lot of them and talk about some of the tremendous flaws I have—I think a lot of some of what I am is, deep down there are certain insecurities," Blagojevich told them earnestly. "And one of them was, and is I think, it's an insecurity that can drive you to work hard and try to make yourself better, but it's also an insecurity that, you know, kind of have petty sides to it and flaws and fear."

It might have been one of the most truthful things Blagojevich would say in more than a week of testimony, but the statement didn't hang in the air long before Aaron Goldstein used it as a bridge for Blagojevich to address one thing that might have been on the minds of some jurors when the tapes were brought up. Blagojevich's blue language was memorable, and there was a church choir director on the jury, for crying out loud, and ten other women who Blagojevich probably would never have dreamed of cussing in front of. Did Blagojevich always talk like that? Goldstein asked, setting up Blagojevich to say he was sorry.

"You know, Aaron, this morning as I was leaving, my daughter—my daughter is Amy and my little one Annie—and they were leaving for school, and I asked them, 'Now kiss your daddy,'" Blagojevich answered. "I told my older one, a teenager, 'Give daddy a kiss for good luck. I'm going to get on the stand and testify, begin to set the record straight,' and my teenager Amy said, 'Dad, I'm to blow you a kiss 'cause I got lip gloss on.' I said OK, so she blew me a kiss and she said, 'Good luck. Watch your language.'"

He had said he was sorry before in front of news cameras, Blagojevich said, but he wanted to personally apologize to the jury. "When I hear myself on the tapes swearing like that, I'm an f'ing jerk, and I apologize," he said.

There was clearly a collection of talking points Blagojevich wanted to make, and Goldstein was trying to get to many without his questioning seeming forced or stilted. Occasionally things sounded a bit scripted, such as when Goldstein joked about Blagojevich failing drafting in high school and later sending a law school application to Harvard, of all places.

But most of the time, a door would open slightly, and Blagojevich would plow forward into something he wanted the jury to know, chiefly that he liked to talk, just in case they were missing that. In addition to being R-rated, the tapes showed that incessant talking was his management style.

"I've used these examples—sometimes the press goes out and says I compare myself to Winston Churchill or Gandhi or somebody like that. I'm not doing that," he started. "But those are historical figures who I have great admiration for, and you can, I believe, draw life lessons from their lives, their struggles, how they dealt with adversities, the things, the principles, the purposes that they committed their lives to. And Churchill had a way of governing that I was always moved by, and that was he would constantly throw out ideas, and one of his adjutant generals or commanders would say, you know, Winston has ten ideas every day and one of 'em is good."

And there it was in a nutshell. The Blagojevich defense, wrapped in freedom of speech and the idea that Winston Churchill could have fallen into the same historical trap he did if the circumstances were the same. Blagojevich obviously couldn't argue that it wasn't him on the tapes or even that what he was saying was being misconstrued. What he was saying was fairly clear, so he needed to adopt the words as his own while at the same time decriminalizing them. What good leaders do, he said, is look at any available option, no matter how outlandish, and whittle the pile of choices down into a manageable list of real options.

"Abraham Lincoln would read out loud because he wanted to hear himself and he wanted to hear himself think," Blagojevich testified.

And just below the surface of the direct argument was something both Blagojevich defenses had tried to hint at throughout. Unable to argue it directly, Blagojevich hoped the jury had picked up the idea that many of the men he was bouncing his ideas off were attorneys who might have warned him to stop if some of his wildest ideas could land him in prison. There was more than one way that the jury could come around to thinking Blagojevich shouldn't face a criminal conviction for just talking.

Another thing he wanted the jury to know was that he had trusted Lon Monk. He had told the jury about loving Monk for sticking by him during his law school struggles. He had described getting Monk's advice when he wanted to ask Patti to marry him and then having Monk stand up at his wedding and read the Twenty-third Psalm. Monk was one of his closest confidants, and when he had taken money from Rezko and gotten himself in some hot water, he had turned on Blagojevich, who didn't know about the payoff. This would place an unfair betrayal at the root of the government's case against him.

And still another idea he wanted jurors to get was that while he had worked as an attorney, he was by no means overly familiar with the law. He wanted the jury to think that independent of the warnings from lawyers that never came, he was unsure whether what he was doing was right or wrong.

"I never, ever took a federal case. I never had a federal case. I never even got close to a federal case or never felt I was capable or competent, remotely, to handle a federal case. I stayed in the state courts," he said.

"Never handled a federal criminal case here?" Goldstein asked. Nope.

The former governor of Illinois, former congressman, and former prosecutor and defense lawyer was a legal field mouse. Clueless in the ways of the law and apparently surrounded by muted attorneys, Blagojevich had taken to his normal habit of spouting off every possibility for political moves such as deciding whom to appoint to the US Senate. Federal agents had taped him in an inopportune moment when he was stumbling through some of those thoughts out loud. It was a position that would seemingly apply to whatever tape Blagojevich wanted to go over on the stand, but it didn't stop him from going through many and layering even more explanations atop his overarching view of the evidence. Even though he thought much of what the jury had heard was just talk, he went through each scenario the government had presented to make specific denials. It was a tricky rope to walk because, in a way, Blagojevich was undercutting himself by explaining too much. It was like he wanted the jury to know that he didn't think he was doing anything wrong, but in case they disagreed, he had explanations for each episode to fall back on.

He would start with the 2006 school grant involving Rahm Emanuel, whom he remembered meeting in 1996 in Washington. Blagojevich was a Democratic candidate for Congress, so he had taken a trip to visit the powers that be. Emanuel was then in the Clinton White House and had shown Blagojevich the Oval Office. It was smaller in person than it is on television, Blagojevich told the jury.

Once Blagojevich became governor, Emanuel took over for him in the US House representing the Fifth Congressional District and had remained a political ally. It was a link that would develop over time, and, like many political relationships, it had its ebbs and flows. But at any rate, the Blagojevich defense contended, they were never enemies, and Emanuel wasn't someone that the Illinois governor would have gone out of his way to cross and squeeze for campaign money. Blagojevich claimed to have only a vague memory of Emanuel asking him for the school grant at all during his first term. He did remember the request itself but said at the time he didn't even pay close attention to which school it was for. The approval was basically reflexive. The school—whichever one it was—was in the Fifth Congressional District, and Emanuel had wanted it, and Blagojevich was eager to help. He said his memory was that he had simply directed some staffer to find whatever money it was that the congressman wanted and make it happen.

Blagojevich said he heard from Harris in August 2006 that Tusk was hearing from Emanuel's office about a grant for the Chicago Academy. The congressman's staff was complaining that the school hadn't gotten its money. Blagojevich told the jury he was actually confused and that he thought the original request had been for a different school, and that the money had gone out long before.

"I think I may have asked him or he told me. I think I expressed a little frustration with Bradley Tusk, our deputy governor, and asked is this—was this Bradley recommitting—committing a new grant or acting without my authority to do something along those lines?" Blagojevich said.

At any rate, Blagojevich said he was puzzled, so he asked Harris to look into what was going on. He wasn't putting a stop order on the grant so he could make some kind of shakedown effort, Blagojevich insisted, just making sure he knew the status of whatever grant it was Emanuel's office was asking about.

"My recollection is I asked him, 'Chicago Academy, that rings a bell,' and then he told me. He described it. It was the former Wright Junior College, which I know a lot because I took the ACT exam there," Blagojevich remembered. "Twice."

Still, Blagojevich said he didn't 100 percent know the grant he was being asked about wasn't actually a second grant for the same school. So just to be careful, he told Harris to pay the money out only as Chicago Academy incurred bills. Again—nothing nefarious. It was just an overabundance of caution, not an attempt to slow drip the money out over the nonexistent fund-raiser.

Blagojevich said he didn't remember talking to Tusk at all about the school and its grant, much less telling him to sit on it over Ari Emanuel raising cash for him. He didn't say that to Lon Monk either, Blagojevich told the jury. He had asked John Wyma to ask Rahm Emanuel to ask his brother about a fund-raiser when they were in California, Blagojevich said.

"I was out in LA on my own fund-raising issues in the Indo-American community with Bollywood stars," he said. "I remember that."

Wyma had known Blagojevich was out there, he said, and asked him to stop by a fund-raiser at Ari Emanuel's home that he was throwing for Rahm. It had turned out to be a memorable night. The governor who would one day spend plenty of time on national television was in his element.

"It was a fascinating fund-raiser because there was Larry David, the guy who created *Seinfeld* with Seinfeld. I'm a big fan of his *Curb Your Enthusiasm*, and I enjoyed talking to him," Blagojevich glowed. "We had somebody in common. We hired a speech writer that was a young comic—"

"Objection," Schar said, finally unable to bite his tongue any longer.

"I knew that was going to happen," Blagojevich said of the prosecutor. Anyway, meeting David had been a thrill. Not quite like meeting Elvis, he said, milking the moment, but fun. The night and the home were beautiful, and Blagojevich recalled asking Wyma afterward if Ari Emanuel might ever host something like that for him. There was no thought of the Chicago Academy, Blagojevich said. It had just been a good night, and he was curious about whether it could be repeated.

———

The fall of 2008 had been a busy time trying to fill the Friends of Blagojevich campaign fund. The governor had been reelected two years earlier, but trying to bring in cash was no less important in the middle of the term. The amount of money raised was a reflection of power, and Goldstein asked Blagojevich why he was still interested in fund-raising in the latter stages of that year.

"Well, the realities of politics in America are that if you want to be competitive politically for most offices, you have to have the campaign resources to be able to take your case in the media age to the people, whether it be through television ads, whether it be through radio ads, whether it be through direct mail," Blagojevich answered.

"Unless you're independently wealthy, this is how our laws are, and there's no accident why something like two-thirds of US senators are millionaires or multimillionaires—"

"Objection again," said Schar.

Goldstein tried to focus things. How about starting with why it was important as a governor? Blagojevich replied that a big war chest meant independence. He could have courage to take positions that weren't popular with the political establishment if he had a lot of money at his disposal, so he wouldn't have to count on party leadership when it was time to run again. A big fund meant the freedom to lose friends and allies in the name of getting things done for people. No matter what the office was, it meant the ability to fight without worrying when you were leading, he said, winding into yet another campaign speech.

"And so my philosophy was from the very beginning based on my understanding of the history . . . of previous governors in Illinois, specifically Dan Walker, who took on Mayor Daley's father in the Democratic establishment and then was defeated—"

"Wait, wait, wait," Judge Zagel said, sounding like an exasperated grade school teacher dealing with a kid who just doesn't get it.

"Sorry, Judge," came the answer, as Blagojevich humbly hunched his shoulders just a bit under the scolding. He would shorten things up. You could afford to make some people unhappy, is what he meant.

He had set deadlines that year, he told the jury. One was the disclosure deadline that would allow the public and the media to see what was in the campaign fund, including at the end of the year. That would let everyone see how politically viable he was. And even more importantly, the end of 2008 would see the ethics bill become law, making it illegal for companies doing business with the state of Illinois from making major campaign donations. That was going to seriously limit what Blagojevich could do in 2009, making the last six months of 2008 even more crucial. Organizations, businesses, and contractors that always had pumped into the Blagojevich campaign coffers were going to be cut off. He told the jury he believed the bill hadn't gone far enough, and he had tried to amendatorily veto the legislation so he could rewrite it and also apply it to state legislators and party leaders. There had been a quiet deal with Emil Jones in the Senate not to override the veto, but Jones had betrayed the deal. That said, Blagojevich told the jury he really did like Emil Jones, bringing yet another objection from Schar.

"That he really likes Emil Jones may stand," Zagel said.

Jones had called the bill to a vote after taking a call from Obama, who thought the stalled ethics bill in Illinois would be a problem for him on the presidential campaign trail. Negative ads were running in Pennsylvania featuring Blagojevich, and Obama wanted to take the air out of the argument that his home state was still an ethics disaster. Blagojevich argued with Jones about sending the broader bill to the Illinois House and having Obama call Madigan and pressure him to pass it, but Jones had eventually decided just to push through the original bill as it was.

So, despite the defeat, what did that mean for the remainder of 2008?

"That you can still raise money from those businesses, contractors, corporations, whomever legally with unlimited amounts up until the end of the year," Blagojevich said. It was an important point for the defense, trying to take some of the steam out of the pay-to-play scenario and show what Blagojevich's mindset was and his lack of criminal intent. He knew what the law was in 2008 and said he intended to follow the new law in 2009, like it or not. There was no problem asking men like Krozel and Johnston for fund-raising help prior to then, Blagojevich said. "It was perfectly, absolutely legal, and it was a common practice up until the law would change after the first of the year."

Johnston's business with the state of Illinois was the recapture bill, which was intended to support horse racing in Illinois and send some casino profits his way. Blagojevich denied shaking Johnston down by not signing the bill until he got a hefty campaign contribution. He had known Johnston and his father for years, Blagojevich said, and had not threatened them. The men were regular contributors who had donated a good deal of money over the years. Blagojevich credited them with widening his network of fund-raisers and seemed especially into the fact the father and son had done business with George Steinbrenner of the New York Yankees.

The Johnstons had even gotten Steinbrenner to host a fund-raiser for him at Yankee Stadium. Patti and his older daughter, Amy, had gotten to go.

"First time I met Donald Trump. He walked in with Regis Philbin and made a contribution at that event," Blagojevich said proudly.

Anyway, between 2002 and 2008, the Johnstons had probably given him $300,000, Blagojevich guessed, hoping to help place in the jury's mind that the father and son were hardly virginal characters who would have recoiled in horror when asked about making another donation prior to January 1, 2009. They were sophisticated and political, Blagojevich said, recalling how he had hung out with them at dinners and seen them at plenty of events.

What they cared about was the horse industry, and they had given money to Republicans and Democrats alike.

Blagojevich's first attempts to explain recordings in the case came the next morning, Friday, May 27, before he could retreat over the weekend and collect his thoughts. He had a number of excuses for why he had held off on signing the racing bill, with none of them having to do with the Johnstons' unwillingness to give Monk a check for him. One was that Monk kept telling him the money was about to come in, so he didn't want to sign the bill and then have the check appear and have things look bad. The media would have been all over it. Instead, he said, he hoped the money would come and he could wait a while before finally signing. The other reason had to do with "Madigan shenanigans," he said. Mike Madigan was as crafty as they came, and every bill had to be scrubbed thoroughly for poison pills that the speaker might attach to legislation that everyone thought was agreed upon. That could include adding "something in that might take free transportation away from senior citizens, for example," Blagojevich told the jury, passing on no opportunities to slip in small reminders of parts of his record that he thought jurors might like.

And Blagojevich also said he had in his mind the call he had with Kelly on Thanksgiving 2008. Kelly had mentioned talking to a friend, former NFL quarterback Bernie Kosar, who lived in Florida and was close to former Florida governor Jeb Bush. Kelly, who had been the administration's earlier link to the Johnstons, had mentioned maybe having Kosar talk to Bush about going to his brother, then the president, about a pardon for Kelly. To Blagojevich, it was possible Kelly was being used to push him to sign the bill and was hoping to get something for himself. Blagojevich tried to explain to the jury how Kelly knew the Johnstons and that Steinbrenner was then living in Tampa. Maybe Steinbrenner would be brought in to talk to Jeb Bush, too, if Kelly could get Blagojevich to sign. Wacky, but the earnest-sounding Blagojevich was really trying to sell it. Quinlan had told him Kelly was interested in the bill, and Blagojevich said he was putting two and two and two and maybe two more together.

"It was a big bold red flag to be very careful with this bill," Blagojevich said, looking toward prosecutors. "I was very aware that the ladies and gentlemen at that table were investigating me."

Monk was doing a delicate dance in the fall of 2008. He was being paid very well by the Johnstons to be their lobbyist and use his rare access to push their agenda with the governor, while at the same time being counted on by Blagojevich to bring in campaign money. When he spoke to the Johnstons, he promised to prod his former boss to sign the legislation they wanted, and when he met with Blagojevich, the focus was on turning around and getting campaign cash from them.

In early December of that year, it was the money-collecting part of Monk's split personality that was captured on federal recordings.

"I wanna go to him without crossing the line and say, give us the fucking money," Monk had said. It was an episode at the Blagojevich campaign offices that prosecutors said was the two men rehearsing how Monk might go about delivering what they considered an extortion message. It was supposed to be a shakedown, just not sound like one.

As he started to describe his version of what was going on in the meeting, Blagojevich had a look on his face like the answer was clear. One had nothing to do with the other. It didn't seem like something he needed to read into, he said, as he pursed his lips and gave half a shrug. He had always known Monk to be smart and honest and understand where the boundaries were. Both men had done this before and could navigate a gray area.

"I took that literally to mean just that: not cross any lines," Blagojevich said, as Niewoehner shot Schar a sideways look at the government's table.

And that innocent explanation carried over into follow-up calls on the Johnstons. Blagojevich's excuse centered on the idea that Monk was trustworthy and that he and Johnston knew what they were doing. It was only later when he started to worry that Johnston could feel too much pressure if he got a call from the governor himself. Blagojevich had never called, leaving the play up to Monk, who told Blagojevich he had gotten in John Johnston's face about the contribution. "Good," Blagojevich had answered.

That was right, Blagojevich repeated on the stand. Good.

"Good, sounds like you didn't cross any lines."

Now Niewoehner was smirking openly, as Schar looked down at the table and visibly shook his head.

＝＝＝＝

By Monday, it was still too early to tell if the jury could be buying Blagojevich's explanation that he was part aggressive fund-raiser and part victim of circumstance. It might be tough to expect them to believe that time and time again—in conversations that they could hear played in court—it was just unfortunate coincidence that Blagojevich was involved in discussions that could be so often misconstrued.

His third day on the witness stand started with his microphone mysteriously going in and out as he answered questions, dropping his voice to only a normal speaking volume in the courtroom over and over again and making it impossible to hear him in the back of the gallery. Off and on it clicked as Blagojevich looked down at it and cocked his head.

"That's not my fault," he said, chuckling toward the jurors, who were ushered from the room so they didn't have to sit there while it was fixed.

One quick look determined the cause. Blagojevich had sat his binder of transcripts on the base of the microphone and on the switch. When he leaned on the binder, it would turn the mic off, and when he lifted his weight up slightly, it was popping back on. Problem solved, so the jury filed back in.

"I misspoke. Apparently it was my fault," Blagojevich told them as Zagel peered down with a look that almost could have been interpreted as pity.

These aren't the moments you're hoping for when you're trying to get the jury to swallow a tale of bad luck and truthiness, but there it was, and Blagojevich had no choice but to plow onward. Back to the fall of 2008, when Krozel said he got the squeeze over the tollway expansion plan. Krozel had said there was no doubt in his mind that Blagojevich was linking Krozel's ability to bring in cash to a larger tollway expansion than the one the governor was first announcing.

There was a reason for all of that, Blagojevich offered, and again it had everything to do with his archenemy, Michael Madigan. He wasn't holding out to extort Krozel and wait for money; he was going slowly to keep the pressure on Madigan to move on the large-scale capital bill. If he gave too much to the road builders right away, they wouldn't have any incentive to keep any pressure on the powerful house speaker to get them the larger package.

Blagojevich acknowledged he did meet with Krozel that September in the campaign office and that both the expansion and fund-raising were discussed. But the two never had been linked, he said. Actually, Blagojevich said he remembered telling Krozel he probably was *not* going to support the more significant tollway plan because he thought it would more than likely have to include a toll hike.

The campaign money "would be very helpful to me" is what he recalled saying, but that was it, Blagojevich said. He hadn't put the arm on the guy.

He would appreciate some money help, is how he said he phrased it, though he said he also did mention that the ethics law going into effect at the end of the year was going to put a damper on such efforts in the future. In the most innocent explanations for his conduct, Blagojevich again said he was on the line with a seasoned political player who should have been able to handle what was happening and not get the wrong idea. He couldn't say it, but Blagojevich wanted the jury to get the idea that when the FBI had come around after his arrest, men like Krozel were willing to shape the meetings in a different way to toe the government line and keep themselves out of trouble.

It was a similar situation with Children's Memorial Hospital. Blagojevich answered "no" at least a half-dozen times as Goldstein asked whether the discussions with Patrick Magoon were a shakedown attempt that fall. He hadn't demanded money, he hadn't threatened him, and he hadn't directed anyone to do it for him. Blagojevich said he never planned to hold up the increase in state reimbursement for the hospital, trying to tell the jury there was a specific reason why. Goldstein started to ask about something in his own life that had crystallized children's health care for Blagojevich, who counted his efforts to make health insurance for families his greatest accomplishments in public office.

"My life experiences shaped my commitment—" Blagojevich started to say, when Schar objected. After another try, it was the same reaction, with Schar even throwing his hands up in protest.

It would take a few minutes before Blagojevich could find a way to tell the jury that a twelve-year-old cousin had died at Children's Memorial Hospital in 1967. Blagojevich was willing to be muzzled some by the prosecutor, but not on that point.

Among the calls Blagojevich and his lawyers had to contend with was the one between Blagojevich and Greenlee, when the then-governor had asked about the rate increase. Blagojevich had asked if it could be held if need be. "Budget concerns, right?" is what Blagojevich had said, which the prosecution argued was Blagojevich facetiously "explaining" the reasoning to Greenlee, who did shelve the plan.

Blagojevich testified that it wasn't a great budget year in 2008 and that he should be taken literally on the call. Things had been so bad that he had been forced to use his veto power to amend the budget, and there were cuts happening everywhere. Still, he had a great relationship with the hospital and was prepared to go ahead with the rate increase. Blagojevich said he had the understanding that his staff—namely Greenlee—was finding the dollars for the plan and carrying out his wishes. Additionally, Blagojevich said he knew that he was going to be the one to call Magoon again in the near future about fund-raising, so he was just checking to make sure the hospital was definitely getting what was pledged.

The budget issues were the reason he asked Magoon not to talk publicly, Blagojevich said. He didn't ask Magoon not to say anything so he could extort him; he just didn't want everyone knowing that CMH was getting more state help when others were being asked to sacrifice and having their funding cut, Blagojevich explained.

"I was very clear to him I was breaking a policy," Blagojevich said. "I didn't want the word to get out because I was making an exception."

⸻

More than two years after his arrest, and after the better part of two federal trials and most of three days on the witness stand, Blagojevich was finally ready to answer questions—under oath—about the allegations he tried to peddle the US Senate seat that had been vacated by the president of the United States to the highest bidder. He had been awakened in his home by the head of the Chicago FBI and carted to court like a criminal. He had been impeached over his conduct. He was facing a long prison term. And he had told anyone and everyone who would listen that it was all a big misunderstanding. Now was the time to explain it away, if he could. Blagojevich was risking much opening himself up to the cross-examination that would follow in a few days, but he was taking a calculated risk his testimony was going to make it worth it.

Blagojevich started his explanations by repeating how his attempts to offer an exchange progressed and agreeing he had discussed his options "incessantly" during those key months.

Much of the talks had happened on calls to and from Blagojevich's house, where he had been "hunkered down" trying to make one of the biggest decisions of his time in office. He had been governor already for six years and wasn't counting on running again. He had made mistakes and done some things he was proud of, but his time as the state's chief executive was not going to last forever.

"I thought that this Senate seat was one of my last, best opportunities" to make a good decision, Blagojevich testified. The strategy involved all of the talking. He wasn't just indecisive; he was throwing out thoughts to see how people would react to them. Most of all, the governor wanted to hear how John Harris would respond to each idea. "The good ones, the bad ones, the stupid ones, the ugly ones," Blagojevich said.

Central for him was the Madigan deal, and he stayed on it throughout the early parts of his testimony. It had been on his mind from the beginning, he said, and was what he actually planned to do by December. His agenda would do good things for people, he said more than once, and he had to placate Madigan in 2008 to get it through before he left the governor's office.

He was also fearful that if Lisa wasn't the pick, a vengeful Madigan would punish him and strain things even more, creating even more gridlock, Blagojevich said.

"Her father was my nemesis," Blagojevich said. But apparently, he wasn't all bad. Blagojevich told the jury that he sometimes spoke with Madigan about raising kids in the glare of politics and that he thought Madigan was a good father. That brought an objection from Schar.

"I just want to say something nice about him, Judge," Blagojevich joked.

At any rate, the actual "deal" that Blagojevich said he was thinking of at the time called for him to appoint Lisa in exchange for the capital bill being passed, an expansion of health care, and a guarantee that there would be no increase in the state income tax while he was governor. Regarding alternative candidates, Blagojevich said the key to him was to replace Obama with another black senator from Illinois. The seat had also been held by Carol Moseley Braun, and Blagojevich said he thought it was important to keep that chain.

One African American who was not going to be chosen, Blagojevich swore, was Jesse Jackson Jr.

"My position was, no, not interested in it," he testified. Blagojevich said he knew what was being offered on that front, and it was not going to happen.

"I wasn't interested in making an appointment of a US senator in exchange for campaign fund-raising or accelerated fund-raising from my Indo-American supporters. I didn't want to do it," he said.

The jury had heard calls where Blagojevich had described Jackson supporters approaching him to "pay to play" and going so far as calling him at home. That was actually irritating, Blagojevich testified, and he had no plans to appoint Jackson regardless of any financial promise.

"It was just over the top."

That seemed believable, as Blagojevich's disdain for Jackson was obvious. And not far-fetched was Blagojevich's contention that he was dangling the idea of a Jackson appointment to the Washington establishment to get DC leadership to reach back and help him get Madigan to agree to his swap. But what was probable was that Blagojevich was simply pushing on all fronts at once. It wasn't necessarily either Lisa Madigan or Jackson in early December 2008. It may very well have been both, with Blagojevich wanting options for a choice he could make later in the month. If Madigan balked and nothing else materialized, Blagojevich would have the Jackson consolation prize.

But that wasn't going to cut it with the jury. The prosecutors' position was that just the asks were illegal and could get Blagojevich convicted. He had to find convincing ways to explain to jurors what he was thinking earlier in 2008 when it sure sounded like he was trying to get a paying position in exchange for appointing Valerie Jarrett. Blagojevich had heard from Harris that there was an Obama preference, and immediately he had asked what Harris thought he could get for that. In suggesting an appointment as secretary of health and human services, Blagojevich said, he was just imagining a way he might promote his main agenda item—health care for everyone, on a national stage. It was just out-loud wishful thinking, Blagojevich said. It was an issue he loved and something that was good for people. But he wanted the jury to think that he wasn't totally serious or at least that he didn't really expect it would ever happen. He might as well have said he would appoint Jarrett in exchange for a ride on the space shuttle.

It was like the poet Robert Browning had said.

"Ah, but a man's reach should exceed his grasp—or what's a heaven for?"

———

The morning of June 1, Blagojevich was ready to dive deeper into the allegations that he had tried to sell the seat and to explain to the jury that he truly believed that even a trade for a cabinet post was legal. Forming the foundation for him was his lifelong study of American history—and particularly presidential politics. Books were filled with examples of US presidents engaging in the kind of horse-trading Blagojevich was talking about, including bartering for appointments and the like.

Blagojevich hoped to walk the jury through his memories of such situations, while prosecutors argued that kind of testimony would only serve to muddy the water for jurors who would be forced to deal with irrelevant testimony from a rambling Blagojevich. Judge Zagel decided he wanted to hear some of what Blagojevich might say before jurors took their seats, so Goldstein began his questioning with the jury still out of the room.

What followed was a ten-minute summary by a finally unbridled Blago-jevich, who threw out the names of more than a dozen historical figures as he tried to explain his thinking.

"When Ronald Reagan was potentially going to challenge President Ford in the Republican primaries for the Republican nomination for president, President Ford offered Ronald Reagan a cabinet position to not run against him. It was the Department of Transportation. Ronald Reagan rejected that. Then President Ford offered him an ambassadorship, the ambassadorship to the Court of St. James, England. Ronald Reagan rejected that," Blagojev-ich began.

"And then after Ronald Reagan created an organization called Citizens for Reagan and became even more likely that he was going to challenge the incumbent president, President Ford dispatched his chief of staff at that time, Donald Rumsfeld, to offer future President Reagan a cabinet position in the Department of Commerce."

In the 1950s, Eisenhower had promised California governor Earl Warren a seat on the US Supreme Court to get him to back the Republican ticket.

"Abraham Lincoln, in order to get the Pennsylvania delegation to back him at the Republican convention at the Wigwam here in Chicago, made a political deal with the governor of Pennsylvania, a guy by the name of Simon Cameron," Blagojevich went on. "He appointed Simon Cameron to a cabinet position, and it was an important one, the secretary of war, at a time when our country was tearing apart and American boys were killing each over the issues of slavery and the union."

Never mind that Cameron was notorious for corruption and resigned his post after a year. That ending was left out of Blagojevich's version, as was the quote attributed to Cameron that an honest politician is one who, once he is bought, "will stay bought."

Even in more recent times, Blagojevich said, political deals are common-place. He said he believed Hillary Rodham Clinton had abandoned her bid for the presidency in 2008 on the promise that Obama would make a large donation to the Clinton campaign fund and then make her his secretary of state. All of his conversations with his staff and his experiences with politics and history had flavored his actions in 2008, Blagojevich said. That was his state of mind, and all of his recorded conversations were brainstorming, with the goal being to land in a place that would be good for people and totally legal.

"I mean, they liked the ideas, some of them, they didn't like others, but no one ever said you can't do it, it's illegal," Blagojevich told the judge. It was all an exploration to come up with the best option in a unique situation.

As far as his personal experience, Blagojevich said he had learned that in Illinois politics, "everything was a deal." He had sometimes complained to Patti that you couldn't just approach another politician and ask for support for something just on the basis of it being good for people.

Reid Schar was not impressed.

The prosecutor said none of what Blagojevich had said had a place in the trial. His opinion on whether what he was doing was legal or illegal didn't matter, and all of the talk of going over ideas with staffers, including Quinlan, was just another attempt at getting an "advice of counsel" defense through the back door. Allow the jury to hear what Blagojevich had just said, and the trial was headed straight for a morass from which it might never emerge.

Goldstein told Zagel the material was relevant because the case was all about Blagojevich's state of mind, and he should be able to explain how he saw the situation. Blagojevich was listening intently as the lawyers went back and forth, and, not surprisingly, he looked very disappointed when Zagel began to explain that he didn't agree with the defense argument. The jury already should have the general idea that Blagojevich was getting advice beyond what they were hearing on the tapes, and as far as normal political swapping, Zagel said the case the jury was considering didn't exactly match up. *United States v. Blagojevich* was nothing like "you vote for my bill and I'll vote for yours," Zagel said.

Worse for the ex-governor was the chatter about the creation of a charitable organization he could be employed to lead. What that amounted to was dollars going into his wallet in exchange for Jarrett's appointment, and that was absolutely a crime. Blagojevich shouldn't be allowed to wander into the world of what wasn't on tape, Zagel said, because it was too vague. What he was being asked to do was allow Blagojevich to say that just because no one specifically told him what he was doing was illegal, he should be justified in thinking it was not a crime. And to what end? That just wasn't the law, and Zagel said it wasn't going to fly in the remainder of the trial.

Additionally, Blagojevich had been taped numerous times saying he knew one thing could not be swapped for the other, so part of the argument went out the window. He could argue one thing *wasn't* in exchange for the other but not climb under the blanket that he thought everything he was doing was fine.

"Not honest belief that it was legal," Zagel said. "His belief was, quite clearly, at least as expressed on the tape, that one for the other was illegal. He is not claiming that he thought that that was OK."

What Blagojevich would say if he told the jury he acted in good faith would be to acknowledge the swapping, Zagel said. That was contradictory anyway to Blagojevich's contention that he never traded one thing for the other.

"So what the defense wants to do, as I understand it, is put him in a position where he can say even if it is one for the other, I still acted in good faith, which I don't think he can say," Zagel finally tried to explain. "What he could say is, or what he wants to say is, one for the other is legal. But the problem with that is, he's got that instruction which says he doesn't have to know it's legal. So the fact that what he thinks is legal or illegal—or the fact that he thinks it's legal, maybe the fact that he thinks it's illegal is not so good for him, but the fact that he thinks it is legal is not relevant here."

That left many in the courtroom scratching their heads, but the bottom line was that much of what Blagojevich wanted to say, the jury was not going to hear. Blagojevich could say he thought he could do what he had done because he did not think he was trading one thing for the other, but he wasn't going to be able to say he thought it was legal. What Blagojevich wanted to do might work on the street, Zagel said, but not in the arena they were working in now.

———

"Did you ever decide what you wanted to do with regard to the Senate seat?" Goldstein asked when the jury finally returned.

"No, I never got there," Blagojevich said.

But in his effort to try, Blagojevich denied ever threatening anyone, demanding anything, or otherwise shaking anyone down over it. Limited to what Zagel had allowed, Goldstein asked whether Blagojevich had taken part in all of his discussions on a Senate pick in good faith. Yes, Blagojevich answered, he had.

Many of his talks had taken place at his home, at a phone near a chair in his "little library" in the front portion of his home on the North Side.

Goldstein showed him photos of it, and then the jurors saw them on a screen in the courtroom. The room was comfortable and warm and smelled of old books, Blagojevich said, just the way he liked.

"There's my bust of Winston Churchill, do you see it?" Blagojevich asked as the jury looked up at the screen. "Blood, toil, tears, and sweat."

Churchill had uttered that phrase to the House of Commons as World War II was beginning. Blagojevich didn't tell the jury that, but he might as well have. If the jury hadn't figured out Blagojevich's love of history yet, they were continuously being bludgeoned over the head with it.

"Charles Dickens, a collection of Charles Dickens, there's Shakespeare, and some American authors like Hawthorne and others. There's different ones," Blagojevich said. "There's some philosophy books. I have a few Bibles in there. There's books on religion. There's a real good book called *God's Politics*—is he going to do that?"

Schar was standing to object as Blagojevich seemed poised to ramble through his entire collection. He had managed to slip in the Bibles before Schar protested. "I'll withdraw that," Blagojevich said on his own, half joking.

"Rod, did you read all those books?" Goldstein asked.

"I'm under oath, right?" Blagojevich continued. "No, but I have to say, I actually read, you know, a pretty good number of them, for better or for worse."

In one photo were the phone and the chair where Blagojevich had sat as he had many of his Senate discussions. There was one talk with Rahm Emanuel and another with former Speaker of the House Dennis Hastert, he wanted the jury to know. There were conversations with Greenlee and many, many conversations with Quinlan. Again, Blagojevich ran up to the line of what Zagel would allow, telling the jury he averaged three calls a day with his chief counsel and sometimes spoke to him five times a day.

To hear Blagojevich say it, Quinlan was nearly his very own Jiminy Cricket, in his pocket at all times. Constantly, continuously, repeatedly, repetitively, Blagojevich said, he was speaking to Quinlan. Before and after and during all of the taping. They had talked about Obama's interest and whether that could be leveraged into billions in federal money for Illinois, and that idea had colored the way he viewed the Senate pick going forward. But a few moments later, when Blagojevich wanted to describe how things that Quinlan had said influenced him, Zagel sustained repeated objections.

At the time, there were to be two parallel streams regarding the pick. One would be the public perception of a process of considering candidates, and another would be the internal machinations. They mirrored each other, Blagojevich said, because he was determined to go slow and be deliberate with his unique opportunity to send someone to Congress with the wave of his hand. The best way to go about it was to throw out every available idea and sift through them, Blagojevich said yet again.

Yes, some of his ideas seemed ridiculous, Blagojevich admitted, but he was just dumping out thoughts unfiltered. He didn't want the jury to think he was being overly serious at the time.

"Although a former governor previously, Adlai Stevenson, was actually a UN ambassador—"

Schar was objecting again.

Blagojevich stopped, and Goldstein asked him whether any decision had been made on the seat. Of course not, was the answer, but Blagojevich was about to hit on yet another theme. Even if Obama had offered any of the posts Blagojevich was dreaming up, Blagojevich still hadn't decided he absolutely would trade. All of it was exploratory, and any actual choice at that stage would have been premature. He was sucking intent out of the equation everywhere he could. He tried to paint everything as happening in slow motion and to give the impression that he had circled the wagons to discuss his options. For example, Balanoff and Stern reached out to him even before Obama was actually elected, not the other way around. He wasn't going to actually seek anything officially until he thought he knew what he wanted to do, period.

———

Blagojevich said his options in 2008 included sending himself or Emil Jones to the Senate, with the idea on Jones being that he would promise only to stay for two years in case Blagojevich ultimately decided he wanted to run. There had been long phone calls with Harris about the possibility of approaching Jones, which Blagojevich explained as keeping an option open and making a political ally feel good about himself. Goldstein asked about Blagojevich telling Harris that either option was better than appointing Jarrett for zilch.

November 4, 2008 was Election Day, and Blagojevich and Harris had continued their discussions first thing in the morning, with Blagojevich catching Harris in a diner having breakfast. Blagojevich had said it was sinking in that he was going to have to make an appointment, and he wanted the

Senate pick to result in something good for the people of Illinois but also good for him. Blagojevich said it was a high bar, and from that day until the morning of his arrest, he struggled with it.

"All these ideas never measured up to that until the very end when I felt the Madigan deal was the good one, and I believe we were close to getting that and me deciding that, but we never quite were allowed to finish," he said.

Blagojevich then described at some length how he had met with Balanoff and Stern, talking political strategy with them and delivering the idea that he had lots of choices on the seat. The Madigan deal was something he had talked about, as was the idea of appointing someone like Jones. Blagojevich had a strong African American base, and a pick like that would be good for him in Illinois, especially if he did for some reason decide to run for a third term.

———

In one of Blagojevich's most infamous rants, the one where he had fumed over unbelievably low approval ratings in Illinois—just 13 percent—Blagojevich had basically said screw everyone. He had worked so hard, giving the "fucking baby" of every disapproving Illinoisan health care and getting their grandmother a free ride on a bus. For many journalists covering the trial, it was their favorite quote. Many recalled Blagojevich announcing the programs he was referring to when times were better, and now the quote crystallized the image of the desperate person he had become. "I gave your fucking baby a chance to have health care" isn't exactly headstone material, but Blagojevich battled through it. He told the jury he was just frustrated by the "unrequited love" he had for the state and its people.

With Zagel bearing down on Goldstein and Blagojevich to be more concise and wrap things up, the lawyer began to push the former governor through a veritable highlight reel of quotes from the wiretaps. They were the ones that were likely to be stuck in jurors' heads, and Blagojevich had to answer each one. It was a rapid-fire sequence that would see Blagojevich take in questions and shoot back his prepared answers until late the following afternoon.

He described Hastert as being like a coach he always wanted to impress. With Harris, he was just "wargaming," and with others, always just talking through options. No matter what jurors heard him discussing about telling Balanoff he would do in exchange for selecting Valerie Jarrett, he never made up his mind. How could it be an illegal quid pro quo if he never thought in his own mind that he would agree to anything, no matter what the other side offered?

It might sound like he was floating the idea of Lisa Madigan to inflate the price of the seat with Balanoff so he could get what he really wanted for a Jarrett pick, but Blagojevich repeatedly promised that was not the case. The Madigan situation was real, and picking Lisa was a way out of it. And if he had picked Jarrett "unilaterally," which apparently was Blagojevich's way of saying "with no job or other escape hatch in return," he was destined to be mired in political gridlock in Illinois for as long as he cared to be governor.

When he told Harris on a call that he wanted to "get the fuck out of Illinois," it was in light of his issues with Michael Madigan and the idea that he might actually be able to become secretary of health and human services. He just wanted to get something good.

"Something good was still to be determined and defined," he said. "That was the whole idea of these conversations. These were the discussions. What would be good that would be good?"

On one call, Harris likened the talks with Balanoff to the kind of negotiations one might have when trying to buy a house. One side or the other would start low or high, depending on their position in the bartering. Balanoff had approached Blagojevich, so the two men agreed it should be the Obama side that offered something. Blagojevich's approach had been to describe his political circumstances and throw out some ideas that Balanoff could see might help the governor resolve them. To Blagojevich, it was the beginning of a political bargain. He had asked Harris about having Balanoff and the Obama people set up a private sector job for him, but the conversation had quickly moved to that job having a public purpose. Maybe he could be named to lead the Red Cross or the Salvation Army, so he had directed Harris to look into what kind of salary he might bring in.

For that, Blagojevich said, he was sorry. Not for pursuing the job, mind you, but for having Harris, a state employee, research things like that for him on government time.

Schar half stood and started to object, but instantly thought better of it and said he would go ahead and withdraw it.

"Thank you," Blagojevich said, looking down from the witness stand. "I'll give you another one in a minute."

All in all, as he ran through many calls, Blagojevich sounded as if he was prepared to stay on message and deliver cogent points to bolster his position that there was nothing criminal about what had happened in the fall of 2008. But there was one call that just about everyone was still waiting to hear him address.

It had started on November 5, 2008 at 11:06 AM. Doug Scofield was on the line in a conversation that began with the men agreeing on how much they hated journalist Carol Marin. Blagojevich testified that he was sorry about that. He was just kind of flapping his gums with an old friend. He had also joked about becoming UN ambassador and staring down those Russian motherfuckers, after all.

"Now I owe the Russians an apology," he said, trying to sound sheepish in front of the jury while suppressing a laugh. "I don't know how to do that."

But then, there was Line 31.

You see, Blagojevich had this thing. It was fucking golden. And he was not just giving it up for fucking nothing.

There was Blagojevich, finally on the witness stand, and a few feet away was the jury with the power to send him out the front door of the court-house with a verdict of "not guilty." They could put the case behind him and send the ex-governor on his way. Maybe Blagojevich had gone through this answer fifty-five million times. Maybe he had started to repeat it in his head while he was brushing his teeth and then had finished it out loud in the mirror after spitting into the sink. Maybe he mumbled his answer under his breath while he was running. And maybe when people were talking to him in 2009 and 2010 and part of 2011, he had seemed to space out, because he was thinking about answering this question in front the jury that was watching him now.

Or maybe not.

"Well, that's the—that's the Senate seat. This is that phrase, 'f'ing golden,' that was heard around the world, and I was saying this opportunity is f'ing golden, and—and that's what I was saying, and I don't want to give it up for nothing," Blagojevich said, seemingly caught off guard. "So we had these discussions."

Really?

Goldstein tried to recover the moment. When Blagojevich had said on the call that he was not "giving it up for f'ing nothing," what was he saying there?

"I'm afraid to answer this. I'd like to answer it," Blagojevich stammered. "I'm not quite sure how to answer it."

"Answer it the best you can, Rod." Goldstein said.

"In my mind, I didn't know. I had no idea other than all these different ideas that we were throwing around—" Blagojevich answered.

Blagojevich would have more to say before Reid Schar got his long-awaited crack at Blagojevich, but to the Chicago press corps, the damage already was done. The headlines on news web pages that day and in newspapers the next would be about Blagojevich's failure to hit a home run when confronted with "the Tape." Blagojevich finished his answer by saying he didn't want to give up the seat without fully talking through all of his ideas. He was trying to figure out what could possibly go into a deal, and even when he had described the chance to make a pick as "golden," he still hadn't made up his mind in any direction, he explained. That was going to have to suffice, and Goldstein plowed onward.

On November 6, Blagojevich had been on the phone with Harris again. As he had said before, he told the jury he was wargaming what the conversation with Balanoff was going to be, believing Balanoff could be bringing him a direct message from the incoming president. Harris advised Blagojevich to tell the union boss about how scarred he had become slugging things out with Madigan all the time. All of it was intended to create a sense of jeopardy. Blagojevich had much to lose and fairly little to gain—unless Balanoff could come through for him. Lisa Madigan was both a realistic candidate, Blagojevich told the jury, and an alternative he could use when throwing around names of other candidates with Balanoff. Blagojevich saw himself as well-qualified to lead a health-care team to Washington to help Obama, and he and Harris talked of settling into a long, slow, political "Kabuki dance" over some kind of trade.

It was during that call that Harris had thrown out the idea that Blagojevich angle to become the head of an organization like Change to Win, SEIU's political group. It would be a paying job with a national profile, but Blagojevich again said at that point he had no idea of jumping and accepting the proposal even if Balanoff agreed immediately and was able to make it happen. Still, Blagojevich had to deal with what sounded on the tape like him being eager to see Change to Win become a reality. He even daydreamed out loud about Patti taking a job there before him. It was evident on the recordings again and again that Blagojevich wasn't really thrilled about being governor any more. He had been depressed the night of his reelection, he had admitted on the call, feeling like he was being sucked into another four-year deal that he really didn't want. On and on he had rambled about Madigan and about not having enough political allies.

It was also on November 6 that Blagojevich had met with Balanoff the second time, after Balanoff had heard from Obama and been cleared to approach the governor. They met one-on-one at the Thompson Center downtown, out of earshot of the feds who were by then listening to much of what the governor was saying.

"We talked about election night, how magical it was. Talked about Jackie Robinson, Joe Lewis, Barack Obama, the history of it, that was amazing. We then got past that," Blagojevich said.

"Then we talked about what he talked to me about the night before, two nights before, when he pulled me aside and said Barack called and he's interested in a senator and we want to work with you, something along those lines, he said. And we brought that up. And then he—the question was, he expressed to me it was Valerie Jarrett. I think that's—I knew that was coming, but I think this is the first time he may have told me directly."

Blagojevich said he told Balanoff that if that's what Obama really wanted, he expected Obama would give him a call to that effect and tell him directly. Balanoff had told him that probably wasn't in the offing.

"He then said, you're a friend of mine, and we've been old friends, something to that effect. Barack's a friend of mine, called him Barack. You know, we're old friends. We were big for him in the election; we were big for you in your election," Blagojevich said. "I'm here to see if we can work together and sort this out, something along those lines. Not quoting, but words to the effect of that."

Blagojevich remembered telling Balanoff that if the new president had an opinion about who should be made the new senator, that would carry a great deal of weight. But Blagojevich had his own political realities. He recalled telling his guest about Madigan and that he would have to consider the wishes of someone like Emil Jones, a longtime ally who also wanted the seat. If he sent Jarrett, he'd have an angry Michael Madigan in his life. It seemed like everyone was going to Washington and doing historic things, and Blagojevich was being left behind. Knowing him, Blagojevich testified, he lapsed into a diatribe while Balanoff listened. He said he had told the Obama emissary that his life would be gridlock and impeachment. He had spelled out how he saw the chessboard, and had thrown the scenario into Balanoff's court.

"You guys won't care after I make a senator. You'll all leave me, and I'll be all by myself," Blagojevich recalled saying. "I love health care, big issue, passionate about health care, that sort of stuff, I'd said. And then I said, let me ask you something, what do you think of this idea? Any chance I can get Health and Human Services? What do you think?"

And Blagojevich remembered the response. It hadn't been the one he wanted to hear, and he remembered Balanoff looking embarrassed when he answered that something like that just wasn't going to happen. It was so bad, Blagojevich said, he felt bad for how uncomfortable Balanoff looked. They kept talking, with Blagojevich mentioning the Rezko problem and saying he understood what everything looked like from Obama's perspective.

But Blagojevich said it didn't really matter. What he wanted the jury to know now was that it was just something he tossed into the air. He was absolutely not "conditioning one for the other." He hadn't decided what to do. Blagojevich said he was in no way conveying a promise to Balanoff that he was not prepared to fulfill if Balanoff's reaction had been the opposite of the one Blagojevich had gotten.

It was a "no," but not one that was fatal to Blagojevich then.

"The rejection of the idea. I was nowhere close to any decision, even if they said yes on Health and Human Services, whether that's what I really wanted to do," Blagojevich said. "I didn't know."

The meeting had wrapped up, and Blagojevich insisted he moved on. He talked to Greenlee about ways to move ahead on the capital bill and ways to negotiate with Madigan.

A call with Scofield was among the next calls Goldstein asked about. Blagojevich could be heard telling him he thought Jarrett was probably out there somewhere, knowing that she could have her coveted seat in the Senate if Blagojevich could be made happy in some way. She had a path to her dream, and it went through Blagojevich. Jarrett had a lot of influence on Obama, Blagojevich recalled saying during the call. Cabinet positions were being filled, and maybe it would all come together. Jarrett was holding the keys to what Blagojevich wanted, and vice versa.

"She's holding hers with two hands, just kinda clinging to, you know, little pieces of it. Me, I've got the whole thing wrapped around my arms, mine, OK?" Blagojevich had said on the call.

So what about that?

"It's a clumsy way of trying to be literary," Blagojevich told the jury. It sounded stupid then and it was stupid now, he admitted. Like so much else, it was being placed under the umbrella of Blagojevich thinking out loud and not thinking for very long before ideas came flying out of his mouth.

Maybe Blagojevich could at least see himself become ambassador to Macedonia, he had joked on the recording. Maybe that's all Obama and his advisers thought he was worthy of anyway.

"Another stupid idea that was going nowhere," Blagojevich testified. "And Macedonia is great. I'm not here to say anything bad about Macedonians," he went on. "The home of Alexander the Great, anyway."

———

From there, Blagojevich's testimony was about what the endgame had been that December.

The governor had gone into the month with seemingly no clear direction, though he believed a final plan was forming. One minute he appeared to be plotting a deft political maneuver to draw Washington leaders into his Illinois fight, and the next he once again seemed to be a man lost in the woods and shooting at anything that moved. Like the time he joked about sending himself to the Senate and going to Afghanistan to hunt down Osama bin Laden. Blagojevich told Goldstein he had said something like that as Schar objected yet again.

Before Blagojevich could be turned over to Schar to face cross-examination, Goldstein had to cover the allegation that Blagojevich seriously considered appointing Jesse Jackson Jr. in exchange for $1.5 million. It was a charge of a spectacular, flat-out sale of a powerful government post and an affront to democracy itself. Prosecutors believed the late calls in the case showed that when push came to shove, that was a likely outcome if Blagojevich could line up everything just as he wanted before Christmas 2008.

Blagojevich's position was that he was floating the idea of the Jackson pick, knowing that leading senators and Obama wouldn't want Jackson anywhere near the capitol, so he could "incentivize" Democratic leadership to push Michael Madigan to give Blagojevich what he wanted legislatively in Illinois. Blagojevich hoped the jury could see the chess move and that the tapes would sound like that was what he was really doing. The Washington establishment wanted a senator who could be reelected, not a thorn like Jackson, who was controversial.

Among the conversations Blagojevich wanted the jury to hear was one with Senator Bob Menendez, who was leading the Democratic committee that steered the national effort to push certain candidates and unify party strategy. Menendez had said his interest was seeing someone appointed who could win again in two years and who wouldn't need a lot of involvement from the national party to raise money. Blagojevich said he explained where he was with Madigan and that he could use help getting a deal going. "He said they generally don't get involved in local fights, but this would be an important one," Blagojevich said. Menendez had told him the party might be able to get behind that kind of arrangement, Blagojevich said, telling the jury that Rahm Emanuel emerged as the go-between who would speak to Madigan.

But there were problem calls during this time period as well.

One of the worst was December 4, when Blagojevich had been on the phone with his Washington adviser, Fred Yang, and Greenlee. He had been recorded telling them about the idea of a Jackson choice, and it certainly sounded real.

He was thinking about the possibility of that pick, he told the pair. There was "tangible support" available to him if he went that direction, he said on the call. So, what about that?

Blagojevich testified that he knew there was an offer of $1.5 million behind the Jackson push and that the congressman himself could even be behind it. But on the call the jury had heard, Blagojevich said he was only talking about political support and that it didn't matter because it was all just a ruse anyway.

Jurors could see that, Blagojevich said, because of the call that came next. He was on the phone with Greenlee again, trying to explain what had just happened on the call with Yang. The talk about Jackson was just that, and he was strengthening his bargaining position. Yang was in Washington and could help spread a perceived message that the Jackson scenario was real.

Goldstein pointed to one part of the call with Greenlee in particular.

"It's a repugnant idea, but I need to leverage that Jesse Jr. with these fucking national people," Blagojevich said on the call. The jury should know that was the real reality, Blagojevich testified. He was trying to explain to Greenlee what he was *really* doing.

"He wasn't picking up on it," Blagojevich testified. "I had no intention of making Jesse Jackson Jr. senator."

When Greenlee had testified, he said he simply hadn't believed his boss and thought Blagojevich was just placating him. To Greenlee, it was much more realistic that Blagojevich was being honest with Yang, whom he had known for much longer, than with him. Greenlee thought "tangible support" was campaign cash, and he said he thought there was a very good chance Blagojevich wanted it and would be willing to sell the seat.

And there were calls from that day where Blagojevich had less room to try to explain himself.

In one of the most damaging, Blagojevich had told his brother that he was considering "elevating" Jackson to the vacancy. Jackson's camp had made promises to him, but "some of the stuff's gotta start happening now."

Blagojevich didn't explain why he would have been saying that to his brother if the pick wasn't a real option, and his explanations fell flatter in the room than some of his earlier ones. He said when he told Robert that things would have to start happening if Jackson were to be picked, he said he meant political support. Jackson would have to start appearing with him and stirring his supporters and backers on the South Side to get behind Blagojevich's political agenda.

Robert was to go and meet with Raghu Nayak, a man that both brothers knew had made the offer of campaign cash. Rod told his brother to be careful how everything was expressed.

"And assume everybody's listening, the whole world is listening," Blagojevich had said on the call, obviously completely clueless to the fact that, oh yes, someone was in fact listening.

Goldstein asked Blagojevich to explain that, and Blagojevich tried his best. In the political arena, when you have conversations like that, keep a clear conscience.

"You don't mind saying it on national television, that's what that phrase means," he told the jury.

Likewise, he had an explanation for why he told his brother not to have his conversation with Nayak on a telephone. Because there had been the money offer at an earlier point, the conversation needed to be crystal clear and not hindered by any language barrier, Blagojevich said. The fine details were going to be key.

"I did not want any miscommunication problem on what we were doing," Blagojevich said. "I wanted him to do it in person so he could properly explain whatever idea I was trying to do here."

Of course the meeting had not happened anyway, with Blagojevich pulling the plug after the *Tribune* reported the next day, December 5, 2008, that the federal investigation of him had led to recordings of his conversations being made. That was a "crisis," he said, and because he wouldn't have time to tell his brother exactly what to say in a Nayak meeting, he had thought better of it and had Robert just cancel.

If the jury thought all of that was a little thick, the Blagojevich defense sought to cover it by playing another call that they hoped would again show the governor's true intention. It was from a few days later, on December 8, with Harris telling Blagojevich about talking to Emanuel again about the Senate choice. Emanuel had not been thrilled at the possibility of a Jackson appointment, which Blagojevich said he took as a signal that his overall strategy could be working. Harris had recounted how Emanuel threw out names like Cheryle Jackson, the former Blagojevich aide, seemingly trying to spur the governor in a different direction. The call with Harris had ended with Blagojevich encouraged. He thought Rahm would be his broker, a powerful hand coming in to sway Michael Madigan.

"I went to bed that night thinking I was a day or two away from making that Madigan deal," he told the jury, almost sounding wistful. Rahm, Harry Reid, Menendez, and Dick Durbin seemed to be getting behind him, he said, "converging and descending" on Madigan to make the deal happen.

In all, he had considered some thirty-four people for the seat. The options had ranged from the politically wise to the ridiculous to some that crossed ethical and criminal lines. What the jury had were scores of recordings of Blagojevich talking about what he wanted to do and days of testimony where he said he was explaining to them what he was really doing. It might be up to history to decide whether Blagojevich was actually planning to do one thing or the other in December 2008 or whether he was really pushing to make all of the options available to him before deciding at the very end which way he would go. But the jury would decide whether Blagojevich headed off to a federal prison, and he wanted to tell them one more time that there was something they could believe.

He hadn't knowingly done anything illegal or shaken anyone down for a seat in the United States Senate, the most exclusive club on earth.

"No," Blagojevich said when Goldstein again asked him if that's what he had done.

"Absolutely not."

———

It was 4:00 PM on June 2, 2009, with just about an hour left in the court day, when Schar finally got to rise from the prosecution table.

He walked around the back of it toward an evidence cart that was pushed up against the jury box. It was from that location that the government typically questioned witnesses at the trial, and Schar was standing there now. He was directly opposite Blagojevich in the room, probably twenty feet away, and closer to the jury than Blagojevich was on the witness stand.

After all the years of government pursuit, all of the press conferences where Blagojevich swore prosecutors were on a witch hunt, all of the TV shenanigans, all of the artful dodging in public, and all of the Blagojevichian head fakes, it was one assistant US attorney versus Illinois's most infamous former governor. George Ryan's conviction had come six years earlier in a courtroom a few floors down from where Schar and Blagojevich were about to square off, but Ryan had not testified in his own defense.

The cross of Blagojevich would be a rare spectacle as anticipated as the examination a few years earlier of Chicago Outfit boss Joey "the Clown" Lombardo by Assistant US Attorney Mitch Mars. And it might be about as entertaining. Schar glared ahead, and Zagel told him he could proceed.

"Thank you, Judge," Schar said quickly. Then he surprised anyone who thought the prosecutor might ease into things. Punch number one was sailing right for Blagojevich's face.

"Mr. Blagojevich, you are a convicted liar, correct?" Schar said sharply. Jurors would later call it the most memorable moment of the entire trial, and they were immediately riveted in their chairs.

Instantly, both Blagojevich and one of his lawyers were talking at the same time. With Blagojevich starting to give an answer that started with "I would—" while Sorosky objected over him. Zagel stepped in to overrule the defense.

"Yes or no?" Schar asked, with no dip in the intensity of his voice. One thing Schar could seemingly produce instantly was righteous anger, and his words were dripping with indignation.

"Yes," Blagojevich answered.

What Schar was getting at was that just after he was convicted in 2010 of lying to the FBI, Blagojevich held a press conference where, the prosecutor contended, he was lying once again. He had told the media that his conviction was unfair, Schar said, leading Sorosky to object again. But it hadn't taken long to draw Blagojevich into a brawl. He spoke right through his own lawyer.

"I have a strong opinion about that if you'd like to hear it," he said, as Zagel told the room that the ex-governor was waiving his attorney's objection. "This is why we have appellate courts," Blagojevich continued.

"It's fair to say that you wanted people to believe you had not lied to the FBI. Yes or no?" Schar pressed.

"I wanted them to know what the truth is, and there's a process that will still unfold, and we're determined to pursue that—that process," Blagojevich said, moving things back to what he was trying to say about an appeal.

"The answer is yes," Schar said flatly.

"Pardon me?" Blagojevich replied, as if he had been talking to someone else and been interrupted.

"The answer is yes to my question," Schar repeated.

"What is your question again?" said Blagojevich.

Well, it was obvious this could take a while. Zagel had the court reporter just read the question back—the one about whether Blagojevich wanted people to believe that he had not lied to the FBI. But Blagojevich just gave yet another answer about truth and the process, leading Schar to ask if what he meant was that Blagojevich wanted it known that "the process" was unfair.

That brought a simultaneous objection from both Sorosky and Goldstein, as both scrambled to try to protect Blagojevich. But it didn't matter.

"No," Blagojevich said to Schar.

What Blagojevich had said at the press conference the year before was that he had been convicted because the FBI had not allowed a court reporter into the room when FBI Agent Murphy interviewed him about fund-raising. The insinuation was that the FBI had blocked the recording of the session, and if it had been taped, the "real" truth would be known and the first jury to hear his case would have thought he was innocent. But he had left something out, right? Schar asked.

"I don't know. I say a lot," Blagojevich shrugged, once again plowing over a Sorosky objection. The questioning was virtual chaos, but Blagojevich seemed almost to be enjoying sparring with his accuser. "What did I say? What did I miss?"

What he hadn't told everyone at the press conference was that the FBI had brought recording equipment to the interview, Schar said. Blagojevich tried to put it on his attorneys, leading the prosecutor to pause and say that his question had been very simple. Didn't he give a statement to the press, and in that statement had he not said that his conviction had been unfair because the FBI hadn't allowed the interview to be taped?

Blagojevich said his lawyers had told him that a court reporter wasn't going to be allowed.

"No court reporter. That's what I said," Blagojevich answered, seemingly trying to draw a line between a tape recorder and a human typing a record. What he had been trying to say was that he did not lie to the FBI. Blagojevich then started to say how he had never even put on a defense in the first case—which Schar cut off with an objection of his own.

"Let me explain something to you that will make this a lot easier, and it will make it a lot easier because, generally speaking, when witnesses argue with lawyers, the witness loses in the end," Zagel finally said.

"If you can answer a question with a yes or no, answer it. You may feel that things are left out that should be added. If that's your feeling, wait for your lawyer to stand up on redirect examination, and you can clarify it. That way we'll go through this in less time and in less suffering for everybody in the courtroom."

Fair enough. Schar went back to his point. Blagojevich had shown up in the lobby of the Dirksen US Courthouse after his conviction and had said that he was unfairly convicted because the FBI hadn't agreed to having a court reporter when, in fact, the agents had appeared ready to actually record the entire thing.

"They never told me that," Blagojevich finally said.

Schar pounded it home by pointing out that the agents had said right in front of Blagojevich that they had recording equipment and that it had been testified to at his first trial. Blagojevich had been the one to refuse a recording. For another few minutes they went around and around, with Schar quizzing Blagojevich on his memory of what had been said before the interview began and Blagojevich insisting he could only remember that a court reporter hadn't been allowed. Blagojevich didn't remember any recording equipment, he said. And Schar was more than happy to keep trying to pin him down and point out the lie to the public, making Blagojevich look shifty and manipulative. Did Blagojevich remember the FBI offering to record the interview?

Blagojevich would only say that he didn't see equipment.

"Sir, over and over again, you have said on TV that you believe the process that led to that interview was unfair because you weren't allowed to have a court reporter," Schar said. Neither man was backing down. "Yes or no?"

"How do you define over and over?" Blagojevich answered. "How many times would that be?"

What was clear was that Blagojevich was no ordinary witness. He was deeply skilled in the political art of asking the question he wanted to answer and finding ways to avoid ones he didn't like or that had an answer that was negative for him. It was like a debate, when the moderator asks a pointed question to a candidate about taxes, only to get an answer about the candidate's position on handguns, or when a politician at a press conference gives a nonanswer to a reporter's question and then points at someone else for a new question. Few politicians in Illinois history were as crafty as Blagojevich when it came to that kind of stick-and-move answer. But there was a slight problem. The "move" part of that combo was not an option in this situation. There was only the witness stand and no one else to point to. Schar was asking the questions, and Judge Zagel was there to make sure the rules were followed.

"You can remember that you were eastbound west of the Mississippi River from the St. Louis *Post-Dispatch* editorial board interview when Dusty Baker called you several years ago, and it is your testimony you do not recall the FBI offering to record the entire interview of you in March of 2005. Is that your testimony?" Schar asked incredulously.

Now Blagojevich was ready to shift the burden again. It was Schar's fault. He had never spoken to Blagojevich about what was or wasn't to be recorded.

"You didn't arrange that meeting with me," he said. "We have lawyers you guys talked to. You guys communicated with my attorneys, not me."

In the end, it took Zagel to move things ahead. He looked down and asked Blagojevich if the answer was that he could not recall an offer to record the conversation.

Schar seemed convinced the point was made. As a politician, wasn't it true that Blagojevich frequently found himself lying to the public?

"I'd object to that," Blagojevich said, seemingly meaning it. Not just saying he didn't like the question, but actually objecting. It didn't matter anyway, as one of Blagojevich's lawyers objected, too, and Schar withdrew the question and asked it in a different way. Did messages go out to the public that Blagojevich knew to be untrue?

Maybe Schar could give him an example, Blagojevich said. He tried to be as truthful as possible.

So the prosecutor brought up November 10, 2008. Blagojevich had been recorded talking to Doug Scofield that day and telling him he wanted a press leak that he'd had a good, long conversation with Jesse Jackson Jr. the prior weekend about the Senate seat. The governor had wanted it in the air that Jackson was being considered.

Right, Blagojevich said on the stand, he had told Scofield to get that information into a gossip column.

"That was a lie," Schar said.

"That was a misdirection play in politics," Blagojevich answered.

Time for rope-a-dope: round two.

It was not factual; that was right, Blagojevich agreed.

So by not factual, did Blagojevich mean that was untrue?

Sure, Blagojevich answered, it was untrue. On that word, they could agree.

OK, said Schar, so it was a lie?

Not so fast. Blagojevich said he didn't see it that way. *Lie* wasn't a word he wanted to adopt. Well, said the prosecutor, it was "false," right? There was no conversation with Congressman Jackson. There had been no meeting, and Blagojevich was telling a longtime friend and adviser to tell someone in the news business that there had been one.

"I had several conversations with Congressman Jackson," Blagojevich said, "just not that weekend."

Hmmm. Well, Blagojevich had not had a long conversation with Jackson that weekend, and he hadn't had a good conversation with him that weekend. In fact, he had not had any conversation whatsoever that weekend. Schar said Blagojevich had floated that idea knowing that no one would contradict it. Congressman Jackson wouldn't deny it, right? Schar asked.

Right, said Blagojevich. It would help Jackson's politics. So Schar asked again. Blagojevich had leaked a lie, on purpose, because he believed it was to his advantage and because he knew he could get away with it.

"For political reasons, I was floating that information because I was trying to develop the dynamic to get the Madigan deal that I've talked a lot about and would love to answer questions about, but I'm sorry, that was a run-on answer," said Blagojevich.

Blagojevich had repeated what he was doing in another call to Harris and Quinlan, Schar pointed out. He had told Scofield to leak the fake rumor to Michael Sneed at the *Sun-Times*. Blagojevich had even said on the call, "Who's going to contradict that, you know?"

The prosecutor stepped forward to show Blagojevich the transcript of the call. There in black and white was Blagojevich saying just what Schar had said he did. No one would contradict that rumor if it hit ink.

Right, Blagojevich finally said after having a look. It would advance the goals of both politicians. He would get it out there that Jackson was being looked at for the Senate, maybe spurring something like the Madigan deal, and Jackson would look good in the press because it would look like Blagojevich was really considering him. Win-win.

But wasn't the point really to deceive? Schar said. The intended recipients of the column item would have been other elected officials.

"It's the quarterback faking a handoff and throwing long," Blagojevich said, sounding proud of the analogy. "It's part of the business. You know what I'm saying?"

Schar did, though the fakery didn't stop there. Wasn't Blagojevich also going to trick the public? Not surprisingly, "no" was the answer. Blagojevich said he saw that as a message designed for the political world. It would be received in the places he wanted it received inside the establishment.

OK, how about November 5 that year? Another press conference, this time just after Obama was elected and Blagojevich was going to be questioned about the process of picking a new senator. He had gone over and over what he might say. Wasn't that correct? Schar asked. Blagojevich knew he was going to get questions on whether he might want the seat for his own. The prosecutor tried to remind Blagojevich that he had been asked about himself when Senate possibilities had come up and that he had told the reporter who asked him, "I'm not interested in the US Senate."

Lie, right? Yes or no, said Schar.

"You know, I hadn't decided what I was going to do, so I would say no, I hadn't reached a decision," Blagojevich said. "I guess, it's—it's a political answer, but I—I can't say that I was completely false."

And so, again, Schar began the task of nailing the proverbial Jell-O to the proverbial wall. Blagojevich had been asked, "How about yourself?" by a reporter at the press conference. And his answer had been that he was not interested. From many, many tapes, it was clear that in "fact," or whatever you want to call it, Blagojevich was interested in the potential of sending himself to the Senate. Still, Blagojevich insisted it was not a lie. He wasn't really *interested* in going to the Senate, he told Schar, he just held out the possibility of sending himself "if things got real bad," and if he ever made a decision, he, Blagojevich, would be among the candidates to think about.

To Blagojevich, this was not a contradiction.

"At that press conference, you looked the camera straight in the eye, correct?" Schar asked.

"Show me if I was looking at the camera or was I looking at somebody else? I don't know," was the answer.

Guessing that could be the response, Schar had the segment of the press conference queued up, and it did appear that Blagojevich was staring ahead toward a bank of TV cameras.

Blagojevich asked for more of the conference to be played. He had said other things the jury might want to hear. Could we hear more? Blagojevich asked.

"Why don't we focus on the lie?" Schar answered, before offering to let Blagojevich have the weekend to look at the tape. If there was a part where Blagojevich had not lied and said he actually was interested in taking the seat, he could let everyone know.

Overall, Schar said, moving past the press conference and Blagojevich insisting he needed the full context of what had been said there, Blagojevich's mantra on the seat seemed to be that he would make a pick that was good for Illinois "and good for me." On, November 4, for example, he had said that to Harris on a call the jury heard.

Right, Blagojevich said.

"I told John Harris that I was going to measure everything up against that, good, bad, ugly things like that," Blagojevich said. "I said good stuff for the people of Illinois, good for me, it's not coming for free, I'm going to make this decision in good faith. On the morning of November the fourth, that's exactly what I said."

Schar's point, of course, was that Blagojevich had said the pick wasn't just about the people of the state. It was about him, and that wasn't what Blagojevich twice had sworn to do when he was elected governor.

"Your oath, sir, doesn't say that you can make decisions based on what's good for you, does it?" Schar said.

"The oath says to follow the laws of the state, the Constitution, to faithfully discharge your duties to the people, and I—I interpret that to do good stuff for the people of Illinois and if it's good stuff for the people of Illinois, that would be good for me," came the answer. "That's what I like about that."

As long as he was getting good things for the people, he felt like that was good for him, too, Blagojevich said. That was why the Madigan deal looked good, he testified.

Well, back at the press conference, did Blagojevich tell all of those reporters he was going to make a decision that was good for the state and good for himself?

"Can I see the press conference?" Blagojevich said again, clearly needling Schar. "I can answer your question."

OK, how about the cabinet post? Schar said, playing right along. Had he said during the press conference that he might make a certain Senate pick if it meant he could be appointed secretary of health and human services?

He'd have to see the press conference for himself, Blagojevich said again, but he could say it was highly unlikely he would have said that.

"Highly unlikely," Schar said, mockingly.

"Highly unlikely," Blagojevich repeated.

And private foundation jobs, how about that? Schar said. Did he say at the press conference that getting a job leading one would influence his decision on Obama's replacement? Blagojevich said he probably didn't say that, but he hadn't seen the press conference. Round three wasn't over just yet, but Schar was finding a way to put a stop to it.

"You don't think you would have stood up and said, 'One of the things I'm considering with this Senate seat is private foundation jobs for me.' You think you might have said that?" said Schar in a tone that made it sound like he could really be searching for that answer.

"I don't think so," Blagojevich admitted.

Schar was circling around the November 4 call with Harris. The governor and his chief of staff had been recorded saying that publicly, the mantra would be what was good for the state, the people of Illinois. They wouldn't be publicly saying it would be what was good for Obama or good for Blagojevich.

Schar was trying to pin that on Blagojevich, who said he would have to see the transcript. It was Harris who had said most of that, Blagojevich remembered, not him. But in any event it was something he basically agreed with, as far as saying that was the public mantra and internalizing it to mean the private mantra also. The prosecutor certainly wasn't going to stop there. If that was the case, could Blagojevich name one time when he had said publicly that the Senate pick was going to be about what was good for him personally?

"You know, I could have said—if I see this press conference, I could have said my commitment to health care, having a senator who believed in my commitment to health care, that was something I was looking for, that would have been good for me," Blagojevich said, sounding earnest.

Not bad, but Schar had more buttons to press, too. How about having the staff research ambassadorships? When had Blagojevich announced that that was happening? When had he told Illinois that he was having aides find out who past secretaries of Health and Human Services had been?

Did he ever tell the public about Change to Win and that he might make a pick dependent on whether he could get a job like that?

"That lasted a day or two," Blagojevich answered. "That went nowhere."

How about that he wanted a salary of $750,000? Did he ever tell the public he might want Obama to remove the president of Families USA and give him that job? Did he tell the public he was attempting to learn how much Patti could make in Washington as a consultant if Blagojevich sent himself to the Senate?

Did he tell the public he was thinking of appointing a placeholder to the Senate who would be willing to give the seat up if Blagojevich ever got in trouble and was going to get impeached?

"Right, the ugly idea," Blagojevich answered. "No—of course—no."

———

Blagojevich would be on the stand for more than another full day, but not until after a three-day weekend. And when he returned, he seemed more comfortable with what was going on and a bit calmer. He had spent time rehashing his first day with a number of his lawyers and advisers, including Sam Adam Sr., who recommended he be much less combative. Schar was trying to draw out the competitive and angrier Blagojevich, to tear away the image he had worked so hard to build up when Goldstein was questioning him. If Blagojevich was abrasive and nasty, it wouldn't be the affable and funny former governor that jurors took in their minds to the deliberating room.

For Schar, it quickly became obvious that his chief goal for the remainder of the testimony was to firm up the ask for the jury. That *was* the crime, since no corrupt deal for the Senate seat ever was consummated before Blagojevich was taken into custody December 9. There could be no ambiguity on whether a message had been delivered that Blagojevich believed was going to the incoming president, Obama. Schar asked whether Blagojevich was telling everyone that during his main meeting with Balanoff, he never "indicated" he was willing to name Jarrett senator in exchange for becoming Obama's secretary of health and human services.

"It's my testimony that I asked Tom Balanoff what he thought of the idea. He didn't think much of it," Blagojevich said. "And that's what—what the conversation was. I did not tell him I would—I made a decision, I did not promise that I would do it, and I didn't say I would do one in exchange for the other."

In fact, Blagojevich said, one thing Balanoff had told him was that Blagojevich needed to talk with David Axelrod about the Senate seat.

But Schar's point was that at the time, Blagojevich expected Balanoff was going to take his thought on HHS back to Obama. Blagojevich was trying to paint it as him just asking what Balanoff thought about the possibility of him taking that position, though he acknowledged it had come up in the context of a Jarrett appointment. Blagojevich would only say he thought there was a good possibility Balanoff would be taking the message back. In other words, Balanoff was a feeler from the newly forming administration. Schar wanted to know if Blagojevich had made it clear to Balanoff that he was proposing a trade, and Blagojevich insisted he had never been that explicit.

"I'm not sure what I would've done," Blagojevich repeated, saying he would have taken the answer and compared it with the Madigan deal or the idea of appointing Emil Jones. Schar was insistent that Madigan was just a stalking horse at that time, but Blagojevich said the reality was all of the options were stalking horses, just "one against the other." In his mind, even at the time, getting named Obama's new leader of HHS was pretty unrealistic.

"Unrealistic? Sir, you made a career out of taking long shots, haven't you?" Schar pushed, poking some fun at Blagojevich's homespun version of his own life's story from the week before. "You applied to Harvard, right?"

Blagojevich's political career had been marked by victories where he hadn't been favored at the outset. The calls were showing that, long shot or not, the Jarrett-for-HHS trade was something Blagojevich was willing to try, and he had attempted to use Balanoff to take the proposal up the food chain. And if he was not named to the cabinet, Jarrett wasn't going to the Senate either, Schar snapped.

The return message eventually had come from Emanuel through Harris. Obama would be thankful and appreciative if Jarrett were named senator. Things weren't going to escalate from there, and Blagojevich had been angered. He had called the Obama people arrogant and told Harris: "Fuck them."

"I may have said something like that," Blagojevich said, dropping his voice a little.

And the calls didn't improve. On November 12, 2008, Blagojevich had a call with Balanoff that was recorded, and he had turned his attention to leading a charitable organization funded by Obama friends. He was hoping it would pay a nice salary and had staffers conducting research on what kind of money he might expect to bring in.

Blagojevich again testified that he never indicated to Balanoff that he had decided to make a trade like that, while Schar said he wanted to take what was or wasn't happening in the governor's mind out of the equation. Had he told Balanoff that he *would* do something like that? Not surprisingly, Blagojevich said he didn't believe he had linked one for the other. On the call itself, Blagojevich could be heard suggesting $20 million could go toward the organization he would lead. If Blagojevich got his millions, couldn't Jarrett be the senator? That seemed to be what was being suggested.

"No, I never—I never told him to go tell Obama or ask Rahm or anybody that I would do that," Blagojevich insisted, despite being confronted with telling Balanoff that $20 million could go toward his advocacy group overnight, "and then we could help our new senator, Valerie Jarrett."

As an Illinois politician, Blagojevich often found himself doing favors for other Illinois politicians. That was an obvious truth. And the former governor readily agreed that was the case. The political landscape was about trades, its art was about give and take, and Blagojevich was among its leading practitioners. He had described it as being like a "favor bank." You do something for someone, and they remember it and help you out in the future when something comes up. It was a human dynamic, Blagojevich told Schar.

But one of the favors he had been asked for in the fall of 2008 was a little unusual, and the government had caught it on the wiretaps. Rahm Emanuel had called, after it was known he would be going to the Obama White House to be chief of staff. It was unclear how long he would be there or whether he might want to return to Congress, so he had asked Blagojevich to appoint someone to his Fifth District seat as a placeholder of sorts. Someone who would be happy to have the spot for a time, who wasn't terribly interested in staying there forever, and who might be thankful for the stint in Washington and then be willing to slide back out of Emanuel's way if that's where he wanted to go back to. Blagojevich had talked with his advisers about whether there was a way to make an appointment since the Constitution called for a special election to be held. Emanuel and people around him thought there could be a loophole, and Blagojevich was taped saying it was a favor "worth doing."

Emanuel had been to Congress and was taking the biggest job on Obama's new staff. He had been a rising star in politics who had now fully arrived, and where he might go next was limitless in 2008. Certainly that was the kind of person Blagojevich would remember doing any favor for and would put that favor in the bank for future help. In 2006 or 2007, Blagojevich had helped Emanuel in Illinois on some legislation for ultimate fighting, which Emanuel's brother, Ari, was involved in representing. It had been memorable for more than one reason, Blagojevich told the jury.

"I'm a traditionalist when it comes to boxing. I like old-time fighting," Blagojevich said. "I was a Golden Gloves fighter. My personal preference is I like that, and ultimate fighting is sort of cutting into the boxing game, and if there wasn't Manny Pacquiao and Floyd Mayweather, there really wouldn't be much pizzaz to boxing anymore. I'm giving you a long answer, but this is sort of my state of mind."

Blagojevich said he had held his nose and signed a bill on the sport and agreed with Schar that he saw it as a favor. Likewise, Blagojevich said he would often ask Emanuel for things too, especially when it came to requesting the congressman back certain legislation. In the same vein, Blagojevich said he had been happy to help Emanuel when he came to the governor for a grant for the Chicago Academy, the one Blagojevich had since been accused of holding up in an illegal bid for campaign money. Schar picked on Blagojevich's testimony that he thought the grant for Emanuel's school might have been a second one, and that was why he had held up the money. Any favor for the powerful politician would have been one Blagojevich would clearly have flagged in his "favor bank."

On the racetrack, Blagojevich's memory was clearer, and the prosecutor worked to suggest Blagojevich's answers were simply unrealistic. Get Blagojevich quibbling over details, and the overall scenario would come into focus.

Schar walked through calls where Blagojevich had told Harris on recordings to sit on the recapture bill, without ever mentioning the idea that he might need to scan the legislation for poison pill language, as he had told the jury. Blagojevich hadn't told Harris he had questions about the bill's makeup. He had testified he was going to sit and review all of the pending bills on his desk himself, when the reality was he was disengaged and had a team of people to do that, Schar said, wasn't that right?

"I guess we'll never know," Blagojevich said somewhat pointedly. "You never let me do it."

Blagojevich's dealings with Children's Memorial Hospital's leader were different from some of the other alleged shakedowns in the case, because the governor had taken a much more active role. Instead of Monk being the sole go-between, as in the Johnston matter, Blagojevich himself had made calls and spoken to Patrick Magoon. On October 17, after Greenlee found money to do the pediatric rate increase, it was Blagojevich himself who called with the good news. The increase would go into effect January 1, the governor had said, but please keep it quiet.

Prosecutors had told the jury that was because Blagojevich wanted to have time to persuade Magoon to make a donation—or even force him to—before the public knew about the state commitment. But Blagojevich said he remembered telling Magoon not to talk about the plan because not everyone was getting such a gift in a tight budget year, or at least that's what he was thinking.

Blagojevich had sounded clear during his direct testimony, but things were sounding squishier under Schar's pressure. That was definitely the reason he told Magoon to keep it under wraps, he said, though he didn't want to get locked into any exact words. It was an opening for Schar, and he ran through it. Blagojevich's memory had seemed exceptional when it came to all kinds of trivia and dates; now he was backing off a key claim. The ex-governor was an expert at recalling all kinds of snips of quotes.

Like what? Blagojevich said from the stand.

"Good for the people of Illinois and good for me, correct?" Schar shot back.

To make his points, Schar had placed the events of the alleged hospital extortion on a timeline. Blagojevich had told Magoon in late September that he wanted to help him, and on October 8, while the money was still unsecured, he had assigned Wyma the task of trying to raise $50,000 from Magoon (or "get Magoon for fifty," as Wyma recalled). Blagojevich hadn't found out the money would be there until October 17. The nine days were important for Schar, because it showed Blagojevich was willing to seek money from the hospital while its rate increase was still in the air.

Blagojevich had then called Magoon himself on the seventeenth to tell him the rate increase would be coming as of January 1.

"And, of course, you understood, did you not, that delivering that type of personal financial news, good news, might put some pressure on Mr. Magoon to help you if you were to turn around and ask him a favor?" Schar asked.

Goldstein objected, but Blagojevich plowed forward and said he would answer it. "Absolutely not," he said, that's why he had called himself. If he thought there was going to be undue pressure, he wouldn't have.

———

Blagojevich's final morning on cross-examination was June 7, 2011, and Schar started it with the Krozel matter. There were a number of facts that the two men could seemingly agree on. There were tollway programs of various sizes that he was considering in 2008, and it was true that during the same time period he did have a desire to have Krozel give him campaign donations. On September 18 that year, Blagojevich had asked Krozel for a meeting and Krozel had shown up. It was clearly a fund-raising meeting, and it had taken place at the campaign offices, where fund-raising activities were supposed to happen. And there had also been some talk of official government action. Blagojevich agreed that he had talked with Krozel about the capital bill, which was something he was trying to make happen in the future, and also about his plan to go forward on a $1.8 billion tollway expansion plan.

Just that set of facts seemed to be a recipe for trouble. If someone like Krozel got that kind of good news, couldn't he feel pressure if the governor then asked for something?

"No, not in my mind," Blagojevich answered. "The word *pressure*, no, sir."

Blagojevich acknowledged he had asked for money, but not in a way that hinged on anything he was planning to do with the tollway proposal. The meeting was before the government wiretaps had been set up, and Blagojevich contended he had never told Krozel he had the authority to do a much larger $6 billion plan. One that big had to be part of a larger state capital bill.

———

Blagojevich did not like Jesse Jackson Jr., and that certainly didn't change with Jackson's little Elvis impersonation on the witness stand. The two men had a history and were destined to be forever linked through Blagojevich's criminal case. It was the most blatant and troubling allegation ever leveled against an Illinois governor. Given the chance to name someone to represent the state in the US Senate, Blagojevich had at least entertained the thought of selling it for $1.5 million and allegedly sent his brother to investigate making it happen.

Prosecutors said problems had started between the men when Blagojevich had first run for governor, and Jackson had appeared in court and told that story. When Jackson refused to give Blagojevich the donation he was looking for, Jackson's wife's shot at a state post had gone out the window.

"That is absolutely not true," Blagojevich said with a hint of anger in his voice as Schar circled for his final questions.

What was true was that by October 2008, Blagojevich had come to learn that his old annoyance, Jackson, was interested in the Senate seat. The jury had heard recorded conversations of Blagojevich talking about messengers from Jackson coming out of the woodwork, calling him at home and making financial offers for the seat. Blagojevich had been approached for "pay to play" and had even used the term.

On October 28, Blagojevich's brother had reported talking to Rajinder Bedi and that Bedi had said Nayak was promising "accelerated fund-raising" for Blagojevich if there was a Jackson appointment. A few days later, at a meeting at an Indian restaurant, Nayak had firmed up the offer in person to Robert. It was an offer of $1.5 million if Jackson were named and was nothing short of a bid to purchase a seat for Jackson among the country's most powerful politicians. Five hundred thousand dollars would be the down payment. Blagojevich had said often from the stand that he was appalled by the thought of taking money to name someone, and he agreed with Schar again that what Nayak was offering, possibly with Jackson's knowledge, would be illegal.

"And, in fact, what they were offering you was bribes, right?" Schar asked.

"They were offering me campaign funds for the Senate seat, which my brother properly rejected on three separate occasions," Blagojevich answered.

"And campaign funds for the Senate seat are bribes?" Schar repeated.

"It's illegal," was as far as Blagojevich would go. For whatever reason, he was afraid of the *b* word, and Schar wasn't going to let him off the hook. Blagojevich looked as uncomfortable on the stand as any politician might with someone like Schar pushing him on this kind of accusation. Winding up in federal court being asked about bribes was the nightmare scenario. And just because it happened often in Chicago, it was no less unsettling for Blagojevich. Schar again asked if Blagojevich considered what the Jackson camp had offered a bribe, and the former governor, as he so often did, deflected with humor.

"Did you see my law school grades?" Blagojevich answered. "I'm afraid to give you an answer. I could be wrong. Whatever it is, it's illegal. You can't do it."

It turned out, with a little more pressing, that the line Blagojevich was drawing was on where the cash would end up. If it had been money for him personally, that would be a bribe. If it was money for his campaign fund, that would be a violation of fund-raising rules. It was clearly illegal and something Blagojevich said his brother had repeatedly rejected. He had never used the term *bribe* in his mind, Blagojevich said, but he knew it was against the law and was war-gaming, not something he was planning to do.

It seemed a small point, but in addition to again making Blagojevich look somewhat evasive, Schar's questioning had established a baseline. It was no small thing to get Blagojevich to plant a flag on any particular moral position when it came to his fund-raising activity, and he had at least agreed that taking the campaign money in exchange for appointing Jackson would absolutely be illegal, whether it was a labeled a "bribe" or not.

Blagojevich's moves in early December 2008 were virtually a blur. Despite telling the jury he was never going to appoint Jackson and that he was using the congressman's possible selection as bait to get the Madigan deal, he had taken steps that could be read either way. He had told Harris to reach out to Emanuel to see if a Jackson pick was still acceptable to Obama, had invited Jackson to a poverty summit to make a public show of their supposed coziness, and had invited Jackson to a meeting at his office to talk about his qualifications for the job. It was no leap to think that at the very least, Blagojevich was hedging his bets if the Madigan deal or any other arrangement fell through. He had even told Patti he was elevating Jackson and not ruling him out as a pick. Why would he need to be duping his wife?

On December 4, Blagojevich was talking to Harris about the war-gaming. He had said he was going to look at the value of a Jackson pick, as offensive as it might be to him. Once again, Harris was supposed to be with Blagojevich behind the curtain. It didn't sound like it was just part of the ploy.

"On line 27 you say: 'I'm gonna begin for the first time to objectively, honestly consider him,'" Schar pointed out.

On the evening of December 4, just before the *Tribune* article about the recordings, Blagojevich had been recorded saying Madigan was out of favor.

One of those calls was with Scofield, when Blagojevich had said he just couldn't pull the trigger on Lisa Madigan.

Just that day, he had spoken to his brother on the phone and told him to reach out to Nayak. It was clear Blagojevich understood what the parameters of a Nayak meeting would entail, because he had told Yang in a call that morning that Jackson supporters had offered "a whole bunch of different things," including "you know, fund-raising." Blagojevich knew what Nayak and Rajinder Bedi were about when it pertained to making Jackson a senator. Don't call it bribes, Schar said, repeating Blagojevich, call it illegal fund-raising.

"Never gonna do it," Blagojevich answered flatly. "Rejected it."

But when he talked to Yang, Blagojevich had been specific. "You cut a deal," he had said on the call. He had to believe the Jackson people when they said they offered him fund-raising including something "up front." In another call with Yang, later the same day, Blagojevich had cleared the matter further. Yang had asked if the deal was that the Jacksons would support him for reelection, and Blagojevich had told him there was more to it. There was "tangible, concrete" stuff from the Jackson group. "You know, specific amounts and everything," Blagojevich had said. It was clear that Schar was locking him in, and Blagojevich tried some last moves to turn what was coming into a more glancing blow. There was political support, that was part of the arrangement, but when he had said "specific amounts," that was, in fact, a reference to campaign money.

"And when you say what was offered, again you are referencing here in the afternoon the money that Raghu Nayak, among others, had illegally offered you, correct?" Schar asked.

"That's what I'm telling Fred, yes," Blagojevich said of the call. Blagojevich had gone on to tell Yang that he realized Jackson wanted the seat desperately and he was the only one to offer things for it. If there was a deal to be made, it was probably with Jackson, despite their past.

And fifteen minutes later, at 2:43 PM on December 4, Blagojevich had called his brother again. His brother, Robert, Schar pointed out, was not a pollster and not in contact with the right people in Washington to throw Jackson out there as some kind of lure. Robert Blagojevich's job was to bring in cash, plain and simple. And the governor's direction was for his brother to reach out to Raghu Nayak, the same person who, Blagojevich had agreed, was offering an illegal payment for the Senate seat.

Blagojevich's brother had said that if Jackson were named, he would have to get tapped into African American money centers and bring in even more money. In response to that, Schar said, Blagojevich had not told his brother to forget about that, he had not said he was never, ever going to really appoint Jackson. Instead, Blagojevich had directed his brother to reach out to Nayak. He was to tell Nayak about the history with Jackson and about how Blagojevich had difficulty trusting him. If there was going to be "tangible" support, it had to start happening immediately and not be based on a vague promise. And another thing, Blagojevich had said, be careful, and assume the whole world is listening.

In some contexts that could mean, be careful, and don't get caught.

"Yes," Blagojevich said, before returning to what he had said before. If you're doing things right, you don't care if everyone knows. Assume the whole world is listening and do it the right way. Do things like everyone can see what you're up to.

Don't do it on the phone, Blagojevich had said. And tell Nayak there was urgency to move forward.

Blagojevich was growing more agitated on the stand, clearly seeing where this was going. Schar was twisting his words, he said. All he meant was that his brother should put the meeting together quickly. He wasn't trying to strike while the iron was still hot, he just wanted his brother to move forward and schedule something with Nayak. And as it turned out, Robert did. He had planned to sit down with Nayak the next day, December 5, to deliver Blagojevich's message.

But it was a meeting that would never occur.

Blagojevich learned that the *Tribune* was publishing its story about Wyma's cooperation and about the federal endgame. In the morning of December 5 it was there. Newspapers all over Chicago with the headline "Feds Taped Blagojevich."

The governor's next move was to cancel the Nayak meeting. Blagojevich had told the jury he pulled the plug because the story had sent him into crisis mode. He was too busy trying to figure out what was happening to him and how to handle the situation to tell his brother how to handle Nayak, he said, so he had thought better of it. Besides, Blagojevich told Schar, the "negative leverage play" he was imagining with Jackson had grown less important.

OK, said Schar, but Blagojevich's world hadn't crashed down enough to prevent him from going to more fund-raisers that weekend or to have a conversation with Harris about getting street signs put up in the honor of the Chicago Cubs general manager.

"No, that was a higher priority than the Raghu meeting. Yes, the Jim Hendry street signs. I'm a Cubs fan," Blagojevich said, trying to throw up a joke in a room that was getting very quiet. Blagojevich was rapidly running out of real estate. Schar pointed out that Blagojevich had told Robert why there was to be no meeting. It wasn't because he had public relations work to do.

"In fact, just do it," cancel it, Schar said. The prosecutor was once again reading what had been captured on tape.

"Go ahead and just call him and say, well, it's too obvious right now because of this story."

Too obvious.

"Were those your words?" Schar asked, bearing down.

Blagojevich paused.

He seemed to be searching again for something else to say or one more explanation to give. But the silence in the room didn't last for more than a second or two, and Blagojevich was filling the space and giving the only answer he really could.

"Yes," he said.

"They were my words."

A Time of Reckoning

It's unlikely Abraham Lincoln rolled over in his grave because of Rod Blago-jevich, but the man who may be the country's most beloved president is credited with a quote that lands at the heart of the Blagojevich story.

"Nearly all men can stand adversity, but if you want to test a man's char-acter, give him power."

Blagojevich, who had been the state's fortieth governor, was convicted June 27, 2011, of seventeen criminal counts, making him the fourth chief executive of the state to be convicted of felonies since 1973.

The jury found him guilty of wire fraud, attempted extortion, bribery, and conspiracy, deciding he had abused the powers of his office, including attempting to sell a US Senate seat. The sweeping verdict came on top of Blagojevich's earlier single conviction for lying to the FBI. He showed little reaction in court when the verdict was read, first staring forward and then pushing back in his chair with pursed lips. He looked toward his wife, Patti, and whispered, "I love you."

The second jury was unable to decide if there was enough evidence to convict Blagojevich on the charge that he shook down Rahm Emanuel over the school grant when Emanuel was still in Congress or that he tried to get a campaign contribution from Krozel in exchange for the larger tollway announcement. By and large, jurors found Blagojevich a frustrating speci-men: a likable guy but a schemer who crossed lines too easily for his own good and who was buried by overwhelming criminal evidence.

"He's a very personable gentleman," juror Rosemary Bennett, a grand-mother from the Chicago suburbs, told the *Tribune* after the verdict.

But others saw signs of manipulation in Blagojevich's testimony. There were many times he seemed to be tailoring his message for them as indi-viduals, trying to get into their heads. The lone man on the jury had Mas-sachusetts ties, so Blagojevich on the stand mentioned liking Boston. The woman who was the jury's foreman, Connie Wilson, a church choir direc-tor, noticed how Blagojevich stressed the Bibles on his bookshelves, seem-ingly just for her. One worked in a library and one had a restaurant in her family, so Blagojevich talked of how much he liked studying in libraries and how he would go to a Greek diner beforehand.

"He kept rambling on," juror Kimberly Spaetti told the newspaper. "Peo-ple were writing 'blah, blah, blah' in their notebooks, and I drew pictures of my cats."

Those close to Blagojevich said he felt condemned from the moment he was arrested and that he didn't have a fair day in court. The judge was against him, his lawyers complained, as evidenced by how few tapes the ex-governor was allowed to play in his own defense.

Sam Adam Sr. thought Zagel was egotistical and Fitzgerald had gotten carried away in his investigation. He likened the case to the infamous Chi-cago Seven trial, when Judge Julius Hoffman had severely limited what the defense could present. That trial had been a show, Adam said, and the con-victions in the case overturned. Many tapes Zagel barred would have shown Blagojevich had no criminal intent, Adam believed, and he was hopeful an appeal would be successful. As for Sorosky, who had known Blagojevich lon-ger than anyone on the defense team, the Blagojevich story was simply sad. Blagojevich was fundamentally honest, Sorosky thought, and was caught in a long progression of bad decisions. The governor thought of Rezko as a millionaire who didn't need corruption to make money, so he never thought to watch him closely. And he had surrounded himself with yes-men who didn't have his back. It wasn't unlike how Lyndon B. Johnson was entangled in Vietnam by advisers who journalist David Halberstam dubbed "the best and the brightest." Aides like Scofield, Wyma, and Greenlee were supposed to be elite minds but had helped Blagojevich find his undoing.

"They weren't his type of people," Sorosky said.

What the case ultimately demonstrated, though, was that Blagojevich sur-rounded himself with aides who went along with his erratic and sometimes aggressive behavior even when they disagreed. His power and personality had marginalized anybody who stood up to him, leaving those who remained in his inner circle with little foresight about where he was taking them and not enough courage to stop him. It had disastrous results for all of them, but especially Blagojevich. At a time when he most needed someone to yell at him that what he was doing was illegal, the warning never came.

He was delusional about his reality then and stayed that way after he was charged. He told one young court observer that Patrick Fitzgerald's claim that he had engaged in a political corruption crime spree "would go the way of weapons of mass destruction" and often predicted his acquittal.

"I can't wait to get my job back," he told one young man in court one day. "I didn't let you down."

Well, yes, Blagojevich did, and his place in history is now sealed, as is that of many of the men who were close to one of the most confounding politicians Illinois has ever seen or who found themselves in his orbit, taking the test that power brings.

Nearly six months later, in December 2011, Judge Zagel sentenced Blagojevich to fourteen years in prison following a hearing that felt as if Blagojevich were pleading for mercy from the judicial branch of the same federal government whose legislative branch he had sought to sell out.

The former governor's lawyers argued Blagojevich's crimes—which they finally acknowledged were crimes—were not as serious as prosecutors contended, especially compared to numerous examples across the country of politicians pocketing cash. They asked for a sentence less than the six and a half years George Ryan received in 2006. Even more importantly, they argued, Blagojevich was a good father whose family would be destroyed by a long prison term.

Prosecutors argued the amount Blagojevich tried to bring in through his schemes called for guidelines of thirty years to life. That would be too much, Reid Schar told the judge, asking instead for fifteen to twenty years. It was important to give Blagojevich a stiff sentence to finally communicate to politicians in Chicago and around Illinois that "pay to play" and other forms of corruption that had thrived for too long were not acceptable.

Schar told Zagel that in the government's view, Blagojevich was corrupt when he first took office and was corrupt when the FBI arrested him at his home. He was only interested in himself, putting the needs of the state behind his own. Most shockingly, he had committed the staggering crime of trying to sell a US Senate seat, compromising the government in an extreme way. Practically speaking, Blagojevich left Illinois with just one vote in the Senate during the fall of 2008, a crucial time when the economy was imploding and votes of national significance were taking place.

Citizens' faith in government must be restored.

"The people have had enough," Schar said. "They've had enough of this defendant. They've had enough of those who are corrupt like him. . . . They should have the highest expectations that their elected leaders will honor that faith the people put in them."

———

When Blagojevich finally stood to speak, he seemed to brace himself on the lectern in front of Zagel, leaning forward with both hands on the sides of it, gripping tight.

He was standing there, convicted, he said. And he was unbelievably sorry. He said the jury had found him guilty, and he accepted it, though he did not flat-out tell the judge he believed he had done something worthy of being labeled a convicted felon.

"I have a tendency sometimes to speak before I think. And I've had plenty of time over the past several months to do a lot of thinking and reflecting and to think about all that's happened and all the things that have led up to me standing here before your honor and not being anywhere near the places that I dreamed of and hoped I'd one day be," Blagojevich said.

He wanted to apologize to the people of Illinois and to the court for his mistakes.

"If there's any consolation that I can offer the people, to you, and to myself, it is that I honestly believed—let me withdraw that. Let me—I—I never set out to break the law. I never set out to cross lines," he corrected himself. He had caused all of his own troubles and said he was blaming nobody but himself.

He was also sorry for dragging the case into the media and for criticizing prosecutors while Chicago and America watched. He was sorry for the disrespect.

"I was very keen on your comments yesterday when you described how I saw it as a duel and a boxing match. You captured me," Blagojevich told Zagel. "I saw it exactly that way, for whatever reasons. Alexander Hamilton in dueling Aaron Burr back in the eighteenth century I've read a lot about. The boxing experience I had, I did see it in those terms, and I should have known better."

He was self-absorbed and childish, he acknowledged. Much of what he had done had been unproductive at best and foolish at worst.

"My life is ruined—at least now," he said, signaling ever so slightly the personality of the man who refused to quit. "My life is in ruins."

It was taking until right then, standing in front of a judge who held the rest of his life in the palm of his hand, for Blagojevich to realize what his future was.

He wanted to apologize to his brother for dragging him into his descent. But most of all he wanted to apologize to Patti, who sometimes leaned forward in her seat in despair nearby, and to his family. Home was the only place Blagojevich had wanted to go after the jury found him guilty, he told the court. He had been able to distract Annie by getting her to play, but Amy, who was fifteen years old, had been much harder to assuage. The press was still swarming the family home, and Amy had wanted her father to go outside as he usually did and explain again why he was wrongfully accused, to tell the world why he was being misunderstood and prosecuted for nothing at all.

"And she asked me and begged me, 'Daddy, please go outside and talk to the media and tell them that you didn't do it and tell them that this was wrong,'" Blagojevich said, telling Zagel he had been forced to accept what had happened to him as his girl cried. His selfishness had jeopardized the one thing he should have held most dear: his ability to be there for his children. To protect them and watch them grow through some of the most precious years a father can have with those he loves the very most.

"And I asked her not to be ashamed of me, and I hope I didn't let her down. But that was the moment where I had to teach my daughter to try to accept what had happened, and it was a moment where I began the process of accepting the new reality."

———

Zagel took a break to consider all he had heard and then emerged from his chambers at almost exactly high noon. He strode to the bench in his normal slow and plodding way, placing papers down in front of him and then taking a seat.

It was no surprise he had much to say about the case that he had overseen for three years. There had been two trials, much argument, and seven days of Blagojevich on the stand trying to explain himself. Then lawyers on both sides had argued about what the former governor's sentence should be. In Zagel's mind, though, some of the arguments had been the wrong ones. The defense had said five years in prison was enough of a deterrent. What government official would trade five years of their life for the potential benefits corruption brought?

"Some are never caught. And then, to cite a not so hypothetical example, after they die, huge amounts of cash are found in their closets," Zagel said, in a reference to the infamous Paul Powell. "If you think you're not going to get caught, you do it. The problem with deterrence always is that you have not only the price to be paid if you are caught but the chances of your being caught. And while economists know how to discount this probability, we don't have reliable statistics on the good way to do it."

Then peering down at the once ever-buoyant man who had overshot all expectations to become governor, he added, "If you are a corrupt public official and you are an optimist, there's a much better chance you're going to do it than if you're a pessimist."

So what of Blagojevich?

It was impossible to dispute what the federal government captured on its wiretaps. That evidence had left the ex-governor to argue he had been misunderstood. Had Blagojevich been played by those in his inner circle? Zagel didn't think so. It seemed Blagojevich had called for certain actions and his minions did as they were told.

The judge also did not believe Blagojevich had gotten bad legal advice from them—or no legal advice at all from some who might have stopped him. The truth was, Blagojevich didn't ask for such advice, because the fact was he did not want the answer.

"A few of his plans may, arguably, have been legal. The ones he was convicted of were not," Zagel explained. "In the end, his defense morphed into a claim that he did not believe his proposals were quid pro quo, which he did know was an illegal exchange. The jury did not believe him, and neither do I."

Ultimately, what Zagel said he heard on the recordings was a man who had the personality of someone who was arguably not fit for public office at all. What had been caught on tape was what happened when that man sank in over his head.

"Much of what I heard in the recordings and both heard and saw in your testimony support this view, some unfortunate elements of immaturity," Zagel told Blagojevich, who sat sometimes looking down toward the defense table and sometimes managed to glance toward the bench. "The unwillingness to admit, even to yourself, that you have done something seriously wrong until you are forced to do so, blaming others for your misconduct, the impatience, the endless talking, the lack of focus, and the need for praise and plaudits say from people whose grandmothers got a free ride on the free bus."

Zagel said he did believe what Blagojevich had told him that day, that he was no longer blaming anybody but himself. That had caused the judge to give the former governor an ounce of good credit. And the judge said he was sympathetic to the plight of the Blagojevich girls. It was a sad reality that hung in the courtroom like a chill, no matter how those in court had viewed Blagojevich, and Zagel was just pointing it out. Blagojevich did, in fact, clearly love his girls. He doted on them. Why hadn't that fatherly devotion stopped him when nothing else would? It had been foolish to even approach the line with what Blagojevich had at stake.

Finally, the judge shifted in his chair slightly and seemed ready to give Blagojevich the sentence he would announce minutes later, the fourteen years. Above all else, it was the judge's duty to be concerned with the times that Blagojevich had used his tremendous power not for the millions whom he had led but for himself. The office of governor was among the very worst to corrupt, he said, second only to the office of president of the United States. The harm in the case was not about money and property. It was not about the money Blagojevich had or hadn't tried to get. It was about the erosion of the public's trust in government. For the American system of government to prosper, it was best when people trust their leaders to do the right thing most of the time, the judge said, and to try to do it all of the time.

"When it is the governor who goes bad, the fabric of Illinois is torn and disfigured and not easily or quickly repaired," Zagel told Blagojevich.

"You did that damage."

———

There are many who came from more humble beginnings than Blagojevich and who climbed over more life obstacles, but few with his kind of working-class roots rise to the heights he did. He finished law school, but his academic career was largely average. He got a government job as a state's attorney but showed little promise there as well. What he eventually became was a man who ascended to places he probably shouldn't have reached and who won jobs he couldn't have attained without the right connections, propelled by an extreme personality. That reality carried the day, until Blagojevich blazed out in frenzied desperation while federal investigators recorded him. He overcame adversity but ultimately failed the character test. He asked for the public's trust and received it, elected amid promises to reform a money-fueled system that ultimately swallowed and destroyed him.

Even his policies left much to be desired. His plan to import prescription drugs from Canada failed. His idea to spend millions to import flu vaccines ended up not helping anyone in Illinois or Pakistan, where he ultimately sent them and where they were destroyed because they had expired. His fight to ban youngsters from buying violent video games never went anywhere amid claims it was unconstitutional. He borrowed billions of dollars to balance the budget, leaving Illinois in a deeper hole ($13 billion) than when he found it ($5 billion). Even what he described as his greatest achievement—the All Kids insurance program—had serious problems. He never provided enough funding for it, seriously increasing the state's deficit.

Those policies were often questioned by the press or lawmakers during Blagojevich's time as governor. Some wondered if they were done more for publicity than policy. Others thought they might even be illegal. But Blagojevich usually dismissed the criticisms with a wave of his hand. He wouldn't be held back by the rules of man-made law or governance. He had a higher rule that guided him: the Golden Rule.

"You should do unto others as you would have others do unto you," he lectured.

As Zagel said, Blagojevich the man was not fit for public office. But what does it say about our political system that he excelled at it?

From the beginning, he was a man of clear contradictions: He was privately conservative yet publicly hewed to a liberal ideology solely because it was in his political interest. He was a true narcissist who overcame inherent shyness with an electric personality that won over nearly everyone he met. He was the "neighborhood guy" who loved fine clothes and high-end schooling. He was the younger brother who idolized his older sibling and nearly destroyed his life. He was the nobody who needed the help of his father-in-law but resented the assistance even as it made his career. He was a politician who hated authority yet yearned for power more than anything.

But the responsibility does not rest on the former governor alone. Just as Republicans had with George Ryan, nearly every Democratic staffer and politician in Illinois backed Blagojevich's bid for higher office, even those who knew his tremendous flaws and helped hide them from voters. They are all accessories to the shame Blagojevich wrought. When it all collapsed, each of them piled on. Some impeached him, others voted him out of office, and still others pretended they hadn't at some point stood alongside Blagojevich on stage in an effort to ingratiate themselves with him. They too were yearning for power. And still are.

The citizenry is also to blame. None of our leaders is perfect, but questions surrounded Blagojevich for years. Voters either didn't pay attention or ignored those questions and purposely set them aside amid a blur of flashy TV spots and witty one-liners. When glitziness trumps substance in picking a winner at the polls, we all end up losers.

The reminder came again in one other thing Zagel told Blagojevich before changing his life forever. He simply pointed out that throughout both trials, he had often called Blagojevich "governor," even though nobody else addressed him as such, as he had been impeached and removed from office.

"By protocol you are entitled to that honorific if, for no other reason, you won elections as governor twice," Zagel said.

"But I also do it because it serves as a reminder to those of us who vote and those of us who don't. It reminds the voters of the maxim: the American people always get precisely the government that they deserve."

Afterword

Rod Blagojevich became Prisoner 40892-424 in March 2012, waving to onlookers for a last time as he entered the Federal Correction Institution at Englewood, Colorado, not far from Denver, with the Rocky Mountains as a backdrop.

He left his Chicago home as he so often had during his trials—with a crowd standing outside on the sidewalk waiting to hear him speak. And when he finally did, it was typical Rod, as he told the gathered reporters, neighbors, and curiosity-seekers that his first thought as the state's leader was always to do what was right for people. Even though everyone knew why he was addressing them and where he was going, Blagojevich couldn't bring himself to say the word *prison*.

Once again craving the spotlight, he signed autographs on scraps of paper for nearly all who asked, even to the point of ignoring the pleas of eight-year-old Annie Blagojevich, who begged him to stop and come back inside the house. Finally, he retreated.

"I'll see you around," the former governor said to the press.

In Colorado, he had his final meal outside the prison walls at a local hamburger place, ordering a double patty melt and fries. But his appetite may have been one casualty of the troubling day, as observers said he didn't eat much. Helicopters hovered to catch every step of his journey to incarceration.

Another thing Blagojevich was expected to lose in his long stint behind bars was the deep color of his hair. In the days after the gates locked behind him, his longtime barber was among those to weigh in on his Blagojevich experiences. The ex-governor's famous hair wasn't naturally dark brown, Peter Vodovoz told the press, and it would probably go gray quickly with then fifty-five-year-old Blagojevich having no access to any cosmetic treatment. "He dyes it himself," Vodovoz said.

A few months after Blagojevich was found guilty, William Cellini stood trial on charges of trying to extort a Blagojevich campaign contribution from Thomas Rosenberg, the Hollywood film producer. Cellini's trial was the last from the Operation Board Games probe. He was convicted in November 2011 but was appealing.

Stuart Levine, who was last working at a suburban mall selling electronic cigarettes, was scheduled to be sentenced in summer of 2012. By then, Patrick Fitzgerald, the longest-serving US attorney in Chicago history, had stepped down from his post.

And not long after Blagojevich entered prison, the last of his former close allies learned their fates from Judge Zagel, who had sentenced Tony Rezko to more than ten years in prison in late 2011 after the convicted fund-raiser was never called as a witness.

Lon Monk got the two-year prison term he was expecting in his deal with the government, but John Harris turned out to be the big winner. Zagel sentenced Harris, whose early cooperation had been so crucial and whose testimony so important for prosecutors, to just ten days in prison. The judge said he understood the kind of position Harris had been put in as he tried to deal with Blagojevich as a boss on an hour-to-hour basis. Harris was continuing to try to rebuild his life.

The relatively light punishment for Harris surprised many, including Patti Blagojevich, who wondered aloud "what planet are we on" in a status update on her Facebook page. Her husband was expected to spend several thousand more days than that in the custody of the government.

The Federal Bureau of Prisons listed Blagojevich's expected release date as May 23, 2024.

Acknowledgments

We'd like to thank staff at Chicago Review Press for their patience and hard work. Susan Betz, who first helped conceive of this book and shepherded it through its first stages, deserves our sincere thanks. We'd also like to thank CRP publisher Cynthia Sherry and especially Lisa Reardon for her deft editing.

We've been honored to work for the *Chicago Tribune* for more than a decade, and we'd like to thank the *Tribune*'s editors for encouraging us to do this project, most notably Editor Gerould Kern and Deputy Managing Editor Peter Kendall. Thanks also to editors Ann Marie Lipinski, Jim O'Shea, George de Lama, Hanke Gratteau, and Terry Brown. We'd especially like to thank editors and fellow reporters who worked with us on a daily basis on the Blagojevich story including Jim Webb, Bob Secter, Eric Krol, Matt O'Connor, Ray Long, Rick Pearson, Christi Parsons, David Kidwell, David Mendell, Stacy St. Clair, Annie Sweeney, and Monique Garcia, and photographer Nancy Stone for taking our author photo.

For their exhaustive work back in 1996 documenting Rod Blagojevich and Dick Mell, we'd like to thank former *Tribune* writers Patrick Reardon, Laurie Cohen, Ray Gibson, and Robert Becker.

Thanks to all of those who agreed to be interviewed for this book and to those who supplied material for it. All of them cooperated with the goal of helping us put together the most complete account possible.

From Jeff Coen:

There are times when a writing project becomes a way for a journalist to make peace with a story, and so it was for us with Rod Blagojevich. After covering him for years—a large block of our professional lives to date—it was a chance to put everything we had gathered in one place and stitch together the full arc of the story. It was rewarding for me professionally and was made all the better by being surrounded by friends for the duration of the work.

When I think back on putting this book together, I'll always recall getting to work closely with John Chase. We had become good friends well before this project, and neither of us would have considered taking it on without the other. In addition to it being fun (most of the time), it was a great pleasure to work with a reporter I respect so much.

I also want to give special thanks to the *Tribune*'s Bob Secter, who was my partner covering the trial of Tony Rezko in 2008 and both Blagojevich trials. Bob had a rich background as a political reporter and editor and is widely known as one of the paper's better writers. Getting him as a trial partner felt like having an unfair advantage, and many long trial days passed quicker by getting to constantly joke around with him. Likewise, special thanks to the paper's Stacy St. Clair, who often took on the duty of covering the publicity side of the Blagojevich defense machine, including following him to New York. She's another good friend, and she was a living encyclopedia of Blagojevich trivia who was more than handy to have around as the book came together.

Finally, thanks to Doug and Kathy Coen, Jeremy and Denise Coen, Chris Coen, Mike and Sharon Marsalis, and Michael and Megann Marsalis for the constant support. To friends Vince and Laura Cook, another thank-you for the encouragement.

To Meredith and Liam, thank you for tolerating all the time this took on days when we could have been doing other things. Because of you I'm as blessed as anyone can be. And finally, I am most grateful to my wife, Michelle. There's nothing I could say in a million words. But thank you—for everything.

From John Chase:

In the midst of writing this book, my sister made a masterful discovery in the Chase family tree. A great, great uncle we all knew to be just a saloonkeeper, John Joseph Brennan, was actually a Chicago alderman for more than two decades. She uncovered that Brennan was a quintessential Chicago ward boss in the late nineteenth and early twentieth centuries (never a good thing). He did favors almost only for his political friends and was jailed for literally buying votes. The discovery helped me understand something about myself and my long-held love of Chicago's seedy political history: it's apparently in my blood.

I hope I've washed away a few family sins by writing this book, which was produced with the help of so many people it's impossible to list them all. I'd particularly like to thank my coauthor, Jeff Coen, who has been a constant source of calm amid sometimes troubled waters.

I'd also like to thank all those who have helped me along my career in journalism, from the Logansport *Pharos-Tribune* and City News Bureau of Chicago to the *Daily Herald* and *Chicago Tribune*. Many at the *Tribune* are listed above, but I'd particularly like to again thank Jim Webb and Bob Secter for being my direct editors during my six years covering Rod Blagojevich as governor.

Thank you to my friends and family who suffered through missed parties and constant complaining and the loss of my dogs Algren and Daisy and cat Emerson while I was working on this, especially: Rick Sloan, Bob Walsh, Señora Neli, the String, the Cypriot Brotherhood, Doug and Donna Novak, Carey Chase (amateur genealogist), my mom, Theresa Chase, and my late father, John Brennan Chase, who I wish could have seen this.

I'd like to thank my daughter, Josephine, for constantly putting a smile on my face and love in my heart. And I'd mostly like to thank my beautiful wife, Shanna, whose constant support and unending patience guided me through this project. I've got one thing to say to her: the book is done.

Index

473